The Films of Jean-Luc Godard
Seeing the Invisible

The Films of Jean-Luc Godard examines the work of one of the most versatile and influential filmmakers in the history of cinema. With a career ranging from France's revolutionary New Wave movement in the early 1960s, through a period of drastic political experimentation in the late 1960s and 1970s, to a current introspective period in which he explores issues of spirituality, sexuality, and the aesthetics of sound, image, and montage, Godard's work defies easy categorization. In this study, David Sterritt offers an introductory overview of Godard's work as a filmmaker, critic, and video artist. He then traces Godard's visionary ideas through six of his key films: *Breathless, My Life to Live, Weekend, Numéro deux, Hail Mary,* and *Nouvelle Vague.* Also included is a concise analysis of his work in video, television, and mixed-media formats. Linking works by Godard to key social and cultural developments, *The Films of Jean-Luc Godard* explains their importance in modernist and postmodernist art of the past half century.

David Sterritt is Film Critic of *The Christian Science Monitor* and Professor of Film at the C. W. Post Campus of Long Island University. Author of *The Films of Alfred Hitchcock* and *Mad to Be Saved: The Beats, the 50's, and Film* and editor of *Jean-Luc Godard: Interviews,* he has contributed articles on film, theater, and music to a wide range of periodicals.

CAMBRIDGE FILM CLASSICS

General Editor: **Ray Carney, Boston University**

The Cambridge Film Classics series provides a forum for revisionist studies of the classic works of the cinematic canon from the perspective of the "new auterism," which recognizes that films emerge from a complex interaction of bureaucratic, technological, intellectual, cultural, and personal forces. The series consists of concise, cutting-edge reassessments of the canonical works of film study, written by innovative scholars and critics. Each volume provides a general introduction to the life and work of a particular director, followed by critical essays on several of the director's most important films.

Other Books in the Series:

Peter Bondanella, *The Films of Roberto Rossellini*
Peter Brunette, *The Films of Michelangelo Antonioni*
Ray Carney, *The Films of John Cassavetes*
Sam B. Girgus, *The Films of Woody Allen*
Robert Phillip Kolker and Peter Beicken, *The Films of Wim Wenders*
Amy Lawrence, *The Films of Peter Greenaway*
Scott MacDonald, *Avant-Garde Film*
James Naremore, *The Films of Vincente Minnelli*
James Palmer and Michael Riley, *The Films of Joseph Losey*
Scott Simmon, *The Films of D. W. Griffith*
David Sterritt, *The Films of Alfred Hitchcock*
Maurice Yacowar, *The Films of Paul Morrissey*

Seeing the invisible is exhausting.

– *Hélas pour moi*

The Films of
Jean-Luc Godard

Seeing the Invisible

David Sterritt

Long Island University

CAMBRIDGE
UNIVERSITY PRESS

PUBLISHED BY THE PRESS SYNDICATE OF THE UNIVERSITY OF CAMBRIDGE
The Pitt Building, Trumpington Street, Cambridge CB2 1RP, United Kingdom

CAMBRIDGE UNIVERSITY PRESS
The Edinburgh Building, Carnbridge CB2 2RU, UK   www.cup.cam.ac.uk
40 West 20th Street, New York, NY 10011-4211, USA   www.cup.org
10 Stamford Road, Oakleigh, Melbourne 3166, Australia
Ruiz de Alarcón 13, 28014 Madrid, Spain

First published 1999

Printed in the United States of America

Typeface Sabon 10/13 pt.   *System* QuarkXpress®   [MG]

A catalog record for this book is available from the British Library

Library of Congress Cataloging in Publication Data
Sterritt, David.
The films of Jean-Luc Godard : seeing the invisible / David Sterritt.
p.   cm. – (Cambridge film classics)
Filmography: p.
Includes bibliographical references and index.
ISBN 0 521 58038 2 (hb)   ISBN 0 521 58971 1 (pbk)
1. Godard, Jean-Luc, 1930– – Criticism and interpretation.
I. Title.   II. Series.
PN1998.3.G63S73   1999
791.43´0233´092 – dc21   99-12443
CIP

ISBN 0 521 58038 2 hardback
ISBN 0 521 58971 1 paperback

All photo stills are reprinted with the kind permission of

As always, for Ginnie,
Craig, and Jeremy

Contents

List of Illustrations   *page* xi

Acknowledgments   xiii

1 Introduction   1

2 *Breathless*   39

3 *My Life to Live*   61

4 *Weekend*   89

5 *Numéro deux*   129

6 *Hail Mary*   161

7 *Nouvelle Vague*   221

8 Video and Television   247

Notes   265

Select Bibliography   279

Filmography   281

Index   291

Illustrations

Strange adventures: Jean-Luc Godard with Anna Karina during the
shooting of *Alphaville* in 1965   *page* 11

Manufactured meanings: Woman as commodity in *2 or 3 Things I Know
about Her* (1966; Raoul Lévy, Anny Duperey)   25

Sunny charm: *Breathless* (1960) protagonists Michel Poiccard (Jean-Paul
Belmondo) and Patricia Franchini (Jean Seberg) on the Champs-Elysées   41

Hanging out: Michel (Jean-Paul Belmondo) and Patricia (Jean Seberg)
pass the time at Patricia's apartment in *Breathless*   43

Very real violence: Michel (Jean-Paul Belmondo) fights with an
antagonist in *Breathless*   49

City as character: Patricia (Jean Seberg) and her American friend
(Van Doude) against a Parisian backdrop in *Breathless*   55

Cultural studies: Patricia (Jean Seberg) juxtaposed with an Auguste
Renoir painting on her apartment wall in *Breathless*   59

Cinephilia: Nana Kleinfrankenheim (Anna Karina) as she watches
Dreyer's *The Passion of Joan of Arc* in a scene of *My Life to Live* (1962)   71

Happiness is no fun: Nana (Anna Karina) plies her trade in *My Life
to Live*   77

"Le zo": Nana (Anna Karina) on the street in *My Life to Live*   81

Violence: Nana (Anna Karina) is murdered by the pimp Raoul in
My Life to Live   87

Death: Nana (Anna Karina) lies dead before the Restaurant des Studios
in *My Life to Live*   88

Verbal orgy: Corinne (Mireille Darc) spins a sex-filled monologue while
her nameless friend listens intently, in *Weekend* (1967)   95

Jarring and fractured: Roland (Jean Yanne) and Corinne (Mireille Darc)
fight and bite their way through a country excursion in *Weekend*   101

Dramatis personae: Roland (Jean Yanne) asks directions from Emily
Brontë (Blandine Jeanson) and Tom Thumb (Yves Afonso) in *Weekend*   107

Escalating horror: Roland (Jean Yanne) and Corinne (Mireille Darc)
make their way through an increasingly surreal landscape in *Weekend*   111

Rock revolutionaries: Death and drumbeats intermingle in the Seine
and Oise Liberation Front scenes of *Weekend*   121

Dziga-Vertov duo: Jean-Luc Godard and Jean-Pierre Gorin when *Tout
va bien* was released in 1972   130

Acting and activism: Jacques (Yves Montand) and Susan (Jane Fonda)
are media workers ambivalent about their professions in *Tout va bien*   131

Another comeback: Isabelle Huppert and Jacques Dutronc star in
Sauve qui peut (la vie) (1979)   163

Provocateur: Jean-Luc Godard at the time of *Hail Mary* in 1985   165

"The Book of Mary": The title character (Rebecca Hampton) of Anne-
Marie Miéville's brief drama sings Beethoven while scrutinizing an egg
about to acquire much mysterious meaning   173

Mary and Joseph: Emotions run high between the frequently confused
and troubled protagonists (Myriem Roussel, Thierry Rode) of *Hail Mary*   183

Female forms: *2 or 3 Things I Know about Her* with Marina Vlady
and Anny Duperey   185

God's-eye-view: Joseph (Thierry Rode) and Mary (Myriem Roussel)
grapple with physical and metaphysical urges in *Hail Mary*   199

The skull beneath the skin: The agonized writhing of Mary (Myriem
Roussel) evokes the mortality of her human nature in *Hail Mary*   205

Multifaceted metaphor: Mary (Myriem Roussel) applies lipstick in the
enigmatic last sequence of *Hail Mary*   217

Unrelenting radicalism: Berengère Allaux in *For Ever Mozart* (1997)   229

Images, signs, people: Marina Vlady as Juliette Janson, and her self-
reflective mirror image, in *2 or 3 Things I Know about Her* (1966)   237

Man with a movie camera: A reflexive moment in the sensuously filmed
For Ever Mozart (1997)   261

Acknowledgments

I have viewed, discussed, and debated Godard for so many years with so many people that it would be impossible to trace all those who indirectly helped with this book. They know who they are, though, and I hope they know how grateful I am for the interests and insights we have shared. I owe special thanks to those who have helped more directly, in ways both large and small. Vlada Petrić got me started on sustained thinking about Godard with his invitation to speak at a Harvard University conference on *Hail Mary* more than a decade ago, and his scholarly rigor and good-humored friendship have been a valued part of my life ever since. Also appreciated are the ideas and support of Maryel Locke and Charles Warren, who included my conference essay in their fine book on that film, and of the sharp-witted scholar Sidney Gottlieb, who invited me to lecture on Godard at Sacred Heart University as my project was lurching into high gear. Peter Brunette and Seetha A-Srinivasan kindly invited me to edit a volume of Godard interviews for the University Press of Mississippi series Conversations with Filmmakers, which prompted me to gather more such material than I had anticipated and considerably enlarged the primary resources upon which I have drawn. Pierre Rissient and Jean-Pierre Gorin made helpful comments in conversations that probably seemed more casual to them than they were for me, and David Wills had the great idea of cross-checking the filmography data we assembled for our different Godard projects. A major grant from the C. W. Post Research Committee of Long Island University helped me complete the book in a timely way. My friend Vanessa Young has helped more than she realizes with her extraordinarily sensitive taste in movies from her native Paris and everywhere else. Ditto for Vasanthi Mariadass, who has shared information and taken a steady interest in my work, as I have in hers. Lucille

Rhodes has always been there when I needed her, and many of my critical and programming colleagues – Phillip Lopate, Stuart Klawans, Richard Peña, and others too numerous to list – have helped to make it all worthwhile. Sasha Berman of New Yorker Films was cooperative far beyond the call of duty in aiding me with the illustrations, confirming yet again my admiration for Dan Talbot's utterly invaluable establishment. Ray Carney and Beatrice Rehl, my gifted editors for Cambridge University Press, have been as helpful and supportive as ever, and Michael Gnat made the production process a pleasure. As always my greatest thanks goes to my wife Ginnie, who continues to put up with me, and my sons Jeremy and Craig, who grew up on Godard and weathered the experience just fine.

The Films of Jean-Luc Godard
Seeing the Invisible

I

Introduction

I am a painter with letters. I want to restore everything, mix everything up and say everything.

– Jean-Luc Godard[1]

Mention the films and videos of Jean-Luc Godard, and superlatives will flow from his admirers. He is "the one film-maker who never disappoints me," says D. A. Pennebaker, a documentary filmmaker who once worked with him. His 1963 drama *Contempt* is not just an excellent film but "the greatest work of art produced in post-war Europe," according to Colin MacCabe, a longtime supporter. "The unspoken debt to Godard," writes critic Michael Atkinson, "has become a holy tithe filmmakers can never, it seems, hope to pay in full."[2] Others revive the out-of-fashion word "genius" to convey the extent of their enthusiasm.

It was not ever thus. *Positif,* one of France's most respected film magazines, described him in the early 1960s as a "bureaucrat with a taste for celluloid . . . a pretentious canary . . . an unrepentant spoiler of film . . . a press agent for himself." French director Jean-Pierre Melville, who played a minor character in Godard's early *Breathless,* later said his movies were "anything shot anyhow." The communist newspaper *L'Humanité* called the erstwhile Marxist a "parlor nihilist."[3] Superlatives indeed.

As these comments show, Godard's reputation has undergone more than its share of ups and downs. A journalist writing in 1963 called him both "the most idolized of the New Wave directors" and "the most unpopular man in the French cinema."[4] His renown within the art-film establishment reached a high point in the middle 1960s, when such movies as *A Married Woman* and *Masculine/Feminine* played in commercial theaters on both sides of the Atlantic and his peregrinations at the Cannes and New York filmfests attracted a bevy of fans who literally followed in his footsteps every moment they could. By the late 1980s, however, even many film students were just dimly aware of him, and one mid-1990s critic regretfully called him "an invisible film-maker for almost a decade."[5]

There are many reasons for this decline. Those not attributable to Godard himself include a climate of increasing political and cultural conservatism, a slide in the international prestige of the French film industry, and a lamentable dwindling of American interest in non-English-language films. To these must be added Godard's own penchant for provoking and at times alienating his audience. Even his most accessible works contain an unusual share of challenging material, and when he actually sets out to be difficult – as in the politically radical films produced in the years around 1970 – the results are almost as troublesome for devotees as for the uninitiated. Then too, people who admire one phase of his career often find themselves puzzled or put off by another; and those who study one phase in an effort to plumb its mysteries – delving into Brecht, for example, as a key to his 1960s aesthetic – may discover that another period is shaped by a very different set of concerns.

Such problems notwithstanding, Godard's stock has been rising once more as cinema heads into its second century. Moviegoers interested in postmodernism and multiculturalism have recognized his work as a precursor and paradigm of important developments in these fields. Videocassettes and laserdiscs have made his complicated films available for the repeated and detailed viewings they demand. Perhaps most important, Godard himself has never stopped plugging away at his activities; by the late 1990s he has become such an integral part of the moving-image landscape that any scholar, critic, or buff is likely to be at least vaguely acquainted with his importance as an artist, innovator, and provocateur. As of 1998 his filmography contains more than seventy works, from short and feature-length movies to videotapes and television series of various lengths, and it is still growing at an impressive rate. Skeptics whose sensibilities are out of tune with these works may find such prolifigacy to be one of Godard's problems, complaining of "too many images," just as the emperor in *Amadeus* complained of "too many notes" in Mozart's music. Nonetheless, expressivity bred from spontaneity and improvisation has been central to Godard's methodology from the start, and the speed of his production is inseparable from its fecundity, variety, and complexity. Equally important to his approach is a healthy disdain for what might be called the Cinema of Common Sense, rooted in stories that appear "compelling" and "entertaining" because they reinforce the illusions by which we have learned to live. Such cinema has dominated the commercial film industry for most of its existence, and Godard's career amounts to a continuous mad dash to outstrip, outfox, and outrage it.

These two qualities – a love of spontaneity and a rejection of transparent storytelling – form clearly visible threads tying together even the most disparate works of Godard's career. They will also link the different readings and analyses in this book. In the pages that follow, it is worth bearing in mind an anecdote Godard has repeated many times in many circumstances, including the momentous *Histoire(s) du cinéma* video series that sums up his personal view of motion pictures. When he was a boy, fond of inventing tales to excuse the mischief he often got into, relatives and teachers would invariably tell him to be more responsible and *not make up stories.* When he grew up and became a filmmaker, fond of using cinema as a philosophical tool rather than an entertainment machine, producers and collaborators would invariably implore him to be more responsible and *make up stories.* Like his alter ego Jerzy, the filmmaker-hero of his extraordinary *Passion* (1982), he has never lost sight of this lifelong irony. He has never capitulated to the grownups, either.

Although few would guess it from the rebellious and even revolutionary tendencies that have guided his career, Godard's roots are anchored solidly in Europe's upper middle class. He was born in Paris in late 1930 but became a citizen of Switzerland when his parents (both from Protestant families) moved there during his infancy.[6] His father was a respected physician, and although his mother also had interests in this direction, she pursued a life of culture in accord with tastes acquired during her wealthy childhood. Jean-Luc went to school in the Swiss town of Nyon, where his father had a private medical clinic, but traveled often to Paris, where his mother's family lived. He attended the Lycée Buffon in Paris and then the Sorbonne, starting there in 1947 and receiving an ethnology certificate after three years, although some accounts say his attendance at classes was sporadic at best. Between the late 1940s and middle 1950s he held various modest jobs, some of which – as assistant TV editor, camera operator, and gossip columnist for a French newspaper – pointed toward his future as a cinéaste. He also traveled briefly in North and South America, courtesy of his father, whose relations with Jean-Luc then turned sour enough to end his financial support and make the young movie lover increasingly dependent on employment in and around the film industry. A more abrupt family trauma came in 1954, when his mother died in a traffic accident that clearly inspired more than one searing moment in his films, including the fatalistic crash at the climax of *Contempt,* made nine years after the tragic event.

It was in the late 1940s that Godard became a regular patron at the Paris Cinémathèque and various Left Bank film clubs. There he met André Bazin, editor of the journal *Cahiers du cinéma,* and four future filmmakers – François Truffaut, Jacques Rivette, Claude Chabrol, and Eric Rohmer – who would later join him as core members of the New Wave group. Approaching his cinematic self-education with the same enthusiasm and originality that would characterize his work as a director, he began contributing articles to a number of publications: the *Gazette du cinéma,* which he founded in the early 1950s and for which he wrote under the Germanized pen name Hans Lucas; *Les Amis du cinéma,* another minor periodical; *Arts,* where he published numerous reviews, interviews, and polemics; and *Cahiers* itself, which had been founded by Bazin and Jacques Doniol-Valcroze in 1951 and became Godard's best-known affiliation.

A clear picture of the *Cahiers* scene is essential for understanding Godard's early career and subsequent development as an artist. Bazin, one of European cinema's most influential critics and theorists, had an admirable openness to new talents and fresh voices. His views on film were shaped by a firmly held set of aesthetic and moral principles, however. Most important, he had invested much of his critical capital in the idea that realism is the essence of cinema.

This countered the view of such influential theorists as Sergei Eisenstein and Rudolf Arnheim, who believed cinema's power comes less from its ability to replicate the actual world than from the filmmaker's ability to manipulate visual representations – through camera work, lighting, laboratory processes, and above all editing – into original creative forms. Not so, wrote Bazin in many essays. Cinema's natural calling is to reproduce reality, he contended, and the filmmaker's job is to facilitate this process. The aim of great directors should be to photograph and record the realities around them as directly and objectively as possible, then transfer those images and sounds to the screen with a minimum of interference. If the subject is compelling, and if the filmmaking is clear and conscientious, art will be served and audiences will be deeply moved.

In accord with this view, Bazin's favorite films included dramas by Italy's gifted "neorealist" school of the mid-1940s to mid-1950s, which told homely human-interest stories (*Umberto D., La Terra Trema*) and topical tales (*Paisan, The Bicycle Thief*) via straightforward, no-nonsense techniques. He also admired American productions by Orson Welles and William Wyler that used imaginative camera positions and lengthy deep-focus shots to include a great deal of visual information in a single take rather than cutting frequently from one shot to another. His most compelling arguments often grew from his opposition to unnecessary editing, which can disrupt the illusion of reality by calling attention to a controlling human hand. A single cut will destroy the credibility of a filmed magic act, he pointed out, since spectators will assume the rabbit was sneaked into the hat while the camera was switched off! In such a case, the celebrated device of montage badly serves all aspects of the cinematic enterprise – the skill of the performer, the integrity of the performance, and the audience's desire to believe what it sees.

Godard and his friends shared Bazin's excitement over Roberto Rossellini's eloquent compositions, Jean Renoir's superb organization of deep-focus space, and Welles's brilliant camera maneuvers; but the young critics also had interests that diverged from Bazin's concerns. For one, they had no prejudice against montage: quite the opposite, in fact, since a clever or expressive cut seemed just as admirable to them as a long "sequence shot," a series of "reframings" within a single take, or any of the other devices that Bazin saw as aesthetically (and morally) superior to editing.

More broadly, they developed keen enthusiasm for a notion that would have profound influence on their criticism and their filmmaking: the ideal of personal cinema. Bazin was not hostile to this, but he disagreed with some of its implications and foresaw negative results – such as an unhealthy emphasis on subjective impressions over objective representations – if it were elevated into a critical principle, a filmmaking credo, or (as quickly transpired) both. Undeterred, the New Wave critics pushed ahead with their *politique des auteurs,* a phrase that is often translated as "auteur theory" but actually signals a policy of support for filmmakers as personal "authors" of their works. Inspiration for this came from critic Alexandre Astruc, whose concept of the *caméra-stylo,* or "camera pen," suggested that filmmakers should use their equipment as spontaneously, flexibly, and personally as a writer uses a pen.

Taking this literally (so to speak), Godard and his colleagues pieced together a new value system based on the degree of personal expression they could locate in a filmmaker's work. To facilitate this, they refined the definition of the word "auteur," using it to indicate the single individual most responsible for whatever personal expression (if any) a movie yielded up under critical analysis. Most movies are not works of art, they recognized, but mere entertainments assembled with varying degrees of competence; such films are made by technicians and craftspeople who may be skilled at their trades but cannot be called auteurs. The marks of the latter are (a) a distinctive vision of the world comparable to that of a capable novelist or painter and (b) enough strength of personality to channel the efforts of all the film's contributors (writers, designers, performers, editors, musicians, and so forth) in such a way that this distinctive world view is effectively conveyed by the finished work. Since directors are usually in the best position to exercise such creative control, auteurs usually tend to be directors, although strong screenwriters, cinematographers, and even performers have been known to usurp this function. (No matter who directed a Marx Brothers movie, one auteur theorist notes, it always came out a Marx Brothers movie.)

Armed with these ideas, the young *Cahiers* critics combed through world cinema – especially that of Hollywood, which impressed them with its vigor and variety – on the lookout for signs of personal expression in pictures dismissed by "serious" reviewers as soulless commercial products. They continued their personal-cinema adventure when they became filmmakers, launching the New Wave movement with works whose sensibilities were forged not within film schools (which barely existed) or studio apprenticeship systems (a conservative force) but within the private confines of their own personalities. Central to their project was a desire to escape the inauthenticity of French studio productions. Instead they sought the living immediacy of the streets, shops, apartments, and other settings that had shaped their own young lives. This linked them with the neorealists, who likewise favored real-life environments for their films.

Unlike their Italian contemporaries, however, Godard and his peers also welcomed a different kind of realism – the realism that grows from a cheerful acknowledgment that cinema is in fact cinema. Leapfrogging over some of Bazin's convictions, they were less interested in film as a "tracing of reality" or a "window on the world" than as a pliable art form whose sophisticated formal elements (framing, texture, editing rhythm, etc.) are just as pleasurable as narrative and representational content. Hence the freewheeling combination of openly fictional storytelling, vividly real backgrounds, and brashly cinematic articulation in such early Godard films as *All Boys Are Called Patrick* and *Breathless,* as well as other seminal New Wave statements such as *The 400 Blows* and *Paris Belongs to Us,* which put Truffaut and Rivette on the map of brilliant new talents.

Theory does not translate into practice automatically, of course, and Godard had to work his way toward *All Boys Are Called Patrick* and *Breathless* through a series of preliminary experiences. In 1954, two years after his *Cahiers du cinéma* writing debut, he took his earnings as a laborer on the Grand Dixence dam in Switzerland and financed a seventeen-minute film about the structure, *Opération Béton* – a conventional nonfiction movie, in the view of most critics who have commented on it, despite its use of music by Bach and Handel, composers not usually encountered in the context of public-works documentaries. During the next year he produced and directed a ten-minute short about a prostitute, *Une Femme coquette*, which he also photographed, edited, and wrote under his Hans Lucas pseudonym. (It was inspired by "Le Signe," the Guy de Maupassant story that would figure in *Masculine/Feminine* years later.) In 1956 and 1957 he parlayed his modest but growing list of credentials into film-editing jobs and a stint in the Paris publicity office of Twentieth Century–Fox, one of the most powerful Hollywood studios. After directing the twenty-one-minute short *All Boys Are Called Patrick* from a Rohmer screenplay, he spliced together *Une Histoire d'eau*, often regarded as one of his most revealing early works since it accompanies documentary footage – shot by Truffaut for a film about a flood, then scrapped when the project was abandoned – with verbally complex dialogue invented by Godard independently of his colleague, who was nonetheless credited as screenwriter and codirector.

The final pre-*Breathless* short was *Charlotte et son Jules,* with Jean-Paul Belmondo as a man trying vainly to entice his former lover back into his life. Godard directed it from his own screenplay, and also dubbed Belmondo's voice, showing the multitalented confidence needed by a fledgling auteur with ambitious hopes for the future. This confidence emerged more forcefully than ever in the feature-length *Breathless,* where key contributions from many collaborators – among them Truffaut, who wrote the initial scenario, and Belmondo, who got to speak with his own voice this time – were woven into an artful, edgy tapestry that clearly reflected Godard's still-emerging but already recognizable artistic personality.

Fascination with filmmaking as an avenue for personal expression, shared by all the young critics-turned-directors of the New Wave group, allowed Godard a quick start on what would become a career-long project: turning cinema away not only from the tired clichés and studio-bound artifices of mainstream entertainment films, but also from the fundamental roots of these formulas in what he increasingly saw as a sadly unjust and materialistic society. This meant rejecting or at least questioning many social, cultural, and political notions generally accepted as the common sense of our age.

Godard's rejection of commonsense filmmaking takes different forms at different stages in his career, and in the early work especially it is grounded more on intuition than on fully elaborated theories. *Breathless* (1960) behaves like a "normal" naturalistic movie when the camera travels through a palpably real world hunting for palpably real images; yet a combination of factors, including a need to make the film shorter and tighter, led Godard to counterbalance his reality effects with editing strategies so conspicuously eccentric that they sparked debates over his basic competence as a filmmaker. The most widely noted of these strategies was his use of jumpcuts that catapult the action from one image to another without the smooth transitions that nearly all directors since D. W. Griffith had taken care to provide. Quick-witted critics immediately grasped how this jagged, unruly montage heightened the jagged, unruly mood of a story propelled more by the whims of its characters than the dictates of a predetermined story. Others sniped at the movie's collisions between realism and formalism, calling these arbitrary and even anarchic.

Ever unpredictable, Godard stayed on the experimental trail that *Breathless* had blazed. At the same time, he came close to agreeing with that movie's detractors, commenting in 1962 that a goal of his second picture, *The Little Soldier* (1960), was "to discover the realism . . . the concreteness" that *Breathless* had missed.[7] The images of *The Little Soldier* are certainly "concrete," recalling the documentarylike realism that Godard admired in Rossellini's films; but again his reality-based shooting style merges with storytelling tactics – shifting attitudes toward characters, a protagonist with whom it is hard to identify – that transform what might have been a straightforward show-and-tell drama into something much more elusive. Godard described it as a "film about confusion" made "from the viewpoint of someone who is completely confused."[8] Not completely missing are confusions of his own, rooted in political and cinematic ideas that are still half-formed in many respects.

Godard's next movie, *A Woman Is a Woman* (1961), turns in a different direction, placing "reality factors" such as improvised dialogue and direct-sound recording into counterpoint with studio sets and musical-comedy conventions. The result is full of "discontinuity . . . changes in rhythm . . . breaks in mood,"[9] alternately confirming and contradicting the film's seeming affection for old-fashioned Hollywood entertainment. Different in style and content from the earlier pictures, it also gives little hint of the deep-rooted seriousness that would characterize Godard's subsequent features. *My Life to Live* (1962) and *Les Carabiniers* (*The Riflemen,* 1963), more mature in both artistic inventiveness and sociopolitical analysis, use urban prostitution and the rapaciousness of war as metaphors for the dehumanization Godard increasingly associates with industrialized society. *Contempt* questions the very possibility of personal and artistic integrity in today's world through its story of a screenwriter facing a marital crisis as he rewrites *The Odyssey* for a mercenary Hollywood producer.

Although these films combine radical sociocultural critiques with bold conceptions of film aesthetics, they do not entirely discard the grammar and syntax of traditional cinema. The same is true of *Band of Outsiders* (1964), an experimental comedy-drama about tangled romance and bungled crime; *Alphaville* (1965), an allegorical reworking of science-fiction themes; and *Made in U.S.A.* (1966), an offbeat thriller with political overtones. Godard's impatience with the legacies of conventional film continued to grow during this period, however, reaching unprecedented intensity in *A Married Woman* (1964) and *Pierrot le fou* (1965), which transform familiar genres (domestic drama, road movie) into shapes so unfamiliar that unadventurous critics wrote them off as irrelevant avant-gardism. The stakes escalated further in a string of extraordinary features stretching from *2 or 3 Things I Know about Her* (1966) and *La Chinoise* (1967) through *Weekend* (1967) and *Le Gai Savoir* (1968). The latter film, consisting largely of political dialogues between two young Maoists named Émile Rousseau and Patricia Lumumba, marked the last straw for Godard skeptics and the end of the road even for many sympathizers, who found the photogenic performances by Jean-Pierre Léaud and Juliet Berto to be scant compensation for the rigors of Godard's near-total commitment to eradicating traditional (read: bourgeois, superficial, commonsensical) pleasures from his work.

Little did these anti-Godardians dream that far from reaching the limits of his experimental trajectory, the ornery director was just warming up for some *really* audacious pictures. Deciding that the very act of signing his films betrayed lingering influences of decadent individualism, he joined with Maoist filmmaker Jean-Pierre Gorin and a small number of like-minded associates to form the Dziga-Vertov Group, a collective dedicated to overthrowing capitalist–imperialist ideologies of all shapes and sizes. In the words of *Pravda* (1969) – the movie, not the newspaper – information conveyed through sound and image "isn't enough" to change society "because it is only the knowledge perceived by our senses; now we must rise above this perceptive knowledge, we need to struggle to transform it into rational knowledge."[10] Godard's break with the wellsprings of common sense – consensus, tradition, even perception – was now close to complete. In their place was a single-minded determination to understand social reality afresh via the rejuvenating insights of Mao Zedong's philosophy. Godard called the project "making political films politically." Detractors called it replacing one set of epistemological blinders with another.

Several factors converged to end the Dziga-Vertov Group period. The most urgent was a near-fatal motorcycle accident that Godard suffered in the early 1970s, one result of which was his close relationship with Anne-Marie Miéville, who – in addition to helping with personal care – supported his interest in video experimentation and encouraged him to engage with narrative again, albeit in forms that remained thoroughly unconventional. A more generalized reason was the conservative sociopolitical climate that developed in Europe and the United States as the tumultuous 1960s gave way to the disillusioned 1970s and the reactionary 1980s. Godard remained a stylistic and philosophical radical, but his filmmaking became less overtly ideological, replacing its passion for political issues with a focus on aesthetic and spiritual matters. He pursued a growing curiosity about television and video technology; he renewed his exploration of traditional European culture in offbeat narrative features like *Passion* and *First Name: Carmen* (1983); and he revealed a genuine (if eccentric) religious streak in *Hail Mary* (1985), the last of his films to receive widespread attention from the general public – no thanks to its challenging style or exuberant beauty, but rather to a noisy controversy stirred up by Christians who disliked the idea of exploring the Virgin Mary's story through working-class characters trying to figure out God's will in a contemporary Swiss setting. Godard spent the rest of the 1980s and 1990s alternating between film and video production, directing art-house features like *Hélas pour moi* (1993) and *For Ever Mozart* (1997), and completing his long-term video series *Histoire(s) du cinéma,* perhaps the greatest capstone of a career at once incredibly varied in its interests and incredibly single-minded in its refusal to do any of the things other people expect of it.

Such are the basic facts of Godard's life and work, many of which will concern us again at appropriate points in the chapters to come. Before proceeding to close readings of individual films, however, it will be helpful to discuss some key aspects of his approach to cinematic style and content. In this area, few issues are more important than his fundamental stance toward the influence of entertainment, diversion, and spectacle on everyday social and political life. *Alphaville,* the 1965 science-fiction movie that has become one of his most frequently revived works, provides

Strange adventures: Jean-Luc Godard with his then-wife and frequent star, Anna Karina, during the shooting of *Alphaville: Une Étrange Aventure de Lemmy Caution* in 1965.

some fascinating clues to this. Two of the most telling appear about half-way through the film.

The first: Lemmy Caution, a secret agent visiting a futuristic city in a distant part of the cosmos, observes an execution room run by Alpha 60, the artificial brain that controls the community. Dominating the place is a large swimming pool surrounded by spectators, men condemned to die, and – incongruously but unmistakably – a lineup of young women in bathing suits, looking as if they're ready for a watery production number in a Busby Berkeley musical. Each prisoner is taken to the edge of the pool, allowed to cry out a few last words, shot full of bullets by a rapid-fire weapon, and left to fall clumsily into the water. The swimmers then dive decorously into the pool, finish off the victim with knives, and re-trieve his corpse, accompanied by polite applause from the onlookers. Thus does Alpha 60 deal with people convicted of behaving illogically, an inexcusable crime in this logic-obsessed city.

The second: Probing further into *Alphaville*'s way of life, Lemmy ponders the way Alpha 60 eliminates "foreigners" who can't be "assimilated" into the city's stiflingly homogeneous life. The usual procedure is to seat them in rows of theater seats and electrocute them as they watch a show. The seats then tilt to a slanted position, dumping the bodies into a bin below so the next "audience" can take its place for the same treatment.

What's going on here? Why does Alpha 60 use these grotesque methods of executing people who fail to obey its rules? More to the point: Why has Godard dreamed up such weird details for his story, when less bizarre metaphors might have moved the plot along without striking moviegoers as jarringly odd?

To give a short answer, Godard enjoys the prospect of jarring, jolting, and generally shaking up his audience. Some of his reasons are political, based on a desire to portray our world in unfamiliar ways that stimulate active thought rather than passive emotionalism. Others are personal, reflecting a mischievous streak that delights in frustrating ingrained expectations.

A deeper motivation for these scenes is so important, however, that it deserves special attention. The presence of the bathing beauties, their graceful performances, the courteous clapping of the spectators – all in service of a mass execution carried out with weapons as crude as they are deadly – reveal a terrible truth that applies to our own time and place as much as to *Alphaville* and its inhabitants. This truth is that *anything* can be turned into entertainment, and *will* be if the results are profitable for a privileged élite behind the scenes. The visit to the electrocution theater reaffirms this message in slightly different terms. Show business, it tells us, can be *bad* for you.

Godard never states this notion in such uncomplicated terms, but it could serve as a motto for much of his career as a filmmaker, video artist, and critic of contemporary life. It's an unexpected motto, to be sure, for someone in these particular lines of work. One might expect a world-renowned cinéaste to show more affection for the traditions of art and entertainment that paved the way for his own work as a creator of movies, television programs, and articles on cinema-related topics, many of which indicate that he has derived much pleasure from those traditions over the years. Show business may be bad for us, but it has given Godard a professional home, cultural power base, and inexhaustible source of subject matter from the early 1950s to the present day.

Faced with this contradiction, one might accuse Godard of intellectual laziness or diagnose him with cultural schizophrenia. (Will the real

Jean-Luc Godard please stand up?) More generously, one might chalk up his vacillations to the energetic gear-shifting of a notoriously restless sensibility. In the end, the most appropriate response might be to follow his own example and throw consistency to the winds, recognizing the existence of different "Godards" at different stages of his career. At some points he is a harsh sociocultural critic; at others he is more forgiving of the failings he finds at the heart of modern civilization; and at times he is downright indulgent toward humanity's frailties, probing them not with the objectivity of a surgeon but the sympathy of an artist who wants to unearth whatever fragile beauties they may hold.

To approach Godard in the spirit of these ever-changing visions, which often jostle against one another within a single film, is not to suspend critical judgment or allow a favored auteur to escape the reasoned analysis he himself has applied to other filmmakers. It is simply to recognize the energy, complexity, and multiplicity that have made him unique among his contemporaries, and to acknowledge the critical pliancy and flexibility that must be brought to bear on his diverse body of work.

In sorting through this diversity, it is helpful to remember that, despite appearances in *Alphaville* and elsewhere, Godard has been a movie fan during most of his career. A goal of his early writing was to reveal the aesthetic depths of entertainment pictures largely ignored by "serious" critics, and while his own films usually take off in unpredictable directions, they frequently use conventions of mainstream entertainment as handy guideposts. *Breathless* is a love story about a Parisian gangster and his American girlfriend, steeped in Hollywood ingredients from start to finish. *The Little Soldier* treats a political subject in the style of a film-noir thriller. *A Woman Is a Woman* is a musical shot in a studio. *Les Carabiniers* is a war movie, *Band of Outsiders* is a crime comedy, and *Alphaville* is a science-fiction adventure. Godard keeps using mainstream reference points long after these early films, moreover. *Détective* (1985) parodies its eponymous genre. *King Lear* (1987) reworks Shakespearean tragedy. The short "Armide" (1987) moves an operatic scene to a weightlifting gym. *Germany Year 90 Nine Zero* (1991) resurrects *Alphaville* hero Lemmy Caution for a pensive road movie probing the uncertainties of Europe after the cold war; and so forth.

These and many other Godard films show not just grudging tolerance but actual affection – albeit a cranky, indirect sort of affection – for the kinds of movies that everyday spectators have flocked to ever since cinema was born. In every case, Godard is both celebrating and criticizing the conventional materials that have found their way into his scenarios; and for all the twists and turns he puts them through, many conventions remain intact enough to engage and entertain us in the completed film. This indicates that Godard likes and respects them, despite the profound skepticism he perennially shows toward commercial culture and all its works. One must conclude that Godard is not so much cynical as deeply *ambivalent* about the long heritage of cultural production in which his own work constitutes a series of ambitious, fascinating, often problematic, frequently uproarious interventions.

Ambivalence is a useful concept when confronting Godard's career, and I mean to employ it here in its most positive sense. It allows for diverse perspectives, staves off the dryness of either–or thinking, and embraces the productivity of paradox. Ambivalence also challenges the ordinary wisdoms of "common sense," which points in opposite directions, thriving on either–ors and treating paradox as its enemy. Godard is cinema's great wizard of ambiguity, resisting neat categories and tidy theorizations from the outset, starting with his love–hate attitude toward traditional cinema.

Alphaville again provides a good illustration. The computer Alpha 60 ranks with the most outrageous villains in screen history – turning death into entertainment and theatergoing into a facade for murder – and Godard portrays this electronic autocrat in bitingly negative terms. The movie has other cautionary messages, too, warning that technology can deaden thought and feeling, and that materialism can stifle love and compassion. Obviously, high-tech pitfalls like technocracy and materialism are not just fictional devices in a fantastic tale but regrettably real tendencies in our own modern world – and mass-media communications, including movies like *Alphaville,* have played an important part in forming that world. Herein lies a contradiction that has fascinated Godard ever since he began thinking seriously about cinema. Film technology permits true artists to create aesthetically profound works that can stir us to the depths of our souls; yet the same technology has an uncanny knack for seducing us with shallow imitations of genuine thought and feeling, all in the service of society's most acquisitive and materialistic instincts.

Godard's response to this contradiction has been to draw on cinema's best possibilities while turning its worst impulses against it – attempting to subdue the beast even as he enjoys riding it, one might say. *Alphaville* thus sets itself up as a science-fiction thriller ("A Strange Adventure of Lemmy Caution") with a linear story, psychologically real characters, and enticing images. At the same time, by delving into Hollywood's bag of tricks to assemble this clever entertainment, Godard knows he is in danger of promoting a set of traditional movie values that he deeply opposes: voyeuristic spectatorship as opposed to critical thinking, vicarious problem solving as opposed to engagement with reality, passive consumption as opposed to active dialogue with the movie's ideas. Deftly skirting these traps, he proceeds to undermine the conventions that give rise to them, fragmenting the story and stylizing the visuals so flamboyantly (e.g., freezing a kinetic fistfight into a series of motionless shots) that they lose their ability to lull the audience into its accustomed state of receptive daydreaming.

This is a risky maneuver, and *Alphaville* has come in for scathing attacks from viewers who resist, reject, or simply fail to understand its approach. Others have welcomed it with enthusiasm, however, finding *traditional* pleasure in the conventions that survive Godard's manipulations as well as *innovative* pleasure in the ingenious methods he devises for casting these conventions into unlikely new forms.

The important point here is that Godard has always liked movies with as much passion as any cinephile in the business, and that his career has been less an attack on cinematic tradition than a concerned, even loving critique. Far from destroying an adversary, his aim in most of his oeuvre has been to help a friend and ally find paths that will finally lead to the long-delayed realization of its vast expressive potential.

In sum, Godard's stance toward traditional cinema is too complex to be boiled down to pithy formulations. His own efforts at self-clarification, often more cryptic than helpful, have frequently proved this. He has certainly not hesitated to reject simple imitation of the past, including splendid and inspiring aspects of the past; yet his quest has not been to negate the legacy of cinema (and other arts) but rather to interrogate and illuminate it. In doing this he hopes to accomplish two things. One is to reconfigure the shape of a hugely popular and persuasive medium so that its aesthetic, political, and philosophical richness will be greatly enhanced. The other is to guide audiences toward a new understanding of the domains of experience that Godard sees as cinema's necessary concerns: the aesthetics of sound and image, the knotty moral challenges posed by human relationships, and (most daunting of all) the interactions between material and spiritual modes of being, which must be grasped on intuitive rather than empirical levels.

As cinematic aspirations go, this is an imposing collection. What saves Godard from a terminal case of hubris is the important fact that he does not claim to possess answers for the vast set of questions he raises. Indeed, one reason for both the seductiveness and the elusiveness of his films is that he refuses to hide his innocence vis-à-vis the subjects he explores, preferring to make his very uncertainty an ingredient – an invigoratingly human ingredient – of his exploration. As his most perceptive critics have recognized, his movies are best approached not as definitive statements but as works in progress. It is as if most of his shots, scenes, and films are intended not as assertions of "what happened was . . ." but rather "if this were to happen, then perhaps. . . ."

This is not a formula for seamless storytelling or stylish entertainment, and nobody recognizes this more acutely than Godard, who is forever signaling his uncertainties in the very titles and subtitles of his films. *Weekend* is "a film found on a scrapheap" and "a film gone astray in the cosmos." *La Chinoise* (1967) is "a film in the process of making itself." *A Married Woman* is "fragments of a film shot in 1964." *Masculine/Feminine* presents "15 precise acts" rather than an all-encompassing narrative. *King Lear* is "a film shot in the back." It is hard to imagine a more modest title than *2 or 3 Things I Know about Her,* and Godard wrote in 1967 that this work "isn't a film, it's an attempt at film and is presented as such."[11] Ditto for the earlier *Pierrot le fou* (1965), which, he wrote in 1965, is "not really a film. It is rather an attempt at cinema."[12]

None of this means Godard lacks confidence as an artist. On the contrary, it takes a highly confident artist to unveil such exploratory works in the movie world, which is accustomed to very different attitudes. What it does mean is that he has little interest in a declarative cinema obsessed with self-contained stories and simplistic psychological models. He prefers visionary excursions into a genre that barely exists outside his oeuvre: the essay film, devoted not to the spinning of fantasies but to the weaving of ideas, chosen less for their clarity or transparency, as in conventional movies, than for their suggestiveness, allusiveness, and open-endedness. Speaking of his second feature – *The Little Soldier,* accused of political sloppiness by some critics – he insisted in 1962 that its "confusion" is not a defect but a virtue, since the movie is devoted to existential problem posing rather than philosophical problem solving. "If one thinks after seeing the film, 'he [the filmmaker] showed this [problem] but not the solution,' one should be grateful to the film, not angry with it," Godard said. "The questions are asked badly? But it is, precisely, the story of a man who asks himself certain questions badly."[13] A story told, we might now add, by a filmmaker who explores the question of questions-badly-asked with admirable honesty and conviction, if not the full sophistication he would be able to apply in later years.

Godard's investment in ambivalence points to a facet of his artistic personality that has not been sufficiently appreciated: his belief that representation of our physical world should not be considered a goal of worthwhile cinema but only a means – and a highly imperfect one at that – of accomplishing more ambitious things. He has a great interest in recording the real world, of course, and his insistence on minimizing the barriers between off-screen and on-screen "reality" is legendary. (He insisted on redoing a shot for *My Life to Live,* for instance, because a slight camera-equipment noise – which audiences would never have noticed – reduced the shot's fidelity to its real-world material.) Indeed, much of his work can be understood as a sort of dialectical wrestling match between documentary and fiction, setting fabricated plots and characters against vivid real-world backgrounds. Still, some of his most compelling films, especially in the second half of his career, go in directions that are hard to explain through normally useful terms like fiction and documentary. *Hail Mary* places a mythical story in a contemporary setting with the hope that this cinematic contradiction will give birth to spiritual insights. *Nouvelle Vague* (1990) combines immaculately filmed images with a remarkably unglued "plot" conveyed through a largely random screenplay. In such movies Godard reaches toward a drastically new form of expression, using fiction and documentary elements as entry points into a realm so uncharted that even he has trouble naming or describing it, beyond less-than-satisfactory phrases like "an attempt at cinema" and "sometimes . . . a show, but other times an experimentation."[14]

Central to this endeavor is Godard's intense recognition of a basic truth about cinema: that *mise-en-scène* (the content of individual shots) is continually inflected, articulated, and transformed by *montage* (the editing that drives a film from one shot to another). One way of understanding Godard's approach is to contrast it with that of François Truffaut, one of his most respected New Wave colleagues. As a self-described atheist, Truffaut took special pleasure in the materiality of cinema, noting that no photographic image can be obtained without real, physical light making direct contact with a real, physical object in the immediate presence of the camera. I mentioned this to Godard during a discussion we had in 1994, and he took a tack directly opposite to Truffaut's, stating that montage has the power to wipe out the seeming materiality of individual images. Picture A and Picture B might be wholly material, but the cinematic splice that joins them gives birth to something new, which may be so wholly *conceptual* that notions of materiality are beside the point.

This idea has a long pedigree, of course. In language, every pupil learns that words can evoke abstract concepts (justice, freedom, truth, etc.) that exist in principle but cannot be rendered through concrete description. In cinema, Sergei Eisenstein made a pioneering contribution to film theory when he observed that since a movie reveals itself one image at a time, it does not really exist anywhere but in the mind of the spectator who perceives it, remembers it, and assembles its bits and pieces into a coherent mental whole.

Godard shares this view of cinema as a largely psychological (and individual) phenomenon, which is why he labors so hard to give his cinema a social impact that goes beyond personal psychology. He also agrees with Eisenstein on film's ability to conjure up nonmaterial ideas; as early as 1957 he praised Nicholas Ray's western *The True Story of Jesse James* for images "which somehow manage to make ideas as abstract as Liberty and Destiny both clear and tangible."[15] These notions come into play with special force in such late Godard works as *Hail Mary, Nouvelle Vague,* and *Hélas pour moi,* which rely less on narrative meanings contained *within* shots than on suggestions arising in the space *between* those meanings, so to speak. That is, their most important messages are conveyed not only by the images we would see in a collection of film stills but also by the collisions between those images as they follow one another on the screen – and by the relationships between different parts of images as they appear before us in the fragmented forms that Godard tends to favor. Again we can trace this to Godard's early career through a comment on a Nicholas Ray movie. "A gulf yawns between the still and the film itself," he wrote in 1958 of *Bitter Victory,* a movie in which the viewer "is no longer interested in objects, but in what lies between the objects and which becomes an object in its turn." His next observation is a remarkable foreshadowing of transcendental tendencies that would preoccupy him many years later: "Nicholas Ray forces us to consider as real something one did not even consider as unreal, something one did not consider at all. *Bitter Victory* is rather like one of those drawings in which children are asked to find the hunter and which at first seem to be a meaningless mass of lines." Viewers who wonder at the apparent obscurity of Godard's mature works can find here a tantalizing clue to his intentions.[16]

Godard's approach to dichotomies often considered basic to cinema – image and editing, fiction and documentary, and so on – is therefore not one of simple (or even complex) dialectics, as if he enjoyed flinging different modes together just to see what syntheses this might produce. He seeks neither to oppose these elements nor to fuse them, but to achieve unprecedented effects by treating them as complements. He does this by subjecting real-world material (photographic images, recorded sounds) to formal procedures (disjunctive editing, offbeat juxtapositions) that abandon the familiar rules of linear narrative, creating new meanings that grow as much from the intuitiveness of the spectator as the inventiveness of the filmmaker.

The most important point to remember here is not the difference between Truffaut's notion of cinema, stressing the materiality of images, and Godard's, stressing the allusiveness of image combinations and juxtapositions. Rather, it is the difference between the *goals* of the two filmmakers: for Truffaut, to evoke the world in its rich physicality; for Godard, to do the same while also conjuring up unseen and perhaps unseeable dimensions. In early films like *Breathless,* these dimensions are connected with the unquenchable energy of human personalities and the social worlds they spin around themselves. In middle-period films like *Le Gai Savoir,* they are linked with visions of political action that might catapult society toward a radical new phase. In later films like *King Lear* – a movie in which the words "no thing" are a continuing motif – they are inseparable from spiritual concerns too ephemeral to photograph but not too evanescent to *suggest* or *evoke* through the magic of cinema in its larger-than-life totality.

For a variety of reasons, then, Godard has always wished to subvert traditional (and limiting) ideas by subverting traditional (and limited) cinema. To understand how he has gone about this, one must start with an understanding of the norm he is rejecting – classical film structure – and how this normative style operates on us while we watch a movie. As described by film historian David Bordwell and others, the "classical Hollywood style" results from a cluster of principles, practices, and procedures that Hollywood studios (and others eager to emulate their financial success) have promulgated since the 1920s. Among its main characteristics are

- "invisible editing" that calls minimal attention to itself;
- "shot–countershot" and "eyeline match" montage that allows the audience to see what the on-screen characters see;
- three-point lighting that maximizes the visibility and clarity of images;
- synchronized sound that matches and supports the visual material;
- alternating dialogue that allows clear understanding of the characters' words;
- a standardized narrative "grammar" that guides spectators through the story; for instance, new scenes generally begin with long-range "establishing" shots followed by medium-range views and then more intimate close-ups.

These and other classical conventions have a common purpose: They reduce the audience's awareness of the filmmaking process, enhancing the illusion that "reality" is unfolding on the screen. We always know we're watching a film rather than real life, of course, but reducing this awareness – bringing about the "willing suspension of disbelief" long valued by fiction writers – is particularly prized in a medium celebrated for its "realism" and its ability to "sweep us up" in its stories. Classical filmmakers are like puppeteers who want us to forget their string pulling and accept the actions of their marionettes as natural events. By contrast, modernist puppet masters like Godard insist on waving to us from behind the stage, reminding us of their presence and inviting us to enjoy their string pulling as an essential and *meaningful* part of the spectacle.

The result is a brand of cinema more self-aware and proudly artificial than classical stylists find acceptable. Editing may be not only visible but aggressive and even disruptive, vying for attention with the story itself. Lighting designs may be expressionistic, symbolic, or otherwise compelling in their own right. Dialogue and other sounds may compete with each other, or be presented for pure noise value rather than for coherent meanings. Above all, the grammar of screen storytelling may be radically altered, forcing viewers into new relationships with the material they're seeing and hearing. Even the plot line might be (and often is) bent into innovative shapes that bring out unexpected meanings at the expense of ordinary values like momentum and suspense. Asked by a bewildered colleague whether his movies have any kind of structure – even a beginning, middle, and end – Godard famously replied, "Yes, but not necessarily in that order."[17] No semiologist could better sum it up.

Transgressions of tradition like these can operate in terms of form alone, or they can be deployed with a definite political intention. Some critics claim that departures from classical style automatically have a subversive political effect, since they force viewers into a stance of active curiosity toward the material; but a glance at almost any TV commercial (including those Godard has made!) shows that innovative structures can be effortlessly mobilized to serve conventional and even reactionary purposes. Godard's importance as a cinematic rebel comes not from his reconfigurations of film and video form per se, but from the way his dissections and reshufflings interact with the subjects he chooses to explore. One of those subjects is always cinema itself; the others change as his career moves from one stage to another. What remains consistent, however, is his deep-seated desire to refute two ideas taken for granted by the vast majority of filmmakers: (a) that cinema captures a "direct" and somehow "natural" view of the world and (b) that cinema's standard psychological devices are somehow equivalent with "human nature" and thus provide accurate, commonsensical insights that can be accepted and enjoyed at face value.

To this end, he gives his movies a self-questioning structure and a self-critical attitude meant to lead his audience away from passive consumption and toward an active, alert engagement with his works and the sociopolitical milieu in which they were made.

Like all cultural and political ideas, Godard's critical attitudes toward modern society and its mass media did not evolve in a vacuum. Some of this century's most influential currents in French art and philosophy (often intertwined, as in Jean-Paul Sartre's work) have explored concerns related to his and have raised similar questions about their own place within the contemporary world's complex of "power/knowledge relationships," to borrow a term from French philosopher Michel Foucault, whose analysis of modern society has much in common with Godard's views.

Foucault sees today's world as a vast network of interlocking social systems. Some are global entities (e.g., the empire of mass communications) whose influence is virtually omnipresent; others are "capillary" offshoots (e.g., local schools and community groups) that operate on a smaller and subtler scale. All are sites where knowledge and power – inextricably linked with each other – may be tapped into and manipulated. Within this universal framework, individuals and institutions vie with one another in a never-ending struggle for privilege and position.

If knowledge and power are closely intertwined, as Foucault contends; and if cinema replicates information and ideas with unprecedented efficiency, as Godard contends; then no ethical filmmaker could maintain a clear conscience without keeping a critical eye on the impact made by cinematic works – especially the filmmaker's own – on the world in which they're unleashed. Ethics have always been at the center of Godard's career, as a concept and as a set of practices needing continual scrutiny and redefinition. Undergirding his ethical view is a determination to harness and limit the ideological *power* of cinema by calling into question the social *knowledge* it claims to represent.

The sights and sounds of cinema, according to Godard, do not present us with self-evident truths. They are merely scraps of evidence assembled by a particular set of personalities and technologies under the conditions of a particular time, place, and sociopolitical system. If we often accept these sights and sounds as accurate representations of the real world, this is because they effectively mimic the impressions conveyed by our eyes and ears – the two "distance senses" that can provide information to our brains without being near the things they're perceiving. In this age of relativity theory and quantum mechanics, though, it should be clear that even direct sensory evidence can be inadequate and misleading, if not downright illusory and false. This goes double for mediated evidence filtered through the technologies (however advanced) and ideologies (however sophisticated) of the individuals and institutions that control the media.

To expand a bit on these crucial points, the things we see and hear within a society may indeed contain valuable clues to its nature. We may therefore turn to cinema, with its finely developed mechanisms for recording images and sounds, as a useful tool for understanding aspects of that society, whether for purely intellectual reasons or to foster social change. Generations of socially concerned filmmakers have acted on this seemingly reasonable premise, but it turns out to have a major theoretical downside. The problem is that cinematic sounds and images do not exist in some "objective" realm outside the social system that's being examined. Material contained in a film must be selected from many possible alternatives; it must be captured on equipment designed and manufactured inside the social system; and it must be viewed within an exhibition system (movie theaters, TV networks, etc.) whose standards of "appropriateness" might seem arbitrary and even unreasonable under different circumstances.

In short, movies – even critical ones like those of Godard and his colleagues – are products of the very sociopolitical system they set out to explore and expose. Moreover, this is just the start of the problem. The senses and interpretive skills we use to perceive cinema are also conditioned by the sociopolitical system, compounding the difficulty of "objective" analysis twice over. Indeed, not even this criticism of objectivity can be called pure or disinterested, since it too emerged within the prevailing power/knowledge regime!

Recognizing these difficulties, Godard operates on the principle that "the 'evidence of our senses' cannot be trusted and is no basis for analysis," as critic Colin McCabe summarizes it. Godard never forgets that our senses are shaped by "the common sense of the dominant ideology ... which takes truth as evident and thus ignores our place in that truth."[18] He is not opposed to "common sense" when this means getting beyond humanly made obfuscations in order to reaffirm contact with the bedrock world of objects and places, as he indicates poignantly in the narration of his 1966 essay-film 2 or 3 Things I Know about Her:

Why are there so many signs everywhere, so that I end up wondering what language is about – signs with so many different meanings that reality becomes obscure, when it should stand out clearly from what is imaginary? Images can get away with everything, for better or worse. Ordinary common sense reasserts itself before my very eyes and comes to the rescue of my shattered sense of logic. Objects are there, and if I study them more carefully than people, it's because they are more real than people.

Yet another part of Godard is always on the lookout – skeptically, even suspiciously – for social agendas being foisted on unwary people by powerful forces that disguise their self-serving views as "natural" or "common sense" positions.

This wariness reaches its peak in his revolutionary films of the late 1960s and early 1970s, where he sees all of Western society as so outrageously decadent that only a sort of scorched-earth cinema can hope to confront and counteract its dehumanizing influences. In these films, Godard's tendency to examine human issues on a large, sweeping scale makes him less a cultural critic than a social philosopher, concerned not with details of the moment but with what Foucault calls the "episteme," the epistemological grid that underlies the thinking of a historical era. This grid determines the taken-for-granted knowledge (and power) that sets invisible boundaries around possibilities of thought and action. The beliefs accepted within these boundaries are often known as common sense. As indicated in the lines from 2 or 3 Things I Know about Her quoted above, Godard accepts such conventional wisdoms when they rescue the clear, productive reality of objects and images from the artificial signs and manufactured meanings that glut our contemporary world. Common sense becomes his enemy, however, when it lures us into uncritical acceptance of those signs and meanings. The eccentricities and idiosyncracies of his work are a decades-long howl of protest against cinema that contents itself with reflecting instead of questioning the assumptions of the society around it. For an artist, moreover, to question society means to question oneself – making "attempts at cinema" rather than definitive statements that take their own wisdom and objectivity for granted.

Godard is convinced, then, that since a society's guiding assumptions are considered to be self-evident, they are seldom brought to light for thoughtful examination. He has long been bedeviled by the idea that the everyday actions of just about everyone (himself included) are strongly influenced by social forces that few people ever look at closely and critically.

Particularly irksome for him is the fact that widely seen movies – exactly the sort of arena where such scrutiny should take place – contentedly buy into this dubious cultural arrangement. On the screen, they seduce us with stories that "sweep us away" by appearing to have a "life of their own." Behind the scenes, however, they are carefully manufactured by people with strong commercial and ideological interests that go largely unexamined by all concerned. Godard's disruptions of classical film style are meant to break down this insidious setup, making us aware of cinematic elements that gain much of their power by remaining invisible not to our eyes but to the consciousness *behind* our eyes: the way sound and picture reinforce each other's credibility, the way editing controls our responses to a story, the way slick "production values" lure us into passive acceptance of attitudes we might reject if we were truly aware of their implications.

All of which is to say that Godard's works are haunted by the invisible. It may seem odd to use a ghostly word like "haunted" in connection with an artist known for dissecting worldly matters in so many of his works, but his effort to ferret out invisible forces – and his growing sense that such forces take many forms – are reasons behind his shift from films with sociopolitical concerns to works with more metaphysical interests. In his early films he upset conventions partly to assert his own artistic freedom, and partly to set his audience free from unseen cinematic structures that commonly dictate the form and content of screen entertainment. During his overtly political period he carried this practice to extremes, attempting not only to expose but to destroy the power of moviegoing pleasures rooted in unexamined (and hence invisible) assumptions of capitalist–imperialist ideology. Eventually concluding that a sociocinematic revolution was not at hand, he turned to a more philosophical/spiritual notion of the invisible, suggesting that the unseen forces guiding our world are more profound than mere sociopolitical influences. Indeed, they are too profound and unworldly for cinema to capture; the best to be hoped for is an allusive form of filmmaking that can evoke, suggest, and hint at dimensions of reality not available to our physical senses or the technological devices based on those senses.

Uniting these different phases is Godard's steady conviction that *something* not directly visible must be taken into account if we are to gain control (or at least understanding) of our relations with the world around us. Almost every element of his filmmaking can be traced in one way or another to his aim of stripping away the conventional veneers that hide unseen forces from view, and thereby limit our options for thought and ac-

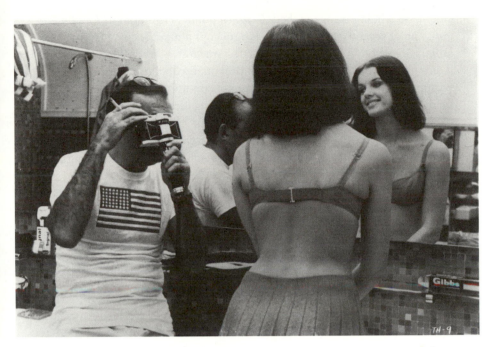

Manufactured meanings: Woman as commodity in *2 or 3 Things I Know about Her* (1966; Raoul Lévy, Anny Duperey).

tion. This ambition is implicit in some films and explicit in others. One that foregrounds it is *Comment ça va* (1976), virtually an essay on invisibility, in which a character played by Miéville notes that what is *not seen* is always the controlling factor in today's economically and ideologically shaped world. Our opportunities, our experiences, our very personalities are molded by social and political factors that we would like to think of as transparent, in the sense of clear and understandable, but are really invisible, in the sense of hard to locate, hard to identify, hard to pin down and understand. Godard also warns us, in *Comment ça va* and elsewhere, that in cinema the filmmaker is invisible too; but this is one invisibility Godard knows he can do something directly about. Instead of hiding his power through commercial-film tricks, he pokes his active presence (and in some movies his entire body) into the audience's perception so we can engage with him and decide for ourselves whether his ideas, strategies, and tactics are to our liking.

Taken to its limits, this approach to filmmaking (and communication in general) implies peeling away artifices and superfluities until a kind of cinematic tabula rasa is reached. Godard ponders this goal in *Le Gai Savoir,* one of several films in which language is a main focus. Here he sees language as both a stumbling block for freedom – when ideologues use it as a power/knowledge tool – and a potentially liberating force for those wishing to investigate and heal the human condition. As noted earlier, the main characters are Émile and Patricia, young idealists who take up most of the movie with a long conversation about "the prison-house of language," to use philosopher Friedrich Nietzsche's phrase. What excites them is the possibility of weakening this prison's hold by cultivating new ways of living and thinking. Assuming they can brush away society's existing patterns at will, Émile is eager to "start from zero," like children acquiring words for the first time; but thoughtful Patricia reminds him that "first we have to go back there. Back to zero." Freedom from ingrained assumptions, she recognizes, cannot be attained through idealistic determination alone. Rather, this great "zero" must be earned through active struggle – that is, a willed forgetting of convention (perhaps resembling what Foucault calls "countermemory") and a conscious investment in new ways of perceiving and being. Patricia conveys Godard's message that neither the linguistic past nor the cinematic past can be scuttled at will. The task of renewing consciousness must be long and exacting, and all a film like *Le Gai Savoir* can do is "suggest . . . effective ways" for starting the process.

Godard's self-analysis at the end of this movie shares the modest, tentative tone of other statements he has made about his works, calling this "not the film which should be made" but one that shows certain "paths" potentially helpful to future ventures. While this is hardly a ringing peroration, it's an honest and self-probing one, demonstrating Godard's awareness of his own place within the prison house of language, and his need to glimpse what lies beyond its walls so real rethinking and renewal can begin.

What is it that lies beyond those walls? The answer suggested by Godard's later work is vast and mysterious, as he looks past the political sphere to a new set of questions about both kinds of sense – common sense and the physical senses – that concern him.

I have already observed that in many of Godard's mature works, such as *Hail Mary* and *Nouvelle Vague,* meaning comes not only from the manifest content of images and sounds, but also from the evocative "space between" different elements of the film. This space seems deeper and wider in Godard's works than in most others, since he emphasizes the disjunctions and discontinuities built into cinema – cuts between shots, contrasts between sound and picture, and so forth – that conventional movies cover with devices stressing narrative flow instead of poetic allusiveness. Behind this practice is Godard's double goal of *demystifying* and *remystifying* the cinematic experience. Demystification takes place when he pulls sound and image from behind the cloak of classical style, bringing them into our awareness by freeing them from their usual servitude to psychological storytelling. Remystification takes place when he discovers within a sound, an image, or a sound–image combination some secret, enigma, or conundrum that ordinary cinema would scarcely acknowledge, much less tease out and explore.

For pursuing these interests, Godard's films are sometimes accused of forsaking coherent meaning. There is truth in this charge – if by coherent one means unitary, monologic, and unmindful of the expansiveness and complexity of human experience. Godard tells us it is tautological, however, to say that human minds can fathom their own intricacies. Still less can they fathom the inklings of spirituality that suggest themselves to restless, intuitive sensibilities like his own. Clues to such cosmic puzzles can be found in philosophical inquiry and also in imaginative rumination on the people, places, and things of everyday life. Both ends of this spectrum figure in Godard's most ambitious works, such as 2 or 3 *Things I Know about Her,* which ranges from thoughtful speculation on the nature of language to astonishing close-ups of a coffee cup whose swirls of steaming liquid resemble the star-filled spirals of a distant galaxy. As luminous as such an image is, Godard treasures it less for its visual beauty than for the hint it gives that physical and metaphysical realities are separated only by a thin shell of materiality that the camera's probing gaze can *almost* penetrate. Equally important to him is the resonance this moment has for fellow film-lovers willing to abandon commonsense constraints and follow the screen's mysterious inscriptions wherever they may lead.

To summarize, Godard refuses to separate areas of experience that are normally confined to distinct categories in both film and life. His sounds and images oscillate between documentary and fiction, linear narrative and free association, crisp iconography and dense collage, the symbolic power of language and the pure presence of music, the contingency of spontaneous events and the calculations of creative labor – and so on, in a list that could grow very long. Conventional divisions between "high" and "low" culture are equally blurred in his mature works, which join the venerable and the contemporary as readily as 2 or 3 *Things I Know about*

Her swings between the ideas of Ludwig Wittgenstein and the story in a comic book. We have noted that, for the first two decades or so, his movies focused most intently on social dysfunctions, political ideas, and the inner workings of contemporary aesthetics, and that his later work has veered increasingly toward a preoccupation with invisible components of experience, expressed through what might be called the invisible components of cinema: subliminal connections between scenes, shots, and frames, and intuited spaces beyond the edges of the screen and the limits of the lens. Parallel with this has been his ever-shifting engagement with sound – more tactile and less linear than light, and capable of supple tricks like going around corners, quivering our flesh with its vibrations, and reaching out to surround us in the dark. Sight appears to be privileged in Godard's early features, whereas sound holds the best cards in the Dziga-Vertov Group films, which are meant to overthrow the empire of visuality that props up commercial cinema. In his films and videos since the early 1980s, image and sound reach a rough parity, alternately supporting and contradicting each other in a rich counterpoint that carries a strong sensual thrill along with its deeper aesthetic and metaphysical implications.

Another element we must consider in Godard's restless, thoughtful approach to film is the notion of cinema as personal expression, with which he has long been associated as both critic and artist. In much theoretical writing of recent years, the very idea of personal expression has been called into question by postmodernist and poststructuralist thinkers who find it an unacceptable remnant of romantic idealism, steeped in concepts of "individuality" and "originality" that have outlived whatever questionable usefulness they ever had. The so-called individual is not a site of uniquely shaped thoughts, feelings, and creative acts, these theorists say, but simply a "locus of enunciation" for socially and materially determined currents that pass through human "subjects" as mere relay points in their discursive travels. Language speaks us, rather than the other way around.

What does Godard, champion of personal cinema and auteurism, think about all this? Ever surprising, he heartily agrees with much of it. His longtime love of quotation and pastiche stems from a similar suspicion of anyone's ability to be truly original after so many centuries of sociocultural expression. Then too, his insistence on direct-sound recording (along with a distaste for artificial lighting) indicates his feeling that human artistry does not genuinely "create" so much as it wanders through a preexisting world, picking up whatever discursive signals capture its (socially conditioned) fancy.

None of this means Godard doesn't champion personal cinema, however. Even as he crams his movies with quotations, allusions, and collage-like concatenations of sound and image, he does so not randomly but according to impulses rooted deep within his own sensibility. Only a critic dogmatically committed to "death of the author" theory could argue that his productions are not intensely and idiosyncratically personal, and almost any excerpt (even from works made in collaboration with partners) will bear his stylistic signature for those familiar with it.

Godard's complex relationship with filmmaking originality in particular and personal creativity in general goes back to his early career. As noted above, he was a founder of auteur theory, as a critic for *Cahiers du cinéma* in the 1950s and as a fledgling director who wanted to express his ideas in a spontaneous *caméra-stylo* manner. Although auteurism remains influential in both popular and academic criticism nearly a half century after its birth, it has been confronted with two strong counterarguments. The first contends that auteurism badly oversimplifies the realities of the filmmaking process, which is collaborative by nature, drawing on what film historian Thomas Schatz, following Bazin, calls "the genius of the system" rather than the genius of individual artists. No single person, this argument states, can credibly be praised or blamed for every aspect of something as large and multifaceted as a feature film. No less an auteurist than Godard himself has acknowledged some merit in this position, admitting that he and his *Cahiers* cohorts exaggerated their auteurist claims for strategic reasons in their well-intentioned fight to establish personal expression as a primary value in film.

The other objection stems from the poststructuralist notions of communication just outlined and from semiotics, the linguistically based study of signs and symbols. Theorists such as Foucault and Roland Barthes have cast doubt on the very concept of "the author," not only in a controversial domain like cinema but even in seemingly incontestable areas like literature and painting, where it seems obvious that a single author takes up pen or brush and produces a work inspired by his or her individual creativity. What do we mean by terms like "individual" and "creativity," poststructuralism asks? Aren't all "individuals" profoundly shaped by the sociocultural milieu in which they live? Aren't all "creative" ideas molded by the limited cluster of power/knowledge relationships that constitute the common sense of a given time and place? Do we really "speak" for ourselves, or are we "spoken by" the social and political forces that surround us? As one theoretician cleverly put it, Ludwig van Beethoven may have been as "individual" and "creative" as they come – but could he have written a rap song?

For all his auteurist credentials, Godard provides ammunition to this antiauthor camp. Since originality is impossible, poststructuralists argue, all expression is basically a form of quotation; and as we have observed, nobody loves quoting more than Godard, who spoke of his "taste for quotation" as early as 1962. "People in life quote as they please," he noted, "so we [filmmakers] have the right to quote as we please. Therefore I show people quoting, merely making sure that they quote what pleases me. In the notes I make of anything that might be of use for a film, I will add a quote from Dostoievsky [sic] if I like it. Why not? If you want to say something, there is only one solution: say it."[19] Or rather, have somebody else say it, perhaps in the words of still another person.

The sort of quotation Godard refers to here – phrases borrowed from preexisting sources – is small change compared with the poststructuralist idea that consciousness itself is the product of a social sphere from which all words, thoughts, and emotions are necessarily derived; yet something like this view emerges from a close study of how Godard actually handles quotations. His practices take two basic forms. One is his habit of quoting from other films – his own, the classics, the nonclassics, pretty much anything that comes to mind. Such allusions are often taken as jokes by cinematically savvy spectators, who enjoy recognizing and decoding them. While jokiness is indeed one of their functions, however, their frequency and prominence point to a deeper intention: the construction of a filmic universe in which all things relate to cinema, and can therefore be expressed in cinematic terms. To put this another way, Godard's continual movie references suggest the existence of a world-as-film that overlaps with the world-as-reality and is no less significant, even though its properties (rooted in meaning and metaphysics) must be very different in key respects. This is a hypothesis that poststructuralists can happily entertain, given their interest in such concepts as "undecidability" and "intertextuality," which challenge taken-for-granted divisions between actuality and representation. It reaches a pinnacle in the *Histoire(s) du cinéma* videos, which are virtuosic in their kleptomania as well as their historiography.

Godard's other form of quotation is the aforementioned practice of having characters speak or write words borrowed from sources outside the cinematic world. What's striking here is how much this grows from his early works to his later ones, mushrooming from a mannerism to a major expressive device. The quotes from William Faulkner in *Breathless* or Edgar Allan Poe in *My Life to Live* are important to the movies that contain them, but the movies would still hold together if they were edited out. By contrast, the screenplay of *Nouvelle Vague* consists almost entirely of quotes, and the Godard who appears in *JLG/JLG – Autoportrait de décembre* (. . . *December Self-Portrait;* 1994) is a veritable fountain of other people's words – plus other people's images and music, appropriated with such passion as to become integral parts of the most autobiographical statement ever made by this keenly autobiographical artist.

What all this evidence adds up to is a demonstration of both the necessity and the impossibility of auteurism: the necessity, since Godard's advocacy of personal cinema helped bring a new awakening of poetic-realist film anchored in the director's rich fund of memories, fantasies, and experiences; and the impossibility, since his taste for appropriation can be traced to a love of artistic legacies dating from millenia before cinema was born, and to his desire to embrace their beauties within new forms determined by all-encompassing modern sensibilities. Godard therefore emerges as an auteurist in spite of himself, delving into his own improvisatory imagination while recognizing that every cinematic act is anchored in the assumptions of a Zeitgeist shaped by social and historical forces.

No wonder commentators (not to mention audiences) have difficulty placing him in any of the critical pigeonholes that suit most cinéastes quite comfortably. Still, descriptive labels can be helpful as long as they are taken as guideposts rather than destinations, and some commonly applied to Godard point to important aspects of his creative personality. It is hard to approach his work without thinking of romanticism, for instance, however much that world view may grate against his postmodernist side. Only a deeply romantic artist – motivated by a strong belief in the possibility of innovative, idiosyncratic expression – would persist so steadily in aesthetic enterprises greeted with so much incomprehension by so many spectators so much of the time. Godard has also courted romanticism in his choices of narrative and theme. An obvious example is *Pierrot le fou,* a story of "the last romantic couple"[20] that focuses on social rebelliousness, psychological angst, and clashes between culture and nature that have preoccupied romantic artists for ages.

Terms of more recent vintage – modernism and postmodernism – also speak directly to his work, however. To begin with the first, many critics have credited Godard with bringing a dynamic sense of modernism to cinema, originally a nineteenth-century art and still indebted to that period for many of its technical and expressive traits. Although this analysis often rests on a superficial identification of "modern" with characteristics like "fast-paced" and "fragmented," there is no denying Godard's deep investment in two fundamental traits of modernist creativity: (a) its self-aware investigation of the processes and motivations of art making in itself and (b) its insistence on the reality and importance of the raw materials used in fabricating artistic works.

Western artists have traditionally seen such materials as ingredients to be transmuted and transmogrified as creativity takes its course. By contrast, modernists revel in the substances they use, seeking less to transform and transcend them than to explore and celebrate them – and by extension, to explore and celebrate the conscious and unconscious thinking that goes into their activities. Painters conceive their works as colors on flat canvases rather than windows on the three-dimensional world; composers explore once-forbidden realms of dissonance and atonality that reveal music as a special form of noise; choreographers preserve the movements of everyday life without bending them into the stylized steps of classical ballet; and so on in every artistic field. Rejecting the notion that cinema is "automatically" modern, with its photographic realism and effortless changes of perspective, Godard and his New Wave colleagues brought to their art a new preoccupation with what Bazin calls its ontological dimension – not subordinating its methods and mechanics to an irresistible narrative flow, but foregrounding its materiality with on-location shooting, conspicuous camera angles, and disdain for the "invisible editing" of Hollywood studios. Montage and mise-en-scène are at least as important as story and psychology, they insisted, and Godard has not wavered on this quintessentially modernist point since he espoused it in the early 1950s. His fascination with editing has strong links to modernist *bricolage* as well, recalling that modernists were the first great collage artists, beginning with the audacious paste-ups of Pablo Picasso and Georges Braque, who pioneered the appropriation of real-world materials as both *presentation* and *representation*. Godard shares their interest in treating such materials as expressive artifacts shaped by the artist's inner vision *and* as physical objects retaining the properties and appearances they possessed before the artist (and viewer) got hold of them.

These aspects of modernism point toward the postmodernism that has held much of the cultural stage in recent years, and in the final analysis Godard's credentials here may outweigh all his others. Modernism paved the way for postmodernism by underscoring the limits of imitation, figuration, and even representation itself; but it is postmodernists who have transformed the cut-and-mix aesthetic of collage from an expressive strategy into a philosophical principle, by refusing not only to act on but even to accept such notions as "category" and "genre," which they find arbitrary and limiting at best, capricious and dictatorial at worst. This accords with the poststructuralist idea that genres and categories reflect a humanistic urge to encompass reality within "master narratives" and other artificial schemes. These schemes promise to organize and illuminate reality, but in fact they warp and distort the very phenomena they're meant to clarify, by twisting them into the likeness of the human mentality itself. This may be comforting for the vanity of our species, but it does poor justice to the ultimately unknowable vastness of our existential realm. In place of categorical thinking, postmodernists seek an art that ranges freely across boundaries, incorporating whatever suits its purposes from wherever this may be found.

Godard has much humanism in his nature, as his broad romantic streak indicates; yet master schemes and philosophical dogmas have long been his enemies. As early as his 1952 article on the "Defence and Illustration of Classical Construction" he attacked thinkers "who seek to lay down absolute rules," including critics who elevate "certain figures of style into a vision of the world" and credit "some technical process or other with astrological pretensions it cannot possibly have."[21] Not for him is a formula-bound cinema that tries to contain the vast diversity of experience within practices and procedures so narrowly construed that only a hardy band of inspired auteurs can leap beyond them. Not for him either is a cinema devoted to reassuring reproductions of a familiar world. He shares with postmodernists an enthusiasm for psychological, intellectual, and spiritual travel through a universe rendered less secure but far more exciting by an awareness of its ungraspable, undecidable nature. The best way to explore this universe is by splitting open its paradigms and preconceptions as precisely as the young heroine of "The Book of Mary" (directed by Miéville in 1985) cracks open the enigmatic egg on her dining-room table, simultaneously closing one story and opening the Pandora's box of another.

This goes a long way toward explaining Godard's penchant for quotation, combination, and pastiche, all indispensable tools in the postmodern enterprise. Perceptive critics have observed that, in Jean-Louis Leutrat's words, he "assembles everything he finds in our world that seems to him apt for creating . . . jarring and accusatory encounters." His respect for tradition often leads him to quote from conventionally respected "works of art or of the mind," but he is less interested in reproducing their aesthetic satisfactions than in reshaping them as cultural "debris" that mirrors the dazzling confusions of our own existential condition. Hence his neverending fascination with "fragments that are badly read, badly spoken, botched, wrecked; corners of images; reproductions of reproductions."[22] The ambiguities, discontinuities, and incongruities of Godard's works are not the slipshod residues of a perversely inscrutable mind. They are the audible and visible traces of an adventure in perception guided by an artist who realizes that for contemporary cinema, as philosopher Gilles Deleuze puts it, "categories are not fixed once and for all. They are redistributed, reshaped and reinvented for each film."[23]

Through his pursuit of such interests Godard has cultivated a cinematic gaze "posed so afresh on things at each instant that it pierces rather than solicits them, that it seizes in them what abstraction lies in wait for," to borrow words he wrote in praise of Jean Renoir's subtle mise-en-scène.[24] This quest for continually renewed freshness, self-invention, and unpredictability helps explain his preoccupation with spontaneity, and also his willingness to embrace an apparent paradox: To produce a sense of spontaneity on the movie screen, great amounts of time and effort may be required. What is ultimately spontaneous as we watch a Godard film is not the story, the characters, or the cinematic techniques, all of which lie frozen on strips of celluloid. Rather, the spontaneity he treasures is found in the mercurial stream of creativity that flows from him and his collaborators as they work. While this creativity is as ephemeral as thought, it leaves unmistakable traces on the work we eventually view.

Godard offered an amusing portrait of his spontaneity obsession in "Montparnasse-Levallois," his contribution to *Paris vu par . . .* , a 1965 anthology of shorts by six directors. The opening titles call his episode an "action film," and one of the characters is an artist who makes "action-sculpture" in his cluttered studio. What is action-sculpture, exactly? "It means that chance enters into the creation of the sculpture," the artist explains to his curious girlfriend. "I take pieces of metal and throw them up, and weld them together the way they fall. It's all very experimental."

This character might be describing the movie he's in, since Godard allowed unusual room for chance in the way he set it up. The basic action was mapped out by the director and his performers, and only then did cinematographer Albert Maysles come onto the set, filming the story as if he were shooting a documentary of real-life events happening before his eyes. Like the fictional sculptor, the real-life filmmaker did not leave everything to chance – the skill and ingredients needed for cohesive, compelling work were carefully assembled so they would be readily on hand when needed; but the way things happened to "fall" played a strong role in determining the final form of this brief movie.

The same can be said for virtually all of Godard's works. A few of them passed from the planning stage to the final cut along pathways that had been laid out from the beginning. Many others benefited (or suffered) from great surprises, inspirations, and changes of direction along the way. One thing can be said, however, about every inch of the oeuvre that resulted: It's all very experimental.

The following chapters offer close readings of works by the director who is perhaps the most protean yet to emerge in European cinema. So prolific and diversified is his output that various attempts to periodize it have come to very different conclusions. By one account, it comprises four major phases: the New Wave period, the "revolutionary" years, the cycle of video experimentation, and the recent "contemplative" period. Another critic finds an early "anthropological" phase followed by a "political" period, then a highly personal exploration of sexual and cultural issues, and finally a specific engagement with the mysteries of sound, image, and montage.

Such analyses are helpful as far as they go, but as this introduction has tried to suggest, to itemize Godard's career so neatly is to miss both the seething intensity and the sprawling range of interests that consistently sweep his work from the grip of conventional categories. Starting with his earliest major films, he has devoted himself to blurring the taken-for-granted boundaries discussed above – not only between fiction and documentary but also between realism and reflexivity, synthesis and analysis, intellect and intuition, the personal and the political, the material and the spiritual. "I'm half a novelist and half an essayist," he told me in 1995,[25] and while his overall career suggests movement from the first part to the second part of that equation, his most resonant films shake off "proper" and "normal" cinema grammars of all kinds. This is one source of their eye-opening impact on spectators willing to shake off the ingrained habits of ordinary moviegoing.

None of this means his oeuvre is too eccentric to be reached by explication and interpretation, as long as these are agile enough to match their demanding subject. Godard's generally firm control over his creative work has ensured that certain themes, concerns, and preoccupations run through film after film, changing their outward forms but retaining an inner consistency that unifies what might otherwise seem an unmanageable explosion of heterdox ideas.

Connecting these is Godard's effort to create what might be called a "subjunctive cinema," in which every important gesture – each image, sound, cut, superimposition, and so on – is less a link in an expository chain than a suggestion as to what such a link might be, subject to immediate questioning and revising by the filmmaker and the film itself. Jonathan Rosenbaum, perhaps the most astute of Godard's critics, observes that in his method "everything remains *in process:* ideas are introduced in order to spawn other ideas . . . and movement invariably takes precedence over explanation."[26] In a radical film like *King Lear,* this reflects not only Godard's restless artistic and intellectual energy but the film's own "refusal to become a commodity, to function as an object – a refusal which . . . threatens and challenges the functioning of the Cinematic Apparatus itself." Such a film wants "to exist and to function as a nonobject: ungraspable, intractable, unconsumable," taking as its subject "ultimate essences rather than fleeting satisfactions."[27]

A movie or method that faces off against the very institution of cinema-as-we-know-it is clearly political to its core, and one more subject that must be discussed before moving to in-depth film analyses is the trio of controversial philosopher-poets from whom Godard has drawn his greatest political inspirations. The first to assume major importance in his thinking was Brecht, who called for an "epic" theater (and cinema) that refuses to entice us with propulsive narrative and psychology but rather induces thought and reflection through "alienation effects" that encourage a critical distance between the spectator and the spectacle.

Brecht's ideas have remained important for Godard in all phases of his career, including the one named after his second great influence. This is the pioneering Soviet director Dziga Vertov, who shared Godard's view that all aspects of filmmaking are different forms of selection or montage, and that the most exalted cinema grows from the artful manipulation of filmed materials drawn not from fictional constructions but from the camera's direct confrontations with the real world.

Godard's third, less enduring mentor was Mao Zedong, the Chinese leader and revolutionary theorist. His appeal for the filmmaker appears to have stemmed from three notions that Colin MacCabe identifies in his thoughtful analysis of Godardian politics: the importance of personal self-analysis as a route to ideological enlightenment; commitment to the Third World as a key site of struggle against bourgeois oppression and superpower imperialism; and a conviction that front-line activism must work hand in hand with theoretical reflection, which spurred Godard to "elaborate systematically the cinematic implications of many of his earlier intuitive choices."[28]

As important as these influences have been, however, the effort to create an ungraspable, intractable, unconsumable cinema has ultimately led Godard beyond political and sociocultural ideas, motivating his growing desire to fuse physics and metaphysics in works more deeply speculative than any he (or perhaps anyone) has created before. He increasingly considers cinema to be the *language of things,* at once firmly material and exhilaratingly conceptual. The heart of his agenda has been to free this language from patterns rooted in simplistic storytelling, one-dimensional characterization, and other commercially driven devices.

As noted, his love for the productive collisions of montage and collage anchors him as solidly in twentieth-century discourse as any modernist or postmodernist around; yet his wish to view existence from a standpoint transcending all limited notions of logic, causality, and representation places him in a visionary realm no other contemporary arist has occupied in quite the same way. This has been his blessing, earning continual attention from critics who enjoy "thinking without bannisters," to borrow Hannah Arendt's phrase; and it has been his curse, earning near-oblivion from a public that craves little more in cinema than soothing reproductions of its own all-too-common sense. Challenger of categories, creator of contradictions, nurturer of paradoxes and impossibilities, Godard stands with the most provocative cultural figures of our time.

In choosing six films for analysis, I have been guided partly by a wish to span Godard's whole career to date, and partly by the recognition – somewhat reluctant – that his works of the 1960s hold more immediate interest (and are more immediately available) for many of today's moviegoers. My selections, with brief indications of the reasoning behind them, are as follows:

Breathless, 1960. A founding masterpiece of the New Wave movement, this innovative gangster-in-love saga introduced Godard to world cinema with an impact that hasn't died down yet, ingeniously synthesizing film-aesthetic currents as different as neorealist naturalism and B-movie melodramatics. It also exemplifies Godardian montage and reflexivity in early stages of development and poses innovative challenges to screen acting styles of the period. It is at once a landmark, a signature piece, and one of the most entertaining movies in Godard's canon.

My Life to Live, 1962. This richly Brechtian drama about a woman turned prostitute represents the first full flowering of Godard's preoccupation with commercialized sexuality as a metaphor for consumerist decadence in capitalist society. It also marks an escalation of his assertive editing style and his reflexive tendencies, and reveals new dimensions in his attitudes toward women. A tremendously moving tale, it calls attention to Godard's strong ability as a dramatic storyteller on those infrequent occasions when he chooses to be one.

Weekend, 1967. At once more sensational and more abstract than the previous works, this harrowing "film found on a scrap heap" starts as a road-movie parody and finishes as an apocalyptic war picture, exploding with noises, colors, and audiovisual rhythms that both embody and critique the bourgeois culture with which Godard has developed a ferocious attraction–repulsion relationship. The hour of revolutionary cinema has come round at last, he tells us here, and this movie waves like a bloody banner on the barricades.

Numéro deux, 1975. Godard hints at a return to popular cinema after his years with the ultraleft Dziga-Vertov Group, but the joke is on his critics as he and Miéville release this complex exploration of the relationships between man and woman, labor and leisure, domesticity and society, and – perhaps above all – film and video, media that encapsulate his twin fascinations with the heritage of Western art and the still-uncharted directions in which its electronic future may lie. Godard turns to new forms of experimentation as cinema turns into television and language becomes ever more inextricable from the concreteness of sight and sound.

Hail Mary, 1985. Godard's growing affinity with the spiritually ineffable and conventionally inexpressible gives birth to this bold, controversial reworking of a Christian master narrative. Aesthetics meet theology as the Godard–Miéville collaboration scales precipitous new heights.

Nouvelle Vague, 1990. A central achievement of Godard's deeply interiorized late period, this mysteriously touching drama combines the visuals of a radically stylized mise-en-scène with the language games of a collagelike screenplay. The result stands with his most hauntingly enigmatic works, providing major clues to his thought in the 1990s.

A final chapter surveys Godard's work in video and mixed-media formats, which range from large-scale television pieces to "scenarios" related to his films. Crowning this facet of his career is the multipart *Histoire(s) du cinéma* project, which is sure to be one of his most enduring legacies.

2

Breathless

It is useless to pretend that human creatures find their contentment in repose. What they require is action, and they will create it if it is not offered by life.

– Charlotte Brontë, quoted by Jean-Luc Godard, 1952[1]

Although I felt ashamed of it at one time, I do like *À bout de souffle* very much, but now I see where it belongs – along with *Alice in Wonderland.* I thought it was *Scarface.*

– Jean-Luc Godard, 1962[2]

Godard's first feature traveled to English-speaking countries as *Breathless,* a suitably snappy title for a speedy, jazzed-up picture that hops to the rhythm of gunshots, bongo drums, and the on-the-run life-style of its hero. Its French title, *À bout de souffle,* points to a different meaning, however: being winded, maybe exhausted, or even at the *end of breath,* as the hero literally is when he collapses in the street at the end of his ultimately fatal career. Of course it's a jaunty title, but it's also an ironic, ambivalent one. In any case, it helped launch the picture – and Godard's feature-filmmaking career – with a roar that still reverberates. *Breathless* remains his most widely known and frequently seen work.

The story is based on a scenario by François Truffaut, a few pages long and providing a reasonably close outline of the finished film.[3] The hero is Michel Poiccard (Jean-Paul Belmondo), a rascally Parisian who makes his living as a stealer of cars, seducer of women, and all-around rogue with lots of connections but few friends on whom he can depend in a crisis.

His first act in the movie is to hot-wire a car, then drive off with hardly a backward glance at the woman who helped him pull off the job. Taking a casual joyride through the countryside, he chatters away to himself – and to us, breaking classical film's strict rule against acknowledging the camera – when he isn't playing with a pistol he's found in the glove compartment. Chased by motorcycle cops for speeding, he dodges them by pulling off the road, but gets spotted when he leaves the car to restart its engine.

"Don't move or I'll shoot," says Michel, who has a flair for melodrama and a taste for clichés; but there's nothing clichéd about the way Godard's camera shoots him shooting the cop: sliding down his arm to his hand, caressing the gun's slowly revolving chamber and implacably aimed barrel, cutting to the cop's falling body just as the shot rings out, then to a distant overhead view as Michel runs frantically away. Michel is clearly a man who breaks the rules when he feels like it – and so is Godard, whose innovative style made its debut with those extreme close-ups of Michel's gun followed by the manic jump cut to his getaway, seen in (alienating) long shot just when an ordinary filmmaker would have used (emotion-filled) close-ups to build the psychological identification that Godard has generally found too easy and manipulative for comfort.

Back in the city, Michel gives us further glimpses of his personality and predilections: stealing from another girlfriend while her back is turned, hunting for a pal who owes him the money he needs to get out of town, playing cat and mouse with two Paris cops trying to solve the Route 7 murder he committed. Most important, he goes to the Champs-Elysées and romances Patricia Franchini (Jean Seberg), a young American who studies at the Sorbonne and hopes to become a writer for the *New York Herald Tribune,* which she sells on the boulevard for pocket money. Michel makes no effort to hide his infatuation with her, but her commitment to their affair is obviously uncertain. They stroll in a lengthy traveling shot while he declares his love, complains about his troubles in Paris, and asks her to move to Rome with him when he collects his debt. She also talks about money, saying she needs her college-student status to keep her family's financial support rolling in; but mainly she banters with her boyfriend and fills the screen with sunny charm. Godard appears to be as entranced with Seberg as Michel is with the character she plays.

Still, the atmosphere is not all romance and repartee. Immediately after they part, Michel walks past a movie poster that reminds us of his reckless side: "Live dangerously until the end!" it shouts, underscored by a brassy chord on the sound track. When a pedestrian gets struck by a car nearby, Michel joins the crowd leaning over his body, gazes at him intently, and crosses himself as he walks thoughtfully away, possibly thinking of his own close acquaintance with mortality. "The future. I'm interested in it," he had told Patricia a little earlier, complaining that the *Tribune*

Sunny charm: *Breathless* (1960) protagonists Michel Poiccard (Jean-Paul Belmondo) and Patricia Franchini (Jean Seberg) stroll through a traveling shot on the Champs-Elysées.

printed no horoscope. His uneasiness and superstition seem justified, given the instability he courts with his criminal ways. During his next date with Patricia he excuses himself long enough to violently rob a harmless-looking man in the men's room of a club, then regales her with a tabloid-worthy tale about a lawless couple. She listens with enough concentration to reveal her own interest in breaking society's rules. She also aims a bit of petty meanness toward Michel, publicly kissing an American journalist who might be valuable to her career.

Later scenes reinforce the impressions of Michel and Patricia given by the film's first part. He dodges the police dragnet that closes in ever more tightly; implores Patricia for love, companionship, and sex; and tracks down the money-owing friend he's convinced is his passport to a clean getaway and a better tomorrow. She hangs out with Michel in her apartment;

covers a press conference with a famous novelist; does her own detective dodging when the police connect her with Michel; and announces that she is pregnant, seeming genuinely upset when Michel receives the news with a shrug of annoyance. Later she caves in with surprising speed (or maybe not so surprising, after the pregnancy scene) when a cop confronts her and demands her cooperation. Still more surprising is her abrupt decision to phone the police and reveal Michel's whereabouts. Returning to the borrowed apartment they've been hiding in, she tells him of her betrayal, and he responds with a mixture of anger, exasperation, and fatigue. "I'm beat anyway and I just want to sleep," he tells the friend who finally shows up with his money. Soon afterward the detective guns Michel down, and he staggers up the street as if trying to escape – or catch? – the death now looming in his path.

Michel expires in the middle of one last misunderstanding, trivial in itself yet important since it makes English-speaking watchers *of* the movie more confused than the French-speaking characters *in* the movie. "It's really disgusting," Michel says with his dying breath, using words ("C'est vraiment dégueulasse") that clearly refer to the situation in which he and Patricia have landed; yet the film's English subtitles translate his sentence as, "You are . . . really . . . ," suggesting a final insult aimed at the woman who caused this tragedy. Patricia has needed help with her French more than once during the movie, and although the word "dégeuelasse" has run like a motif through the film's dialogue, she asks a stranger to translate Michel's dying words. "He said, 'You are really a little bitch,'" the stranger replies, taking the meaning from "dégueulasse" (as if he had read the misleading subtitle!) that would apply had Michel used it as a noun instead of an adjective. More accurately in this case, the word means "disgusting" and even "sickening," with a hint of the "nausea" that Jean-Paul Sartre evoked in describing his existentialist view of the human condition. Michel is not insulting Patricia alone. He is reviling all that has brought them to this sorry state.

The film's ending is a richly ironic coda to a tale of star-crossed lovers with an utter inability to get their signals straight. Michel dies after closing his eyes with his own hand; Patricia gazes into the camera and mumbles, "A little what? I don't understand"; and the screen fades to black as she turns her pertly coiffed head away from us, the filmmakers, and everything that's happened in the past ninety minutes. (Godard originally wanted Patricia to rifle through Michel's pockets, but in a strikingly Patricia-like move, Seberg refused to carry this out.)[4] The finale remains rich even with the garbled subtitling, but it has an extra layer of perplexity for moviegoers who share Patricia's imperfect grasp of her boyfriend's lingo.

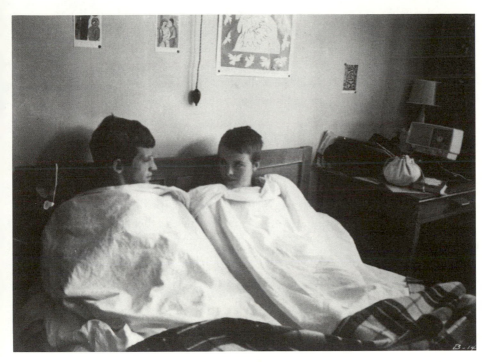

Hanging out: Michel (Jean-Paul Belmondo) and Patricia (Jean Seberg) pass the time at Patricia's apartment in *Breathless*.

Writing some twenty years after *Breathless* was released, a critic observed that one of the "remarkable" things about Godard's work had always been "its closeness to the contemporary moment."[5] Although some later films would stray from this principle, it is generally true of Godard's career, beginning with his first feature-length production.

Breathless was filmed in 1959, an eventful year for French society. On the political front, agitation continued to flow from Algeria's anticolonial war, leading French President Charles de Gaulle to offer a peace plan based on the prospect of (conveniently delayed) independence if Algerian voters approved it four years after hostilities ended. In mass communications, the number of television sets in France reached 1.5 million, behind West Germany and way behind Britain but still in step with Europe's increasingly televisual culture. Elsewhere on the cultural spectrum, playwright Jean Anouilh finished *Becket; or, The Honor of God,* contributing to the antiauthoritarian rumbling that would gather strength in coming years. In film, Alain Resnais made his feature debut with the strikingly fresh *Hiroshima mon amour*, from a script by experimental novelist Marguerite Duras; more important still, Truffaut brought his first major production – *The 400 Blows*, a loosely autobiographical tale about growing up absurd on the streets of Paris – to the hugely prestigious Cannes International Film Festival, where he walked away with the coveted Best Director award, instantly making himself and his New Wave friends significant players in world cinema.

Still, as busy as France was at the tail end of the 1950s, the eyes of Godard and his colleagues were also fixed on the United States, thanks to their ongoing fascination with Hollywood and American popular culture. Without question, 1959 was a noteworthy year on that side of the ocean too. Edward Albee's short play *The Zoo Story* helped bring avant-garde expressionism to popular attention in theater, just as the opening of Frank Lloyd Wright's audacious Solomon R. Guggenheim Museum did in architecture. Robert Rauschenberg gave a major impetus to pop art with *Monogram*, perhaps the most influential of his collagelike "combine paintings." The sexually frank novel *Lady Chatterley's Lover*, by British author D. H. Lawrence, reached American printing presses some thirty years after authorities had banned it for obscenity. Even more pungently, Beat Generation writer William S. Burroughs completed his *Naked Lunch*, bringing a radically disjunctive style to drugged-up subject matter that mainstream publishers would have found unthinkable a few years earlier. A more prolific Beat author, Jack Kerouac, virtually flooded the market with significant works, from the *Evergreen Review* essay "Belief & Technique for Modern Prose" to the major novel *Doctor Sax; or, Faust Part Three*, the minor novel *Maggie Cassidy*, and the epic poetry cycle *Mexico City Blues*.

All the while, directors lauded by the New Wave group were filling movie screens, making expansive use of their mature talents under the new expressive freedom made available by the continuing breakdown of Production Code censorship rules. A few examples will suffice: Howard Hawks's *Rio Bravo*; Alfred Hitchcock's *North by Northwest*; Douglas Sirk's *Imitation of Life*; Otto Preminger's *Anatomy of a Murder*; John Ford's *The Horse Soldiers*; Budd Boetticher's *Ride Lonesome* and *Westbound*; new pictures by Vincente Minnelli, Samuel Fuller, and Frank Tashlin; and the extraordinary *Suddenly Last Summer* by Joseph L. Mankiewicz, who had been the subject of one of Godard's first articles in the short-lived *Gazette du cinéma* at the beginning of the decade.

Godard wrote more about French films than Hollywood productions in 1959, and his ten-best list is French from start to finish. Nevertheless, he did find time to praise Sirk, applaud Anthony Mann, and give Blake Edwards a mild pat on the back in articles for *Cahiers* and *Arts;* and his general interest in American film remained strong, as his next ten-best list showed by including Hollywood pictures from Hitchcock, Nicholas Ray, Stanley Donen, and Fritz Lang. Explaining the *Cahiers* group's predisposition toward American film, critic Jim Hillier cites "the ways in which American cinema was perceived to relate to American society: it was, often enough, socially 'critical,' but critical without being directly 'political,'" a position many French artists found appealing. He also notes film historian Thomas Elsaesser's observation that French intellectuals looked to American culture for "works of fiction that could serve as creative models, representative of their own situation and embodying specifically modern tensions – between intellect and emotion, action and reflection, consciousness and instinct, choice and spontaneity."6

These were prominent among the tensions that preoccupied Godard, and they were chief obsessions of an American group so journalistically notorious by 1959 that Godard must have been aware of it: the aforementioned Beat Generation, a band of authors, poets, and cultural provocateurs whose influences ranged from American literature and Asian religion to France's powerful existentialist movement and, more modestly, the French movies loved by Kerouac ever since his French-Canadian upbringing in a New England town. I have written about the Beats elsewhere,7 and I invoke them here not to reindulge a personal interest but to suggest that an awareness of the Beat sensibility – a way of thinking, feeling, and being that fascinated European as well as American artists – provides important clues to the making of *Breathless* and its galvanizing impact on international cinema. Although he has not referred specifically to the Beats in his comments on the film, Godard's sympathy with the directness and spontaneity embodied by their work shines through numerous remarks he made during this period – in 1962, for instance, when he praised American screenwriters for employing "the kind of simplicity that brings depth." American filmmakers "are real and natural," he went on, adding that his compatriots "must find the French attitude as [Americans] have found the American attitude. To do so, one must begin by talking about things one knows. . . . Filming should be a part of living, something normal and natural," full of "seeking, improvising, experimenting" rather than a "mental departmentalizing [that] also corresponds to a departmentalization of social truths."8

Like these words, *Breathless* bristles with the Beat spirit, which had reached a peak of fame and influence at precisely the time when Godard set to work on his film. Of all the writers who developed and promoted that spirit, Kerouac was the one most directly in sync with Godard's artistic personality. I am not suggesting that Godard was directly influenced by Kerouac, and there is no clear evidence that he had read Kerouac's books or articles. However, both were iconoclastic thinkers with a zest for experience and ideas; both were impatient with the 1950s mindset of conservatism, consensus, and conformity; and both sought release from this questionable Zeitgeist in a torrent of creative activity that challenged sociocultural norms with a charged-up mixture of impulsiveness, irreverence, and flamboyant rejection of common sense.

Central to this attitude was the concept of improvisation. Kerouac had embraced this in the novel that made him famous two years earlier: *On the Road,* written on long rolls of paper in nonstop bursts of "bop-trance composition." He had then shown its continuing value with *The Subterraneans* and *The Dharma Bums* in 1958. Kerouac was so committed to improvisation ("first thought best thought") that he crusaded against all forms of rewriting and revising, even chiding his Beat colleague Allen Ginsberg for correcting the errors made when his fingers slipped on the typewriter keyboard. Behind his quest for spontaneous "wild form" was a conviction that living, thinking, and art making are inseparable from one another, and that only the most unmediated forms of creativity – such as his spontaneous writing and the improvised jazz that often inspired it – can capture the quicksilver flow of lived experience in all its energy, diversity, and mutability.

Godard in 1959 was a somewhat more prudent and methodical artist, but his sympathies leaned in similar directions. The production history and the final form of *Breathless* bear this out. "I improvise, certainly, but with material which goes a long way back," he said in 1962, managing to endorse spontaneity and preparation at the same time.[9] He is hedging his commitment to in-the-moment creativity here, of course, by acknowledging that his material has undergone much thought before being commited to celluloid; yet even this accords with Kerouac's practice, since the Beat author thought obsessively about events prior to his marathon writing sessions.[10] Putting things on paper was the continuation of composition by other means. Ditto for Godard, who saw every aspect of a cinéaste's life and work as part of the filmmaking process.

Before the shooting of *Breathless* began, Godard supplemented Truffaut's scenario with a fully written beginning – featuring Patricia on her Champs-Elysées paper route – and many notes for subsequent scenes. Still worried about his lack of a completed script, he abruptly decided to rely on speed and confidence alone, reasoning that "in a single day, if one knows how to go about it, one should be able to complete a dozen takes. Only instead of planning ahead, I shall invent at the last minute."[11] Thinking of this as "last-minute focusing" rather than full-fledged improvisation, he enlisted his cast as accomplices in the experiment but limited their contribution by filming without sound. This allowed him to supply them with their dialogue, written shortly beforehand, by simply calling it out while the camera rolled; their voices were dubbed in later, synchronized with their lip movements. In a medium far more cumbersome and collaborative than the typewritten page, Godard thus approached Kerouac's ideal of spontaneous authorship, literally speaking the film's words through the mouths of his performers.

The film's quality of off-the-cuff inventiveness was further enhanced by Raoul Coutard's supple cinematography, using a hand-held Arriflex camera rather than "the usual equipment, which would have added three weeks to the schedule," as Godard later noted.[12] One scene was shot with a camera hidden (along with its operator) in a canvas mail cart, others from a wheelchair in which Coutard was whisked around by the director.[13] During the postproduction process another innovative element was added: impetuous jump cuts that replace ordinary "continuity editing" at key moments in the story. Sometimes these propel the action precipitately from one episode to another, denying the smooth transitions afforded by classical films. At other times they wipe out individual frames of an otherwise continuous scene, lending it a jagged energy. The director found his unusual filmmaking process "tiring" and even "killing," but in retrospect he justified it on grounds that recall Kerouac's love of immediacy and authenticity. "One feels that if one is sincere and honest and one is driven into a corner over doing something," he observed, referring to the breathless schedule he had set for himself, "the result will necessarily be sincere and honest."[14]

Breathless shares the Beat sensibility in content as well as form. Michel may not be a beatnik, but he has many features of a closely related type: the hipster, defined by a 1950s journalist as "an *enfant terrible* turned inside out," and by author Norman Mailer as "the American existentialist" who knows that in a culture threatened with extinction by war, oppression, or conformity, "the only life-giving answer is to accept the terms of death, to live with death as immediate danger, to divorce oneself from society, to live without roots, to set out on that uncharted journey into the rebellious imperatives of the self."[15] This certainly sounds like Michel, who has had an excellent relationship with his rebellious imperatives since long before we met him. He accepts death's terms not in the self-conscious style of a Hollywood hero but in the casual, taken-for-granted manner of a loner whose divorce from society is so complete he may never have realized there was a choice about the matter. Thrusting away the constricting comforts and straitjacketing safety of bourgeois life, he courts instability, precariousness, and the everyday possibility of disaster as fecklessly as any jived-up hustler in any neon-flashing city of the postwar world.

Although he talks a great deal, a trait shared by most Godard characters, Michel expresses his ever-shifting states of mind less through words than through gestures, body language, and a general inability to remain still. In keeping with his peripatetic nature, he shares Kerouac's view of automobiles as allies in the self-propelled movement from stifling rootedness to exhilarating liberty. His story can be traced through the cars he steals, uses, and abandons in the naïve belief that freedom is a matter of physical transit – if he can just get his money and zoom to Italy, everything will be all right – rather than difficult options like political struggle and spiritual regeneration, which Godard will explore in later works.

There is a sad and touching quality to Michel's unexamined faith that a different place will bring a different life. This idea has animated great migrations in the past, but it breathed its last during the 1950s, when unexplored space finally ran out and modern geography confirmed that no location on earth has some exotic property that can transform the self in ways once fantasized by Beats, hipsters, and other romantic go-getters. Michel doesn't realize this ideal is dead, and his ingenuousness helps win our affection, or at least our commiseration, despite his sometimes malevolent behaviors. Something similar goes for Kerouac's roadrunners, who are rarely models of social responsibility, and for some of Hollywood's most enduring characters – Norman Bates in Hitchcock's *Psycho,* for example, who elicits our sympathy through the apparent artlessness of his personality. Michel belongs in their company. So childlike is his pursuit of Patricia's love, so unavailing are his encounters with cops and crooks, so transparent are his efforts to present a cool-and-collected image to his lowlife cronies, that one is tempted to empathize with his misadventures and minimize the very real violence he commits, with a nonchalance that would be bone-chilling if the conventions of his movie's genre didn't smooth its edges.

Although he is less bluntly autobiographical than Kerouac often was, Godard also shares the Beat writer's willingness to "talk . . . about things one knows" and invest a story with material familiar from his own life. The tightly wound rhythms and mercurial riffs of *Breathless* echo Go-

Very real violence: Michel (Jean-Paul Belmondo) fights with an antagonist in *Breathless*.

dard's personality as an aggressive young artist who wanted to make "the sort of film where anything goes,"[16] and Michel's character – including its more menacing side – draws some of its dark power from the filmmaker's own brushes with this territory. After passing through a "shy and uncharming" adolescence, Godard as late as 1952 was known as a chronic thief (relatives and the *Cahiers* office were among his targets), a failed homosexual prostitute, and enough of a social misfit to be committed by his father to a psychiatric hospital for what one biographical sketch describes as "a considerable period."[17] Godard had cleaned up his act long before his feature-filmmaking career started – his cameo appearance in *Breathless* ironically casts him as a nosy passerby who helps the police track Michel down! – but he had lived the downside of hipsterdom that Beat commentator John Clellon Holmes captured when he critically observed (in a quarrel with Mailer's account of hipness) that "the destiny of the nervous system, accumulating Sensation the way Faust's mind accumulated Knowledge, is inexorably violence."[18] To be sure, Godard was never the thug Michel turns into when irritated by the stolen-car dealer he roughs up, tempted by the men's-room visitor he mugs, or – in the explosive moment that thrusts the film into high gear – threatened by the highway cop he kills. However, the filmmaker was neither innocent nor naïve with regard to the more sordid possibilities of the free, unfettered life. *Breathless* acquires its unsettling force from this semi-insider status as well as its freewheeling performances and bold stylistics.

Reflecting different aspects of Godard's personality and imagination, Patricia is many things Michel is not: a woman, a worker, a reader and writer, an American with parents back home and prospects for a respectable future.

In some ways she is a dead ringer for Michel, however, beginning with her penchant for unpredictable acts and her refusal to be defined or delimited by the people around her. Peddling her papers on sunny Parisian afternoons, enrolling in the Sorbonne so her family's checks will keep on coming, juggling romances with men who couldn't be more dissimilar, she has all the appearances of a self-sufficient spirit freely inventing her identity to suit her changing whims. Still, among the things that distinguish her from Michel is a growing realization of something he grasps only in a fitful, semiconscious way: that thought and behavior are functions of each other and our interactions with the world, not of some inner essence that presides over our lives from birth to death.

Common sense generally says otherwise, of course. Each of us has a unique and consistent nature, it tells us, with a coherent set of distinctive properties that last a lifetime, however much they "evolve" and "mature" along the way. We know, however, that Godard is no great friend of common sense, seeing this as a hazy substitute for real analysis and insight; and although he hadn't yet developed his views on this matter in 1959, he had his suspicions. So did some American artists, including social dissidents like Kerouac, who turned to rebellious adventure (e.g., hitting the road) and radical creativity (e.g., bop-trance writing) as escape routes from the traps of consensus-bound thinking. So did some European intellectuals, including existentialist thinkers who aimed particular criticism at the notion of "human nature" as they explored the predicament of sentient beings in a fundamentally absurd universe. Existence precedes essence, they argued, suggesting that our selves are determined by our behaviors – the choices we make and the actions we carry out – rather than the other way around. If we do have a nature, it is not fixed: It is infinitely mutable, precarious, and contingent on the circumstances in which it finds itself.

In addition to being two of the most artfully developed characters in Godard's early work, Michel and Patricia are vivid embodiments of his still-coalescing ideas on this multifaceted subject, which was of urgent interest to many people as the conservative 1950s showed their first tentative signs of giving way to the tumultuous 1960s. Testifying to Godard's thoughtfulness about such existential issues is the fact that these characters represent two different perspectives on them. At issue is the problem of reconciling personal will with existence in a world that is at once intricately social, profoundly subjective, and utterly irrational in the long run. As suggested above, Michel has a groping, instinctive approach to this dilemma, whereas Patricia has a still-embryonic but somewhat more alert position.

We can tell from our first glimpse of Michel's cocky, rakish persona that he sees himself as a confidently free agent with a swinging city at his fingertips, and that he's proud of his ability to cast aside convention and pursue the gratification that's his primary goal in life. The way he sees himself doesn't necessarily mesh with the way the world sees him, but one of the things Godard invites us to like about him is the fact that he doesn't particularly care what society thinks of his inner self, as long as his outer self can keep dancing through the city and having enough gangster-film adventures to distract him from worries about tomorrow. Michel is the first of many Godardian figures who don't know their own minds, or rather, who perceive at least dimly that knowing one's mind is beside the point. This is because a person's consciousness is as much a *result* as a *cause* of the things one chooses to do. Then too, the experiential reality of one's mental life may be just tenuously connected with the existential reality traced on the physical world by one's activities. When his interior and exterior lives appear to conflict in some way, Michel takes for granted that authenticity lies not in his own consciousness – split between conflicting motives and priorities, fond of deluding itself along with others – but in the real-world results of what he actually does and says.

To put this in moral terms, truth and fakery are separated by thin and slippery lines, and Michel would rather exploit this fact than think about it. "There's no need to lie," he tells Patricia during their long scene in her bedroom. "Like in poker, the truth is best. The others still think you're bluffing, so you win." Godard seconds this notion by moving his camera from Michel to a drawing mounted on the wall, showing a man (beardless, young) holding a mask (bearded, old) over his face. Continuing the appearance-versus-reality motif a few moments later, Patricia says to Michel, "I want to know what's behind that mask of yours. I've watched you for ten minutes and I see nothing, nothing." She is struck by the gap between her boyfriend's external appearance – hard to ignore, since few faces are more magnetic than Belmondo's in this movie – and the interior psychology that she assumed had shaped this appearance. Indeed, she is beginning to doubt the accessibility and even the relevance of this psychological dimension, at least as a meaningful factor in her relationship with him.

Patricia is in a good position to benefit from this doubt, since she has been spiraling toward the realization that her own existence is defined more by her real-world behaviors than by the unreliable stream of consciousness she carries around inside. More intellectual than Michel, and possessing an intuitiveness more refined than his comparatively gross instinctiveness, she is starting to become authentically aware – and more important, ironically appreciative – of the yawning gulf between the abstractions conjured by her mind and the actualities projected into the social sphere by her voice and body.

"I don't know if I'm unhappy because I'm not free, or if I'm not free because I'm unhappy," she tells the American journalist during their conversation over drinks, signaling a growing sense that her social and individual selves are at once habitually at odds *and* inextricably bound together, so tightly that they hardly have their own existences. A short while later, she elevates this philosophical glimmer into a behavioral guide. "I stayed to find out if I was in love with you or if I wasn't in love with you," she tells Michel after betraying him to the police. "And because I'm mean to you, it proves I don't love you." Rather than introspectively ponder her feelings – surely the commonsense way of charting one's emotional response to another person – Patricia has acted out her impulses and observed the results with an almost clinical curiosity, seeing the outward manifestations of her behavior as coequal with the "real self" that prompted it. Michel listens to her words with more resignation than rage. These ex-lovers are clearly two of a kind, and in her explanation he hears echoes of his own outlook on life.

In addition to their similarities with each other, Patricia and Michel are refracted yet recognizable reflections of the filmmaker who (as noted earlier) speaks through them like a ventriloquist to his audience. "I see no difference between reality and an image of reality," Godard said in 1979. "I always say, 'A picture is life and life is a picture.' And when I make pictures it's making life. . . ."[19] Godard is discussing the interplay between his private and professional activities, but his attitude is mirrored by Michel and Patricia as they go about their day-to-day lives. Outward signs – images for Godard, actions and behaviors for Patricia and Michel – cannot be separated from the realities "behind" them, since all are interrelated parts of an endless loop. Arbitrary social rules may warp or distort this arrangement, leading to various crises – the difficulty of uniting love and work, for instance – that Godard explores and often weeps over in his later films. The main characters of his first feature are oddly in tune with it, however, and if this fails to bring them happiness (perhaps an impossible commodity in our profoundly flawed world) at least their capacity for spontaneous action lends them a measure of existential energy that merely commonsensical creatures could envy.

All of which is to say that Godard and his *Breathless* protagonists agree with F. Scott Fitzgerald that "action is character" – and, they would add, vice versa. Michel is especially impatient with anything that threatens his extroverted approach to life, including Patricia's occasional efforts at philosophical thought. "Between grief and nothing I will take grief," she quotes from William Faulkner's book *The Wild Palms,* and then asks Michel which he would choose. "Show me your toes," he less than helpfully replies. It's a funny and revealing moment, and when Patricia presses him again to make Faulkner's choice, he reconfirms his dislike for introverted thinking. "Grief is idiotic," he says. "I'd choose nothing. It's not any better, but grief is a compromise. You've got to have all or nothing."

Given this refusal of anything partial or incomplete, it is not surprising that the adventures of Michel and Patricia generally unfold in bursts of concrete activity, choreographed by Godard to reveal character on both individual and social levels. Some of these moments are as broadly melodramatic as one would expect in a movie dedicated to Monogram Pictures, a low-budget Hollywood studio whose lean, energetic productions Godard had admired as a young critic.[20] Michel first shows his antisocial streak, for instance, by stealing a car and then abandoning the woman who helps him pull off the heist, and all this is just a prelude to his murder of the highway cop who's been sharp-witted enough to chase him down. Other revelations of character through action are subtle or almost subliminal, however. Consider the car-stealing scene, when Michel's accomplice follows the couple whose sedan Michel is about to take, and all three of these figures – the lookout and the impending victims – walk exactly in step with one another as they make their way down the Parisian sidewalk. This suggests that despite their very different places in this narrative, they are all linked components of the city's violent, unpredictable ambience.

Another element linking *Breathless* with the hipster sensibility is the fact that the city is a vitally important character in it. I realize that calling the city a character is the sort of observation made so often by commentators – the house is a character in *Psycho,* the ship is a character in *Battleship Potemkin,* and so forth – that it has become a critical cliché. However, it suits *Breathless* as well as any movie I know, in part because Godard was heavily under the influence of Italian director Roberto Rossellini during the entire first stage of his career, seeing in the great neorealist's work a model for his own conviction that the relationship between character and environment is as imposing as any subject a filmmaker could hope to tackle. "He alone has an exact vision of the totality of things," Godard said of Rossellini in 1962.[21]

It follows that Godard's concern with place is hardly limited to the artful depiction of expressive background locations. What interests him is the way people relate to the places they are in, and conversely, the roles environment plays in determining how people move, how they present themselves to one another, how they interact with the physical world as a whole. Writing in 1965 that his sketch film "Montparnasse-Levallois" was "constructed on the actors," he immediately added that what compelled his attention was "fluidity, being able to feel existence like physical matter: it is not the people who are important, but the atmosphere between them. Even when they are in close-up, life exists around them. The camera is on them, but the film is not centred on them." One notes Godard's typical ambivalence as he says his film is "constructed on" yet not "centred on" the people in it. "The film is a district," he adds, "a particular time."[22] Sure enough, what it conveys most vividly is not the psychology of its characters but the rhythm of their passage through a specific place at a specific moment. Much the same can be said for *Breathless,* which gives a similar sense of building upon characters who remain parts of a greater whole – the city they are in, and also the movie through which that city lives and breathes for us.

Godard's fascination with the interactivity between individual and environment returns us again to his view of interior (character, personality,

City as character: Patricia (Jean Seberg) and her American friend (Van Doude) against a Parisian backdrop in *Breathless*.

psychology) and exterior (action, behavior, image) as shifting points on a loop that defies analysis via commonsense notions of cause and effect. Cinema is an ideal arena for exploring this conundrum since, as Godard noted in 1965, in this medium "the real and the imaginary are clearly distinct and yet are one, like the Moebius curve which has at the same time one side and two, like the technique of cinéma-vérité which is also a technique of lying."[23] This comment on cinéma-vérité – a type of documentary that presents real-world material in seemingly direct, unmanipulated form – is not as negative as it may appear, but reflects Godard's view of fiction and nonfiction as interlocked approaches to an existential world in which "truth" and "lying" can never be wholly separate modes of either communication or consciousness. The interface between them is imagination, as Godard indicates near the beginning of a much later film, the 1982 drama *Passion*. There a movie-director character asks for an explanation of a difficult scene on which he is working – actually a tableau based on a Rembrandt painting – and an associate replies, "It's not a lie, but something imaginary. It's never exactly the truth, but not the opposite either. It's something separated from the real world by calculated approximations of probabilities." This is consistent with Godard's comment, made shortly before *Breathless* went into production, that "great fiction films tend towards documentary, just as . . . great documentaries tend towards fiction. . . . One must choose between ethic and aesthetic. . . . But it is no less understood that each word implies a part of the other. And he who opts wholeheartedly for one, necessarily finds the other at the end of his journey."[24]

Navigating this journey along the Möbius strip of the imaginary is at once an exhilarating adventure and a daunting challenge. "It's pretty disconcerting, to say the least," Godard admitted in 1965. "Doubtless that is why it is difficult to say anything at all about the cinema, since . . . the end and the means are always confused" by a "double movement" that "projects us towards others while taking us inside ourselves."[25]

Like many of Godard's statements, the remarks quoted here may seem more cryptic than the phenomena they're meant to explain; but they appear to suggest that by partaking of both reality and artifice – associated with "ethic" and "aesthetic," respectively – film demonstrates the inseparability of our mental lives from our perceptions of the social world we inhabit. Godard's view of ethics and aesthetics as overlapping domains will become an explicit concern in his second feature, *The Little Soldier*, where the protagonist says that "ethics are the aesthetics of the future," implying that a more enlightened age will make no distinction between the imperatives of beauty and morality.[26] At the time of *Breathless*, however, Godard is less interested in idealistic projections than in here-and-now experiences. His film techniques mingle the truth of fiction with the fictionality of truth – Michel and Patricia are invented yet realistic characters, Paris is an actual yet poetically expressive setting – while illustrating the power of social images to infiltrate and influence the selves that Michel and Patricia think they are inventing under their own imaginative steam.

The fact that Michel and Patricia are not totally free agents is a crucial point. Godard's decision to explore existentialist issues through hipster-style characters and Beat-style improvisation might appear to presume that, as some existentialist thinkers argue, individuals have absolute freedom of will and may steer their destinies in unexpected directions. Godard is willing to question philosophical notions as readily as cinematic

conventions, however, and he takes issue with this proposition in no uncertain terms. One of his methods is to show how both of his main characters draw key aspects of their seemingly anarchic personalities from the
culture in which they live.

The opening scene provides an example. It begins with Michel buried
in the pages of *Paris-Flirt* and muttering to himself, "I'm no good. If you
have to, you have to." The words catch our attention, but their meaning
is vague. Then he lowers the paper and reveals his face, glowering in our
direction from beneath a hat brim yanked down so far it almost covers
his eyes. In order to see he has to tilt his head backward, which gives him
an arrogant air, enhanced by the cigarette dangling from his mouth. Looking directly toward the camera, he surveys the scene around him and lifts
his hand to his mouth, rubbing his thumb across his lips in a nervous
back-and-forth motion. There's something theatrical about it, and indeed,
everything about Michel seems slightly larger than life – the cut of his hat,
the jut of his jaw, the burly knot of his necktie, the way he checks out his
surroundings without a wasted move. Later we'll learn that his thumb-
to-lips gesture is borrowed from the tough-guy persona often adopted by
Hollywood star Humphrey Bogart, and even now it seems obvious that
Michel is performing or at least posing, playing the role of a rough-and-
ready character who either knows every trick in the book or has his weaknesses wrapped in a huge amount of protective armor. In short, he is an
actor without a theater – or with one, if we remember that all the world's
a stage, especially in a modern city overflowing with potential spectators.
Michel may or may not be a genuinely cool character, but his moves are
definitely not those of a totally self-possessed personality. They are borrowed from one of the most obvious sources imaginable: the movies.

Godard reconfirms this cultural kleptomania when he explicitly shows
us that Michel is a Bogart fan. He does this through one of the film's most
thoughtfully worked-out episodes, a sort of cadenza that temporarily
stops the main action in its tracks. A movie theater is showing *The Harder They Fall,* a 1956 prizefighting drama directed by Mark Robson; the
stars are Rod Steiger, Jan Sterling, and Bogart as a down-on-his-luck
sportswriter who becomes a hard-bitten press agent. Michel stands gazing at the display in front of the theater, and while numerous pictures
from the movie are on view, the one that transfixes him is a standard portrait shot of Bogart in a generic movie-star pose. Godard cuts back and
forth between the photo and Michel pensively removing his sunglasses,
puffing his cigarette – one shot shows the picture with smoke drifting
across it – and saying "Bogey" in a quiet voice. This may be childish hero

worship on one level, but on another Michel is renewing contact with a wellspring of both his behavioral repertoire and his self-image as a tough, glamorous fellow who has mastered "the American attitude" as thoroughly as one of its most powerful icons. He replaces his dark glasses and moves on, and mirrored in the theater's glass facade we see the two cops who are vainly trying to tail him. The scene ends by irising out on their distant reflections, using a deliberately antique bit of cinematic punctuation to underscore the motion-picture artifice that links Michel's brief epiphany with the movie in which he himself is the star.

Another sign that Michel is embedded in a web of social role-playing is his habit of making faces. Three faces, to be exact, always done in the same order: mouth wide open in a gaping yawn, mouth stretched sideways as if saying "cheese," mouth pushed frontward beneath a wrinkled brow. He does this often, teaches Patricia to do it in her bathroom mirror, and uses it for his valedictory gesture to the world in the moment before his death. Facial expressions are essential for everyday communication within a culture, and also for projecting a persona for public consumption. They mean a lot to Michel, and while these particular ones are so stylized that they're nonsensical, it comforts him to carry them around and run through the sequence now and then. He uses the Bogart gesture just as frequently, rubbing thumb across lips with a contemplative look as he thinks of favorite movies, or events of the moment, or perhaps nothing at all.

Patricia is no less culturally influenced than her boyfriend. She also faces life through a series of unconsciously assumed masks, and her performative moments are even easier to read. She conspicuously compares herself with an Auguste Renoir painting, angling her head to make the likeness as close as possible. She whimsically mentions Romeo and Juliet as role models for Michel and herself. She play-acts in front of a mirror, addressing herself with a military salute and a brisk "Dismissed!" She even tries out different attitudes in the midst of a decision-making situation. When her journalist friend presumptuously tells her that "of course" she will follow his suggestion and spend more time with him, she repeats the "of course" three times with three different inflections – first mock-serious, then questioning, then smugly cheerful – in a sort of vocal variation on Michel's three-part facial tic.

What makes these moments significant is the way Godard uses small gestures – often whimsical and offbeat, never particularly meaningful or original – to indicate the contagiousness of the behavioral twitches we pick up from our social surroundings. Michel and Patricia are not self-

Cultural studies: Patricia (Jean Seberg) juxtaposed with an Auguste Renoir painting on her apartment wall in *Breathless*.

inventing hipsters but are molded or "spoken" by their society in a sort of cultural ventriloquism, obliquely echoed by the ventriloquism that Godard used to control the movie's dialogue. Although they are continually trying on different poses, expressions, and intonations, they must always choose from the options available to them as inhabitants of one specific milieu at one specific point in history. There is some variety within this constraint, of course – Michel has his little-boy facial twists, on one hand, and his tough-guy thumb gesture, on the other – but the constraint is nonetheless real, frustrating would-be free spirits who think they have far more psychological and spiritual autonomy than could ever be available to them. This explains why Michel is in a chronic state of fatigue, and why Patricia fairly pants to throw off her almost-a-gangster status and get into the newspaper business, where adventures are vicarious and the illusion of free will is harder to indulge and therefore far less tempting.

"Language is the house man lives in," a philosophical character will say in 2 or 3 *Things I Know about Her,* six years after *Breathless.* As noted in Chapter 1, some thinkers consider that house a prison, and Godard would agree (at least until the later, more spiritual phase of his career) that human thought cannot effectively venture beyond the limitations of the language, verbal and nonverbal, that carries it. Michel and Patricia think they are masters of their fates, but in fact their capacity for spontaneity runs no deeper than the imitative phrases and gestures that compose their sadly circumscribed vocabularies. Try as they might to deny it, their lives are caught in roles that existed long before they arrived on the scene. Michel seems dimly aware of this when he observes that "squealers squeal, burglars burgle, killers kill, lovers love" – a catalog of character types from which he and Patricia have selected during the course of their story.

Consistency matters little to them – indeed, Michel reels off that catalog in response to Patricia's hugely ironic statement that she hates informers – but it would hardly make much difference if the opposite were true. In the end, their goal in life appears to have been nothing more lofty than transforming "It seemed like a good idea at the time" from a trite rationalization into a metaphysical principle. The highest compliment one can pay them is to acknowledge that they come precariously close to succeeding.

3

My Life to Live

Would one blush for the religiously realistic art of the cinema if we were not eaten away by an unhappy desire to change the world? But here artistic creation does not mean painting one's soul in things, but painting the soul of things.

– Jean-Luc Godard, 1952[1]

Breathless boosted Godard to the rank of New Wave leader – along with Truffaut, his prizewinning colleague – by introducing him to critics, audiences, and fellow cinéastes as a certified enfant terrible with a taste for the innovative (those jump cuts!) and the offbeat (that ambiguous ending!) rivaled by few others on the contemporary scene.

He quickly started work on *The Little Soldier,* his second feature. Here he continued his exploration of film-noir terrain, adding a political inflection via its protagonist: an undercover agent combating a left-wing organization during the acutely controversial war for Algerian independence. The drama puzzled many observers with its lack of political coherence, but Godard promptly explained that this was one of its most admirable qualities; his intention, after all, was to depict an ethically confused character in a film meant to seem "like a secret diary, a notebook, or the monologue of someone trying to justify himself before an almost accusing camera, as one does before a lawyer or a psychiatrist."[2] Godard's own justifications are as problematic as the "thriller" itself – among other things, he suggests that to understand the movie one must somehow "sense" his often-shifting "distance" from the characters – and it is tempting to write off both the film and the self-analysis as honorable failures in a still-young career. Carefully considered, though, the film and the retrospective comments show Godard's growing recognition of how conventional cinema joins other instruments of cultural control – including law and psychiatry, which he specifically names – in producing and reproducing social norms that hinder freedom and happiness. Foucault and Louis Althusser are among the philosophers who have developed this idea, and Godard rings interesting variations on it.

Moving to color cinematography and a radically different genre, Godard then wrote and directed *A Woman Is a Woman*, a musical shot on studio soundstages. Calling it "my first real film" and "the one I like best," he said afterward that his inspiration had been Charles Chaplin's observation that "tragedy is life in close-up, and comedy, life in long shot." Ornery as always, Godard turned this dictum on its head, attempting to make "a close-up comedy." He claimed after its highly uneven reception that it had been most popular in "countries noted for their wit," not including France, where it "didn't go down well."[3]

His next production was "Sloth," a 15-minute contribution to the 1961 anthology film *The Seven Capital Sins*. Unfazed by its less-than-gracious treatment from the critical corps, of which he still considered himself an active member, he plunged swiftly into his next project: *My Life to Live*, the story of a young woman named Nana who becomes a prostitute – the first of several Godard heroines to take this desperate route – and meets a tragic end. He began shooting on Paris locations in early 1962 and emerged a few weeks later with one of the most emotionally and intellectually rich achievements in all of New Wave filmmaking.

Before a full discussion of *My Life to Live*, it is worth taking a closer look at Godard's ideas and working methods in the period after *Breathless* launched his career. His interests certainly changed in some respects. Although his second feature recalls *Breathless* with its cars, travel, and skepticism toward bourgeois mores, for instance, its political themes and thriller atmosphere have little of the Beat-hipster spirit about them.

Still, one aspect of the Beat sensibility remained very much in view: improvisation. This was partly a professional tic that Godard had trouble shaking; even his first short movies had been "prepared very carefully" but "shot very quickly," as he described the process.[4] It was also a deliberate way of maintaining the sense of immediacy that had raced through his earlier features.

Although his comments on the shooting of *The Little Soldier* are somewhat vague, Godard appears to have begun the film by writing a partial scenario giving key moments of the story. He also decided it would take place in Geneva, perhaps because this is a "capital city of capitalism," in one critic's phrase,[5] and perhaps because he had visited the city as a child (during stays with his mother's wealthy family) and knew the area well. Other aspects of the narrative were so uncertain that shooting lasted four times longer than the two weeks he had anticipated. Scenes were frequently written the same morning they were to be shot, as Godard wrestled with bouts of "thinking" and "hesitating" brought on by the challenge of exploring longtime interests while avoiding the "anything goes" mentality of his first feature. (Dialogue for *Breathless* had been dashed off the evening before scenes were shot, an almost leisurely pace by comparison!) One important scene, an interview centered on Anna Karina's character, was shot in a completely improvised style – "she didn't know in advance what questions I would ask her" – inspired by Jean Rouch, an ethnographic filmmaker who became a hero for Godard and other New Wave directors by using spontaneous cinema to explore diverse cultures and personalities. Godard's academic background was in ethnography, and while he has rarely emphasized this in comments or interviews, it attests a long-lasting interest in real-time, on-the-spot probing of subjects that have caught his attention.

The scriptwriting for *A Woman Is a Woman* was equally unorthodox. On one hand, Godard started with a "very detailed scenario" and "followed it word for word, down to the last comma."[6] Yet while that sounds very responsible, the writing of specific action and dialogue was more of a down-to-the-wire process than ever, with Godard jotting material at the studio while the performers applied their makeup. Once again he was rediscovering a knack he shared with Kerouac: being able to weave spur-of-the-moment inspirations from familiar material that had already been bouncing obsessively around his mind. As he described it later, "one only thinks of things [for insertion into a film] one has been thinking about for a long time."[7]

Despite his gift for improvisation, Godard realized throughout this period that there is something to be said for writing a movie before directing it. Indeed, he tried to say "never again" to spur-of-the-moment creativity as early as 1961, when *The Little Soldier* was completed. Since he kept sliding into last-minute shooting patterns anyway, however, he eventually decided to call this his "method" and simply live with it – arranging five-week shooting schedules while knowing that the actual photography would occupy only two weeks, so the rest could be devoted to thought and reflection. *My Life to Live* was shot over four weeks, but the entire second week was a hiatus, giving Godard time to think. This irritated his performers, who disliked hanging around an idle location with no idea when their director would decide to roll the camera again.

What he sought in this film was so unconventional that one doubts a more commonplace methodology would have proved any more efficient. While he wasn't looking for any "particular effects," he wanted to explore some of his most deeply felt themes through an approach he later called *théâtre-vérité*. By this he meant a sort of "theatrical realism" that combines the arbitrariness of stage drama – unfolding in continuous "blocks" that cannot be "retouched" by the director – with film's unique ability to capture "chance" events in a "definitive" way.

To this end, he designed scenes that would be shot one time only, in the same order as the story – itself an unusual procedure, since in standard filmmaking scenes are generally shot more than once, in a chronology different from the final movie.[8] Then he spliced the shots together with a minimum of editing. The result of this procedure has a mood very different from the breathlessness of *Breathless,* the elusiveness of *The Little Soldier,* and the effervescence of *A Woman Is a Woman.* Still, the sense of spontaneity remains strong, reflecting Godard's success at making a complex and multilayered "impromptu" film "right off the bat, as if carried along, like an article written at one go." Again he used the Beat-like values of honesty and authenticity to justify his methods. "I didn't know exactly what I was going to do," he reported later. "I prefer to look for something I don't know, rather than be able to do better with something I do know." Karina felt "a little unhappy because she never really knew beforehand what she would have to do," he added. "But she was so sincere in her desire to make the film that between us we brought it off."[9]

Perhaps the strongest influence on *My Life to Live* is that of Bertolt Brecht, whose connection with Godard was briefly discussed in the first chapter. Brecht's spirit had suffused *A Woman Is a Woman* from its opening moments – when the filmmaker's cry of "Lights! Camera! Action!" rings out over the credits – and here it reaches its first full flowering in Godard's work.

Brecht's great breakthrough as a dramatic theorist stemmed from a problem he faced as a politically committed playwright. The more effectively he involved spectators in the flow of his story and the psychology of his characters, he realized, the less likely they were to focus on (or even notice) the sociocultural critiques he was trying to convey. To solve this dilemma, he developed a new form of drama – the epic theater – in which various devices purposely "alienate" audience members from the show they are watching. This is meant to promote active thought instead of passive emotionalism, leading the audience to think *about* the drama instead of sinking *into* it.

Brecht recognized the value of theatrical conventions, including effective storytelling, for attracting an audience and holding its attention. Therefore he found it acceptable for playwrights to illustrate points by dramatic means – assailing the evils of capitalism, say, by showing an avaricious factory owner laying off a conscientious worker who has no other way to support his hungry children. However, he also knew that if a writer crafted such a scene in a truly spellbinding way, spectators might be so consumed with worry over the worker's fate that the evils of capitalism per se would never occur to them. Hence, the practitioner of epic theater might interrupt the episode with a parade of picketers carrying signs ("The Evils of Capitalism") across the stage, or perhaps the cast would break into a song that spelled out the message in its lyrics. If done too didactically, of course, such shenanigans might alienate the audience clear out of the theater; so Brecht made his "A-effects" as entertaining and stimulating as possible. He also worked out a theory of acting that countered the introspective tendencies of Konstantin Stanislavski's influential "Method" with a "presentational" style, calling for performers to reveal their own attitudes toward the characters instead of psychologically "disappearing" into their roles.

Godard had Brecht firmly in mind when he designed *My Life to Live* as a series of twelve scenes or "tableaux," with a self-consciously "theatrical" feel and a deliberately episodic structure. "I wanted to show the 'Adventures of Nana So-and-so' side of it," he recalled later. The division into separate tableaux, he added, "corresponds to the external view of things which would best allow me to convey the feeling of what was going on inside. . . . How can one render the inside? Precisely by staying prudently outside."[10]

This is another in Godard's long list of murky clarifications, but it points to an idea that is indispensable in understanding this film and most of his others: that cinema, like painting and other visual arts, is a valuable yet problematic tool for casting light on human beings and the existential reality in which they dwell. Godard recognizes that externals are all the camera and sound recorder can grasp, and that such outward signs – superficial by definition – may seem sadly inadequate if one is looking for the "inner selves" of psychologically defined characters. Nevertheless, he also rejects "the Antonioni error" that claims "non-communication" is cinema's most natural subject. "I think it is wrong to say that the more you look at someone the less you understand," he said in 1962. The externals captured by cinema can be highly suggestive if one accepts the notion that inner selves are inseparable from the external actions they trace on the world around them. "A painter who tries to render a face only renders the outside of people; and yet something else is revealed," Godard says. "It's very mysterious. It's an adventure." *My Life to Live* was thus "an intellectual adventure: I wanted to film a thought in action – but how do you do it? We still don't know."[11]

We still don't know, but we have been trying to find out since the early days of cinema. Another of Godard's heroes, American film pioneer D. W. Griffith, stated many times that "movies are the science of photographing thought,"[12] and while Godard brings far more philosophical sophistication to his efforts, on a fundamental level he is exploring the same set of problems faced by his illustrious predecessor. It must be remembered, however, that in seeking to film "a thought in action" it is the action more than the thought – that is, the traceable behaviorial activity more than its evanescent psychological content – that Godard takes as his main concern. This is not because he finds psychology uninteresting, but because it is more a hurdle than a stepping-stone on his road to intuiting and embracing the mysteries of being human. He signals this in an early scene of *My Life to Live* that stands with the most resonant moments in his work. Nana and her former husband are finishing a bumpy but not entirely unpleasant conversation by having a friendly pinball game. He mentions some school assignments that his father has been reading, and says some of them are quite remarkable. The camera makes a small but deliberate movement that isolates Nana in the center of the frame, underscoring her thoughtful attitude as she listens to a quotation from a pupil's essay: "A bird is an animal with an inside and an outside. Remove the outside, there's the inside. Remove the inside, and you see the soul."

This summarizes much of Godard's cinematic and philosophical project. All movies consist of "outside" material, that is, visual and auditory records of exterior realities. Movies aspiring to "artistic" status attempt to take things a step further, going "beyond" surface representations to suggest "inner," psychological realities that cannot be directly depicted. Godard wishes to go further still, stripping away psychology in order to expose something more profound and mysterious – a "something else" that can only be approached through oxymoronic genres like *théâtre-vérité* and eccentric creative processes like the one to which Godard cryptically alludes when he says the film "was made by a sort of second presence."[13]

My Life to Live announces its structure – "a film in 12 tableaux" – at the beginning of its opening credits. True to Godard's opinion that the "greatest tableaux are portraits," it then presents a portrait of Nana/Karina's face, seen in three leisurely shots (left profile, front view, right profile) as credits continue to roll. The lighting is dark, shadowy, sad. More important, Nana/Karina is not posing prettily for the camera. Her face is quiet, yet mobile; still, yet charged with an emotional current that seems compelling even though the film has not defined it yet through word or action.

Accompanying this portrait is the first statement of Michel Legrand's remarkable music score, a series of brief passages played by a chamber orchestra. In conventional films the background score is often used to communicate a character's inner feelings to the audience, and although that certainly happens here – the music reinforces our impression that this is not a happy woman – the psychological effect is deliberately thrown off kilter by apparent mismatches between sound and picture, which seem to be following their own schedules instead of trudging along in Hollywood-style synchronization. The music comes and goes at unexpected times, and much of the sequence passes in silence, focusing attention on the visual image with rare intensity. This all amounts to a bold violation of classical-film structure – and a highly effective one, since it signals that although this movie will contain familiar elements of ordinary cinema, these will not assume their conventional roles of soothing, distracting, and entertaining the audience. Instead, each will maintain its own aesthetic integrity even as it contributes to the film as a whole. It will be up to the spectator – the active, participating, Brechtian spectator – to perceive their interrelationships and ferret out their meanings.

First tableau: A CAFÉ. NANA WANTS TO LEAVE PAUL. THE PINBALL MACHINE. In keeping with its strategy of separation and fragmentation, the film introduces each of its twelve scenes with a full-screen intertitle that interrupts the story and announces the main events that are about to happen. Working against traditional notions of cinematic suspense, this formal maneuver seems surprising in conjunction with a story that could have been treated as a thriller or film noir if the director had chosen.

The first scene throws the audience into even deeper Brechtian waters through its disorienting camera work. Nana and Paul, her former husband, are having a long conversation at the bar of a café, and everything about Raoul Coutard's cinematography is designed to make their alienation from each other not just a narrative point but a living, discomforting reality for the audience. Positioned directly behind the characters, the camera persistently films the backs of their heads, refusing the psychologically revealing facial expressions that ordinary film grammar would demand at such a moment. Their faces are occasionally visible in a mirror over the bar, but the view is distant and intermittent as the camera moves from one spot to another, often preventing even their backs from appearing together within the frame. Nana's hand touches Paul's head in a fleeting gesture near the end of their talk, and the effect is almost jarring in a scene (and a movie) where physical contact looms as a constant threat (violence, prostitution) while physical affection (caressing, embracing) is largely unknown.

By starting with this Brechtian flourish, Godard introduces *théâtre-vérité* as a means of engaging us with characters who do not fit any of the standard movie categories. On one hand, they are not fully developed figures inviting us to identify with them emotionally; we have little idea who they are (the husband's part in the story never becomes entirely clear) and for a long time we can barely make out what they look like. On the other hand, they are not just abstract embodiments of sociocultural types either; their main concern here – clearing the wreckage of a shattered relationship – is recognizably human and poignant. In any case, if their vagueness makes them seem elusive, our resulting curiosity leads us to focus more closely on whatever clues the scene does offer about them, and thus to enter the world of the movie all the more intently. Most impressive of all is their concreteness, the quality Godard pursued in *The Little Soldier*, and obviously an important trait for any film described by a term like *théâtre-vérité*. Photographed almost as if they were objects that happen to be in the room, Nana and Paul are more like two-dimensional graphics than three-dimensional personalities. This is because they are not "fleshed out" psychologically, and also because of two reasons directly linked to the cinematography: (a) Their images are conveyed partly by reflections in a mirror, and (b) the camera's lateral movements (a gesture Godard will use vigorously in later works) tend to flatten space sideways instead of exploring it in depth. Still, this very two-dimensionality, brooded over by Coutard's obsessive lens, gives them a pictorial presence that effortlessly dominates the scene's black-and-white images, allowing the couple to make up in physicality what they lack (so far) in context and psychology. This is enhanced by the film's use of directly recorded sound, free of the mellifluous mixing that makes Hollywood-type sound tracks at once seductive and inauthentic.

The dialogue also contributes to Godard's quest for concreteness. Answering one of Paul's inconsequential questions with a question of her own, Nana asks "What do you care?" and then repeats the phrase several times in a row. At first she might be mimicking Patricia's repetitions

("Of course. Of course? Of course!") in *Breathless,* and to some extent her role playing is similar; Nana once appeared in a movie with Eddie Constantine, we will learn later on, and still wishes to become an actress, which might help her navigate more effectively through life by projecting a more practiced persona. Her reiterations have less to do with performing, however, than with a desperate attempt to grasp the mercurial meanings she feels within her conflicted self – to understand her turbulent "inside" by projecting it "outside," through words and behaviors that can be held and examined like other physical phenomena. "I wanted to be very precise," she explains to Paul, lamenting the difficulty of holding onto meaning long enough to express it accurately. Paul misses the point, telling her not to "parrot" words, since she's not on a stage. "The more we talk, the less words mean," she says a little later, but the anxiety produced by her alienated emotions ("I'm fed up. I want to die") is equally lost on her companion, who accuses her of "parrot talk" again.

Parrot talk it may be, but its purpose is deadly serious. Nana seizes upon the sounds of words in a compulsive effort to possess the meanings they presumably contain, and thereby to reconfirm her own sense of existence, which has been shaken by the destabilizing events in her life. Godard's camera records her plight at once dispassionately and compassionately. This approach might be contradictory in less gifted hands but is made effective by Godard's conviction that cool, attentive observation ("staying prudently outside") is a reliable route to honest concern with Nana's predicament and the social circumstances that cause it. The impersonality of the setting, the distanced placements of the camera, the repetitive rhythms of the dialogue, and the hard-edged realism of the sound combine to amplify the scene's implicit cultural critique; who wouldn't have trouble holding their lives together in such an atmosphere? At the same time they mute the melodramatic undertones that a less Brechtian filmmaker might readily have exploited.

The episode concludes with the pinball game, Paul's parable of the soul, and Nana's silent gaze at a world (visible in its wintry bleakness through the window beside her) that is both more absolute and more enigmatic than her sad experiences have prepared her to expect.

Second tableau: THE RECORD SHOP. 2,000 FRANCS. NANA LIVES HER LIFE. Pursuing his agenda of foregrounding the filmmaking process – motivated partly by Brechtian politics, partly by New Wave cinephilia – Godard begins the next tableau by removing all sound during two documentary-style shots of Paris streets. He then replaces the restless shot-to-shot editing of the café scene with lengthy pans, showing Nana at work as a record-store clerk. She seems less alienated here than in the café, and the camera's easy movements lend a supple attractiveness to the scene. They almost suggest that unremarkable working-class life might not be a terrible burden if Nana didn't long for something better, symbolized by her movie-acting ambitions.

Her uneasiness is as profound as it is perplexing, however, and her "thought in action" is too intricate and mysterious to be contained by the commonsense experiences of ordinary work in ordinary places. The limits of any merely rational approach to her existential plight (by the character or the filmmaker) are underscored when one of her coworkers reads a lengthy excerpt from a magazine story that includes the cautionary sentence, "You attach too much importance to logic." Rebelling against the prison houses of logic and language alike, Nana is determined to live her one and only life on terms of her own invention – a heroic ambition that cannot be fulfilled in the confines of a middle-class record shop that deals in exactly the sort of prerecorded, predigested sounds that Godard has rejected for the purposes of telling her story. Like the first tableau, the second concludes with Nana in a pensive pose, listening to her colleague's droning voice as Coutard's lens slips past her and focuses on the flow of city life streaming past the store window in all its crisp materiality.

Third tableau: THE CONCIERGE. PAUL. THE PASSION OF JOAN OF ARC. The beginning of the next tableau seamlessly joins the distancing of Brechtian stylistics with the psychological suspense of traditional narrative. Nana lives in an apartment complex separated from the street by a forbidding wall. She wants to enter her apartment even though she has not paid her rent, and knows the concierge will not permit her on the premises. We know nothing of this situation as the episode begins, however. Positioned inside the courtyard, the camera shows the gateway to the area, flanked by large patches of shadow cast by the wall. Nana appears in the gateway, making a conventional entrance into the scene, but abruptly turns and hops back through the entryway, disappearing from view. Immediately the same action recurs twice again, exactly as if Nana were not a character but an actress who had stepped within camera range (or onto the stage) before her scene had begun. Only after these false starts does Nana actually enter the space of the episode, where she is promptly accosted by the concierge and forced into a series of quick activities (photographed from an all-encompassing overhead angle) that make up a small catalog of performative maneuvers: a contrite apology, a sneaky grab for her key, and finally submission to her opponents. These adversaries show enough satis-

Cinephilia: Godard fills the screen with expressive close-ups of Nana Kleinfrankenheim (Anna Karina) as she watches Dreyer's masterpiece *The Passion of Joan of Arc* in a scene of *My Life to Live* (1962).

faction in their little victory to remind us of the (Brechtian) point that we might be identifying with them, instead of with Nana, if Nana were not given a privileged position within the narrative.

After a nondescript meeting with Paul, who holds even less interest for her than he did earlier, Nana goes to a movie theater – and no ordinary theater, since it's not only showing a silent film made more than three decades before she bought her ticket, but also displays the film's title (*The Passion of Joan of Arc*) in huge neon letters, as if this were the only attraction that ever played there. The visual importance given to the title is appropriate, since while Nana seems to approach this as an everyday visit to the movies – complete with a date who seems romantically interested in her – her response to the film is profound and all-consuming, enveloping her in a set of emotions as deep as any she encounters during her story.

In a broad sense, this scene is another sign of the historically minded cinephilia that Godard shares with his New Wave colleagues; he sees nothing odd in the notion that a working-class Parisian would select a religious silent film of 1928 from her local movie listings, and he makes the most of his opportunity to fill the screen with indelible images from Carl Dreyer's masterpiece. Much more is also going on, however, as Godard cuts with a slow, steady rhythm between Dreyer's expressive close-ups and his own close-ups of Nana's transfixed, often tearful gaze.

- The scene plunges us into the heart of Nana's emotional life, allowing us not only to observe but to feel the intensity of her identification with Joan of Arc, the peasant girl who chooses to suffer an awful death rather than renounce her belief that God has a special destiny in store for her. The destiny of which Nana dreams is more modest and secular – to be appearing in movies rather than watching them – but it's no coincidence that her onetime acting job with Eddie Constantine was in a picture called *No Pity,* a title that applies both to Joan's plight and to the fate Nana will meet at the end of her adventures. Nana's tears flow for Joan, for herself, and for a world in which the pitiless have a monopoly on power.
- The pitiless are often men. Although we are still near the beginning of Nana's story, it is already clear that men have offered little to enrich her life. Paul doesn't interest her much, Eddie Constantine is in a different orbit, and few other males appear to have much relevance for her; in later scenes they will provide more harm than help. No wonder she gazes with awe and sympathy as Joan looks into the masculine face of affliction. Ironically, the rigid grasp of this affliction is embodied by a handsome young monk who commiserates with Joan even as he reveals her fate's horrible details. The silence of the scene adds to its power, which culminates when the screen fills with a single word spelled in implacably black letters against a pulsing white background: "La mort," the death that will still Joan's mortal voice and allow her the spiritual deliverance her sufferings have earned.
- The silence of the episode derives from Dreyer's silent film, of course, but it also anticipates a scene near the end of *My Life to Live* when a minor character will be filmed without sound so that Godard's own postsynchronized voice can be substituted for his, mingling artistic expression with personal confession. The later scene is foreshadowed here, suggesting that Godard's personal feelings about the story he is telling – including its double nature as a *théâtre-vérité* fiction and a portrait of Karina, his wife and collaborator – are linked with the cinematic admiration and philosophical wonder that *The Passion of Joan of Arc* inspires in him.

- The monk, Jean Massieu, is played by Antonin Artaud, a figure of great relevance to Godard's career. A radical French theorist with extreme ideas about the morality and philosophy of art, he wrote voluminously during a long career that included forays into acting and filmmaking. He also underwent recurring bouts of schizophrenic behavior that led to long-term incarceration in an asylum. Among his most influential ideas is his call for an innovative "theater of cruelty" so deeply immersed in humanity's naked suffering that its performances would resemble the contortions of condemned prisoners burning at the stake and signaling through the flames to onlookers at their immolation. Godard pays tribute to him twice over in *My Life to Live:* by incorporating his image within the film, and by doing so via the specific scene in *The Passion of Joan of Arc* where his character informs Joan of the tortures she will shortly have to undergo. The sight of mad, tormented Artaud with doomed, tormented Joan – two figures at once transfigured and nearly crushed by enigmatic revelations – adds greatly to the resonance of this extraordinary moment. (Godard's colleague Jacques Rivette invokes Artaud with a more sweeping gesture in his masterful film *Out One: Spectre,* the setting of which is identified as "Paris and its double," an obvious reference to Artaud's most famous theoretical work, *The Theater and Its Double.*)
- Just as Nana's double becomes the threatened and imprisoned Joan, so Karina's double becomes Maria Falconetti, who plays the heroine in Dreyer's film. Dreyer's method of filming Joan's interrogation has become famous (and infamous) in cinematic circles: By taking repeated shots of arduously dramatic moments under physically demanding conditions, he subjected Falconetti to hardships almost as difficult and unpleasant (though of course not so terrifying and interminable) as some of those that were inflicted on the real-life character she portrayed. The result is a performance that partakes, in a small but authentic way, of the awful ordeal it is meant to represent. This is *théâtre-vérité* with a vengeance, and Dreyer's comments on his use of relentless close-ups to convey Joan's anguish apply with surprising force to Godard's employment of the same device. "The records give a shattering impression of the ways in which the trial was a conspiracy of the judges against the solitary Jeanne," the Danish filmmaker notes, "bravely defending herself against men who displayed a devilish cunning to trap her in their net. This conspiracy could be conveyed on the screen only through huge close-ups that exposed, with merciless realism, the callous cynicism of the judges" and thereby moved the audience so greatly "that they would themselves feel the suffering that Jeanne endured."[14] Go-

dard's portrayal of Nana as a pawn ensnared by male-generated greed and power shares much with Dreyer's view of Joan as the victim of a power/knowledge network manipulated by men hoping to further certain ideological aims. Another contact point between the two filmmakers is their insistence on the material presence of the images that anchor their stories. Both want to stay in intimate touch with what critic Raymond Carney calls "the accidental and particular . . . the undeconstructable human being with a real body who is at the center of the role, and who emphatically won't be reduced to . . . a mere semiotic function of a film's systems of artistic expression."[15] Godard could not have said it more directly. Neither could Dreyer, another thinker with a leaning toward Brecht-like politics and a profound sympathy for the plight of women trapped within patriarchal societies as rigidly as Joan and Nana are trapped by the hard-edged borders of their close-ups.

After the film-within-a-film concludes, Nana shakes off her date, who expresses irritation at this; he paid for her movie ticket, after all. This is a small but meaningful detail, since the man's expectation of a payoff on his investment foreshadows the commercial arrangements Nana will enter as a prostitute. It also shows the ubiquity of a sex-as-commerce ideology – the power of masculine money to command feminine sexuality – in contemporary society.

Still dreaming of a show-business career, she then meets with a man who offers to compile nude photos she can use to market her charms in the movie world; again we see the prevalence of commercial sexuality in the realm of "respectable" business, "popular" entertainment, and "responsible" self-improvement. Nana is interested, but right now she's preoccupied with getting 2,000 francs to pay her rent and get her life in order. The camera follows their conversation in another intrusive variation on "normal" cinematic style – swinging from one side to another as it frames first Nana, then her companion, then both together in a conspicuously long, fluid take. It then lingers on the empty bar after they leave, again stressing the transience of Nana's presence within a material environment that exists quite independently of her activities.

Fourth tableau: THE POLICE. NANA IS QUESTIONED. Nana sits before a window, thrown into silhouette by the glare shining through the dirty glass. Her appearance in silhouette is significant, suggesting that individuality is hard to sustain when one is hauled into an impersonal office and subjected to questioning by a near-anonymous minion of the law.

Responding to the police officer's questions, Nana tells a new tale of sadness. She admits she tried to steal 1,000 francs by placing her foot over a banknote dropped by someone on the street, but lost her nerve under a long, hard stare from the woman who lost it – a mean-spirited woman, Nana complains with fiery emotion, who had her arrested even though she returned the money. The policeman takes down her story impassively, framed by Godard as if his typewriter were more important than he is.

The most interesting visual element of the scene is a framed image, hanging on the police-station wall, showing a few male figures underneath what appears to be a giant-sized arm and hand stretched over their heads. This may be seen as literally the long arm of the law, signifying the power/knowledge complex that makes all the decisions here – following its own dictates and unlikely to care about the social circumstances that have led someone like Nana into her current plight. Alternatively, it may be taken as another Artaudian allusion, this time invoking *The Spurt of Blood,* a dramatic work published in 1925. In this play a chaotic episode involving a prostitute and a priest climaxes with God's enormous hand reaching across the stage and setting fire to the woman's hair, whereupon she becomes "naked and hideous," bites God on the wrist, and sexually embraces a young man until the arrival of a dead girl who is dropped on the ground, "where she collapses and becomes as flat as a pancake." Godard's film will reach an ending somewhat similar to that of Artaud's scene, etched in terms that are no less abrupt and upsetting, if far more naturalistic in tone.[16]

Also significant is the end of the episode, when the officer asks how she will now take care of herself. "I don't know," she replies. "I . . . I is another." Nana does not usually slide into sloppy syntax, or into the unconventional language of avant-garde literature – her second phrase is a famous one, written by Arthur Rimbaud in an 1871 letter – so we must think seriously about these hesitant words. On one level, she is manifesting the existential alienation produced by a society that sadly lacks the capacity for guiding, nurturing, and consoling its inhabitants; in such circumstances, one's self may seem almost as alien (an other) as the glaring stranger who hands you to the cops despite the need and desperation flickering through your eyes.

At the same time, Karina the actress is showing both her close identification *with* and critical distance *toward* the character she plays. She achieves this double state through the Brechtian technique of not burrowing into Nana, but standing alongside her so as to "observe" her actions and "quote" her words – "staying prudently outside" in order to refract "inside" realities. Legrand's music makes a strategic return to render the moment even more dramatically effective. Note too that the purposeful lapse of grammar in Nana's unwittingly quoted sentence ("Je est un autre") again marks Godard's willful resistance of common sense – shared with Rimbaud, who called for a "systematic derangement of the senses" as a pathway to social and aesthetic liberty – as it destabilizes "correct" communication with an openness of which a child, a visionary, or a poet could be proud.

Nana turns her face into profile after speaking, and the camera eye zips away into empty space an instant before fade-out. This signals the end of what might be called her "normal life." She will now become a victim of the sexual commerce that she sees as her only escape route from loneliness and fear, which surround her like Joan's rough, uncomforting cloak.

Fifth tableau: THE BOULEVARDS. THE FIRST MAN. THE ROOM. The camera tracks down a Parisian boulevard. Then we see Nana making her way down the sidewalk, and we view the neighborhood's prostitutes through her curious eyes. A man picks her up; they enter a sad-looking little room; and we observe the details of their preparations – including Nana's uncertainty about her price, which turns out to be 4,000 francs – in a long scene with quick, almost clinical editing. The tableau ends with one of the film's most agonizing scenes: another Dreyeresque close-up, as the camera moves in for a relentlessly long take of the client's attempt to kiss Nana on the mouth. She resists by swinging her face frantically from side to side, vainly trying to evade the intimacy her new trade will force on her until the end.

Sixth tableau: MEETING YVETTE. A CAFÉ IN THE SUBURBS. RAOUL. GUNSHOTS IN THE STREET. Nana has a sidewalk conversation with her friend Yvette, filmed from a vantage point behind Nana's head; we don't see their faces until Coutard's camera belatedly swings around when the scene is well under way. Moments later the camera makes an equally conspicuous gesture when it moves from the women on one side of a café to a young man named Raoul on the other, where he's pumping away at a typically Godardian pinball machine. These are elegantly Brechtian visuals, contributing to the film's narrative intelligence while discouraging facile immersion in its emotional and psychological levels.

Back at their café table, Yvette tells Nana the story of her unhappy marriage and her entry into prostitution; the camera focuses mainly on Nana as she sympathetically listens. In an unexpected shift of tone, the film then

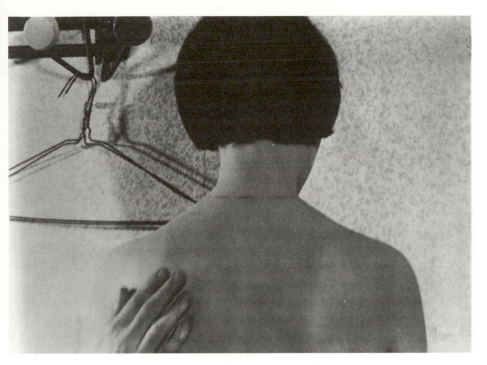

Happiness is no fun: Nana (Anna Karina) plies her trade in *My Life to Live*.

makes a strikingly explicit statement of the existentialist viewpoint that Godard brings to this story and the issues it raises. Responding to Yvette's claim that life is depressing but it's not her fault, Nana states her belief that

> we're always responsible for our actions. We're free. I raise my hand, I'm responsible. I turn my head, I'm responsible. I am unhappy, I'm responsible. I smoke, I'm responsible. I shut my eyes, I'm responsible. I forget I'm responsible, but I am. I told you, there's no escape. Everything is good. You only have to take an interest in things. . . . After all, things are what they are. A message is a message. Plates are plates. Men are men. And life is life.

It is clear from this speech that existence still precedes essence in Godard's work, and our selves are still determined by our behaviors. Nevertheless, we should not take Nana's words as a manifesto by the filmmaker, since she is expressing what might be called a pop-culture version of existentialist thought. Stated in repetitive, ritualistic phrases that frame its meaning in terms closer to religious rhetoric than logical argument, her litany has the sophistication of, say, a self-help manual or a greeting card. Godard's decision to focus on her ideas in this way reflects his perennial skepticism toward logic itself, even when logic might bolster the philosophical views to which he feels closest. The scene also renews our sense of Nana's vulnerability, revealing her need to convince *herself* of her liberty even as she preaches freedom to her companion.

Left out of her statement, of course, is any hint of political awareness, with which Godard is becoming increasingly concerned as the 1960s progress. Nana may feel she bears responsibility for the conditions of her life, but the seductions of Raoul the pimp and the realities of Parisian prostitution – about to be revealed in a documentarylike scene full of facts and figures – will soon show how easily the illusions of individual choice can be shattered. Bearing out this theme, Yvette chats with Raoul while Nana listens to a foolishly romantic pop song about the simple pleasures of the poor. Happiness is a matter not of socioeconomic status, its music and lyrics suggest, but of having an attractive lover to cuddle up with between shifts on the assembly line.

The illusory nature of Nana's supposed freedom is underscored by the next incident in her story. Raoul administers a "test" to determine whether she is a "lady" or a "tramp," and although she "passes" this exam – laughing instead of bristling when Raoul showers her with insults – her response verifies his view of human nature as a matter of stereotypes and categories. (He starts his insults, incidentally, by accusing her of "parroting" his words – recalling the charge of artificiality and unoriginality that Paul made against her in the first tableau.) If she were truly a free agent, moreover, Nana might end her relationship with Raoul after glimpsing the book in which he records the accounts of his prostitutes, reducing them from full humanity to the degraded level of mere numbers in a ledger; yet she makes no move to reduce her involvement with this sleazy new acquaintance.

It is during her glance at this book that the awful sound of gunfire bursts into the café from the street outside, magnifying the implicit violence of Raoul's dehumanizing trade into the explicit violence of a whole society steeped in antagonism, exploitation, and commodification of bodies and souls. The mayhem is as random as the action of Raoul's pinball machine, as inevitable as the markings on his account sheets; yet lingering naïveté makes Nana as blind to its deeper meanings as the victim who staggers into the bar with blood smeared over his eyes.

As if compensating for their tragic inability to see, Godard injects the gunfire's horror into the very fabric of his film, blasting frames out of Coutard's rapid pan shot in a display of jump cutting whose likes we haven't seen since *Breathless*. Nana makes a panicky exit as the material world closes suffocatingly in and the cinematic world blows explosively apart. Raoul will later say "some political thing" caused the madness. He will be correct.

Seventh tableau: THE LETTER. RAOUL AGAIN. THE CHAMPS-ELYSÉES. Seeking a better place to ply her new trade, Nana writes to the madam of a nearby brothel. Godard uses the occasion to reinforce the link between his improvisatory *théâtre-vérité* and the human lives – fictional (Nana) and nonfictional (Karina) – that are its subjects. Peering over Nana's shoulder as she composes her letter, we witness not only the continuation of the film's story through the words she writes, but also a documentary account of Karina's physical movements as she performs an activity whose very ordinariness blurs the line between acting and simply being. Behind her, a huge photomural of the Champs-Elysées underscores the photographic nature of the scene, at once emphasizing its realism (like the photo, this movie is a lifelike account of Paris in 1962) and complicating our attempt to read it literally (this is not reality but a construction, with its own agendas and priorities).

Raoul walks up and speaks with Nana, placing her into more of the categories (ladies and tramps, profitable and unprofitable hookers, etc.) that organize life for him. "The classic letter," he says of the page she has written, relegating her carefully composed words to the lowly status of tried-and-true cliché. She asks his opinion of her, and he says she is "very good," with "great goodness in [her] eyes." She expresses surprise at this "Catholic" answer to what she thought was a simple question, but her feelings of security and authenticity have grown so shaky that she encourages Raoul's judgmental views and the social pigeonholes to which these assign her. She asks what "category of women" he places her in, and he announces that there are "three types of girl," depending on the number of "expressions" they have.

Godard films this conversation in accord with the movie's generally Brechtian tone. The camera starts with left-to-right movements from a position behind Raoul, whose head sometimes hides Nana from view. Then it changes to a position at the end of their table, shifting from one side to the other until Raoul asks Nana to smile. The camera views both of them as Nana protests and maintains her thoughtful expression; then it swings excitedly toward her as she breaks into a sudden grin. Her happiness is short-lived, as she quickly resumes her pensive look and gazes at Raoul with apprehension. They leave the café in a jaunty mood, though, playfully exchanging a puff of cigarette smoke during an affectionate kiss. Nana asks when their new business arrangement will begin, and Godard cuts from the photomural's daytime Paris to a shot of the city at night, enticing and forbidding in its suggestion of unknown possibilities.

Eighth tableau: AFTERNOONS. MONEY. WASHBASINS. PLEASURE. HOTELS. This tableau's title names pleasure as nothing special – just one in a series of everyday nouns, and near the end of the list at that. The tableau itself consists largely of a *faux* documentary on the subject of prostitution in Paris, showing places, objects, and gestures used in the trade. Bodies also appear, filmed in bits and pieces to reflect (among other things) the dehumanizing effects of impersonal sex. The busy montage is accompanied by an "informative" commentary, but rather than invoke the "objectivity" of traditional "voice of God" narration, Godard structures the voice-over as a series of answers to Nana's curious questions. One might call this a catechism for the capitalist age, especially since Nana's recent religious allusion (responding to the "Catholic" remark) is still fresh in memory.

Ninth tableau: A YOUNG MAN. LUIGI. NANA WONDERS WHETHER SHE'S HAPPY. Just as the eighth tableau consisted largely of information that most narrative films would exclude for being too dry, this one is full of Brechtian digressions that nudge us out of the story, allowing room for thought and portraying some of the uneventful "dead time" that occupies real life far more than it occupies conventional movies. We wait with Nana at a bar while Raoul confers with a friend. We wait some more while a young man fetches her a pack of cigarettes. We follow her as she dances to jazz on a jukebox, hovering near her body, and sometimes look through her eyes at the men who stare at her.

The scene's most outlandish digression takes place when Luigi, a minor character, does a comic impersonation of a child inflating and exploding a balloon; while this is an apt metaphor for Nana's ultimately tragic naïveté, it is presented as a sort of vaudeville routine that deliberately postpones the story's development and again foregrounds its artificial, performative nature. Spectators may well find this frustrating, and of course that is the point. Godard's satisfaction with such devices is demonstrated by his repeated use of them – a poem delays an execution in *Les Carabiniers*, a lengthy joke interrupts a dramatic scene in *Alphaville*, a comedian's routine delays the climax of *Pierrot le fou*, and so on. Even the jazz that

"Le zo": Nana (Anna Karina) on the street in *My Life to Live.*

prompts Nana's dance is riddled with brief pauses (momentary rests built into the music, much as printed intertitles are built into this movie) that reinforce the film's interruptive strategy. Beneath its artfully composed shots and carefully recorded sounds, *My Life to Live* is built on a foundation of absence: the absence of tones during the silences in the jazz piece, the absence of words during the *Joan of Arc* sequence, the absence of images during each tableau's introductory title, and finally the absence of Nana, toward which the entire tragedy is wending its way.

Tenth tableau: THE STREETS. A BLOKE. HAPPINESS IS NO FUN. Nana is hooking on the street, more settled into her profession than before. Smoking, surveying the scene, and waiting for trade, she stands before a wall covered with ragged posters; a fragmented phrase directly over her shoulder reads "le zo," evoking the Greek root meaning "life." We may see this as an accident of the shot's composition, but since Godard often fills his frames with carefully selected words and syllables, we may also see it as a reference to the movie's title, and a sign that one particular "life to live" has now enveloped Nana, excluding other possibilities that may once have been available to her. Depending on our interpretation of her story, we may feel she has selected this life with her own individualistic will ("We're always responsible for our actions. We're free") or that it was subtly imposed on her by an alienated, materialistic society. Supporting the second hypothesis over the first, the fragment "zo" also suggests "zoo," a place where animals are confined for the enjoyment of other, more privileged creatures. We may also note another poster alongside Nana, promoting Hollywood star Paul Newman in his popular movie *The Hustler* (*L'Arnaqueur*), a sardonic allusion to the tenacity of hustlers and hustling in her daily round.

In any case, we observe Nana in her "cage" as she socializes with other prostitutes, and we visit a typical session with a client, watching her smoothly negotiate the price and make the rounds of nearby rooms when he asks for an additional woman. (The sound track momentarily drops away as he makes his request, weaving another subliminal silence into the texture of the film.) Arbitrarily ignored by the client, who evidently prefers the new member of his ménage, she again sits in silhouette before a window as Legrand's mournful music swells. This may be considered a Brechtian interlude, undermining melodrama by pushing its conventions (sad music, romantic pose) to the breaking point; but it might also be seen as patently, even desperately heartfelt, using clichés of the Hollywood "woman's picture" to sympathize with Nana over how easily her contentment can vanish into puffs of lonely cigarette smoke. Either way, Godard is honoring two Hollywood giants here: Alfred Hitchcock, whose masterful profile shots in *Vertigo* and *Psycho* could have inspired Nana's pose, and Douglas Sirk, whose use of glass to separate isolated individuals from the plenitude of nature (as in the 1955 *All That Heaven Allows*) prefigures her place before a window revealing an inviting but unreachable world.

Eleventh tableau: PLACE DE CHÂTELET. A STRANGER. NANA THE UNWITTING PHILOSOPHER. Rapid tracking shots capture people walking down city sidewalks. Music and ambient sounds come and go. Nana enters a booth in a café, sees a man reading and smoking in an adjoining space, and asks if he'll buy her a drink.

"Why are you reading?" she asks after a little small talk. "It's my job," the philosopher matter-of-factly answers. Nana admits that she suddenly doesn't know what to say – a recurring situation in her life – and we remember the first tableau, when she repeated a phrase many times instead of developing a thought at length. This prompted Paul's "parrot talk" insult and her own conclusion that "the more we talk, the less words mean."

As a man of words, the philosopher – played by Brice Parain, a respected scholar – would probably not agree with Nana's earlier statement about talking; but she is interested in another side of the question now, and she raises it with him. "I know what I want to say," she observes. "I think about whether it's what I mean . . . but when the moment comes to speak, I can't say it." The philosopher responds with a rambling account of Porthos's death in Alexandre Dumas's novel *Twenty Years After*. Here the dullest-witted of the Three Musketeers lights the fuse on an explosive, starts to flee, but suddenly begins wondering how it is possible for the human body to coordinate the activities used in moving; paralyzed by the paradox of unconscious action translated into conscious thought, he stands transfixed and becomes the victim of his own bomb. "The first time he thought, it killed him!" the philosopher summarizes.

"Why did you tell me that story?" asks Nana with real anger. "No reason," he replies, "just to talk." This begins a lengthy conversation about the nature and purpose of language, in which certain observations and exchanges clearly reflect Godard's current preoccupations. One is Nana's repetition of her point that "the more we talk, the less words mean," coupled with a wish that people could live in silence. The philosopher says this is desirable but unattainable, for two reasons: "We must think, and for thought we need words. . . . To communicate one must talk – that is our life."

He goes on to elaborate his notion that speech and silence are two different states of being, with the former a result (or even a rebirth) of the latter. "We swing between the two because it's the movement of life," he says. "From everyday life, one rises to a life we call superior: the thinking life. But this life presupposes one has killed the everyday, too-elementary life." Thinking and talking are basically the same – "one cannot distinguish the thought from the words that express it" – and both inhabit a separate plane from ordinary existence in the world of things.

This does not mean, of course, that thought or language is isolated from falsehood and error. "Lies too are part of our quest. Errors and lies are very similar," says the philosopher; and Nana adds a bit later that "there is truth in everything, even in error." Godard certainly likes this idea, which he used to justify the "touching" confusions of *The Little Soldier*.[17] Still, persistent effort and existential responsibility are needed to locate truth-through-error and benefit from it. "One must speak in a way that is right, that doesn't hurt," the philosopher goes on, adding (as Nana stares directly into the camera, signaling Godard's fascination as well as her own) that it is best if one "says what has to be said, does what has to be done without hurting or bruising." Again one hears a plea for good-faith integrity – one of the few human qualities that can help us through the raging absurdities of our existential condition.

The conversation keeps rambling along, very much on the philosopher's terms – a sentence like "Leibnitz introduced the contingent" probably means little to Nana – but spurred and sustained by his companion every step of the way. "What do you think about love?" she finally asks, as music hauntingly returns to the sound track. "The body had to come into it," the philosopher replies, and when he veers off into a series of references that Nana can only find obscure, she steers him back to her wavelength by asking, "Shouldn't love be the only truth?" No, he responds, arguing that love cannot be dependably "truth" since it is not dependably "true" but rather a matter of "bits and pieces" and "arbitrary choices"; still, with maturity one can hope to be "at one" with a lover (the words "at one" imply equality, not possession or control) in a way not possible when one is young. "That means searching. This is the truth of life," he concludes. "That's why love is a solution, on condition that it is true."

It is well that the scene ends here, since the philosopher appears to be growing more pretentious and self-involved as he goes along, and Nana lacks the verbal facility to debate him effectively, much less debunk his more dubious notions. What she desires from this conversation is less the philosopher's wisdom, however, than the opportunity to journey through her own thoughts by speaking the words that embody them. She wants to test their truth by hearing their sound, and by watching them register on one of the rare acquaintances who (unlike Raoul and her clients) will listen to her seriously.

What the scene offers to Godard is different but no less valuable: another chance to blur the boundaries between reality and artifice, joining fictional and nonfictional "characters" in a setting at once invented (Nana's narrative) and discovered (Karina's discourse with Parain). "We must pass through error to arrive at the truth," says the philosopher, and it would be hard to convey the rationale behind *théâtre-vérité* more concisely.

Twelfth tableau: THE YOUNG MAN AGAIN. "THE OVAL PORTRAIT." RAOUL TRADES NANA. Sitting in an apartment, the young man who fetched Nana's cigarettes in the ninth tableau holds a volume of Edgar Allan Poe's complete works, the book covering the lower half of his face. Nana is before the window. He lowers the book to converse with her – but instead of hearing their words, we read the conversation in subtitles as Legrand's ever-mournful refrain fills the sound track. They discuss trifles, revealing the comfortable nature of their relationship. Then we hear a voice as the man, apparently Nana's boyfriend now, reads from Poe; at first the screen is darkened, and as the image fades in, we again see only the upper portion of his face over the book he holds. "I thus saw in vivid light a picture all unnoticed before," he reads. "It was the portrait of a young girl just ripening into womanhood. I glanced at the painting hurriedly and then closed my eyes."

The extraordinary thing about this moment in *My Life to Live* is that we are hearing Godard himself – not the young actor on the screen, whose mouth is invisible behind the book – speak Poe's words by reciting the passage into a microphone outside the camera's range. "The portrait, I have already said, was that of a young girl," he continues. His words are accompanied by Karina's immaculately framed image, as if the movie were taking its cue directly from Poe's words.

"It was a mere head and shoulders, done in what is technically termed a *vignette* manner," he goes on, as Nana poses in silhouette before the window. "The arms, the bosom, and even the ends of the radiant hair melted imperceptibly into the vague but deep shadow of the background. As a thing of art, nothing could be more admirable than the painting itself." Nana now gazes toward the camera in close-up, with only a plain white wall behind her. "But it could have been neither the execution of the work nor the immortal beauty of the countenance which so vehemently moved me. Least of all could it have been that my fancy had mistaken the head for that of a living person. At length, satisfied with the true secret of its effect, I fell back within the bed. I had found the spell of the picture in a lifelikeness of expression." Nana is now in profile, sharing the frame with a small portrait reproduction tacked to the wall (not unlike Patricia's decorations in her *Breathless* apartment).

"Is that book yours?" asks Nana, and the man – still speaking in Godard's off-screen voice – repies that he just found it in the room. Then, in an act of ventriloquism that is startling even by Godard's audacious standard, the filmmaker speaks directly to his actress-wife through the young man's persona, as if the latter had no other reason for appearing in the scene. "It's our story," he says to Nana/Karina, "a painter portraying his love! Shall I go on?"

She answers affirmatively and he continues, Poe's words now transformed by their new meaning in the film-and-life that Godard and Karina share. "And in sooth, some who beheld the portrait spoke of its resemblance as of a mighty marvel, and a proof not less of the power of the painter than of his deep love for her whom he depicted so surpassingly well." Becoming increasingly obsessed with his work, Poe's narrative goes on, the painter "turned his eyes from the canvas rarely, even to regard his wife. And he would not see that the tints which he spread upon the canvas were drawn from the cheeks of her who sat beside him." When the painting was complete "save one brush upon the mouth and one tint upon the eye, the spirit of the body again flickered up as the flame of the lamp. And then the brush was given and then the tint was placed, and for one moment the painter stood entranced before the work he had wrought. And in the next while he gazed he grew tremulous and aghast, and cried with a loud voice, 'This is indeed life itself!' and turned suddenly to regard his beloved. She was dead." Nana slowly fades to black as melancholy music swells once more.

Film critic Angela Dalle Vacche has detected a strain of "iconophobia" in Godard's work, suggesting that his obsession with images and their power results from fear and dread as well as devotion and respect.[18] His lengthy quoting of "The Oval Portrait" supports this diagnosis, as does the silent, subtitled conversation that now resumes between Nana and the young man. A request, "I'd like to go to the Louvre," is answered with, "No, I don't like looking at pictures." An aphorism, "Art and beauty are life," is answered with a change of subject.

Turning from the arts to a more immediate concern, Nana agrees to break off with Raoul and move in with her young boyfriend. The next scene then fades in on an outdoor location as Raoul roughly pushes her across the pavement, criticizing her for not accepting "anyone who pays" as a client. "Sometimes it's degrading," she protests, still clinging to her elusive dignity. They drive off, and we see some of the places they pass from the window of Raoul's car. One is a movie theater showing Truffaut's romantic *Jules and Jim,* which prompts someone in the car to complain that there's always a queue when you want see a film. Another is the cast-iron sign of a business called Hell & Sons (Enfer et ses fils). As before in Godard's work, no scene is too serious for a joke to disrupt its mood and delay its outcome.

The film's last joke is the ironically named Restaurant des Studios, in front of which the story ends. After a long, static shot of the street corner, the camera pans with Raoul's car as it swings into view. Coutard then positions the camera some distance from the curb to allow for smooth lateral movements, filming the action in a single shot marked by the flattened-

Violence: Nana (Anna Karina) is murdered by the pimp Raoul in *My Life to Live*.

out, sideways space that Godard has started to favor in his cinematography.

With horror, we realize that Raoul has arranged to sell Nana to another pimp. He pulls her from his car and pushes her in the other man's direction, receiving a packet of cash in return; but the money is short, and he pulls Nana back, refusing to be cheated on the deal. Deciding to destroy the merchandise if he can't drive away with it, the prospective buyer aims his gun at Nana, whose terror is conveyed with poignant force by Karina's barely controlled voice ("No! No!") and harrowingly expressive gestures. His gun fails to fire, and with a tough-guy casualness that borders on caricature ("You shoot. I forgot to load mine") he orders his lackey to finish the job. The thug's bullet smashes into Nana, and a subsequent gunshot – this one from Raoul – ends the little life she still has left to live.

Raoul drives off, leaving Nana's corpse alone within the frame. Godard's camera makes a final abrupt gesture, moving sharply downward so the cold, empty street fills the lower portion of the screen. Nana's lifeless body is thus elevated to the upper portion – a faint, materialist echo

Death: Nana (Anna Karina) lies dead before the Restaurant des Studios in *My Life to Live*.

of the heavenward journey that Joan of Arc might have expected from the God she faithfully served.

Nana shared Joan's tears at an earlier point in this story, but Godard's final portrait of her is less redemptive (not to mention inspirational) than the opposite camera movement – upward to a finer, loftier realm – that ended Dreyer's film. Nana has passed through error, but the philosopher's words notwithstanding, it is far from clear that she has arrived at truth.

4

Weekend

Only violence helps where violence rules.
– Bertolt Brecht[1]

At the beginning of *Weekend*, as described in the published edition of Godard's screenplay, "we find ourselves in the penthouse of a Paris apartment block, looking out through some french windows to a terrace with green trees beyond. Two men, Roland and a Friend, are seated outside, chatting, a table laden with drinks in front of them."[2] This sounds like the first-act setting for some thoroughly traditional play or movie. The location is comfortable, even luxurious, and the people appear to be members of the privileged classes enjoying their privileges, as Hollywood director George Cukor once described some of his characters. Entering this world, our first reaction might be pleasurable envy, as we settle back for two hours of vicarious enjoyment with a movie whose very title signifies leisure, diversion, and respite from workaday cares.

We are in for a bumpier ride than the screenplay's bland description lets on, however, and Godard signals this promptly. The movie's first printed words are not the title but a bizarre label: A FILM ADRIFT IN THE COSMOS. The first sounds evoke not the cozy routines of bourgeois living but the cacophony of modern society – the roar of traffic, the hum of conversation, the insistent ringing of a phone – in all its multitudinous complexity. Soon the movie will offer another enigmatic self-description, A FILM FOUND ON A SCRAP HEAP. Only after a burst of dialogue about death ("Wouldn't it be great if both of them died . . .") and chaos ("Did you know that seven people got killed . . .") will the title finally appear, in this startling form –

```
END  WEEK  END
WEEK  END  WEE
K  END  WEEK  EN
D  WEEK  END  WE
EK  END  WEEK  E
ND  WEEK  END  W
EEK  END  WEEK
```

– printed in the red, white, and blue colors of the French and American flags.

The movie's way of presenting its title merits consideration, since it carries a number of meanings relevant to the picture as a whole. For spectators who saw it in 1967, when it was new, an obvious reference point would have been the pop-art style being catapulted to prominence by Andy Warhol and others who shared (like Godard) a refusal to draw boundaries between rarified conceptualism and earthy materialism. Pop prides itself on absorbing the products and processes of commodity culture, defamiliarizing them through rhythmic repetition and self-referential irony, and transforming them into art objects that are mechanical embodiments *of* and critical commentaries *on* the relentlessly productive society from which they emerged.

The title frame of *Weekend* announces its pop affinities in two major ways. One is the use of red, white, and blue as its (literally) primary colors. These colors have become hopelessly hackneyed – almost invisible, one might say – through their use in national flags; yet they carried a major expressive punch during a decade when politically alert individuals were ratcheting up their skepticism toward governments that wrapped these hues around themselves as they pursued imperialistic policies, jingoistic wars, and other ill-founded projects. Leftists like Godard were increasingly repulsed by manifestations of brute nationalism in France and also in the United States, which had inherited one of France's most tragic colonial follies (the effort to keep Vietnam under Western control) and carried it to extremes that even moderate politicians were beginning to reject in the second half of the 1960s. Godard was drawn to the red-white-and-blue with a sort of morbid fascination, using the colors with aggressive irony in *La Chinoise* and other works. This was at once an aesthetic gesture (in themselves, the colors are a vivacious trio) and a sarcastic commentary on current events in the sociopolitical sphere.[3]

The title frame also evokes the assembly-line aesthetic of pop, which rejects the once-sacred notion that art must have "unique" or "special" properties – a sort of "aura," in philosopher Walter Benjamin's term – if it is to be considered genuine or authentic. The mid-1960s saw a great flowering of cultural production that chose not to hide or camouflage its mass-manufactured origin but revealed and even flaunted the mechanized processes that produced it. Godard was very interested in this development, which both excited his aesthetic imagination and suggested a new departure point for his escalating critique of the culture industry – as in his 1968 film *One Plus One,* also known as *Sympathy for the Devil,* which chronicles the creation of a Rolling Stones rock recording, with emphasis on the calculated, repetitive labor that goes into it. Godard readily included theatrical cinema in his expanding list of cultural products that were being deprived of their souls by commercialization and commodification; indeed, not long after *Weekend* he renounced commercial film altogether, pouring his energy into a search for alternative modes of production, distribution, and exhibition. The design of the *Weekend* title, stamped out repetitiously and mechanically in a sleek parody of industrial chic, joins additional elements in that movie and other recently made Godard films – the pop-music recording session in *Masculine/Feminine,* the ad-slogan party scene in *Pierrot le fou,* the landscape of commercial products in *2 or 3 Things I Know about Her,* and many more – to provide a vivid foretaste of his ultrapolitical phase, which would begin with *Le Gai Savoir* the following year.

Finally, the title reflects an important aspect of Godard's artistic method: his habit of putting words and pictures into productive competition with each other. With its eye-catching design and runaway multiplicity, the WEEKEND logo captures the spirit of an age that often values quantity over quality. Equally important, it captures Godard's growing fascination with cinema that "disassembles language into images and makes language out of images," as Angela Dalle Vacche describes the process.[4] He knew that all movies turn images into language; one of his first published articles praised Soviet cinema for giving "the idea of a shot . . . its real function of sign,"[5] that is, for integrating visual material into a languagelike structure with a recognizable "grammar." Doing this equation in the opposite direction, the WEEKEND title card turns language into image, since its verbal meaning is considerably less striking than its shape, color, and overall visual impact. In addition to this double operation – language becoming image and vice versa – Godard gives both image and language a distinctly rhythmic function in many portions of *Weekend,* often using them to provide more of a "musical" pulse than a "literal" set of meanings. His collagelike conjunctions of the verbal, the visual, and the musical demonstrate his wish to throw different systems of communication into eccentric new configurations that may (he hopes) produce meanings and ideas not available via more traditional routes.

Along with his affection for Brechtian devices and pop-art irony, this ambition explains the frequent out-of-the-blue wordplay that fills the screen in *Weekend* – reappearances of the title, pointless reminders of the day and hour, vague indications of Godard's underlying agenda for a scene, and so on. Most interesting are the typographical blocks that attack conventional language head-on: "ANAL YSIS" and "FAUX TOGRAPHY," for instance. These point up similarities between Godard and provocateurs in two radical French movements of the 1950s and 1960s: the Situationist International and its predecessor, the Lettrist International, which proclaimed the limitations of logic by seeking to liberate the letters of the alphabet (innocent building blocks) from the words and sentences (ideological tools) that imprison and control them. Godard was not a card-carrying member of these groups, which have roots in the earlier surrealist and dada movements; indeed, his allegedly "pretentious pseudoinnovations" were attacked more than once in the *Internationale Situationniste* journal published by Guy Debord and company.6 Nevertheless, his films often share the Lettrist mixture of deadpan whimsy and dead-serious outrage, and his characters have a frequent habit of spray-painting their slogans onto the scrubbed facades of polite society, a practice the Situationists themselves honed into a fine art during the late 1960s.

Weekend reached the screen in 1967, when the era known as the sixties was approaching its European climax. Social unrest and political protest were on the upswing, and many French dissidents expected full-fledged insurrection against a capitalist–imperialist order they despised.

These hopes were disappointed the following year, when revolt fizzled and the powers-that-be reasserted their dominance; but the electricity of the period was still building as Godard went into production on increasingly radical films like *2 or 3 Things I Know about Her,* with its subversive critique of capitalism and its discontents, and *La Chinoise,* with its wry look at Marxian alternatives to commonsense norms. *Weekend* is perhaps the most explosive of these movies; yet while Godard clearly wished to carry the cinematic and political implications of his earlier work to new extremes, he was not quite ready to throw off all traces of traditional moviemaking. What places *Weekend* among his most exciting films is the fact that within it we see the most drastic transition of his career – from liberal skeptic to radical mutineer – gathering speed and energy before our very eyes.

The growing urgency of this transition appears to be an integral part of Godard's plan for the film, as it builds from its chatty opening in a bourgeois apartment to its ferocious finale in a decimated countryside. The deceptively conventional beginning hints at the craziness to come, since its main reference points in Hollywood cinema are derived from the film-noir cycle of the 1940s and 1950s, which specialized in tales of intrigue, treachery, and betrayal. Many self-respecting noirs might have inspired the dialogue between our heroine, Corinne, and a friend who's visiting her and Roland, her husband:

> FRIEND: Wouldn't it be great when Roland drives your father home if both of them died in an accident? . . . Did he get his brakes fixed?
> CORINNE: No. I managed to make him forget.
> FRIEND: Did you know seven people got killed last Sunday at the Evreux junction?
> CORINNE: Yeah, that would be great. . . .

And here is Roland on the telephone, a few moments later: "Listen, you're not to phone me here any more. It's dangerous. . . . I've got to be cautious after those sleeping pills and the gas. . . . She may be dumb, but she'll start getting suspicious. . . . Anyway, the main thing is for her old man to croak. Afterwards, when Corinne's got the money, we'll deal with her. . . . Of course I love you. . . ."

Has this movie stumbled into some outlandish den of iniquity where civilized values have inexplicably been forgotten? Quite the opposite: Civilized values aren't what they used to be, and for Godard, the violence-prone household of Corinne and Roland catches the spirit of the late 1960s as well as Ozzie and Harriet Nelson's home represented aspects of the previous decade. In an age when greed and belligerence have overtaken the Western world at large, people like Corinne and Roland hardly stand out from the crowd.

Rather than simply preaching this proposition, Godard weaves his disturbing vision into the substance of the film itself. This clarifies further why he punctuates the action with those jarring, disruptive blocks of typography. In other ways, too, he surrounds the story with signs of social disjunction and dysfunction. The first such outbreak comes between Corinne's conversation and Roland's phone call, when two motorists have a furious fight after their cars collide on the pavement below. This introduces automobiles as the film's main symbolic objects, embodying the materialism and aggression of a society being crushed by its own fetishized commodities. Important too is the look and feel of the brawl as Godard presents it. As filmed from the apartment's balcony, it would appear pointless and absurd even if it weren't so wildly hyperactive (the Three Stooges were never more frenetic) and so wildly out of proportion to the trivial fender-bender that prompted it. The movie is still in its opening moments, but already we see that the sociocultural center cannot hold, human relations are falling apart, and mere anarchy is being loosed upon a world that indeed seems adrift in the cosmos.

Weekend might be too volcanic to watch if it kept up this pace indefinitely. It shows signs of subsiding as Roland's phone call concludes with a (visual) fade to black and a (verbal) riff that repeats his last words with the inanity of a broken record, recalling Nana's repetitive "parrot talk" in *My Life to Live*. The following scene has a very different rhythm, with ramblingly long takes and a numbingly long speech by Corinne to her still-nameless friend.

The film has not settled down as much as first appears, however, and "numbing" doesn't quite describe Corinne's monologue. Prompted by her friend's curiosity, she sits on a tabletop in her underwear and interminably describes a small-scale orgy she had with two companions, Paul and Monique, at their home. The beginning of her speech might have been lifted from an ordinary melodrama: "He started in the Mercedes. . . . We necked for a long time in the parking lot. . . ." Then the scene being described changes to Paul's place and Monique enters the tale, adding a new layer of perversity: "She asked me if I didn't think her ass was too big . . . and she turned round, spreading her legs open. . . . She asked me to describe them. . . ." Her voice stays as flat as the table she's sitting on, making wild statements and banal ones in the same affectless tone.

Is this some new kind of sociopolitical critique or just a dose of old-fashioned pornography? Godard's later film *Numéro deux* asks this question explicitly about its own content, and the answer turns out to be both. The same goes for *Weekend*, where the ironic absurdity of Corinne's monologue grows increasingly clear, culminating in a round of carnivalistic sex (e.g., Corinne masturbating while Monique squats in a dish of cat milk) that eventually peters out in what can only be called an anticlimactic climax:

> FRIEND: Did all this really happen or was it a nightmare?
> CORINNE: I don't remember.
> FRIEND: I adore you, Corinne; come and excite me.

Fade to black. Whether all this "happened" or not is moot, of course, since Corinne's words pack a sensationalistic punch regardless of any

Verbal orgy: Corinne (Mireille Darc) spins a sex-filled monologue in a tone as flat as the table she's sitting on, while her nameless friend listens intently, in *Weekend* (1967).

"real" past events. What matters about the scene is that it escalates Godard's war against the tyranny of images. Convinced more than ever that show business is bad for us, he now wants to undermine the very idea of cinematic spectacle. He does this through a sort of verbal flank attack, combining contradictory elements – prurient speech and puritanical picture – that throw movie-sex conventions into a deliberate muddle. (Adding to the irony is the fact that Corinne is played by Mireille Darc, widely known for sexy roles in commercial films. Roland is played by Jean Yanne, a more conventional choice. Many other characters have no fictional names within the film, incidentally, and are called by the names of the performers who portray them – e.g., the revolutionary leader is called Kalfon after the actor Jean-Pierre Kalfon.)

The tactics of this scene are based on Godard's conviction that a basic strategy of commercial film (in keeping with the commodity system as a whole) is to stimulate our visual appetites, then gratify this artificial desire by providing the material it has teasingly promised. This is built into the most common pattern of movie editing, where "eyeline match" shots alternate between *someone looking* and *what the person sees*. The same strategy is behind almost every kind of narrative scene, from sophisticated suspense sequences (What will the outcome be?) to exploitative sex episodes (What will we see next?). The sound track is usually limited to a supporting role, designed to make the visual tease more alluring and the eventual payoff more gratifying.

Determined to thwart such manipulative uses of film, Godard has pioneered a provocative (and highly Brechtian) approach that turns image and sound into equal partners, each with its own aesthetic and expressive integrity. Democratized like this, sight and sound have new freedom to interact in unexpected ways, challenging our analytical powers instead of lulling us into passive spectatorship. This is why Corinne's monologue cannot be called gratuitous, to borrow a favorite term of would-be censors. While its subject cries out for pictures, Godard's refusal to supply them makes us keenly aware of (a) how effective movies are at sparking superficial desires, and (b) how much more interesting it can be when a filmmaker calls sardonic attention to these instead of pandering to them on the screen. If show business is bad, how about a cinema that doesn't show?

Weekend returns to its film-noir roots as Corinne and Roland begin the journey that dominates the movie's fractured story. Jumping into their Facel convertible, they start for the distant town of Oinville, where they hope to pin down Corinne's inheritance and speed the demise of her father so they can collect it – each dreaming of the other's death, meanwhile, so the loot won't have to be shared.

They don't get out of the parking lot, however, before encountering more of the slapstick-style buffoonery that punctuated the opening scene. Roland bumps his car into a parked sedan, leading to a quarrel with the owner's little boy, who pockets a bribe and calls his mother anyway. She arrives in a rage; Roland and Corinne fend her off with a paint gun; she retaliates with a blitz of tennis balls; and her husband joins in with a shotgun as their son shouts, "Bastard! Shitface! Communist!" Godard labels the episode with a blue intertitle reading "SCENE FROM PARIS LIFE," as if this were a nineteenth-century literary vignette. His view of urban living is plain: Honoré de Balzac meets Moe, Larry, and Curly.

On the road at last, Corinne and Roland promptly run into one of the most bravura sequences in any Godard film: a cinematically stunning traffic-jam scene that brings together many of his most original and subversive ideas. Automobiles are central to this scene, and it is interesting to note how the metaphorical meaning of cars has shifted in Godard's value system. In the early *Breathless* they represented a Beat-style dream of liberation via speed, flexibility, elusiveness. They played a more somber role in *My Life to Live*, introducing Nana to the sad pavements she would walk, and carrying her to the lonely street where pimps would gun her down before speeding away to safety. *Weekend* veers even more sharply in this cynical direction, paralyzing cars altogether by cramming them into a self-suffocating gridlock so devoid of action and energy that the movie itself almost stops moving.

The scene begins as Corinne and Roland steer their Facel down a country road that's backed up with cars as far as the eye can see. Godard's camera runs parallel to the road, gliding along the shoulder at about the same pace as the convertible. Since everything takes place on the roadway, the action seems stretched and flattened into a two-dimensional spectacle, as shallow as the society that has allowed everyday life to degenerate so badly.

Sound also plays a key part in the scene, filling the air with horn honks so loud and persistent that they lose any potential meaning as greetings or warnings. This is cacophony as sheer self-assertion, blaring away with no regard for purpose or utility; yet it conveys a bitter sort of beauty all the same, celebrating its own belligerence with a heedless panache recognized by critic Pauline Kael when she described the horns as triumphant, "like trumpets in Purcell."[7] In addition to its metaphoric value, the noisiness also serves a clever cinematic function – counterpointing the flatness of the image with a direct assault on the audience's eardrums, stamping the scene's immediacy on our bodies as we experience it.

This goes on for hours of narrative time, as Roland maneuvers his Facel through the tie-up with even more edginess and impatience than most of his fellow drivers show. The panorama that he passes, and that Godard captures on film, amounts to a microcosm of social activity: On view are recreation (card playing, a chess match), sports (ball tossing, sailboat rigging), culture (book reading, radio listening), personal hygiene (relaxing, urinating), and so forth. The most arresting images are two that stand out for their own pictorial value as well as the fact that Coutard's camera gives them a bit of extra attention. One shows a traveling menagerie including monkeys, lions, and a llama staring back at us with the calm assurance of a creature that knows its dignity and integrity are leagues above those of the *Homo sapiens* so chaotically surrounding it. The other is a gigantic Shell Oil tank truck. It greedily sucks up screen space with its intimidating bulk and aggressive red-and-yellow colors; yet it's even more stymied than the other vehicles, stuck in a nose-to-nose stalemate with a white Fiat headed in the opposite direction on the same stretch of roadway. This is a prototypical Godardian symbol, transforming the personal car crash that climaxed *Contempt* into a socioeconomic car clash (Shell vs. citizen) with darkly comic undertones.

Many arguments, insults, and altercations later, Roland and Corinne finally approach the end of the congestion and discover its cause: a horrifying accident that has left wrecked vehicles and mangled bodies strewn along the street. Not surprisingly, our heroes couldn't care less. They zip past the catastrophe, turn off the main highway, and enter a rural area that holds forth the possibility of a calmer, cooler atmosphere.

Roland wrecks the calm about two seconds later, bowling over a trash can as the Facel screeches into a town square and careens up to the curb. We know by now that such reckless behavior is normal in the *Weekend* world, but more tumultuous upheaval is about to transpire. No sooner has the Facel lurched to a stop than we hear an off-screen crash between a farmer's tractor and a Triumph sports car holding a young woman, who survives the accident, and her wealthy boyfriend, who does not. Roland and Corinne ignore this ruckus, discussing instead what will happen to their plan if Corinne's father uses his "little Japanese tape recorder" to dictate an updated will. "Why have we been sweating it out for the past five years, putting poison in his mashed potato every Saturday?" whines Corinne, dismayed that her work might come to nothing. "Did you see the Triumph?" she adds, finally acknowledging the collision that just occurred. "If only that could have been Mommy and Daddy, it would have made everything a whole lot easier."

Like many film-noir couples, Corinne and Roland have a strained relationship; but at least they share a middle-class background, which saves them from the class warfare that explodes between the tractor-driving farmer and Juliet, the surviving sports-car passenger. The personal rage displayed by these two is so great that their shouting match seems at first like mere emotionalism. There is no mistaking the gender-based inflections and class-coded subtexts of the insults they hurl at each other, however, and Godard underscores this political dimension with on-screen labels –

SS
SS STRUGGLE
THE CLASS STRUGGLE

– all in bold blue letters. Juliet fiercely belittles the farmer: "It makes you sick that we've got money and you haven't. . . . You're pissed off because we fuck on the Riviera and you don't. . . . I bet you don't even own [your tractor] and it belongs to one of those rotten unions or some fucking co-operative. . . ." The farmer shows more political intelligence, but bogs down in ideological argument: "If it weren't for me and my tractor, the French would have nothing to eat." Juliet trumps him with "You big lump of shit!" and other colorful yelps.

With its unhappy premise and outrageous dialogue, this episode is an uneasy blend of tragedy and farce, leaving us uncertain how to respond. Piling on more ambiguity, Godard inserts an incongruous shot of Juliet posing with an advertising billboard (flanked by a brassiere ad and an Esso tiger) wearing a pensive expression on her face. Later, when the farmer launches into a reasonable-sounding criticism of Roland's awful driving, a similar cutaway shows three men we've never seen before, perhaps bystanders listening to the argument, or perhaps Brechtian intruders who are not part of this story at all. Subsequent shots show a smiling man, his girlfriend, and another fellow in a baseball cap. The published *Weekend* screenplay assumes these figures are watching the fight between Juliet and the farmer, but their stiff, apathetic poses suggest complete separation from the narrative. In any case, these shots serve the same purpose as the movie's full-screen titles, disrupting what might otherwise be an absorbing – and therefore morally unacceptable – melodramatic scene.

Godard finishes off any lingering traces of normal melodrama with a sardonic plot twist. Arguing so fiercely that they come to blows, Juliet and the farmer appeal to Corinne and Roland as witnesses of the fatal crash. Roland scoots his convertible past them with scarcely a nod, naturally infuriating them – and radicalizing them, to the point where they instantly unite against the outrageous couple. "You can't leave just like that! Aren't we all brothers like Marx said? Bastards! Bastards!" hollers the farmer. Juliet's parting shot at the motorists is far more scandalous – "Jews! Filthy rotten stinking Jews!" – but the farmer sympathizes without hesitation, wrapping an arm around his erstwhile enemy and escorting her from the scene. By satirizing anti-Semites and Communists in almost the same breath, Godard proves he is far from the party-line Marxist for which some critics still mistook him in 1967. Indeed, this scene shows his skepticism toward all parties in the "SS CLASS STRUGGLE," including the often-idealized working class.

The screen then fills with FAUX TOGRAPHY in blue letters, and all the dislocated strangers from the preceding episode pose neatly before the billboard. Roland is there too, comforting himself over Corinne's momentary absence by embracing Juliet, still covered with blood from her recent accident. What's going on here? The answer is murky, and again that is precisely Godard's point. All we know for certain is that strange days are increasingly upon us.

Together again, Roland and Corinne are confused as well. Red and blue numbers tick off kilometers as their Facel zooms along a country road, bringing them closer to their destination but hardly reducing their hostility toward each other.

"When did civilization begin?" asks Corinne, taking a break from their bickering. Her question seems slightly odd, since their surroundings are rural, not conspicuously "civilized" in the way an urban setting would be. What she is discovering – along with us in the audience – is that *Weekend* finds the countryside more conducive to true civilization than the city or suburbs. This is not because "nature" carries some essential grace, à la Rousseau, but because its comparative distance from the power/knowledge networks of mainstream society makes it a productive place for romantic outlooks, utopian daydreams, and revolutionary experiments. This outlook defines "civilization" in an ornery way, suggesting that the bursts of rural anarchy in this increasingly anarchic story are more civil and refined than the suburban milieu Roland and Corinne have left behind. *Weekend* is an ornery movie, however, and Godard – whose passionate love of the natural world will radiate through the postpolitical landscapes of later films – sees the countryside as an appropriate place to unleash the purgative powers of his growing sociocultural rage. The characters we meet in this rural "civilization" are like the "uncivilized" protagonists in *Band of Outsiders* two years earlier. "They have neither the mentality of thieves [nor] of capitalists," Godard metaphorically described the *Outsiders* figures. "They're like animals. They get up in the morning. They have to find a bird to kill so they can eat at noon, and another for the evening. Between that, they go to the river to drink. And that's it. They live by their instincts, for the instant. The danger would be to make a system of it."[8] Later in *Weekend* we will spend harrowing time with people who *have* made a system of it, and "dangerous" is a mild word for the results.

For now, Corinne is still trying to fathom the previous scene. "I don't understand," she gripes, referring to the farmer's comment about Marx calling all people brothers. "It wasn't Marx," replies Roland, "it was Jesus – another commie." For once, Godard has put a coherent thought into Roland's muddled mind, recalling that Marx and Jesus shared certain

Jarring and fractured: Roland (Jean Yanne) and Corinne (Mireille Darc) fight and bite their way through a country excursion in *Weekend*.

notions about genuinely "civilized" life. Corinne has already lost interest, though. "Even if it's true," she asks, "who cares? We're not living in the Middle Ages." Her fleeting philosophical moment gives way to a series of highway encounters, as jarring and fractured as the traffic-jam scene was prolonged and hypnotic. Quick-cutting vignettes show furious battles with other motorists, complete with biting, hitting, hairpulling, and outrageous insults. Civilization may exist alongside the roadway, but on the asphalt a Three Stooges mentality remains alive and well.

Corinne's casual question about entering civilization gathers more ambiguity as *Weekend* proceeds, since evidence suggests that everybody involved (i.e., the characters in the film and the audience watching it) is leaving an old, familiar world and sliding into a new, disorienting mode of existence. While this new realm is superficially the same as the one it replaces, rational structures and reasonable controls seem mysteriously missing. Godard finds this both exhilarating and terrifying, and encour-

ages us to experience it with the same ambivalent wonder. Lest we under-
estimate how drastically the movie's world has changed, the next scene
makes this so evident that even the most resistant spectator must recognize its radicalism and confront its implications.

The convertible roars down a country road in a teeming rainstorm. A
woman, decked out in a red raincoat and white boots, waves for it to stop
alongside an accident site with two smashed-up cars. She asks for a ride,
and Roland responds by checking out her body, even lifting her raincoat
to inspect her derrière. (This echoes Michel's evaluation system for hitch-
hikers in *Breathless;* the woman puts up with it as normal masculine behavior.) Deciding she meets his specifications, Roland motions her toward
the Facel's back door. However, like many a hitchhiker, she has a companion waiting nearby, and he now crawls from one of the wrecks, wearing
a coat that matches hers and carrying a slender tree branch in one hand.
He demands a ride in the opposite direction; when Roland demurs he fires
a gun, brandishes his leafy stick, and prods Roland through a U-turn, just
as a lion tamer would put a circus animal through its paces. Filled to
capacity with its four passengers, the Facel heads back in the direction
whence it came, and the scene gives way to a full-screen intertitle that
changes as we watch:

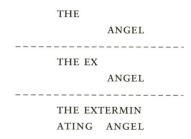

This is a typical Godardian joke, making a film-buff reference to Luis Buñuel's masterpiece *The Exterminating Angel* (1962), about a dinner party
that spirals into chaos when the guests discover they are incapable of leaving. By invoking its title in his own movie, which takes a similar dark pleasure in confrontations between the ordinary and the inexplicable, Godard
cleverly cannibalizes its blend of existentialist angst and surrealist drollery.
He also injects another Brechtian break into the story's continuity (already
shaky), and foreshadows a supernatural/religious element in the episode
about to unfold.

Claiming to be the product of "buggery" between God and Alexandre
Dumas, the hitchhiker-hijacker may be the angel of Godard's film, but he

certainly doesn't seem like one. Jammed in the back seat, he uses his pistol to keep Roland and Corinne under control – not that other motorists pay any attention to their yowls for help – and snaps pictures of them with a camera. Corinne asks about the photos, and he answers that they are "for the Ministry of the Interior," explaining that "even God has His police." Roland parries that he and Corinne have nothing to fear, since they are married, which legalizes their sex acts. The ensuing dialogue reveals a feminist awareness that is surprisingly strong for a film produced in 1967, when the modern feminist movement was just beginning to pick up speed:

HITCHHIKER: Tell me your name, lady.
CORINNE: My name is Corinne Durand.
HITCHHIKER: No it's not. That's your husband's name. What's yours?
CORINNE: My maiden name is Corinne Vitron.
HITCHHIKER: No, that's your father's name. What's yours?
CORINNE: What? My name? Well, I . . .
HITCHHIKER: That just shows you. You don't even know who you are.

This critique of patriarchal power, which traverses the kinship system to gain control of identity itself, is followed by a reference to language and religion. "Christianity is the refusal to know oneself," the hitchhiker says. "It's the death of language."

Language and religion are such significant topics for Godard that we should pause to see how their relationship has been evolving in his films. He set forth his deep respect for language in *My Life to Live*, seeing it as a precondition of thought itself. Another slant on this appears in *Masculine/Feminine*, made a year before *Weekend*, when the main characters watch a pornographic film showing a woman being abused by a man who communicates in grunts and barks. The brutality of this scene, one critic suggests, derives "as much from the absence of language as . . . from the man's rape of the woman."[9] Also significant is an observation by one of the *Masculine/Feminine* characters that the porno movie is presented in its "original language." Combining these elements – "absence of language" and "original language" – with the idea that "language is the house man lives in," as *2 or 3 Things I Know about Her* stated, it follows that the "original language" must be "no language, man before language, a beast."[10] At this stage in his career, Godard apparently sees language as a progressive medium for "purifying sexuality from brutality and violence," in critic Yosefa Loshitzky's words.[11] This means that a force like

Christianity, bringing "death of language" and "refusal to know oneself," is limiting and destructive.

Godard will change his mind in eighties and nineties films like *Hail Mary* and *Nouvelle Vague,* seeing the "original language . . . no language, man before language" not as bestial, but as blessed and inspired; yet *Weekend,* in its own obstreperous way, already points in this direction. Although the obnoxious hitchhiker does not make a very appealing prophet, he has a definite mission to perform: "I am here to proclaim to these modern times the end of the grammatical era and the beginning of an age of flamboyance in every field," he announces, "especially the movies." Since this is an accurate summary of *Weekend* itself, we are evidently watching not just a movie but an annunciation – a scruffy, belligerent, chaotic annunciation, but flamboyant enough to suggest that the grammatical era may indeed be having its apocalypse even as we watch.

Godard is no less determined than the hitchhiker to jettison commonsense stylistics. Accordingly, he continues the intruder's scene with an increasingly eclectic mélange of images and sounds. Trying to impress Roland and Corinne with his semidivine nature, the hitchhiker offers them "whatever you want" in return for a ride to London; to prove his worthiness as a credit risk, he performs a hilariously trite magic trick, conjuring up a white rabbit under the dashboard. Corinne responds with equally hilarious ambivalence, squealing "Shit! A miracle!" as she hauls the animal into the open. Realizing they've stumbled on a gold mine, she and Roland deluge the hitchhiker with their wish list, and it's just the sort of mindlessly materialistic catalog this pair would be expected to dream up: a large Mercedes, a Saint-Laurent evening dress, a Miami Beach hotel, a headful of blond hair, a fleet of Mirage IV aircraft "like the yids used to wipe out the wogs," and a weekend with James Bond – a prospect that turns both Corinne and Roland on. Less of a lowlife than he appears, the hitchhiker refuses to gratify the couple, although his reason is unclear. "Is that really all you want?" he asks, not specifying whether he is disappointed by their materialism or by the banality of their demands.

So far, *Weekend* has been a bitter parody not only of film noir but also of Hollywood's cultishly popular road-movie genre. Now it becomes more of an action picture, as Corinne snatches a pistol from the hitchhiker's companion and helps Roland chase them across a grassy field. The genre and tone of the picture then become indeterminate for a moment, as the hitchhiker runs toward a wrecked car, raises his hands, and demands silence, like a patriarch in some old Cecil B. DeMille epic. He appears to be working up another miracle, and Godard accomplishes it for him, cutting to a shot nearly identical to the first, except that the characters are surrounded by a huge flock of sheep that has materialized out of nowhere – or rather, out of Buñuel's film *The Exterminating Angel,* which ends with a similarly mysterious image of sheep swarming through a public place for no earthly reason. Grabbing the gun in this confusion, the hitchhiker chases Roland and Corinne back to their Facel, yelling "Vade retro! Go home!"

Are we under the Exterminating Angel's spell? If so, who embodies this apparition? It could be the hitchhiker, who has performed two miracles; it could be Godard, who actually accomplished these, using tacky mise-en-scène tricks (the rabbit) and extravagant montage feats (the sheep) that recall Hollywood's version of biblical supernaturalism; or it could be the Spirit of Intertextuality, presiding over Godard's clamorous call for a cinema as cluttered, tumultuous, and flamboyant as his own moral imagination.

Speeding along in their Facel again, Roland and Corinne pilot the car like infantry soldiers battering their way through hostile territory. Honking and hollering, they force a bicyclist, another small auto, and a pedestrian off the road, meanwhile swerving into a couple of near-collisions and running over a hapless chicken. Scrambling the movie's time sense as much as its geographical bearings, Godard propels us prematurely into the next scene with lightning-quick flash-forwards, showing a horrific accident engulfed in flames and smoke. We then plunge into this purgatory as Roland drags himself from under the pileup, while Corinne screeches her agony in one of the movie's most savagely satirical moments. "Help! My Hermès bag!" she shrieks in infinitely mournful tones, oblivious to the horror and suffering (including Roland's bloodstained condition) all around her.

Narrative time, space, and consistency – the chronotope of the movie – continue to bend and wobble as Roland and Corinne trudge along a path after their catastrophic crash. Striding with them is none other than Louis Antoine Léon de Saint-Just, a major figure of the French Revolution, dressed in eighteenth-century clothing and reading from a book in stentorian tones:

> Freedom, like crime, is born of violence . . . as though it were the virtue that springs from vice . . . fighting in desperation against slavery. . . . The struggle will be long and freedom will kill freedom. . . . Can one believe that man created society . . . in order to be happy and reasonable therein? No! One is led to assume that, weary of the restfulness and wisdom

of Nature, he wishes to be unhappy and mad. I see only constitutions that are backed by gold, pride, and blood, and nowhere do I see . . . the fairness and moderation that ought to form the basis of the social treaty.

These words clearly relate to Godard's radicalized social philosophy, lamenting the human strife bred by capitalist vices of greed and competition, which have corrupted the natural world. They also relate to Godard's filmmaking strategy, whereby the virtue of freedom – that is, a liberated cinema – must be born from a violent, take-no-prisoners assault on "slavery" to classical style and conventional narrative. Since the kind of filmmaking represented by *Weekend* is all but unprecedented, Godard's audience must decide whether he and his troops are winning this battle on our behalf, or whether "freedom is killing freedom" in a political-aesthetic skirmish that may prove Pyrrhic at the final fade-out.

Slicing the film's continuity into more collagelike fragments, intertitles reading "SU ND AY" and "STORY FOR MONDAY" appear in confusing alternation. Saint-Just leaves the screen, then returns long enough to repeat his last words. A new pan shot of Roland and Corinne makes two false starts before proceeding beyond its first few frames; and though Saint-Just has indeed gone, the actor who portrayed him (Jean-Pierre Léaud) is still around, now playing a young man who opens the sequence with an off-screen cry: "I'm calling out in the emptiness."

These words may sound like another outburst of angst and absurdism, but the fellow is merely singing a message to friends from a conveniently placed phone booth. (An intertitle has labeled this portion of the movie FROM THE FRENCH REVOLUTION TO WEEKENDS WITH DE GAULLE, and the two characters played by Léaud embody this chronotopic leap.) Roland and Corinne soon arrive and, as we might expect, patience at public telephones is not among their virtues. Roland pesters the man to finish. The singing man persists, altering his lyrics ("I'm afraid I've got to hang up now/There's some people outside, they can't wait") to suit the circumstances. Roland prods him by climbing into his Honda and starting its motor. The young man buzzes out of the phone booth, and another slapstick struggle ensues, which he wins, using a jack handle and tire as a sword and shield. Roland and Corinne limp into the next scene among burning and exploding cars, asking directions from corpses scattered along the roadside. "These buggers are all dead," says Roland, with his usual degree of compassion.

The next sequence requires only one false start before it actually begins: a glimpse of countryside that immediately fades, then reappears as Roland and Corinne arrive. We are DU COTÉ DE CHEZ LEWIS CARROLL, as a blue

Dramatis personae: Roland (Jean Yanne) asks directions from Emily Brontë (Blandine Jeanson) and Tom Thumb (Yves Afonso) on a country path in *Weekend*.

intertitle soon informs us, and the scene's mood of wry parody echoes the tone of Carroll's fiction – although its whimsical blend of literary references (Blake, Brecht, Brontë) goes far beyond the dramatis personae of Wonderland.

Roland and Corinne meet two characters on this stretch of road: Emily Brontë, perusing a book as she strolls, and Tom Thumb – or Gros Poucet, his French equivalent – reading from pieces of paper pinned to his clothing, as though he were a child who might otherwise lose them. In the background is a gate that serves no real purpose, since there is no fence alongside it; the words "No Entry" are inscribed across the top. Perhaps this was suggested by William Blake's poem "The Garden of Love," which describes a garden once filled with flowers but now a domain of graves, tombstones, black-gowned priests "binding with briars my joys and desires," and a newly built chapel with "Thou shalt not" written over its door.

The first words Tom recites are taken from Brecht, telling of a time when the German-born playwright was robbed – in Los Angeles, the moviemaking capital "where dreams are for sale" – but kept quiet about the incident since a fellow immigrant was responsible. This anecdote suggests a tellingly ambivalent attitude toward stateless or nomadic individuals, on one hand, and the malaise of materialistic social systems, on the other. Tom has a pebble collection, and Emily helps him build it up with bits of stone found alongside their path. Meanwhile she converses with Roland and Corinne, answering their inquiries about the road to Oinville with a philosophical counterquestion ("Are you looking for poetic or concrete information?") and the dubiously relevant observation that "physics does not yet exist, only individual physical sciences. Perhaps they're not yet physical, even."

The scene rambles on like this for a long time, establishing at great length how unable these characters are to communicate on even the simplest level. The travelers keep asking for directions, but the literary figures refuse to budge from their more abstract interests: Emily reels off nonsensical syllogisms, which one critic connects with the Logician's irrelevant exercises in Eugène Ionesco's absurdist play *Rhinoceros;* meanwhile Tom portentously denounces "the real thieves, the big ones," whose sociopolitical crimes bring "night" and make "the world . . . full of horror." One could almost sympathize with Roland and Corinne, whose questions seem reasonable enough to deserve reasonable answers. Godard appears to be satirizing hyperintellectuality that loses touch with human needs.

Once again, though, Corinne and Roland eventually cross the line between understandable frustration and sheer viciousness. A little earlier in the scene, Roland had directed anger not only at Emily and Tom but at *Weekend* itself, complaining that the movie is "crap . . . full of crazy people." Corinne now assaults Emily with the argument that "this isn't a novel, it's life. A film is life!" The travelers then physically attack the English author and her friend. Emily moves to escape, panting, "We must cover the flowers with flames, we must stroke their hair, we must teach them to read." Savagely parroting her – "So you want to cover the flowers with flames!" – Roland sets her dress on fire while Corinne holds her from running away. Emily shrieks off-screen as the killers gaze in her direction, and their words reiterate Godard's insistence on blurring all distinctions between the realities of fiction and the fictions of reality:

> CORINNE: We are beasts. We have no right to burn anyone, even a philosopher.
> ROLAND: Can't you see they're only imaginary characters?
> CORINNE: Then why is she crying?
> ROLAND: I don't know. Let's go.
> CORINNE: We're not much more than that ourselves.

Corinne's attitude seems close to compassionate for a moment, but the reality of the feral violence she and Roland have committed is underscored by a close-up of Emily's blazing remains. It is not far-fetched to associate this fiery death with the slash-and-burn destructiveness of the war in Vietnam – always on Godard's mind during this phase of his career – and with the self-immolation used by some courageous protestors to denounce that war. (One such was a short-lived character in *Masculine/Feminine*.)

Tom ends the scene with a long recitation summing up Brecht's pessimism about a society that relegates artistic and intellectual activity to the status of culture-industry commodities:

> I said to myself, what's the use of talking to them? . . . All they're looking for is cheap knowledge they can sell for a high price. . . . They don't want to be oppressed, they want to oppress. They don't want progress, they want to be first. They will submit to anyone as long as he promises that they can make the laws. What can one say to them, I wondered? Then I decided, this is what I will say to them:

And the scene fades into darkness, suggesting the inability of literary words or cinematic images to ameliorate such evils. If the goal of the oppressed is not to eliminate oppression but merely to take control of its operations, what solution can there be but an end to laws, controls, and social systems of all sorts? Yet such anarchy could carry an exorbitant price of its own, as *Weekend* will show as its grim progress continues.

Since the movie's chaos and mayhem have now approached combat-field intensity, it is hardly surprising to read the next intertitle, in red and blue letters: ONE TUESDAY IN THE 100 YEARS WAR. Next comes a close-up of a common worm on a patch of muddy earth. On the sound track, Roland and Corinne chant an assessment of the human race that seems particularly accurate with regard to themselves:

ROLAND: We don't know anything.
CORINNE: Yes, we are entirely ignorant of our own natures.
ROLAND: As ignorant about ourselves as about this worm.
CORINNE: Both of us are enigmas.
ROLAND: And whoever denies this is the most ignorant of the ignorant.

To the extent that this is a self-analysis by our troublesome protagonists, few moviegoers are likely to argue with it.

Roland and Corinne are resting in another rural field, rousing themselves only when they spot some spiffy clothing on a corpse in another of the horrific auto wrecks that still litter the story. Corinne says her mother has surely changed the all-important will by now, but Roland has not given up. "We'll just have to torture her to make her change her mind," he says. "I remember when I was a lieutenant in Algeria, they taught us a trick or two." They pause so Corinne can hail a big yellow truck by lying in the street with her trousers off and her legs open, giving "on the road" a smarmy new meaning.

Godard's interest in Brechtian digressions has not diminished, and now the title MUSICAL ACTION introduces a scene with more of the former than the latter. After agreeing to help the truck driver in return for a ride, Roland and Corinne wind up at a farmyard piano recital, where their new acquaintance plays a Mozart sonata with rough-hewn sensitivity. (Different critics have come up with different motivations for this episode: One says the musician is a piano salesman demonstrating his product; another finds the scene a satire on the French government's policy of bringing culture to the people.) Coutard's camera travels in an elegant circular movement, contrasting the crispness and concision of Mozart's musical patterns with discursive, modernistic visuals. The piano's conspicuously displayed brand name – Bechstein, a ready-made echo of Brechtian – reminds us that commodification pervades the world of high as well as low culture. Meanwhile, various people we haven't seen before stand, roam about, and listen to the performance, caught almost casually by the roving camera. (A recognizable one is Anne Wiazemsky, a new Godard collaborator and love interest who will become a star in some of his later films.)

Speaking as he plays, the pianist (Paul Gégauff, a New Wave screenwriter) criticizes his own talent, praises the teacher (Artur Schnabel) under whom he studied, and deplores the social injustice that allowed the sublime Mozart to die a pauper's death. Surprisingly for a Godard character – especially in a wildly innovative film like this one – he also attacks the forms of contemporary music that reject classical harmonic structures. Mozart composed "the sort [of music] you listen to," he says, adding that "the sort of music people don't listen to is so-called serious modern music. Let's face it, almost nobody goes to hear it." Ironically, it's hard to hear Gégauff when a passing airplane almost drowns out his voice, but he makes a valid point when he notes that much modernist music (in the atonal, twelve-tone, and aleatory styles) have never attracted large audiences. Still, we might expect a tradition-questioning radical like Godard to consider the public's indifference to "difficult" and "obscure" music a tragedy of laziness rather than a sign of populist common sense. Instead the pianist states that "the real modern music" is built on Mozart's ideas,

Escalating horror: Roland (Jean Yanne) and Corinne (Mireille Darc) make their way through an increasingly surreal landscape in *Weekend*.

and that alternative routes have led only to "the biggest damn disaster in the whole history of art."

Do these words reflect the filmmaker's opinions, or are they a spontaneous outgrowth of this movie's explosively dialogic nature? As usual with Godard, the answer is both. He is obviously no enemy of modernist cinema (e.g., Rivette, Straub–Huillet) that diverges as sharply from Hollywood classicism as modernist music (e.g., Schönberg, Cage) diverges from the eighteenth-century sonata; ditto for Godard's predilections in painting (e.g., Picasso) and literature (e.g., Faulkner). Nonetheless, his musical taste is undeniably steeped in the traditional; examples abound, from the Beethoven quartets in *First Name: Carmen* to the Mozart pieces in *Breathless* and the very title of *For Ever Mozart*.

Be this as it may, Gégauff finishes his ruminations with a revealing remark. "He rarely tackled Mozart," the pianist says of his teacher, "because he used to say Mozart was too easy for children and beginners, and too difficult for virtuosos." This comment prefigures an aesthetic turn Godard will take immediately after *Weekend,* in such movies as *Le Gai Savoir* and *One Plus One,* which contain passages of mise-en-scène so spare and stylized that they're almost cartoonish. A child might indeed think too little goes on in such scenes, whereas an adult unfamiliar with Godard might find the material esoteric and demanding. In all, it appears Gégauff is speaking for Godard's growing interest in uniting simplicity and sophistication. If one more clue is needed that Gégauff is close to Godard's heart in some ways, it might be the cigar-smoking habit the pianist shares with our tobacco-prone filmmaker – and blames for the clinkers he hits on his keyboard!

THE WEEK OF 4 THURSDAYS reads the next disorienting title, as Roland and Corinne bid farewell to the pianist and his yellow truck. They continue on their journey, taking turns giving each other piggyback rides. Time travels fast as another title, ONE FRIDAY FAR FROM, takes them past three onlookers who identify themselves as "gli attori italiani della coproduzione," that is, Italian actors in the coproduction. Roland steals a jacket from a car-crash corpse, and Corinne plops down for a rest after her last turn as a piggyback chauffeur. A young man roars up in a sports car, and his companion asks Roland the provocative question, "Are you in a film or are you for real?" Roland replies that they are "in a film," and the driver shouts, "Liars!" as he takes off down the road.

More depressed than ever, Corinne hops into a ditch and announces that she must sleep or die. Roland advises her to do the latter, then sits to smoke a cigarette. A wandering derelict happens along, asks Roland for a light – holding a flaming match, Roland says he doesn't have one – and then asks Roland if that is "his girl" in the ditch. Roland won't dignify him with an answer, so the derelict lowers himself into the trench and rapes Corinne so savagely that the sound track fills with her cries of pain and pleas for help. This scene would be horrifying even if Godard did not present it with such matter-of-fact casualness; yet Roland sits impassively, not bestirring himself until another car comes rolling down the road. He approaches the well-to-do woman in the back of the American sedan and asks if Oinville is on her route. The matron responds by asking, "Would you rather be fucked by Mao or Johnson?" Roland gives the wrong answer ("Johnson, of course") and the woman calls him a "dirty fascist" as her chauffeur drives on. Roland resumes his seat, the wanderer emerges from the ditch, and the camera gets bored with the dull-eyed

glances they exchange, tracking down the road until both characters disappear from view. Reversing its course a few moments later, it travels
back to show Corinne rejoining Roland, clearly bruised by the assault but
fairly impassive all the same. She asks another passing motorist about
Oinville, interrupted by a particularly bizarre intertitle series –

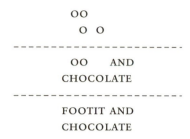

– and gets asked a question in return, "Who attacked first: Israel or
Egypt?" Corinne's answer, "Those bastards the Egyptians," is evidently
incorrect, and the driver calls her an "ignorant fool" as he departs. The
pair resume their piggybacking, and Roland cheats shamelessly, counting
out his allotted number of steps (ten per turn) much faster than he actually walks.

Of all the incongruous elements in this scene, the questions asked by
the passing motorists seem particularly out of place; yet they serve a serious purpose, joining the movie's *faux* film-noir parody to more explicitly
political interests. The next scene carries this further, foreshadowing the
imminent "radical phase" of Godard's career so vividly that we can almost see it being born. Another truck heaves into view (a garbage truck
this time, but yellow like its predecessors), and the workers on board offer
Roland and Corinne a ride. The travelers pitch in to help the laborers,
trudging along a path carrying loads of garbage and trash. Not an enthu-
siastic helper in the best of times, Corinne soon drops her load in a heap.
Roland does better, managing to dump his garbage into the truck. Tired
and hungry, he searches for something edible amid the mess, then asks one
of the truckers – they are an Arab and a black man – for "just a bite" of
his oversized sandwich.

This modest but distinctly human gesture opens the film's most voluble,
didactic, and confrontational journey into the twin territories of power
and ideology, expanding Godard's challenge to conventional spectacle
with an extravagantly Brechtian interlude meant to drive an enormous
wedge between our craving for entertainment and what little is left of the
movie's linear narrative.

Roland's request for a morsel of food leads his black acquaintance to take a hearty bite of sandwich for himself, pause thoughtfully for a moment, then hand Roland a scrap that he eagerly accepts. Roland asks for more, but the laborer takes another large bite for himself and observes that the crumb Roland just ate was appropriate for him – since it "represented exactly the same proportion of my sandwich as the proportion of its overall budget that the U.S. gives the Congo." Corinne shows up with a load of trash, dumps it into the truck with Roland's help, and follows his example by asking the Arab for something to eat. He teases her and demands a kiss. When she begins to eat a scrap he's given her, he strikes her, saying he is "applying the law which the big oil companies apply to Algeria." Sharing the meager bite she has extracted from the Arab, she and Roland ask what law he is invoking. "The law of the kiss and the kick in the ass," the Arab answers. "Just because you're underprivileged doesn't mean you have to be mean!" retorts Corinne, as a blue title appears:

WORLD

3

Once again, Godard is refusing to idealize or sentimentalize the working class, which can clearly be as arbitrary and bullying as its more privileged sociocultural cousins.

"My black brother will now express my views," says the Arab, and we watch him devour his sandwich while his companion delivers a long, discursive speech. Africa is experiencing a new wave of optimism, the black worker says. This is not the result of any new bounty on nature's part, nor is it the outcome of "less inhuman" or "more benevolent" behavior by the people who once brought colonial oppression to the continent. Rather, he continues, political and military actions by the African masses are what have improved the region's morale. He then compares the exploitation of Africa to the "physical and spiritual liquidation" brought to Europe by Nazi terror, and he calls for native Africans to combat "the French, English, and South African manifestations of this evil" while also staying on the lookout for other possible outbreaks. "We, the African people, declare that for more than a hundred years the lives of two hundred million Africans have been held cheap or denied, haunted continually by the spectre of death," he goes on. Hope lies not with "the good will of the imperialists" or "the mechanical development of . . . natural resources," but with the "hands and brains" of the people as they set in motion "the dialectics of the continent's liberation."

This is quite a declamation, and it is worth quoting at length for two reasons. For one, it expresses precisely the sort of political ideas that Godard – prone to ideological "confusion" as recently as *The Little Soldier* in 1960 – now sees as useful tools for improving our badly damaged world. It also escalates his recently instituted campaign against the tyranny of images. Not only does the movie stop in its tracks for this long monologue, but we don't even get to see the speaker as he speechifies; instead we watch the Middle Eastern worker eat his sandwich, an unseductive sight if ever there was one. This view is relieved only by a couple of quick flashbacks – one to the hitchhiker prodding Roland and Corinne with his branch and pistol, the other to Saint-Just reciting in the countryside. Although both flashbacks seem calculated more for rhythmic impact and alienation value than for conveyance of any specific message, it is noteworthy that the nasty-hitchhiker flashback takes place just as the African likens colonialism to Nazism, and that Saint-Just appears when the speaker mentions "the dialectics of [a] continent's liberation." Hardly coincidental, these juxtapositions point up the carefully calibrated method underlying the apparent madness of this movie.

The same polemical pattern then repeats itself as the African introduces his Arab companion, chews his sandwich in close-up, and listens while an even longer oration takes place. Again it begins with one of the men saying the other will speak for him; but whereas the black man's statement applied to black Africans and Arabs alike, the Arab's speech pleads the cause of black people quite specifically. He begins with an attack on "nonviolent men" and "pacifists," perhaps influenced by the militant career of African-American leader Malcolm X, whose life had been cut short by assassination (just when his work was turning in a more nonviolent direction) two years before *Weekend* was made. Declaring that "a black man's freedom is as valuable as that of a white man," the speaker claims that freedom cannot be won through "nonviolence, patience, and love." On the contrary, the "war" between black people and "the United States and its friends" can only be resolved through guerrilla fighting. Black partisans are already present in such "strategic points" as factories, fields, and white homes, he adds. Sabotage against transportation, communication, and technological networks will "bring the West to its knees by ruining it economically," but economics is only part of the story. Also needed are "bloodthirsty" deeds inspired by Vietcong tactics, carried out with Molotov cocktails and other low-end weapons deployed by black Americans who learned modern guerrilla methods in Vietnam.

Viewers who already know the ending of *Weekend* may find a particularly grim fascination in the Arab's monologue when he calls for absorbing the power of white American society – infiltrating its strategic areas, learning its combat techniques, understanding its transport and communication systems – in order to turn this potency against the enemy that created it. In metaphorical terms, appropriating and reversing an adversary's strength amounts to "anthropophagy," or cannibalism; in political terms, this includes what film scholar Robert Stam calls "a devouring of the techniques and information of the superdeveloped countries . . . in an effort to struggle against colonialist domination."[12] *Weekend* will reach its riotous finale in a burst of cannibalism, as outrageously gruesome and exhilaratingly subversive as anything in Godard's career, which is itself partly dedicated to cannibalizing the conventional cinema. Ultimately, cannibalism is the carnivalesque link between theoretically minded guerrillas like the African and the Arab, on one hand, and self-serving goons like Corinne and Roland, on the other. These characters occupy very different places on the revolutionary spectrum, but all are products of a sociopolitical system that breeds its own devourers with ironic ease and efficiency.

Another blue title –

CID   THE OCCIDENT   DENT

– evokes the Western world flanked (trapped?) by history and biology: medieval heroics (El Cid) on one side, material presence (dent = teeth, the body's only visible bones) on the other.

Working together now, the African and the Arab offer a refresher course in Marxist sociology, identifying civilization (in a different sense than that used earlier in the film) as the basic condition of group oppression. "To be civilized means to belong to a class society," the African intones, "to a reality full of contradictions" that lead inevitably to slavery, serfdom, and exploitation. The characters continue in this vein, tracing society's movement from savagery to barbarism, from tribal confederation to military democracy. The scene closes with Friedrich Engels's idea that Western social evolution can be understood through the study of certain Native American cultures, which had "reached the final stages of their independent histories" and were about to start "their history as a class society" when the Columbian invasion changed their path forever.

Much of this tirade is accompanied by the blandest possible images: close-ups of the African eating his sandwich, or Roland and Corinne resting, smoking, listening. This portion of *Weekend* prefigures Godard's strategies in the Dziga-Vertov Group period, when he will put even more energy into inverting commercial film's preference for spectacle over substance, diversion over discourse, visual seductiveness over verbal significance.

Still, the images grow more restless as the episode proceeds, and more material from elsewhere in the movie intrudes on the speechifying. Words about destroying the established order are accompanied by a flashback to the bloody ending of the traffic-jam scene, a vision of society choked by self-generated contradictions. Words about capitalistic greed summon another traffic-jam image, juxtaposing the car of Roland and Corinne with an old-fashioned horse and cart. Words about "private property, the monogamous family, and the state" bring back the parking-lot fight from the beginning of the film. Words about social evolution are paired with Roland and Corinne walking a road that has become a corridor of twisted, flaming automobiles. A description of ancient military democracies is counterpointed by surreal Exterminating Angel material. As Native American societies are mentioned, we see Tom Thumb's recitation over Emily Brontë's smoking ashes. Perhaps most important, the Arab's talk about Iroquois and Seneca cultures is accompanied not by a flashback but by a flash-forward, showing a rifle-bearing young woman; she could be a traditional American Indian, or a hippie from the 1960s. Sharing the screen are two similar figures, one sitting near a river and one dancing to music we cannot hear.

This ideologically complex, cinematically daunting scene then concludes in a surprisingly conventional way: As the garbage truck continues through the countryside, Roland and Corinne realize they have arrived in Oinville at last! Jumping from the trash, they run happily toward the village, bickering over who'll have the first bath.

Conventionality soon vanishes again, however. WEEKEND flashes three times in blue letters, and Roland worries that he and Corinne have missed the death of Corinne's dad. The scene changes to a bourgeois bathroom, with Corinne in the tub and a painting of a nude woman on the wall. (This is another instance of the interaction among art–painting–reality–cinema that Godard has explored through similar framing in most of his previous films, and as critics have noted, it perpetrates a mischievous irony by contrasting the unseen breasts of Corinne – played by Darc, a sexy movie star – with the visible breasts of the "respectable" nude hanging behind her.) Roland tells Corinne that her mother is reneging on the "50–50 split" of her father's estate, and Corinne fumes at getting so little return after enduring so much aggravation. "She won't get away with it," the dutiful daughter vows.

The scene changes again, sort of, as the camera jumps to exterior shots while the sound track stays with Corinne and Roland in the bathroom. We see a sunny Oinville view complete with a peaceful road, a small-town church, a billboard with a gasoline ad, and a second street with a bit of traffic. Blue titles invoke Balzac again –

LIFE IN THE / SCENE FROM

LIFE IN THE

PROVINCES

– and remind us that we are still watching A FILM ADRIFT IN THE COSMOS and A FILM FOUND ON A SCRAP HEAP. What we hear during this sequence is Corinne trying to get Roland's attention as she continues her bath and he reads at length (another common Godard mannerism) from a borrowed book.

At first this appears to be another purely Brechtian digression, since nothing could be more irrelevant than the "just-so story" that Roland recites – about a hippopotamus who asks God for permission to live in the water, promises not to eat the fish who dwell there, and agrees that "every time I want to shit I'll spread the shit out with my tail, so you can see for yourself there aren't any fish bones in it." The fable acquires deeper meaning when Roland reads a commentary on it, however:

> By day, the hippopotamus is a completely different creature. At least the night conceals his astonishing display of ugliness – his bulging eyes, his gigantic mouth, his misshapen body, his absurdly short legs, and his grotesque tail. Perhaps, from a hippopotamus's point of view, this represents the acme of beauty, but I am not a hippopotamus. I look upon him not only as the most ungainly beast of all, but also as an infinite abyss of stupidity. I would not have dwelt at such length on the disgust that this horrible creature inspires in me were it not for my conviction that the servile way in which he accepts collective life is the most abject side of his nature.

The first section of this paragraph includes a catalog of (animal) body parts, as if Godard were parodying the lists of (human) body parts we encounter in several of his earlier films – either spoken by characters (e.g., Patricia in *Breathless,* Camille in *Contempt*) or constructed by the camera (e.g., the opening of *A Married Woman,* the brothel scenes of *My Life to Live*). However, the most striking aspects of the hippo inventory are its savagery, its gratuitousness, and its lack of charity toward what is, after all, a dumb animal that cannot help its appearance or the reactions it may inspire in others. The quotation suggests a nightmarish reversal of romantic notions (the felicities of nature, the bounties of physical beauty) that have crept into otherwise tough-minded Godard films like *Pierrot le fou* and *Masculine/Feminine*. Beyond this, the latter part of the passage ("the servile way in which he accepts collective life . . .") constitutes a bitter attack on the (metaphorical) ugliness of any creatures that fail to question the premises of their social and political surroundings. Near the end of *Weekend,* the revolutionary Kalfon will utter a key line: "We can only overcome the horror of the bourgeoisie with even more horror." Roland's hippopotamus embodies both kinds of horror in all their unreflective ugliness.

So does the flayed rabbit that Corinne's mother fetches from Flaubert the butcher, as her daughter and son-in-law vainly beg her to share her late husband's estate; and so does the mother herself, after Roland and Corinne strangle and stab her to death. Mother and rabbit wind up in equally awful shape on the patio floor, and Godard depicts this appalling outcome through a close-up of the rabbit bathed in pale red blood from an unseen source – perhaps the slashed-up body of Corinne's mom, as she screams bloody murder on the sound track. This scene is an extraordinarily risky mixture of parody, grotesquerie, and flat-out gruesomeness, staging the homicide as a burst of mayhem that's almost farcical in its exaggeration – Roland starts to garrote the mother while Corinne hacks her with a huge knife that pumps up and down behind some bushes, recalling the detective's murder in *Psycho* – followed instantly by the sickening sight of the blood-drenched rabbit. (The rabbit shot is an unusual sort of synecdoche, inverting that trope's ordinary purpose of allusiveness and discretion.) Rarely has any filmmaker thrown audiences such a stunning one–two punch of contradictory emotional cues in such a hypercondensed period of time.

Faced with the familiar Hollywood problem of how to dispose of the corpse, the parricides consider some solutions associated with celebrity killers of the past – burning her à la Dr. Petiot, who conducted a sort of private Holocaust in Nazi-occupied France, or following the example of Dr. Tarr and Prof. Fether, another of the film's Edgar Allan Poe references. Finally they settle on an ideal method for *Weekend:* stashing the cadaver in a burning accident site along the highway. Chortling over their perfect crime and cooing their affection for each other, they incinerate their victim by setting fire to a plane-and-car wreck, which explodes as they scurry into the Oinville woods. The film's moody, repetitive music roars its ambiguous response.

From the beginning, everything about *Weekend* has been more Brechtian and clinical than personal and engaging. Few spectators are likely to walk away from it with vivid memories of facial expressions, vocal intonations, or psychological details. Even in this context, however, the film's last portion is shot in ways that seem conspicuously distanced and removed, with the camera placed in "incorrect" positions very far from the action; it appears determined not merely to discourage but to prevent the possibility of emotional rapport between characters and audience. Remember the long-distance shot of Michel after the cop killing in *Breathless,* multiply this several times over, and you have some sense of the detachment enforced by Godard's camera style here.

The characters don't get any more appealing, either. In the forest they have just entered, Roland and Corinne ask directions from the first person they meet (they are lost again, hunting for Versailles this time), and he answers by hiding his face with a novelty postcard and squeaking its bird-twittering soundbox at them. This is less than helpful, as is the red-and-blue intertitle that appears at the same moment –

F L / F L / F L
S   S O

Later this cryptogram will be filled out with white letters to identify the Seine and Oise Liberation Front – an imposing name, although rendered less impressive by an implacable white X crossing it out.

The postcard man, Yves, disappears into the woods, and we return to Roland and Corinne as they barge into a family picnic, grabbing food and drink from the group. Yves then reappears with his girlfriend, Isabelle, and a second accomplice; the latter two are dressed like hippies, but armed with submachine guns – an interesting mixture of "love generation" and "guerrilla underground" iconography, evoking the 1960s era in contradictory ways. They terrorize the family, stealing its provisions and torching its car. Then they slaughter the husband, wife, and child with Yves's gun, and hustle a remaining picnicker, Louis, into the woods along with Roland and Corinne.

If one knew this picnic-massacre scene only from reading the screenplay, one might imagine a Hollywood-style episode fraught with drama and emotion. Godard defuses any potential suspense or pathos, however, rendering it as bizarre and uninviting as the postcard-man who introduces it by twittering an idiotic consumer gimmick. Alienation devices continue to proliferate with stepped-up energy and frequency – in the unpredictable editing, the mise-en-scène and sound (e.g., the drums at which Kalfon

Rock revolutionaries: Death and drumbeats intermingle in the the Seine and Oise Liberation Front scenes of *Weekend*.

and Yves thrash away in their countryside lair), and the full-screen titles (usually bearing historical and literary references) that intrude on the action more jarringly than ever. We have passed the point of no return on our journey into the film's new "civilization," and we have no more chance than Roland and Corinne of changing our minds and returning to the social order we left behind. At least we are here voluntarily, which is more than Roland and Corinne can say as they plod farther into the wilderness, with guns at their backs and increasingly weird company by their sides.

Their new revolutionary companions include Yves and Isabelle, who abducted them; Gerald, who wears a butcher's apron and hails the kidnapped Louis as an old friend from the Ethiopian war; Kalfon, evidently the leader of the group; and Ernest, a guerrilla chef with a bloodstained hat on his head and a huge butcher knife in his hand. Isabelle greets him by pushing the abducted girl in his direction and saying, "You can fuck her before you eat her if you want." Ever discreet, the camera spares us more of this episode by panning to Isabelle strolling away and Yves whacking his drums. Fade to black.

Such is life at the Seine and Oise Liberation Front, where revolutionaries radio one another with cinematic code names ("Battleship Potemkin calling The Searchers") while Louis reminisces about wartime sex and Ernest drops eggs on a heap of cadavers. The scene is repellent and incoherent by the standards of "normal" filmmakers like Eisenstein or Ford, the directors alluded to by the radio codes. It makes sense, however, if we view it in terms of the carnivalistic "grotesque body" tradition that critic Mikhail Bakhtin has traced through Western art and literature (Rabelais, Dostoyevsky, etc.) for centuries – a tradition that challenges ruling-class decorum (and power) by cultivating impropriety, incongruity, and unruliness in outrageous tales governed by boisterous impulses that are as profoundly human as they are wildly excessive. To be sure, the carnivalism of *Weekend* is as dark and dystopian as it comes; yet this tradition provides many precedents for the uproarious vulgarities that litter the movie, from Corinne's early monologue to Ernest's sick activities in the outdoor kitchen. One thing the Seine and Oise Liberation Front wants to liberate us *from* is the notion of "decency" and "discipline" that bourgeois society uses to keep our anarchic bodies under suffocating control.

To liberate our potential for great, glorious creativity, however, is also to unchain our capacity for frightful, terrifying evil. The tension between these aspects of the human condition is as fundamental as that between rationality and emotion, ego and id, conscious thought and unconscious desire. Godard signals his recognition of these tensions by punctuating the Liberation Front scene with the title TOTEM AND TABOO, borrowed from Sigmund Freud's late study of primal human impulses, including the desires for incest and murder. Freud links the repression of these urges with feelings of dread and guilt, and with the growth of social prohibitions surrounding sex and food – the very activities that are mixed so indecorously in this film's most outlandish moments. Bringing the increasingly mad fusion of sex, food, and death to a deliberately barbaric climax, the Liberation Front scene serves a double purpose. First, it unmasks the abhorrent urges that dwell in all human hearts, prompting repressions and denials that evolve into the psychosexual norms of civilized society. Second, it argues that a "return of the repressed" might readily occur if the social order were attacked with enough vigor by forces believing that, in Kalfon's words, the "horror of the bourgeoisie" can be dislodged only by "even more horror."

Some revolutionary thinkers of the 1960s believed exactly that. Godard's own stance appears to be deeply ambivalent, divided between excitement over cinema's ability to unveil society's foul secrets, and genuine disgust at the putrescence that crawls into view when civilization's rock is overturned. (This ambivalence is itself a carnivalistic attitude, open-ended and flexible rather than closed-minded and determined.) The scene culminates when Corinne's weirdly comic speech near the beginning of the film, about a kitchen-counter sex party with orgasms amid eggs and milk, is transformed into nightmarish farce as Ernest places ritualistically broken eggs and then a massive fish between the open thighs of a captive woman. While this is perhaps the most pointedly repulsive moment in all of Godard's work, it serves at least two purposes that justify its ferocity. For one, it pungently exposes the flamboyant irrationality of the libidinal energies held tenuously in check by social convention. For another, it points to male sexuality as a primary breeding ground for those energies, and for the aggression and violence they produce. Since the words TOTEM AND TABOO put this portion of *Weekend* into explicitly Freudian territory, we must remember the insistence of psychoanalytic theory that castration anxieties (acquired in childhood and never successfully shaken) are at the root of countless male behaviors aimed at assuaging subconscious feelings of lack, inadequacy, and fear. By this view, Ernest is grotesquely repairing the "universal wound" of the "castrated" female, replacing the missing phallus with materials whose size and shape (fish, eggs) identify them as obvious dream symbols for the male organs that these revolutionaries are desperate to reclaim. The fact that a woman helps Ernest reminds us that victimized classes are often complicit in their own oppression – a point that will shortly be reinforced when Corinne switches from guerrilla hostage to active member of the marauding band.

Full-screen titles become more plentiful than ever as *Weekend* continues its journey to the end of the revolutionary night. Four appearances of TOTEM AND TABOO are followed by LIGHT IN AUGUST, another in Godard's long string of Faulkner homages. (At this stage in Godard's career it is worth noting that Faulkner's work steered a similar course between high-art experimentation, à la *Absalom, Absalom!*, and gut-stirring melodrama, à la *Sanctuary*.) LIGHT IN AUGUST is also a punning reference to one of Godard's favorite filmmakers, Auguste Lumière, whose last name translates into English as "light." Lumière's statement that cinema is "an invention without a future" is ironically inscribed on a projection-room wall in *Contempt;* it seems apt that Godard invokes his name in this portrait of what appears to be a society without a future.

Back in the narrative, the guerrillas move stealthily through the overgrown countryside with their hostages, and suddenly Roland makes an unexpected bid to escape, charging away from the startled group. This move has a certain dramatic impact, but one is hard-pressed to say whether Roland's motive is courage or cowardice, since the camera keeps its strict Brechtian distance, denying us the psychological information that a classical film would heap upon us at such a moment. A female guerrilla – none other than Juliet, the upper-class woman who clashed with the tractor-driving farmer many episodes ago – aims her rifle in his direction. Kalfon intercedes, not to save Roland but to kill the fleeing captive himself, using a carefully aimed slingshot. Roland yowls in his death agony as Juliet prods Corinne along with her rifle. The story has reached a decisive juncture – the demise of a major character – but in keeping with its hallucinatory tone, this turning point is tossed out in an off-screen moment, purposely abrupt and absurd.

The next red intertitle announces THERMIDOR, the eleventh month of the new calendar established during the French Revolution as part of its effort to institute a new era in human history. (Thermidor ran from late July to the middle of August, by the old calendar, so the chronology of *Weekend* shows a sort of fever-dream consistency by placing LIGHT IN AUGUST and THERMIDOR next to each other.) We now see the mortally injured Roland as he lies bleeding near the path, and a brief off-screen dialogue assures us that his violent death will have no more dignity than his disreputable life –

CORINNE: Why have you opened his stomach?
ERNEST: Because it's the best part.

Corinne responds, "How horrible," and it is now that Kalfon utters his epigram about mobilizing excesses of horror to defeat the horror of the bourgeoisie.

The group marches on as time marches on, indicated by more red and blue intertitles –

- SEPTEMBER MASSACRE: A policeman dies in a gunfight with a female guerrilla.
- SEPTEMBER MASSACRE again: Two men slaughter a pig (in real, unsimulated footage) with a sledgehammer and butcher knife; Juliet levels her rifle at one of the men as he subsequently kills a goose.
- PLUVIÔSE, a winter month in the Revolution's calendar: Kalfon returns by boat to the guerrilla camp; Claude paints the naked body of a wom-

an tied to a tree as Louis placidly watches; Ernest putters in his blood-spattered kitchen.

- OCTOBER LANGUAGE, alluding to the October Revolution and Eisenstein's film *October:* Claude makes radio contact with a distant ally ("Johnny Guitar calling Gosta Berling") while perusing a book.
- OCTOBER LANGUAGE again: Crashing rhythms from the camp's drums accompany a spoken manifesto; its length and declamatory style recall the African and Arab speeches given earlier.

This manifesto is recited by Kalfon as he thwacks away at the drums. Much of it is a salute to the ocean, of all things, phrased in conspicuously flowery language. Like the pianist's barnyard concert, this scene works partly as a Brechtian interruption, and partly as a poetic interlude with sly implications for the film's polemical meaning. The speaker describes himself as a "monster whose face you cannot see," insisting that he is "not a criminal" despite his "hideous" soul. He then mixes panegyrics to the sea ("on first sight of you, a breath as full of sadness as the soft murmur of the wind blows through the soul") with statements conveying a somber vision of humanity:

> Those who love you never fail to be reminded, sometimes unawares, of man's rude beginnings when he first learned the pain which has never left him since. . . . I suppose that man only believes in his own beauty out of vanity, but in fact suspects that he is not truly beautiful. Otherwise, why would he look with such contempt upon the faces of others made in his image? . . . In spite of the ocean's depth, the depth of the human heart is on a whole different scale. Psychology has a long way to go. . . . Tell me if you house the Prince of Darkness . . . O Sea . . . for I will rejoice to hear that hell is so close to mankind. . . .

He concludes, "I cannot go on, for I feel the moment has arrived to return to the harsh land of men. . . . Let us make a supreme effort and, conscious of our duty, fulfill our destiny on this earth. . . ."

This peculiar yet oddly passionate discourse stirs memories of earlier scenes: Roland's hippopotamus recitation, which also evokes a pathetic "monster," and the garbage-truck episode, where the Arab's words about Indian tribes spark a flash-forward to Juliet strolling with other guerrillas while Kalfon drums and declaims. It seems odd for *Weekend* to detour into a poem about the ocean – once again, interruption for its own sake appears to be at work – but Godard's social, political, and metaphysical concerns shine intermittently through its rambling language about humanity's "pain," the "contempt" we show toward one another, and the possibility of a nearby "hell" holding justice for our "harsh land" unless we finally take control of our destinies. Fade-out to darkness and silence.

Brechtian style and melodramatic content join again in the next scene, which provides still another example of potentially stirring action-film material deliberately drained of emotional and psychological appeal. Kalfon forces Corinne onto a lonely roadway, planning to exchange her for another hostage. This plot development strongly resembles the climax of *My Life to Live,* which also shows a domineering man turning a vulnerable woman into a salable commodity. As in the earlier film, the deal goes violently sour, but this time it is Kalfon's accomplices Isabelle and Valérie who are killed, while Corinne makes a panicky escape. Blue intertitles (ARIZONA JULES) punctuate the mayhem, which includes much gunfire and frantic running. The camera then frames the fatally injured Valérie in close-up as she sings a childish song with the unchildish theme of human isolation: "Although one may be suffering agonies/Still to others all may seem right." Her helplessness begins to stir our sympathy, but her lyrics remind us that ordinary feelings are rarely adequate to the complex interplay of reality and illusion in human affairs:

> With a broken heart one can still smile,
> Apparently indifferent,
> When the last word has to be written,
> In a novel that comes to a bad end.

Valérie dies after breathing the final words in a barely audible voice. Three identical titles – FAUX RACCORD, meaning "mismatch" or "discontinuity" – then interrupt a sequence that is not discontinuous at all but coherently depicts Valérie's death, Kalfon's parting kiss, and his flight with Corinne in another flurry of gunshots. (It is also possible that Godard actually sees this sequence as "discontinuous," since its linear construction seems downright weird in this context, surrounded as it is by the wired-up disintegration of *Weekend* in its final throes. FAUX RACCORD might also refer to the incongruous kiss between living Kalfon and dead Valérie, or simply to the interruption of an action scene with static intertitles.)

The penultimate title – VENDÉ MIAIRE, the Revolutionary calendar's first month – indicates that considerably more time has rushed by. Corinne has joined Kalfon and the others in their camp. We see a close-up of Kalfon's fist, clenched in a popular 1960s salute that combines the threat of force with the assertion of solidarity; and we hear his voice in a final expression of revolutionary rage. "When your foot slips on a frog, you feel disgusted," he says. "But when you scarcely touch the human body, the skin of your fingers splits like scales of mica under hammer blows." He opens his fist to reveal a tiny frog; then we see him sitting near Corinne, bedecked in full guerrilla-style regalia. "Just as a shark's heart beats for an hour after its death," he continues, "our insides keep stirring through and through long after we make love."

Corinne is baffled by Kalfon's caustic metaphors; in the film's last extended speech he clarifies his vision of

> the boundless horror that people feel for others of the species. . . . I know there is probably a more terrible affliction than the swollen eyes that come from meditating on the strangeness of human nature, but I have yet to discover it.

All the while, Ernest has been working away at his kitchen fire. Now he scurries over to Kalfon and Corinne with big hunks of meat, which they grab and start gnawing without hesitation. Their closing dialogue, spoken in respectable tones that would suit a well-laid table in a Parisian bistro, ranks with Godard's most memorable:

CORINNE: Not bad.
KALFON: Yes, we mixed the pig with the remains of the English tourists.
CORINNE: The ones in the Rolls?
KALFON: That's right. There should be left-overs of your husband in there, too.
CORINNE: When I'm finished, Ernest, I wouldn't mind a bit more.

Thus does capitalism become cannibalism, in the course of a ninety-five-minute movie about a middle-class weekend on the byways of provincial France.

The conclusion of *Weekend* is outrageous by any reasonable standard, and so are many elements of the mix-and-match mélange building up to it; yet such confrontational stuff is hardly unprecedented in the tradition of subversive cinema. Stam calls attention to anticolonial Brazilian films, for example, which stir up "orgies of clashing allusions and citations" in a spirit of "creative disrespect and irreverence," producing a boisterously chaotic mood in which "dominant cinema is made to war against itself" while the sardonic filmmaker "stands aside and ironizes."[13] Such an artist becomes a carnivalistic cannibal, devouring alien materials – like the Hollywood-style ingredients in the early scenes of *Weekend* – that become increasingly unrecognizable as the movie digests them and appropriates their energy.

"The logic of carnival is that of the world turned upside down," writes Stam, citing Bakhtin's observation that carnivalesque satire treats death as a cheerfully grotesque affair "surrounded by food, drink, sexual indecencies and symbols of conception and fertility."[14] *Weekend* operates on precisely this principle, albeit a ferociously cynical version of it. Godard mocks every sort of power, from middle-class privilege to working-class indignation and revolutionary outrage. As for the place of death in this cannily skewed portrait of our all-too-familiar world, Valérie's dying song is less an affirmation of human dignity than a recognition of life's ultimate absurdity; and Roland's demise is scarcely noticed before his bones turn up in Ernest's potpourri, which his wife proceeds to gobble up with the gusto of a hungry picnicker. This is surely a "civilization" turned upside-down and inside-out, wherein life and death, beauty and horror, reality and illusion become heedlessly confounded with their opposites. The purpose of these inversions and contaminations is to shake us into a brutal new awareness of how tragically our real-world civilization has gone astray.

Indeed, so wrenching are the film's extremes – scrambling fundamental elements of narrative and characterization to the point where they all but dissolve under the strain – that a term like "carnivalesque" may seem too neat and manageable to account for them. Cultural theorist Julia Kristeva defines another level of radical creativity when she argues that "abjection" picks up where "apocalypse and carnival" leave off. By dictionary definition, the "abject" means that which is low, wretched, base; by abject expression, Kristeva means utterances fostering a heightened awareness that "the narrative web is a thin film constantly threatened with bursting." When divisions between subject–object and inside–outside are called into question, the narrative may lose its linearity and enter a new stage in which "it proceeds by flashes, enigmas, short cuts, incompletion, tangles, and cuts." Eventually the fiction's highly stressed infrastructure "can no longer be narrated but cries out or is descried with maximal stylistic intensity (language of violence, of obscenity, or of a rhetoric that relates the text to poetry)."[15]

This describes *Weekend,* and other works of Godard's revolutionary phase, with great accuracy. "If one wishes to proceed farther still along the approaches to abjection," Kristeva adds, "one would find neither narrative nor theme but a recasting of syntax and vocabulary – the violence of poetry, and silence." Small wonder that Godard ends *Weekend* with a final blue title that evokes a final enigmatic silence:

END OF STORY

END OF CINEMA

5

Numéro deux

Abjection – at the crossroads of phobia, obsession, and perversion. . . . Its symptom is the rejection and reconstruction of languages.

– Julia Kristeva[1]

Weekend does not mark the dawning of abjection – that drastic preoccupation with the low, the dejected, the discarded – or the beginning of narrative breakdown in Godard's work. He had been traveling in these directions from the beginning, picking up speed when *My Life to Live* brought new radicalism to his complex relationship with movie conventions. His skepticism toward linear narrative made a major leap with *A Married Woman* in 1964, grew more pronounced in *Pierrot le fou* and *Masculine/Feminine* over the next two years, and became a dominating factor in *2 or 3 Things I Know about Her* and *La Chinoise*, which show their disregard for storytelling by largely ignoring it – rather than disintegrating it in full view of the audience, as *Weekend* does.

Pulverized beyond repair, narrative remains mostly absent from Godard's work for a dozen years after *Weekend*. What replaces it is an ongoing extension of the *Weekend* scene where the Arab and African laborers deliver their ideologically charged speeches – bringing the already tenuous plot to a standstill in order to address the spectator as an alert, thinking presence who is engaged with the film's ideas as actively as Godard himself.

Le Gai Savoir (1968), his first picture following *Weekend*, consists largely of political conversations held by a young man and woman who are seeking what theorist Roland Barthes calls a "degree zero" of language – a verbal "style of absence," to use another Barthes phrase, emancipated from limiting burdens of conventional meaning. Following this in Go-

Dziga-Vertov duo: Jean-Luc Godard and Jean-Pierre Gorin when *Tout va bien* was released in 1972.

dard's filmography is a series of radical cinematic experiments, including a group of collaborative *Ciné-Tracts,* revolutionary essays lasting a few minutes each and intended for distribution outside the theatrical circuit. Other works of this varied and provocative period include *Un Film comme les autres* (1968), the first movie bearing the Dziga-Vertov Group signature; *One Plus One,* alternating record-studio footage of the Rolling Stones with stylized dramatic scenes about race, revolution, and violence; and *Wind from the East* (1969), cinema's first Marxist western.

Adding notions of authorship, individuality, and identity itself to the list of conventions he wanted to interrogate, Godard put a disorienting spin not only on the styles and subjects of his movies during this time but on his own auteur status as well. Seven projects completed between 1969 (the year of *British Sounds* and *Pravda*) and 1972 (the year of *Tout va bien* and *Letter to Jane*) are attributed either to the Dziga-Vertov Group or to Godard and one of his collaborators, Jean-Pierre Gorin and Jean-

Acting and activism: Jacques (Yves Montand) and Susan (Jane Fonda) are media workers ambivalent about their professions in *Tout va bien*.

Henri Roger, both as committed to radical cinema as their famous partner. Still, it was Godard's established (if contentious) reputation that played an essential (if ironic) role in getting such outlandish projects out of the discussion group and onto the screen.

Not many screens, however. Godard's determination to revolutionize society by contesting the pleasures of bourgeois entertainment was audacious in theory, problematic in practice: As one critic wrote, the audience for the Dziga-Vertov Group shrank and shrank until even Godard and Gorin were no longer speaking to each other. In their penultimate project together, *Tout va bien*, they sought wider attention by employing movie stars (Jane Fonda and Yves Montand) and telling the more-or-less linear story of a strike by angry workers against an exploitative factory and the greedy capitalist who runs it. The result was a qualified artistic success but an unqualified commercial failure, reinforcing the growing suspicion that whatever the potential might have been for an effectively subversive cinema in the years immediately after 1968, there was little prospect of its realization now that the 1970s were in full swing.

Events in Godard's personal life – never all that separate from his professional life – provided more impetus for change. His marriage to Anne Wiazemsky, who around 1967 had initiated him into the ways of Maoist idealism, ended as unhappily as had his earlier relationship with Anna Karina. His new companion, Anne-Marie Miéville, helped him recover from his serious motorcycle accident a few months before *Tout va bien* started filming, and soon became his artistic as well as domestic partner. Godard's last collaboration with Gorin was the 1972 essay film *Letter to Jane,* a fifty-two-minute critical analysis of a still photograph of Jane Fonda, star of *Tout va bien* and all-around leftist agitator of the period. This was followed by two years of cinematic silence and then *Here and Elsewhere* (1974), the first of several Godard–Miéville collaborations. *Here and Elsewhere* grew from a 1969 trip that Godard and Gorin had taken to Jordan and Lebanon, where they shot material for *Until Victory,* a documentary on the Palestinian revolution. A year later the Palestinian effort was smothered by events of Jordan's civil war, and the two filmmakers proceeded to terminate both their Palestinian project and the Dziga-Vertov Group itself. Godard was learning to capitalize on seemingly unusable footage, however. Shots from the unfinished *1 A.M./One American Movie* had been recycled into the proudly eccentric *1 P.M./One Parallel Movie* (1971) under a joint Jean-Luc Godard–D. A. Pennebaker signature. In a somewhat similar move, Godard and Miéville now edited material from *Until Victory* into the very different *Here and Elsewhere,* which deals not with the Palestinian movement as such but rather with the ways in which media representations conveyed (and distorted) its meanings for people close to it (here) and in distant places (elsewhere). The result is as radical and polemical as anything the Dziga-Vertov Group produced during its three years of existence; yet along with a now-familiar dissection of political issues and cinematic forms, it also suggests a renewed interest in self-examination by Godard and his collaborators. Much the same can be said of *Comment ça va,* a 1976 docudrama that uses discussion and debate to seek ideologically acceptable ways of spreading information about progressive activities.

It was between these two political-essay films that Godard and Miéville produced their signature work of this period: *Numéro deux,* a picture steeped in dissidence and dissonance. Although rigid sociopolitical norms had been on Godard's enemies list for years, his partnership with Miéville appears to have stimulated his outrage on this subject to new intensity. If moralizing, standardizing, and circumscribing are the weapons used by cultures to enforce "proper" thinking and "correct" behavior, thereby erecting arbitrary borders around our potentially unlimited lives, then he and Miéville would attack these insidious practices without mercy. They would do this not through the abstract theorization that had proved so hard to manage in the Dziga-Vertov Group films, however. Instead they would make an aggressively concrete movie capable of grabbing attention and galvanizing imagination through the sheer extremity of its approach.

The arrival of *Numéro deux* in movie theaters was surrounded by what amounted to an elaborate practical joke. Godard was still a celebrity in 1975, despite his years of "hiding" from conventional audiences behind a barrage of unpopular films. He also knew that revolutionaries of his generation had a tendency to "mellow" and "mature" as they grew older, particularly as the widespread radicalism of the 1960s gave way to a more conservative Zeitgeist. Playing on expectations that he might follow this pattern, he let it be known that he planned to leave radical cinema and return to the "mainstream" filmmaking that he had done so much to energize in bygone years. The impression spread among his admirers that his comeback vehicle was called *Numéro deux,* or *Number Two,* because it was a remake of *Breathless,* the hugely acclaimed film that had launched his filmmaking career; evidently they overlooked the fact that his partner in the production was the same Anne-Marie Miéville who had worked by his side on the demanding *Here and Elsewhere,* and few observers took his hints about the new film to mean it would be as drastic in style and confrontational in content as any of the works that had lately been testing their patience.

Whether despite this misunderstanding or because of it, *Numéro deux* was greeted respectfully by thoughtful critics who looked far enough beyond its sensational elements to see that it contained an effective set of solutions to many of the problems Godard had been posing for himself and his audience. The movie told a story without being enslaved by narrative; it developed characters without being confined by their insular concerns; it probed social, political, and philosophical issues without sliding into rarified abstraction.

None of this means that *Numéro deux* is a remake of *Breathless* in any readily detectable sense, of course, or that it recognizably returns to some earlier form of Godardian cinema. Among its other new departures, it is his first feature-length work to make extensive use of video footage, much of it filmed from video monitors that retain their television "look" within the larger motion-picture frame. During much of the film, two monitors with different images are shown at the same time; filmmaker and critic Harun Farocki suggests that Godard picked up this idea from his recent experience in video production, since video editing is normally done with a pair of monitors showing edited and unedited material, respectively.[2]

The film does mark a clear continuation of theories and practices Godard had explored earlier, however, and its logical place within his body of work is confirmed by three of its central qualities. One is a deep concern with modern society's division of everyday life into separate domains of "labor" and "leisure," allegedly a "natural" arrangement but really an unnecessary attack on human fulfillment, perpetuated by its own alienated victims. Another is a continued interest in sexuality as both human behavior and artistic metaphor, dissected here with a psychosocial intensity that makes *Weekend* look almost well-mannered. The third is an undimmed enthusiasm for discursive interruption, cinematic interference, and creative obstruction of the image flow that seduces us so effortlessly in regular movies.

All three of these interests can be traced back to Godard's early features; yet they acquire extraordinary force and clarity in *Numéro deux*, indicating the undiminished desire of its makers not merely to communicate with but (in proper Brechtian fashion) to stimulate and *activate* the widespread audience they hoped to attract with this "return to mainstream cinema."

As previous chapters have indicated, perhaps the most straightforward way of reading Godard's career is to see it as a steady trajectory away from conventionally seamless cinema (resisted since the early shorts) and toward an energetic fracturing of the film-watching experience. From the impulsive jump cuts of *Breathless* to the collagelike rhythms of *Weekend* and the wholesale rejection of narrative in the Dziga-Vertov Group films, Godard shows growing interest in fragmentation – of movies, of the creative processes that produce movies, and of the places and objects (especially bodies) that appear within movies.

Numéro deux is another milestone on this path, as its very first images make clear. The screen is divided into three distinct areas. On the left is a patch of bright red video static. On the right is a rectangular patch containing close-ups of a man and woman, who turn to gaze into the camera. In the center are printed words, some (the column on the left) steadily readable but others (the two on the right) blinking on and off –

MON

TON

SON   IMAGE   SON

Translations are easy: *mon* = my, *ton* = your, *son* = his, *image* = image. However, the word *son* also means "sound," and we certainly hear sounds as we read these words: chirping birds, distant voices of children, and kitchen or household noises. (Note also that *Numéro deux* is the second film – after *Here and Elsewhere* the preceding year – from the Sonimage production company, set up by Godard and Miéville as an alternative to the commercial studios.) Instead of inviting us into a story, therefore, the movie starts by establishing the screen (and sound system) as a place not of narrative illusion but of visibility and audibility for their own sakes. This explains the barrage of disconnected images, random sounds, and printed words that assert their punning personalities here (also getting in a plug for the outfit that made the film!).

The next scene is equally fragmented. We see two side-by-side video images. On the upper left is a city view with a plaza in the foreground, trees in the midground, and buildings in the background. On the lower right are two children, a boy and a girl. "There was a landscape," the boy says, "and a factory was put into it." The shot of the children then starts alternating with a shot of two adults, a man and woman, puttering in a kitchen and talking about injustices faced by workers who lose their jobs or labor in unsafe conditions. The little girl speaks a variation of the little boy's comment: "There was a factory, and a landscape was put around it." Since this is still the very beginning of the movie, one might hear in this sentence a hint of "Once upon a time. . . ."

Preceding these images, we saw the film's title in provisional form: NUMÉRO 2 / TEST TITLES. Now it returns more formally, with NUMÉRO DEUX fully spelled out; but no sooner does it materialize than it starts to change, one letter at a time, until the screen spells out AU DÉPART, meaning "departure." (The metamorphosis happens in stages, so evocative fragments like ERO and DEO make fleeting appearances along the way. This happens with intertitles throughout the film, and although the transformations are generally simple letter-by-letter replacements from left to right, some produce more puns and double entendres than space allows me to trace here.)

The movie then begins all over again, this time with Godard himself appearing as a sort of host or master of ceremonies. He stands at the right of the screen, resting his hands on a TV monitor that displays his face, which is otherwise hard to see because of the camera's angled position. He faces various pieces of audiovisual equipment, including a couple of movie projectors. Talking in the manner of an introductory speaker leading up to a main topic, he remarks on subjects that have long been important to him: language, politics, control. Given its in-person delivery and its position at the beginning of a major work in a transitional phase of Godard's career, his monologue is worth sustained attention.[3]

"When the delegate makes a speech," he begins, "he reads the words of others. I think it's the paper that gives orders, and that's the trouble." Assuming that Godard functions as a sort of "delegate" in this movie appearance, he is evidently criticizing the scripts that supply conventional films with their prefabricated, predigested content. Like a jazz musician (or Beat poet) warming up some favorite riffs, he then launches into a few vague anecdotes based on puns or slippery definitions. In one he uses the word "machine" in both its standard meaning and its specifically French meaning (*machin*) of "what's-his-name." In another he calls his roomful of audiovisual equipment a "library" with no books. In a third he speaks of "paper" in the different contexts of books, printing, and money.

He then introduces a subject that will be central to the movie as a whole: the factory as a metaphor with a wide range of applications, from the intensely personal to the sweepingly social. "In biology, you know, this is a factory here," he says, still speaking in his free-associative manner. "You could call it a factory. The body's a factory, too. I listen to the machines. That machine's going faster. That machine's going slower. And I'm the boss, but I'm a special boss because I'm a worker as well. And because I'm not alone as a worker, we've taken power."

Godard is probably being ironic here, since his "power" is only that of an independent film artist operating far from the financial resources of commercial cinema. Nevertheless, this speech appears to come from his heart, and its personal nature is underscored by a reference to his still-recent road accident: "I was sick for a long time, and that made me think, about the factory." Also sincere – wistful, even – are subsequent remarks about his "factory" being different from others with names like Fox, Metro, Mosfil'm, and Algerian National Cinematography, all connected to "a multinational company that does the programs." He then complains that people are programmed, too. "You can't ever use what you learn in school," he gripes. "If I did literature, I'd tell you that the government programs people with methods that are full of holes. Stepping stones: workers, the children of workers. They go to school, and after school to the factory. It's all the same."

Good point. Still, in a monologue that slips so mercurially from multi-national film factories to shortcomings of the French school system, we may be wondering by now whether Godard is wholly in earnest or if he has shifted into his stand-aside-and-ironize mode.

Staying a quick step ahead of us, he anticipates our question – "Games with words, you say?" – and affirms the importance of hard-to-pin-down language that ambushes our ingrained habits. "In democracies there's something that doesn't surprise me: Word games are banished in a certain sense. . . . We say they're not serious. But puns – a word that slides on a thing – it's a language, and after all, love taught us language." Wordplay should liberate instead of enslaving, he continues, expanding on a perennial theme. "It slides. That shows short-circuits, interference, and so on. We use it to cure sickness sometimes. So it's serious. We say it's complicated . . . but it's *things* that are complicated. Pain is simple."

The monologue ends with a lengthy anecdote about a friend named Georges (probably Georges de Beauregard, his erstwhile producer) who came to visit, saw Godard's machines, and said the filmmaker should put them to use. Godard replied that he needed money, and the two repaired for a drink at a nearby bus station, where Godard agreed with the proprietor that provincial Grenoble is "smaller, sweeter, softer" than Paris, his former home. Georges then boarded a Paris-bound plane, promising to raise 600,000 francs for a movie. Godard concludes his story, "A newspaper would have said, 'It was a chilly November morn. The tires squeaked on the runway. . . .' But no literature. Money, commerce, beauty."

That last phrase is Godard's three-word definition of modern film-making.

Printed words fill the screen again: À L'ARRIVÉE, signaling the delayed *arrival* of the film proper. Godard starts it off by noting that many kilometers away, the Vietcong are thinking about Saigon – while "three meters away, in this factory, you have to produce. Have to produce. But what to produce? And to go where?"

The notions of work, creation, and manufacture, here centered on the punning word "produce," will be central to *Numéro deux* as it proceeds. For now, the words meaning ARRIVAL turn into THERE WILL BE, and the screen lights up again with a pair of video monitors, showing an old man at a stove and an old woman on a sofa. Looking distinctly unhappy in their domestic setting, they call out impatient phrases like "Always that!" and "No more of that!"

The word REPRODUCTION takes shape, and the video screens display a soccer match on the right and a household scene (grandparents, father, child) on the left. Reproduction has obviously taken place in this family – that is how families are made! – and reproduction now establishes itself as one of the film's subjects.

As the older folks sit in the background, the father leans down to talk with the young girl, then leaves with an abrupt swipe at her head, just as the sports announcer reports a penalty play on the sound track. Have we finally settled into an absorbing domestic drama? Evidently not, since the film's title appears again, and then we are back in Godard's studio, with two stacked-up video monitors dominating the screen. Godard is dimly visible, too, watching and occasionally adjusting the monitors. The upper one fast-forwards through the beginning of *Vincent, François, Paul . . . and the Others,* a French commercial drama (Claude Sautet, 1974) about male buddies whose hard knocks are softened by weekends of shared friendship. The lower one shows a news report on Southeast Asian developments (Saigon's name has changed to Ho Chi Minh City after a "pure and hard" revolution) and on Paris's traditional May Day parade, surely a poignant event for leftists like Godard seven years after the near-revolution of 1968. (May Day now focuses on conventional union demands, according to the report, but left-wing demonstrators are present, suggesting the continued possibility of radical change.) Occasionally the image is replaced by more printed words that change their messages one letter at a time. THIS SCREEN is transformed into A FILM THAT, foregrounding the movie as a material object. The capitalistic MERCHANDISE becomes the cultural MUSIC, calling attention to the Sautet film's lugubrious melody, as well as to the commodification of art in the commercial marketplace. Most important, WORK becomes SHIT and EQUALITY becomes LIBERTY – two pairings that foreshadow major themes of the film.

Numéro deux then undergoes a larger transformation. We still see the video workplace with its two monitors juxtaposing news and entertainment, but we hear the voice of a new narrator: a character called Sandrine, adding her presence (invisible so far) to that of Godard, until now the film's dominating voice. Her delayed appearance suggests a subordinate status – she might be the "Number Two" of the title – but her position within the movie is not passive, as she shows by commenting on its content. "What about this film called *Numéro deux?*" she asks, competing for attention with continued sound from the TV monitors. "It shows incredible things. Ordinary things. Shitty things. Good things."

At about this point, the attentive viewer will notice that the Sautet movie on TV has been replaced by a different production: a hard-core sex picture with an emphasis on oral pleasures. "Pleasure isn't simple," observes

Sandrine, ringing a less melancholy variation on Nana's discovery in *My Life to Live* that "pleasure is no fun." Printed words do another on-screen dance as CINEMA changes to POSSIBLE. "I think pain is simple," Sandrine goes on, ratifying Godard's earlier statement to that effect. "Not pleasure. Unemployment is simple. Not pleasure. I think that when unemployment is pleasurable, then fascism moves in." A sign in the porn movie reads "Dead End."

Sandrine then speaks again about the movie itself. "*Numéro deux* is not a film of the left or the right," she informs us, "but a film 'before' or 'behind.' Before, there are children. Behind, there's the government . . . *les enfants de la patrie* . . . the nation. You learn that it's a factory." As she speaks the words "before or behind," the shot of Godard's audiovisual workshop is replaced with a jarring new image: a composite video picture that combines a little girl's face with a superimposed view of a couple having sexual intercourse; both partners are standing as the man (his pants around his knees) penetrates the woman (her skirt over her hips) from behind.

So much is going on here that again it is necessary to dwell in detail on one fleeting moment. By combining images of a child's face and two adults having intercourse, the composite shot strongly suggests that the girl is watching this sexual activity. This makes it a reenactment of what Sigmund Freud calls the "primal scene": the moment when a child witnesses (or fantasizes) intercourse between the parents, is seized with jealousy at being excluded from this intimate act – and also stunned with fear of such overwhelming physicality – and instantly represses the experience into the unconscious, where it will retain its haunting (and tantalizing) emotional energy forever after.

Heightening this moment in *Numéro deux* is the image's interplay with Sandrine's narration. At first, her replacement of "left and right" with "before and behind" appears to be a whimsical example of the "word games" defended by Godard a little earlier. However, the sense of whimsy diminishes as her monologue continues: "Before, there are children. Behind, there's the government. . . ." If children are "before" or "in front," they must be in the position of the woman on the screen; and if the government is "behind," it must be in the position of the man, mechanically "screwing" its passive and possibly unwilling partner.

If government = power and children = innocence, Sandrine and Godard clearly see modern society as corrupt, brutalizing, and sick. Moreover, the government is not some alien entity that exercises power through its own self-generated strength. Sandrine links government with *les enfants de la patrie* – the "children of the nation," as citizens are called in "La Marseillaise," the French national anthem. She then labels this hydra-headed monster a "factory," thus returning us to the film's opening words, about a factory and a landscape locked into close but uneasy coexistence.

By this point it is clear that *Numéro deux* aims to analyze and criticize a number of interlocking phenomena: the home, where children must cope with such daunting existential challenges as the primal scene and other parental mysteries; the education system, which ill prepares them for present or future tasks; the industrial world, where people's lives are not their own; the government, which uses and abuses us; and the mass media, including the film and video technologies used to make *Numéro deux* itself.

Continuing the latter thread, the shot of Godard's audiovisual workshop returns to the screen, its monitors still showing a commercial movie and a news report. "Film is also a factory," Sandrine observes, "a factory that manufactures images, like television." She then offers a sort of media-savvy nursery rhyme, again confirming childhood (and its comparative innocence) as an organizing factor in the movie:

> Once upon a time there was an image.
> Once upon a time there were two images.
> Twice upon a time there was a sound.
> Once upon a time there were two sounds.
> Number One and Number Two.

This leads (at last!) to the credits of *Numéro deux,* which Sandrine recites aloud. But wait a moment – surprises are frequent in Godardian cinema, and this turns out to be not the credit sequence after all but a "coming attractions" teaser. "*Numéro deux:* coming soon on this screen!" announces Sandrine, with typically deadpan delivery.

Has the film actually started, or are we still in some kind of preamble? Does *Numéro deux* have an "official" beginning at all? It is probably better not to worry about such things, turning our attention to the moment-by-moment progress of whatever it is we *are* watching.

Sandrine encourages us in precisely that direction. "This screen is on a wall," she notes, pointing out the obvious. Then she problematizes her simple statement by asking, "A wall between what and what?" We know from earlier films that Godard loves to challenge the commonsense borders, boundaries, and dividing lines – that is, the conceptual walls – that we customarily use to organize our everyday thoughts and activities. He is willing to grant that movies and videos materialize on screens, and that these screens generally have walls behind them. What, however, do those (metaphorical) walls separate the movies and videos from? Is it the multitude of real-life problems continually thrust at us by families, governments, schools, factories, and the market forces that determine what cinema and television will comprise? If so, our fascination with screens and spectacles – our willingness to gaze at them without really thinking about them – ties in with far-from-ideal social situations that cry out for critical reflection.

The two-sided coin of *separation* and *combination* is a fundamental theme of *Numéro deux*. The movie's interests range from common yet ambiguous categories like "before" and "behind" to such filmic phenomena as the juxtaposition of different shots, which are separated by "cuts" in conventional film, but can merge and combine in video composites like the "primal scene" image we've just watched.

Most profoundly, *Numéro deux* is concerned with the hazy boundaries between different people – boundaries that are both affirmed and erased by sexual activity – and between different aspects of a single person. These aspects may be conflicting facets of the mind, forever split between conscious and unconscious, reason and unreason, influences of the past and imperatives of the present. Then again, they may be various parts of the unruly human body; we have noted Godard's tendency to see the body in fractured terms, using strings of words or images to represent bodies as collections of separate part-objects rather than coherent wholes.

All of which explains why *Numéro deux* is itself simultaneously divided and unified in its interests and methodologies. "So another political film?" Sandrine asks rhetorically. "No, it's not political," she immediately answers, "it's pornographic. No, it's not pornographic, it's political. So is it pornographic or political? Why do you always ask either–or? Maybe it's both at once."

She then restates the phrase "twice upon a time," which is becoming an unofficial motto of the film, and another video screen lights up with a little girl writing on a blackboard. Sandrine proposes that we put aside "talk, talk" and attend to quiet looking and listening.

"Look at what?" she queries. "You don't always need to go far. There's a lot to see. . . . Your sex, for example. Have you ever looked at it? Did you let others know you looked at it? Honestly. Not like in commercials or adventure movies."

The idea of gazing at a part of one's own body, instead of at manufactured body-images in entertainments and advertisements, suggests that visual pleasure can be found by (a) distinguishing between two ways of seeing and (b) choosing the one that is most often overlooked. The overrated way is *institutional,* fabricated for consumption by a wide, lowest-common-denominator audience. The underrated way is *introspective,* focused on the everyday and close at hand.

Another key metaphor of *Numéro deux* then reappears in a new form, further blurring divisions between personal and public, animate and inanimate, natural and artificial. "Didn't you ever ask yourself if Papa is a factory or a landscape?" Sandrine asks. "And if Mama is a landscape or a factory? In my opinion, a factory. . . . Or maybe a power plant. It charges and discharges. And it hurts."

If this "charging and discharging" refers to the body's built-in biological functions, then this "hurt" may simply be the existential pain of what Freud called the "ordinary unhappiness" of life. One suspects Sandrine is less worried about this "natural" human discomfort, however, than about humanly caused sufferings brought by social, economic, and political abuses specific to the industrial and postindustrial eras – sufferings not limited to the "factory" or "power plant" aspects of capitalism, as conventional reformers would often have us believe, but wreaking more havoc as they spill into the domestic sphere with which *Numéro deux* is largely concerned.

The porn movie is back on the upper-left monitor and brassy jazz has joined the sound-track cacophony as Sandrine continues, "We play music. But why play music? To see the unbelievable." The monitor with the little girl now fills much of the screen, displacing commercially jaded sex with a reminder of how promising childhood is before dehumanizing forces have a chance to sour it.

"What is the unbelievable?" Sandrine concludes. "The unbelievable is what we don't see." This is of course a resonant phrase for Godard and Miéville, who are dedicated to exposing the limitations of the visible and locating the *invisible* dimensions where power and influence often reside. Here as before, their goal is to refute two propositions: that seeing = believing (which allows film to deceive us) and that believing = seeing (which allows us to deceive ourselves). *Numéro deux* wants to explore the unbelievable by probing the limits of "what we don't see," as Sandrine puts it. This focuses the film on two sorts of material: that which is socially forbidden – a child should not witness the sexuality of its parents, for instance – and that which is psychologically inaccessible, such as the repressed desires that surge through our subconscious minds. (Later films by Godard and Miéville will approach the "unbelievable" from another angle, using cinema to locate a spiritual dimension within the material realm.)

The child works away at her blackboard, meanwhile, writing a very unchildish slogan: "Before being born, I was dead." As noted, many elements of *Numéro deux* evoke childhood: the girl and boy who speak at the beginning, the nursery-rhyme cadence of "once . . ." and "twice upon a time," the composite image of adult sexuality and a young girl's face. The child's blackboard phrase now implies concern with a still earlier stage, speculating on the nonexistence that precedes birth. What both *separates* and *joins* the obscurity before birth and the self-awareness of life is, of course, the pivotal moment of conception. *Numéro deux* follows Freud in recognizing the disavowed but unbreakable links among *eros*, the sexual drive; *thanatos*, the desire to reclaim the equanimity of nonexistence; and the lifelong urge – beginning in infancy – to understand and resolve the tensions generated by these powerful forces.

More than one contemporary thinker has investigated the territory that Godard and Miéville delve into here, and a glance at some of their ideas will illuminate *Numéro deux* and its place in an important cultural tradition. I recognize that the movie is dense and strange enough in itself, without bringing in a host of cultural references to complicate it further; but Godard and Miéville are ardently intellectual artists, and to trek through a work like this without at least touching on its philosophical "backstory" would be antithetical to their spirit. Since one of the movie's most striking (and controversial) qualities is its fascination with the interplay between sociopolitical norms and the body's indecorous demands, I focus on modern theorists who give intellectual weight to aspects of human experience that have traditionally been considered too "low" or "base" for consideration by serious-minded persons.

One we have already encountered is Mikhail Bakhtin, who celebrates the carnivalism of freethinking works that challenge the social, cultural, and political norms of their day. Such writings frequently dwell on urges of the body (especially the lower body, where sexuality and excretion blur the boundaries between self and other) at the expense of rules, regulations, and laws designed to squeeze the unbridled individual into governable patterns. Another is Georges Bataille, whose concept of the *informe* argues that materiality is irreducible and "unformable," and that theory must resist the impulse to shape it with abstract schemes and systems. Still another is Julia Kristeva, who states that infants pass through an *abject* stage of development, during which they cannot conceive of being either *part of* or *separate from* the mother. At this time they inhabit a borderline mental realm that oscillates among the exhilirating prospect of independence, the smothering fear of being entrapped or reabsorbed, and the dread of unmoored existence in an outside world of solitude and instability.

Numéro deux refers directly to none of these authors, but its concerns are rooted in the tradition they represent. Like the outwardly chaotic *Weekend,* with its casual cannibalism and cartoonish violence, it exudes a subversive spirit through polymorphous sexuality and a seemingly disjointed structure; both movies also have quick-as-lightning mood changes that reflect the proud instability of carnival grotesquerie. The superimposed video images in *Numéro deux* are especially effective in this regard. Although their implications can be unsettling, as in the primal-scene material, their fluid form and provocative content create a transformative atmosphere in which ingrained rules may be bent, broken, or reshaped beyond recognition in the blink of an eye.

Two facets of *Numéro deux* would have earned Bataille's particular applause. One is its rejection of linear narrative in favor of a thematic density that foregrounds the physicality of word and image. The other is its focus on "unformed" materials, defining this territory broadly enough to encompass phenomena as different as the still-developing mind of the young child and the presence of excrement as an intimate ingredient in daily life. Moreover, the film treats such "low" material without necessarily twisting it into shapes held acceptable by social convention. Bataille calls for a new brand of theory that he names "heterology" – actually the opposite of a theory since it "is opposed to any homogeneous representation of the world, in other words, to any philosophical system." Such systems, he says, always aim at deflecting our "sources of excitation" and developing a "servile human species, fit only for the fabrication, rational consumption, and conservation of products." What needs to be reclaimed are the substances rejected by these processes, "the abortion and the shame of human thought," so that philosophy can become a servant of "excretion" and introduce "the demand for the violent gratifications implied by social life."[4] Those gratifications took center stage in *Weekend,* which asked how cultures and classes might "consume" and "excrete" one another in acts of war and revolution. The same gratifications assert themselves in *Numéro deux,* here taking more homely forms (power games linked with bodily functions) but still charged with potentially disruptive power operating within and around the individual human being.

Kristeva's notion of the abject is perhaps clearest of all in a movie preoccupied with intersections of "low" and "high" material, and with a wide variety of borderline conditions: political/pornographic, natural/artificial, public/private, sound/image, attraction/repulsion, and so on. Among the most important of these is film/video, since even the production methods of *Numéro deux* are designed to blur conventional boundaries. For the infant, Kristeva suggests, the abject stage is marked by profound ambiguity as to where the parent leaves off and self-identity begins. Manifesting this condition in cinematic terms, *Numéro deux* embodies the ambivalence of a young medium (video) caught within its parent medium (film) at precisely the moment when its newly acquired powers, purposes, and sensibilities are ready to assert themselves but are still uncertain as to what their own distinctiveness and usefulness will be. One of the qualities that make *Numéro deux* unsettling is the fact that it doesn't just allegorize but vividly actualizes – one might even say incarnates – the abject.

Numéro deux is also concerned with the difficulty of crossing sociocultural barriers, be they physical or psychological. Rarely has a film concentrated on the concept of *blockage* in so many forms. This starts at the beginning, when the title has trouble appearing on the screen, as if the movie were facing some invisible block or obstacle on its way to the audience. The film does get started eventually, but various devices keep the sense of blockage going. Some operate through the film's style: the uneven progress of the story; the frequent interruption of one scene by another; the competition between film and video images, which sometimes seem to get in each other's way. Others operate through the movie's content: the stop-and-start pictures on the monitors in Godard's workshop; the image of a primal scene that must be repressed as soon as it is witnessed; the linkage of birth (commencement) and death (cessation) in the girl's blackboard sentence. When the narrative proceeds a little farther, we will encounter the film's most blunt metaphors for blockage: the constipation and impotence that plague Sandrine and her husband, respectively. When she compares her mother with a "factory" that "hurts" when it "charges and discharges," Sandrine is also describing herself and many others – women who feel cut off from life's flow by the demands of work, and deprived of healthy sexuality by the insensitivity of their husbands. We will also learn that Sandrine's spouse is abusive, using anal intercourse (blocking a channel) to punish and control her.

One more aspect of *Numéro deux* that Kristeva's ideas illuminate is its Godardian use of sound (immediate, surrounding, ungraspable) to combat the tyranny of the image (distant, hard-edged, authoritarian) that dominates commercial cinema. Kristeva holds that early infancy is bathed in sound as the child develops within the "chora," which is both the *flesh-ly* envelope of the womb and the *sonic* envelope of the noises (most notably, the mother's voice) that filter through to the infant's hearing. Nostalgia for this stage of life persists long after its peace and plenitude are ruptured by the rude awakening called birth. This helps explain the power of music (increasingly important in Godard's cinema) to touch us in ways for which rational considerations can't wholly account. It also helps explain the cacophonous sounds in *Numéro deux,* a film that extravagantly favors physical immediacy over coded communication. *Numéro deux* loves noise – noise for the ears, such as the gobbledygook of overlapping sound tracks, and noise for the eyes, such as video static and on-and-off television pictures. Godard told us earlier that language games can cure sickness, so it isn't surprising that verbal and visual puns are a major component of this movie (which was produced after he himself had recuperated from his serious motorcycle accident). The way to heal blockage is with slippage – and nothing slides more easily, or with a more liberating effect, than a word or image whose meaning has no fixed abode other than in-the-moment dialogue with its audience.

Even as it pursues its fascination with the materiality of sight, sound, and cinema, *Numéro deux* has ideological goals in mind, with specific analyses to conduct and sociopolitical messages to convey. Accordingly, some of its mostly brief episodes reduce the frequently high level of verbal and visual "noise," presenting lucid images with synchronized sound – in other words, coherent "scenes" appearing one at a time. Though these often range from difficult to obfuscatory, if measured in ordinary movie terms, they gather significance and force as the movie progresses.

As we would expect, many episodes continue the film's concern with culturally "low" subjects, focusing on women, children, housework, and biological details that transform the "abject" from an abstract category into an everyday affair. Inflecting their meaning are Godard's familiar intertitles, drawing our thoughts from the manifest content of the scenes to the ideas behind them, generally in punning, allusive ways. As the girl writes her "before I was born" statement on the blackboard, for instance, the intertitle REPRODUCTION appears and then changes to REGULATING, suggesting a long list of possible meanings and interconnections.

Soon afterward, Sandrine irons clothing in her kitchen while the little girl, Vanessa, paces restlessly about. Perhaps prompted by the seminudity of her mother, naked beneath an open bathrobe, Vanessa asks whether she herself will have "blood between [her] legs" when she is older. "Yes," replies Sandrine, adding, "You'll have to watch out for guys. They're not reliable." (Intertitle: REGULATING becomes EDITING.)

The composite image of sexual intercourse and the face of a girl (Vanessa) returns, and now the child makes an apparent reference to it: "Sometimes I think what Mama and Papa do is pretty, and sometimes I think it's caca." (Intertitle: MONTAGE becomes FACTORY.) Then we see Vanessa's lower body as Sandrine washes her in a bathtub. "Do all little girls have a hole?" the child asks, and a bit later, "Is that where memory comes out?" Answered with a cheerful "yes," the child asks where memory goes after it "comes out," and Sandrine replies, "It vanishes. It vanishes into the landscape. There's a factory in the landscape now."

The film's chain of associations is becoming more complex: Factory and landscape are still tightly connected, but the latest intertitle uses FACTORY as a link between MONTAGE and the body, which produces memories (residues of images previously consumed?) that disappear into the landscape, where (completing the cycle) they join another factory! It would be a challenging task, and perhaps an endless one, to count up all possible meanings of this visual–verbal rebus; but its most important point may be the comparison of the (female) body to a factory, at once physical (complete with "holes" that produce both excrement and new life) and psychological (there is a memory "hole" too).

We have seen the foregoing shots on a video screen that almost fills the larger surface of the movie screen. Doubling this arrangement, two video screens now appear. A little boy (Nicholas) sits at a school desk, doing calculations and reading from a book about a "stupid wolf" who is ignorant, hungry, and lost. Then we see him at home, sitting moodily apart as his mother and little sister (Sandrine and Vanessa) dance nearly naked to a song with political lyrics. Sandrine likes the song's message that "anarchy is not a bomb, it's justice and liberty."

Intertitle: SOLITUDE becomes NUMBER ONE. A pop singer yowls about loneliness on the sound track, and we cut to Nicholas and Vanessa conversing about pop culture. More accurately, they are trading narratives – obviously borrowed from pulp fiction or B movies – as they gaze at each other across a table. Nicholas begins, "She's the one who betrayed him, eight years ago. . . . She decided to kill everyone in her way." Vanessa continues, "By way of welcome she plowed five bullets into his belly. He'd committed two murders, but he loved her. What an odd time!" The scene is photographed to favor Nicholas, with the camera facing him over Vanessa's shoulder; yet her image often scrolls videographically over his, and her face dominates the whole screen for a moment near the end.

Once again, two important points emerge from a moment with little story or character development. For one, this represents a new approach to improvisation in cinema, made possible by video technology that allows artist(s) to manipulate or "play" the contents of the screen as spontaneously as if it were a musical instrument or the canvas of an "action painting." Godard's longtime interest in improvisation (dating back to *Breathless*) thus finds a new outlet and a host of fresh possibilities.

As for this particular improvisation, it is as if the two makers of *Numéro deux* were making their own voices heard through the on-screen children, with the lesser-known Miéville wrestling the world-famous Godard for her fair share of attention. Reinforcing this interpretation (and the notion that *Numéro deux* deals largely with gender politics) is the intertitle reading NUMBER TWO that appears just as the girl starts to speak. For years now, the names of Godard's films have cropped up at odd moments during the action; but this particular instance does not seem merely random and interruptive, especially since NUMBER ONE materialized just before Nicholas began *his* turn in the spotlight. These intertitles remind us that society indoctrinates even the youngest males and females into their "natural" places: Number 1 and Number 2, respectively. Fortunately, this movie is named after the "lesser" person, and an invisible hand at the video panel makes sure her image gets fair representation, despite the primary camera's all-too-typical position privileging her male companion. This is improvisation with an agenda.

The adult world returns on side-by-side video screens. On the left, the grandfather of the household tries to amuse a clearly bored Nicholas by burning a piece of cigarette paper and exulting over how completely the paper is consumed – a Godardian joke, perhaps, suggesting the minimal value placed on (old-fashioned) paper in the age of (fashionable) *ciné-video*. On the right, Sandrine and her husband (Pierre) quarrel violently as he tries to remove the stereo earphones that allow her a temporary escape from domestic life.

Two new screens then appear. On the right, Sandrine lies sleeping while factory-and-landscape imagery scrolls and unscrolls over her image, as if revealing her dreams. On the left, Pierre soliloquizes about city discomforts and the inadequacies of education; then he explains his job (as a recording technician) to Sandrine. He keeps talking after she leaves the room. "I've had kids," he says. "I never screw them. It's not allowed. I agree with that. I screw my wife, but it's no good. Thanks, boss." This remarkable speech points in three directions at once: toward the id impulses raging within him, toward the social norms restraining his behaviors, and toward the domestic unhappiness brewed by these unresolved tensions.

Intertitle: LANDSCAPE becomes NIGHT. Compressing to a single screen, the film returns to physical blockage as a metaphor for the repression of abject urges. "Shit! It's blocked up again! Awful plumbing in these projects," Pierre complains, moving from the toilet to the bathroom sink, where he urinates after getting Sandrine's permission. Talk then turns to sex:

SANDRINE: Do you want to tonight?
PIERRE: I don't know. We'll see.
SANDRINE: Thanks, boss.

She grasps his penis and massages it, complaining that he or "his job" always determine whether they'll have sex. He agrees with her anger, adding that getting an erection is often impossible for him nowadays. She sympathizes with him, but he makes a wisecrack about her periods and stalks out. "It all has to change," Sandrine wistfully laments. "But where does this [change] happen?"

The quarrel continues in the next scene. As a static-filled video monitor pulses on one side of the screen, Pierre does a household chore on the other, arguing with Sandrine about his reluctance to spend time with her. "There's always other [available] guys," she says – apparently a casual threat, but actually a turning point in the film's minimal story. An abrupt cut brings back the jolting primal-scene image, and Pierre finally reveals what this image means in narrative terms, integrating it into the movie's plot structure for the first time. "Something awful happened," he tells us. "Sandrine screwed another guy. She wouldn't say who. I wanted to rape her. She let me, and then I screwed her in the ass. She screamed. Afterward, we realized Vanessa was watching. Family life – maybe that's what it is."

This is strong stuff, and the filmmakers take immediate steps to defuse any melodramatic effect it may have, following it with a sort of grim comic relief: Pierre tries to help Sandrine figure out the controls of a new washing machine, and Sandrine's bent-over position echoes her posture when Pierre violated her. She wins this round by managing to start the washer – a victory for woman as "domestic engineer" in her household factory – and fixes Pierre with a told-you-so look.

The next scene returns Pierre to dominance, however, as the couple has intercourse in what we learn is his favorite position, with Sandrine straddling him and facing toward his feet. She ostensibly has some control in her on-top location; but the camera views the scene from his perspective, and he tells Sandrine that he likes this position because it allows him to see parts of her that she cannot see herself. He then describes the view, offering (his) words as a replacement for (her) images. His description turns out to be surprisingly poetic, likening Sandrine's body to a river and its banks; yet the scene's visuals are deliberately awkward, as we stare past Pierre's nose to Sandrine's buttocks. His dominance of the situation is suspicious at best and unacceptable at worst, given our knowledge of his capacity for sexual violence.

Accordingly, the film counters this scene with another bedroom episode that privileges Sandrine, who faces the camera across Pierre's body as she masturbates him (without much effect) and delivers a monologue far more practical, poignant, and meaningful than his:

> Every morning you leave. You get out of here. I'm not criticizing, but *I* don't have a job. I see your ass leaving, going off to work. That's a part of you that you never see. At night . . . and when you come home, I see your prick. . . . I think love would have to be a *job* for you. . . . If we were rich, I think I'd pay for it.

They aren't rich, Pierre quickly points out. The next scene finds Sandrine looking for a job of her own, while turning away a politically active neighbor who wants to interest her in the oppression of Chilean women. Problems in Chile are too distant for a woman preoccupied with difficulties close to home; but then again, oppression is a phenomenon Sandrine knows something about. As the right-hand video monitor reminds us of Pierre's sexual problems – his penis remains flaccid as she repeatedly takes its tip into her mouth – on the left-hand screen we watch her read a pamphlet describing female Chilean prisoners who are blindfolded, manipulated, and subjected to the desires of male guards.

"They are other women," she concludes. Then she adds, "Me, too." Could this be the beginning of a radicalized consciousness, or at least a politicized one?

We will not find out right away, since Sandrine must still give most of her attention to household chores, which she does not associate with political thinking. Raising her children is one of these, and a new challenge may be looming here, since Vanessa appears to be brooding over sexual subjects. While this is normal for a growing girl, it is surely more complicated than usual in this case, given the violent sex scene that Vanessa recently witnessed.

Sandrine greets Pierre cheerfully, then scrubs at Vanessa's shoes while the girl questions her about intimate matters: "Does Papa touch your breasts when you sleep together? Is it he who likes it, or is it you?" Sandrine answers directly: "Both of us do. But it's not the same. Sometimes it hurts. I like it anyway." Vanessa asks if she can watch them sleep together, and Sandrine replies with a noncommittal "we'll see," as if they were discussing a favorite dessert or some other casual treat.

This family is uncommonly candid about sexuality, and Godard and Miéville see this as a mixed blessing. It has liberating aspects, such as the parents' willingness to discuss sex with the kids; and it has oppressive sides, such as the sexual threats and abuses thrown heedlessly about the house. In any case, the family's day-to-day dynamics are steeped in the bland regularity of middle-class routine, suggesting that the filmmakers see sexual openness in itself as a weak defense against the bitter forms of alienation brought by blockages and brutalities of contemporary life.

The next few scenes catalog melancholy aspects of that life as Sandrine and Pierre live it. In the first, Sandrine again walls herself off from their quarreling with a pair of stereo earphones, listening to a lugubrious performance about loneliness at night. Pierre tries to break through her isolation with vicious names (whore, bitch) and complaints about their marriage.

In the second, Pierre offers suppositories to Sandrine, who is suffering from two weeks of constipation. She asserts her independence: "It's my kitchen, they're my children, it's my ass." But she admits that "too much" has accumulated, and that the situation is more "complicated" than Pierre's solution implies. He goes off to participate in a strike at his workplace, leaving Sandrine to droop over her coffee and tell Nicholas about her physical problem.

The third scene in this sequence presents two views of Sandrine at home. On one screen she continues to mope in the kitchen. On the other she returns from a shopping trip "all charged up," flops onto her bed, and masturbates, sending Pierre away when he shows some interest in joining her. "When we don't get on with a man we can always leave him," she soliloquizes. "But what do we do when it's a state, a whole social system that violates us?"

The next scene is more positive in tone, yet also more transgressive in its view of sexuality as a family affair. Naked on their bed, Sandrine and Pierre call the children for a sex-education session. Using their own bodies for the demonstration, they describe their genitals as lips (the vagina) and a mouth (the tip of the penis) that embrace during lovemaking. "It's like we're kissing. It's like we're talking," Sandrine explains. "It's love that teaches us how to talk," she adds. "And afterward when it's finished,"

Pierre continues, "death lays a finger on our lips and silences us. Off to school now, kids! Goodbye!" The idea of orgasm as *petite mort* or "little death" smacks of an old-school romanticism out of keeping with *Numéro deux* as a whole. Still, it suits the more conventional aspects of the household's fundamentally bourgeois outlook; and a satirical undertone may be intended.

As an essay on family life, among other things, *Numéro deux* has taken care to show mother, father, daughter, and son in a variety of situations and interactions. Largely missing so far has been the older generation, which now arrives with a near-ferocious energy that opens a whole new dimension within the film.

The grandmother peels vegetables, makes a bed, and scrubs a floor while her off-screen voice speaks on the sound track. Her activities are stereotypical "woman's work," but the words accompanying them – from *The Female Eunuch,* feminist Germaine Greer's pioneering 1971 study – are hardly the innocuous pablum with which a nice old lady might pass her time in a traditional picture of middle-class life. Rather, they continue the movie's focus on abjection – on matters of the body, on female oppression, on oscillation between "high" and "low" states of physical and mental life.[5]

"Women do not realize how much men hate them," the voice-over says. "She is punished as an object of hatred, fear, and disgust because of her magical orifices: the mouth and cunt." The text then indicts masculine domination and suggests that women should "deliver" men from sole responsibility for sexual power. "Women must have rights to their sexual organs," it continues, implying that female subordination results from suppression of bodily awareness and control. "Most women only become aware of their ovaries and womb when something goes wrong," the text goes on. "Which almost always happens."

This is followed by a word-and-image combination that might seem disconnected if not for the film's unifying theme of abjection, centered on "low" social states (the infantile, the feminine) and separation anxieties. On the screen, the grandmother cleans a floor; on the sound track, her voice-over turns to the subject of children, noting their desire to "become independent of adults." What is desirable for children is elusive for women, however, since they face ongoing burdens of social and sexual subordination. Given the difficulties of both celibacy and conjugal life, the narration goes on, "women must learn to view happiness as a victory. The greatest service a woman can provide to the community is to be happy."

This is followed by a key statement that crystallizes much of the film's radical philosophy: "The depth of rebellion and irresponsibility she must achieve to become happy is the only indication of the social metamorphosis that must be effected if there is to be sense in being a woman."

The voice-over repeats what may be the most important words in this statement: *the depth of rebellion and irresponsibility.* At the same moment, the scene's images of domestic drudgery are replaced by the old woman removing her robe and standing naked before a bathroom mirror and the camera.

This gesture confounds commercial-film notions of visual pleasure as exemplified by conventionally "beautiful" bodies. It also gives *Numéro deux* a fresh infusion of vitality, welling from the unembarassed self-exposure of a woman whose nudity would be rigidly excluded from any mass-audience commodity that traded in traditional glamour or eroticism. While she washes herself, her off-screen voice proceeds with a diatribe from Greer that takes on a scathingly sarcastic tone, begining as a utopian celebration of woman-as-Venus-figure ("The sun only shines to gild her skin and hair. . . . She is the crowning glory of creation") but passing to a catalog of death and depredation (pillaging of the sea, slaughtering of fur-bearing animals) committed in the name of fetishized beauty.

Might one argue that *Numéro deux* itself fetishizes woman? Godard's use of female nudity in this and other films – to be discussed further in the next chapter – has led to charges of insensitivity, exploitation, and commodification not unlike the charges he levels at the prostitution business and other forms of sexual trafficking. If the unglamorized female images in *Numéro deux* are simply the other side of this sexist coin, substituting gender-political novelty for old-fashioned titillation, they might be called equally problematic. Evidence can be found for either argument, here and elsewhere in Godard's work. However, it seems to me that the balance is tilted toward the progressive end in *Numéro deux* by the film's innovative focus on cultural abjection, which is examined from a commendably wide range of perspectives, most of them centered firmly and sympathetically on challenges faced by women.

As the film proceeds, it adds to this interest a growing concern with social ramifications of the aging process. By paying sustained attention to young Vanessa and grown-up Sandrine, it examines the "low" status of both the still-developing child and the dominated wife. The grandmother's presence brings in the crucial subject of old age – to which Bakhtin accorded great importance in his carnival theory, regarding the last stage of life as a natural borderline state that should be greeted with humor, good will, and cheerful impropriety. The old characters of *Numéro deux* seem somewhat in tune with such an attitude (the impropriety part, if not the humor or cheerfulness part) as they shed their clothing, bare their bodies and their thoughts, and help the movie accomplish its inversions of narrative-film convention.

Despite their feistiness in some respects, however, their lives are full of frustrations and sadnesses bred by their suffocating society. This becomes mournfully clear as the grandfather reminisces about his years at a war-equipment plant. Death punched in every night at 8 P.M., he recalls. The plant was isolated from its community, he continues, by flowers that made it virtually invisible. (This revives a familiar motif; plants hiding a plant – is it a landscape or a factory?) A strike gave him and his colleagues time to reflect on their work as manufacturers of deadly devices that would inevitably hurt "women and children" as well as combatants. "I don't mind earning my living by death," he candidly admits, "but I won't die in order to live." So he found a new job, in the concession stand of a Gaumont movie theater – an amusing but not-quite-satisfactory outcome for this moral dilemma, as Godard and Miéville hint by throwing in an intertitle that says MERCHANDISE.

Grandpa is a central presence in three more household scenes, all involving the media saturation of daily life. He quarrels with Nicholas over whether to watch a soccer game or a Russian movie on television. He listens to a doleful, somewhat surrealistic Leo Ferré pop song about the modern world, briefly sharing his headphones with Vanessa and Sandrine, and commenting that he sees the world as one sees "the unbelievable," that is, what cannot be seen. Finally, he joins the family to watch a tangled TV show about a secret agent, a financier's daughter, skullduggery in Mexico and Dachau, and international communism.

He then becomes the film's main attraction again, sitting naked in a chair and recounting a misadventure he had in Singapore during his days as a communist organizer. "It was stupid," he comments, "but this is history, not the movies." Further insulting cinema, he says the movies are time-consuming in contrast with words, which can relate forty years of life in two minutes. Taking hold of his penis, he decides to give up movie-going and look at his genitals instead. "This way to the exit, ladies and gentlemen," he sarcastically chants.

The film segues back to Pierre by way of a voice-over about the landscape-and-factory theme. The screen shows Sandrine's sleeping (dreaming) body appearing and disappearing over an outdoor shot. "In the end," Pierre's voice says, "there is not one factory and one landscape. There are two in one. There's a landscape that we cross like idiots, to punch in at home. And a factory, where we can never work while we sleep in the shade of the trees, because there aren't any."

By now we are well-schooled in Godard's criticism of the cultural divide between working life and private life, but he renews its freshness with another revealing household scene. Nicholas asks Pierre why he used the word "impossible" during an argument. Pierre describes the quarrel, saying Sandrine complained that he helped too little with the wash, whereupon he responded that it's impossible for a man to consider his "home" a workplace or "factory," as a housewife naturally would. To ask if her underwear is dirty, moreover, would be as embarassing as asking if her body were soiled.

Pierre's musing continues in the next scene, counterpointed by nonsensical static on two video screens. Nicholas brought home some pornography, he recalls. The boy quickly forgot about it, but Pierre himself fell to thinking about Sandrine's vagina and his irrational anger at the idea of other men occupying it. In their own lovemaking, he says, he sometimes feels their genders are reversed, especially when he asks her to touch his anus. This returns abjection to the foreground, evoking "low" or "dirty" behavior and using anal sexuality to blur divisions between male and female roles.

Indeterminacy also dominates the visual style, as we see Sandrine's face superimposed first over Pierre's body and then a prosaic shot of the couple doing domestic work. Sandrine has taken a shop-assistant job to get out of the house, we learn; but she has already decided to quit, realizing that more extreme measures are needed to make a woman's life fulfilling. "I know how to manufacture tenderness," she says of her role as a culturally conditioned woman. "I know how to cook. I know how to do Nicholas's homework. I know how to suck a cock." In the end, she concludes, there is too much in her life – and yet not nearly enough.

Sandrine probes this condition more deeply in a voice-over linked to images from earlier scenes: Grandma scrubbing a floor, herself touching Pierre's penis with her lips. In other words, two kinds of labor.

"I felt like I was producing," she says, "but they'd already distributed my products. I was producing at a loss. And who profited from this? Not him. Someone behind him. Something between us. Work." Once again the film sees *behind* and *between* as incredibly complicated places, capable of providing great pleasure and taking shameless advantage of anyone not fully aware of socioeconomic pressure points outside and inside the individual body. We have seen that *between* is the natural habitat of abjection, a state thriving on ambiguity and ambivalence. The mention of *behind* recalls Sandrine's opening speech (when she replaces "left" and "right" with "before" and "behind") and Pierre's sexual aggression.[6]

Also important is Sandrine's statement that the "products" of her household work have been distributed in advance, at no profit to herself or anyone she cares about. Godard finds this a great tragedy, feeling that all production should be a joyful process linking creativity and dissemination; and he bitterly resents the frustrations that result when this is blocked or aborted. In a text written fourteen years after *Numéro deux,* he contrasts the authenticity of true cinema – "freedom speaking" – with the commercialized deadness of mass-market television, which "doesn't create any goods" but rather "distributes them without their ever having been created."[7] This describes the flip side of Sandrine's predicament, as she produces real benefits that society simultaneously exploits and undervalues, meanwhile draining away their possible rewards before she ever has a chance to enjoy them.

The text just quoted also supplies another reason why Godard and Miéville use video – a form including TV, although not limited to it – in *Numéro deux,* which takes blockage of private and public fulfillment as a primary subject. "To program is the only verb of television," Godard writes in this 1989 statement. "That implies suffering rather than release."[8] This comment about the public world (television) applies ruefully well to Sandrine's private world. In the next scene, she tells Nicholas of a biological blockage ("I haven't shit for two weeks") that mirrors the social blockages of her domestic life. Her constipation is not a simplistic symbol for psychosomatic discontent, moreover. In another transgressive maneuver, Godard and Miéville stress the *productivity* of defecation by likening it to childbirth, also a natural human activity. "Eight years ago, in a sense, I shit between my thighs," Sandrine muses. That was a normal event, but she can no longer function so harmoniously. "Now everything is blocked," she laments.

> My tissue is cracking. I feel like everything I say is shit. . . . Everything that should happen in my ass happens somewhere else. In my ass nothing is happening. It's me who does the cooking. It goes in and it goes down, but nothing comes out. I'm becoming both a giver and taker of shit. I wonder if there are many women in France like this?

And with this large, difficult question *Numéro deux* starts moving quickly toward its end – not by achieving some conventional sort of closure, but by *falling apart* in a deliberate and purposeful way that echoes its step-by-step coalescence some eighty minutes earlier.

Godard sits in his studio, slumped over a recording console. "Suddenly it's over," Sandrine says, continuing her last voice-over. "Something happens. My role is finished. What are we playing at? He interprets me – but he shouldn't, because it's me who understands." What she understands is the eternal scam whereby men order the times and places for everything from work and dishwashing to sex and vacation – and, too often, filmmaking.

To whom, however, are we listening here? Is it Sandrine the movie character speaking of her problems with Pierre, or Sandrine the movie actress (i.e., Sandrine Battistella, who plays the part) departing from her fictional role to address the deficiencies of our age? And where does Godard figure in the situation, especially now that he has returned visibly to the film?

Answers begin to emerge as Sandrine notes how difficult it would be for a man to occupy or understand her place. Godard raises his head from the console, watching the video screen that now carries her image. He is one who "tells the news about others," in Sandrine's sarcastic phrase. "That's special work," she continues, "especially if you get paid for it. But letting others tell you news about yourself is a crime. Especially if we *don't* get paid for it."

Women conspire in this crime against themselves, she continues. "We go to the movies. We buy a ticket, and in exchange we sell our roles as producers." Also guilty are women and men who purchase "news" as disinterested observers. "You turn on the TV and become an accomplice. Worse, you become the organizer of the crime. We look for news about *ourselves* where there's only news about *others*. We want others with us, but without danger. An animal would never do that. But we are men and women, we are superior," she says with withering irony.

Vanessa's face, visible over the edge of a bathtub, has now appeared on another monitor. Sandrine's voice muses on, offering a brief catalog of paired concepts that correspond to the Number 1 and Number 2 that have run as leitmotifs through the film: again and already, yesterday and today, child and parent, today and tomorrow, now and later.

"And me?" she concludes. "Finally in my place, Number 3. . . . Between my past and my future, between a girl and an old man. I invent the grammar, I find the words – and those 'shes' and 'hes' who have already invented music."

Godard is still at the control panel, but Sandrine is not without power of her own. As she mentions "words" and "music," her image disappears from the monitor (Vanessa has already vanished) and, as if she had willed it, a Ferré song replaces her monologue on the sound track, with lyrics conjuring up nostalgia for the night and the past.

The movie continues toward dissolution by recalling that while society attempts to order and discipline its members, its oppressive efforts face ultimate limitations. Pierre recites the rules for living in a rented home ("The lessee . . . should meet all the orders of the city and the police, and fulfill his role as head of the family") to Vanessa – and she responds by asking whether he'll still be her daddy when he's dead.

The screen fills with a close-up of the sound-control panel. Sandrine and Pierre ask Vanessa two questions: "Do you know what a landscape is? Is Papa a factory or a landscape?" Godard's hand slides a switch on the panel and pop-song lyrics take over again:

> These eyes look at you night and day,
> Not just at numbers and hatred, as they say.
> These forbidden things you're creeping toward . . .

Nicholas's voice returns: "I'm carefully studying my plan. I see that it can't be realized." Vanessa repeats the beginning of the film: "There was a factory and we put a landscape around it." And finally, Godard's gliding fingers fade in the song-poem that terminates *Numéro deux*:

> These eyes look at you night and day,
> Not just at numbers and hatred, as they say.
> These forbidden things you're creeping toward . . .
> which will be yours . . . when you close the eyes . . .
> Of oppression. . . .

Godard closes the cover of the sound console as the song reaches its last lines. His hands leave the frame. Lights go out, one by one, until the screen is dark. A blur of random noise continues for a few seconds, followed by a single orchestral chord. Its orderliness and finality assure us once again that this seemingly chaotic film has been firmly under the control of its makers from first moment to last.

Godard's appropriation of pop-culture material dates to the early stages of his career, but the song lyric that ends *Numéro deux* is almost uncannily apt for its context, and the importance of its message is clear. Godard and Miéville have indeed been creeping toward "forbidden things" in this movie, which oscillates between politics and pornography via purposely transgressive devices – reenacting the primal scene, mixing childhood innocence with adult sex and power games, looking closely at anal sensuality and other manifestations of the abject. This fascination with the forbidden will continue in future Godard films; pungent examples include the father's incestuous fantasies in *Sauve qui peut (la vie)* and the anal sex in *Passion,* where this is not abusive but romantic. Never will it be elaborated as single-mindedly as in *Numéro deux,* however.

In addition to their self-contained meanings, the words of the song join with the film's visual conclusion to create an elegant cinematic equation. The lyrics tell us that forbidden things will be ours when we close the eyes of oppression – and immediately the lights of the screen go dark, closing the eyes of the movie itself. The lesson is clear: image = oppression. This is an enduring Godardian theme, stated directly and economically.

The reference to oppression also takes us back to Godard's familiar feud with notions of "normal" and "decent" in our stifling society. The oppression evoked by *Numéro deux* is identical to the conspiracies of "official" power and "authoritative" knowledge that Foucault warns about in his analyses of social self-regulation. An earlier philosopher calling for rejection of "civilized morality" was Herbert Marcuse, who also anticipated Godard's cry against alienated labor by noting that its limited pleasures have "nothing to do with primary instinctual gratification" or the satisfactions of a healthy erotic sensibility.

"To link performances on assembly lines, in offices and shops with instinctual needs is to glorify dehumanization as pleasure," Marcuse writes,[9] in a critique that Sandrine and even Pierre would surely endorse. Marcuse calls for a new "reality principle" based on freedom rather than repression. "No longer used as a full-time instrument of labor," he predicts, "the body would be resexualized." Sexual energies would spread across all zones of body and personality, "genital supremacy" would decline, and the polymorphous eroticism of infancy would be joyously reborn. "The body in its entirety would become . . . a thing to be enjoyed – an instrument of pleasure," blasting away the suffocating institutions that hold us in their grip, including the "monogamic and patriarchal family"[10] that *Numéro deux* so critically examines.

As dark and disturbing as this film frequently becomes, therefore, its conclusion can be seen as utopian. Freed from the division of labor that bisects life into separate domains of work and domesticity, Sandrine would no longer suffer from blockages of mental creativity, bodily productivity, and sexual gratification; and Pierre would stop channeling his energies into exhausting work, alienating arguments, and alternating fits of sexual aggression and dysfunction. Their relationship with the children might be modeled on the convivial sex-education session rather than the morbid dynamics of the domestic rape scene. The older generation might exchange its drudgery (Grandma) and nostalgia (Grandpa) for a productive and companionable role in the household's daily life.

Might our culture actually see the changes that would enable such bright metamorphoses to occur? Only tentative responses to this riddle will emerge from subsequent films by Godard and Miéville, whose explorations of aesthetics and mysticism will search more for suggestive clues than definitive answers.

In the end, the filmmakers' response to the question may be most clearly visible in the very existence of the movie that raises it. "Art attracts us," wrote Godard as early as 1952, "only by what it reveals of our most secret self."[11] His own secret self is never closer to the surface than in *Numéro deux,* his most radical effort to close the eyes of oppression and glimpse whatever visions this passionate blindness may provide.

6

Hail Mary

Chaos speaks precisely to the abyss or the open mouth, that which speaks as well as that which signifies hunger.

– Jacques Derrida, *The Gift of Death*[1]

Godard and Miéville remained fascinated with video long after their mid-1970s explorations of its unique possibilities, both on its own and in conjunction with film. *Numéro deux* and the other short features made around the same time, *Here and Elsewhere* and *Comment ça va,* were followed by two massive television series: *Six fois deux / Sur et sous la communication,* with six one-hundred-minute segments, and *France /tour / détour /deux /enfants,* with twelve segments of about thirty minutes each. Two major films, *Sauve qui peut (la vie)* and *Passion,* were accompanied by video essays called *scénarios,* brief ruminations on the films and some issues they raised for the artists. Additional video productions have rolled from Godard's camera ever since, most notably the *Histoire(s) du cinéma* series that became one of his major preoccupations starting in 1989.

Some critics responded to these video works as if they were mere sketches, *divertissements,* or minor adjuncts to movies that were the real achievements; others greeted the best of them (such as *Scénario du film Passion,* which some found equal to *Passion* itself) as creative triumphs in a medium that "serious" directors still tended to avoid. Godard's excursion into video proved intense and long-lasting enough to quell any doubts about the sincerity of his commitment; yet his deepest energies continued to gravitate toward feature filmmaking, and full-length film productions must dominate any list of his most thoughtfully received works.

Godard directed four features between *Numéro deux* in 1975 and *Dé-*

tective a decade later. *Sauve qui peut (la vie)* arrived in 1979, written by Miéville and Jean-Claude Carrière, and promoted as yet another "comeback" to commercial cinema. Known as *Every Man for Himself* in the United States and *Slow Motion* in Britain, it tells a relatively linear story and features such stars as Isabelle Huppert and Nathalie Baye among its internationally known performers. Its most aggressive formal experiment involves unexpected jumps into stop-motion cinematography, breaking down the movement of some scenes into analytic strings of static imagery; these provide a measure of Brechtian disjunctiveness while injecting the movie with an eye-catching unpredictability that any director of Hollywood action pictures (or TV commercials) could envy. Many reviewers hailed *Sauve qui peut (la vie)* as an art film of unusually wide appeal, but Godard expressed dissatisfaction with its innovative moments, complaining that the slow-motion sequences had not turned out as he had envisioned them.[2]

Passion, released in 1982, was at first dismissed by critics who looked just far enough beyond its high-powered cast (Huppert, Hanna Schygulla, Michel Piccoli) to find what they considered inward-gazing artiness and self-conscious reflexivity. In time, however, its meditative treatment of longtime Godard themes – including the struggle to create meaning through beauty, the division between love and work, and the relationships among word, image, and narrative – raised it to canonical status among cinéastes who still examined his films with care. *First Name: Carmen* was completed in 1983 from Miéville's screenplay, gaining an international release but puzzling commentators who expected a more literal retelling of the traditional *Carmen* story, or at least a dash of Georges Bizet's music instead of the comparatively abstract Beethoven quartets (plus Tom Waits's gravelly crooning) that accompanies its scrambled tale of lovers, revolutionaries, and filmmakers. Its reception confirmed Godard's reputation in the late 1970s and early 1980s as a respected but disconcerting auteur who obviously possessed the technical skills and fund-raising resources to make any sort of cinema he cared to yet, inexplicably, confined himself to eccentric exercises in what popular culture was learning to call the "deconstruction" of stories, themes, and performances that might be perfectly enjoyable if he would just present them "straight." His declining rapport with general-interest audiences was compounded by a steadily declining patience with film-as-art among Americans and Europeans who – after showing glimmerings of interest during the 1960s – were now embracing a cultural conservatism that paralleled the increasing social and political conservatism of the period.

Another comeback: Isabelle Huppert and Jacques Dutronc star in *Sauve qui peut (la vie)*, also known as *Every Man for Himself* and *Slow Motion* (1979).

It was in this context that Godard and Miéville released *Hail Mary*, a film that seemed every bit as likely as *Numéro deux* to disconcert spectators who felt a movie should be at least partially planted in the sociocultural norms of its day. Indeed, the unorthodox religious content of *Hail Mary* turned out to be considerably more provocative than the "politics and pornography" of *Numéro deux*. One reason is that Godard's approach to the sacred was linked with his still-developing interest in the ambiguities and anxieties of abjection, always guaranteed to make convention-minded moviegoers nervous. Another is that *Hail Mary* had enough superficially appealing qualities (a familiar story line, attractive stars, beautiful nature photography) to position itself as "accessible," and therefore loomed as a significant threat to audiences who had never even heard of *Numéro deux*, a similarly scandalous but more openly avantgarde work.

In any case, controversy erupted around *Hail Mary* even before it made its first public appearance.[3] Two organizations in France – the National Confederation of Catholic Family Relations and the imposingly named Alliance against Racism and for the Respect of French and Christian Identity – mounted a major effort to have the film censored or banned. The presiding judge of Paris's superior court watched the movie with attorneys for both sides of the case, found that it was not "pornographic or even obscene," and rejected the idea of withholding it from "a viewer . . . who takes the initiative, by paying for the entrance-ticket, of engaging in a singular dialogue" with it. Picketers marched at some French theaters showing the movie, but most screenings took place without interference. An exception was the city of Versailles, where conservative Catholics barged into a theater and mutilated two "shocking and profoundly blasphemous" reels. Local authorities then banned the entire film as a public-safety measure, but this was reversed by the same Paris judge who had cleared it on free-expression grounds. The most widely reported European brouhaha took place at the Cannes International Film Festival, where Godard received a pie in the face (actually a shaving-cream concoction) from an experienced protester fond of this particular tactic. The predictable result was far more publicity for *Hail Mary* than its Cannes presentations would otherwise have received.

Reaction to the film in Italy was energized by two special considerations: the fact that the Roman Catholic Church has its headquarters there, and the fact that local and regional elections were scheduled for about three weeks after the film's opening, which rolled the movie into political currents that would otherwise have swept right past it. Its opening in Rome was delayed by twenty-four hours so the theater's manager could obtain a permit personally signed by the national official in charge of entertainment; yet the day after its premiere, some thirty people broke up a screening and physically assaulted the manager. As in France, agitation caused by *Hail Mary* became mixed with rhetoric of "cultural identity," calls for "solidarity" among Christians, and worry over "respect" toward religion. Also noteworthy was the participation by young people in many organized protests, suggesting that the left-leaning youth movements of the 1960s – so close in spirit to the politically radical cinema produced by Godard during that period – had been displaced by groups with similar zealousness but very different goals. A collective prayer for "atonement" was organized by the Ardent Marial Youth and World Fatima Movement, and Pope John Paul II supported this with a message acknowledging the "tribulation of the faithful" over a movie that "insults and deforms" the Christian faith, "desecrates" its spiritual and historical outlooks, and "deeply injures" the religious values of Mary's followers. A few days later, the pope filled an international broadcast with prayers designed to "repair the insult" caused to Mary by the film. With these gestures, John Paul

Provocateur: Jean-Luc Godard at the time of *Hail Mary* in 1985.

II appears to have become the first pope to engage in public combat with a movie. His campaign was supplemented by like-minded articles in *L'Osservatore Romano,* the Vatican newspaper.

Godard did not take the Italian protests lightly. Indeed, he asked his Italian distributor to cancel screenings planned in Rome, although the distributor proceeded with the picture anyway. (Its release in Rome was terminated a few weeks later, despite Godard's growing optimism about its financial prospects there.) At about the same time, Godard sent a remarkable message to the pope via a Catholic official in Rome, along with a copy of his request that the film's Italian release be withdrawn. In this statement, Godard cited a 1980 papal document – published in a collection called *Theology of the Body,* under the title "The Plenitude of Eros in the Spontaneity of Human Love" – and claimed that in light of this text, it "so happens that the Holy Father was one of the screenwriters of this film"! Godard added that his present message was inspired by writings of Flannery O'Connor, an American author who treated sincerely Catholic themes with hugely sardonic wit; and by passages of Saint Paul, whose observation that "the plenitude of the image will be achieved through the Resurrection" might serve as a motto for *Hail Mary* itself.

The film was criticized elsewhere in Europe as well. Theater owners canceled engagements after protests in West Germany and Athens, for instance; demonstrators in Madrid targeted a theater where Godard's earlier *Alphaville* was being revived; and in Latin America, the president of Brazil banned it outright. It also drew support, however – as at the Berlin Film Festival, where the International Catholic Cinema Office gave it a prize.

As in other parts of the world, protests against *Hail Mary* in the United States took two main forms: efforts to obtain some kind of official censorship, and expressions of angry disapproval through demonstrations or other types of direct action. If the latter predominated, this was partly because Americans like to congratulate themselves on a tradition of rowdy individualism. More important, however, was the impact of a 1952 decision by the Supreme Court that overturned a decades-long policy of treating films as mere commodities, instead deeming them a "medium . . . of ideas" that falls under First Amendment guarantees of free speech. (Interestingly, the 1952 case that established this liberalized policy had concerned Roberto Rossellini's drama *The Miracle*, itself a movie with religious content, centering on an ignorant woman who believes her baby has been fathered by a saint.) Banning, expurgating, and censoring of movies still occurred on a local level; but since the 1952 decision, the starting point for any self-respecting protest was less likely to be a court document than a public outpouring of hostility aimed at distributors, exhibitors, and consumers of the offending material.

Such hostility arose promptly when conservative Christians heard that *Hail Mary* was coming to the United States by way of the New York Film Festival at Lincoln Center, where as many as five thousand demonstrators gathered to greet its premiere. Most were members of Roman Catholic groups, many chanting "Ave Maria" or "Shame! Shame!" as they carried placards announcing their dismay with the film and its normally well-respected venue. Armbands and candles in blue, Mary's traditional color, vied for attention with angry signs (e.g., "*Hail Mary* – Tax-Funded Anti-Catholicism") and ritual gestures with holy water and rosary beads. One day before the film's debut, John Cardinal O'Connor of the New York archdiocese branded it "an act of contempt," but by the evening of its second screening the crowd had diminished to about 20 percent of its original size. Godard participated in the festival's press conference, but left New York before the public screenings, after which (in accord with the festival's usual practice) he would have been "spotlighted" and invited to join a question-and-answer session with the audience. *Hail Mary* historian Maryel Locke reports that Joanne Koch, exceutive director of the Film Society of Lincoln Center, implored Godard to remain for these events, noting that the festival had staunchly supported him throughout the controversy. "It's only a movie," the filmmaker replied.

Large-scale protests also occurred in Boston and Chicago; smaller demonstrations were held in Hollywood as well as major cities in Nebraska and Alabama, among other places. This produced anxiety at the company that expected to distribute the movie, Triumph Films, a venture controlled by Columbia Pictures in conjunction with Gaumont, the venerable French studio that distributed Godard's work to European theaters. Letters and telephone calls from angry Catholics bombarded Coca-Cola, the corporation that owned Columbia, and threats of an economic boycott pushed Triumph out of its distribution agreement. New Yorker Films, a highly respected distributor with a longtime commitment to international cinema, joined with Gaumont to bring the movie before American audiences. No noteworthy incidents marred its New York theatrical run.

Things were less satisfactory in Boston, where the powerful Sack Theaters chain rejected the film after a number of modestly scaled protests. Across the river in Cambridge, the art-oriented Orson Welles Cinema showed it successfully despite legal and grassroots efforts to eject it. A theater in Los Angeles removed it on grounds that a "rosary crusade" was causing fire and safety hazards in the mall where the auditorium was located, according to censorship scholar Charles Lyons; he also describes a Chicago protest organized by a coalition of Roman Catholics, Black Muslims, and Greek Orthodox Christians, whose combined strength was enough to coax a condemnatory statement from the City Council but not enough to prevent the movie from finishing a successful eleven-week engagement. A showing at the University of Nebraska was canceled after receipt of a letter from a state senator, then reinstated after a suit was brought to federal court by a law student. A screening at the University of Alabama proceeded despite a campaign launched by the Eternal World Television Network to prevent it. Lyons notes that the defeat of efforts to ban the film in Omaha and Birmingham was "not surprising in a legal climate repeatedly liberal on the subject of censorship," but adds that "the fact that religious groups, especially Catholics, had produced censorious effects in Boston and Los Angeles was a sign of conservative groups' reemerging power over images, and an indication that great religious group censorship successes were possible." (These would reach a climax in the 1988 frenzy over Martin Scorsese's religious epic, *The Last Temptation of Christ,* based on Nikos Kazantzakis's unorthodox yet clearly reverent novel.) As for the career of *Hail Mary* over the long run, Locke reports that New Yorker Films continued to receive protest letters (all cut from virtually the same mold) into the 1990s, and that a "last gasp" of picketing was provided by a Long Island religious sect in 1989, when a hundred of its members turned out for a Lincoln Center screening of the film.

The presence of so much bitterness over *Hail Mary* might lead an unsuspecting observer to think Godard's film is indeed "only a movie" in the Hollywood sense of that phrase – that is, a filmed entertainment that trades more in story than theme and that touches on deep sensitivities only as an incidental part of its business, which is primarily to divert, amuse, and profit from as many ticket buyers as possible.

Weighing against this notion is not only the content of the movie but the overall tone of Godard's career during the period when *Hail Mary* was produced. This was not a time of commercially geared "comeback" films, despite the impression gathered by moviegoers about some of his preceding features. On the contrary, it was an artistically ambitious and commercially troubled period that had announced its seriousness in such uncompromising projects as *Sauve qui peut (la vie)* and *First Name: Carmen* and would continue in subsequent films including *Détective,* an offbeat comedy-drama undertaken to generate revenue so *Hail Mary* could be completed, and *King Lear,* a darkly comic meditation on the loneliness of the creative soul. As a characteristic work of this period, *Hail Mary* is the opposite of "only a movie." It assertively opposes the mass-audience titillation and headline-grabbing contentiousness one might expect if that phrase had been spoken by a filmmaker *not* known for ironic utterances (and behaviors).

In the end, the most preposterous aspect of the *Hail Mary* controversy was its irrelevance to the film itself, which explores its theme with a complexity quite unaccounted for by media and street-corner debates. The controversy also had an unintended effect on members of the general audience, of course, who would scarcely have heard of the picture – much less been roused to activism over it – had protests not conveyed the misconception that it represented a major flashpoint in the movie industry's treatment of religion. This said, what is important for our purposes is not the social uproar raised by the movie but the fascinating convergence it displays of religious material with the unique sensibilities of Godard and Miéville.

As we know, relationships between word and image have preoccupied Godard from the start of his career. One way to approach *Hail Mary,* a film strongly based on biblical material, is to note that the Bible contains many conceptions of *word* in the many books that constitute it. These books travel a long road from the relatively concrete creation stories in Genesis ("Let there be light") to the exalted abstractions of St. John's apocalyptic vision ("In the beginning was the Word, and the Word was with God, and the Word was God"). Concepts of *image* come importantly into play as well, although less directly, if only because the Bible is made not of images but of words. The history of Christianity may be traced through genealogies of word and image – or rather, the Word as sent to humanity by God, and ways in which humans have tried to image this forth in order to comprehend it more deeply.

Word–image relationships in Godard take different forms, too. Some are adversarial, as when printed words intrude on the flow of pictures, or complicate scenes with oblique or obscure commentaries, or make stories difficult to follow. More characteristically, Godard likes to blur distinctions between word and image, seeing them not as rivals but as parts or aspects of one another. Here he joins the tradition of twentieth-century collage art, which has long considered written words to be as suitable as other materials for cut-and-paste combination.

Hail Mary is a collage-film to its bones, starting with the fact that it is really two movies spliced together: the short "The Book of Mary," credited to Miéville, and the feature *Hail Mary,* bearing Godard's signature. Godard's contribution to this diptych contains many other collage elements as well, from discontinuous editing (e.g., cutting between a flying basketball and a stately moon) to interruptive titles, stop-and-start music, and elliptical storytelling that hopscotches among different subplots, omits large chunks of time, and stretches small incidents into major detours from what appears to be the main narrative.

These familiar gambits remind us of Godard's enthusiasm for fracturing words and images so as to (a) prevent them from dragging us into preordained patterns of thought and communication, and (b) disrupt any intimidating or distracting powers they may appear to have, anchoring them in the here-and-now of real intellectual and emotional needs. In the three major films preceeding *Hail Mary,* he took art forms rooted in the physical world – still photography in *Sauve qui peut (la vie)*, painting in *Passion,* music in *First Name: Carmen* – and made them into a sort of aesthetic ballast, using their materiality to keep storytelling or psychology from whisking us into the Never-Never Land inhabited by most narrative films. Two central elements of *Hail Mary* – its historically freighted "Catholic images and Protestant music," as Godard describes them – serve the same function here.

What makes *Hail Mary* a fresh departure for Godard is its investigation of a vast new arena for improvisatory freedom: the spiritual realm, where the interpenetration of word and image may lead not just to the taming but ultimately to the *transcending* of both. Christianity states that Mary was the human vehicle for the Incarnation, the ultimate fusion of impalpable Word and palpable reality. This makes her an ideal vehicle for the next step in Godard's quest for a cinema that will blend language and spectacle, art and life, individual and society, soul and body into an inspired whole that escapes the power/knowledge paradigms of conventional culture. Loosely speaking, this quest took sociological forms in works like *Breathless* and *2 or 3 Things I Know about Her,* political forms in works like *La Chinoise* and *Comment ça va,* and aesthetic forms in works like *Sauve qui peut (la vie)* and *First Name: Carmen.* In their different ways, all those films counterpointed the physics of artistic *production* – involving sights and sounds that must be perceived by the senses – with the metaphysics of artistic *expression,* aimed at evoking the ineffable and communicating the incommunicable. *Hail Mary* and subsequent films like *Nouvelle Vague* and *Hélas pour moi* take the ineffable as their most immediate concern, yet they remain fully realized cinematic works. Among the rewards they offer is a keen sense of the pleasure Godard feels in playing their material properties (color, composition, texture) against more allusive qualities of theoretical reflectiveness and philosophical, even theological, speculation.

As noted, *Hail Mary* is actually a movie in two parts, beginning with "The Book of Mary," written and directed by Miéville independently of the feature-length Godard film. The similarities between the two movies – their elliptical stories, their crystal-clear cinematography, their gaps between sound and image – show the filmmakers to be on very much the same terrain in their cinematic interests. Their subjects are also roughly similar, since both stories have female protagonists facing emotional travails in male-dominated environments.

Miéville's film is fundamentally secular, however, focusing on an eleven-year-old girl whose parents are going through a divorce. The story begins with an argument between the parents, heard in voice-over as we watch a series of elegant still-life shots that bring us step-by-step toward the world of the narrative: a quiet lake, the setting sun, the grounds of a comfortable house, the flower, fruits, and furnishings of the house's interior, and finally the people who are speaking, although their voices continue in unsynchronized voice-over. Godard's film will also start with nature shots and off-screen voices, but that will be to evoke a sense of mystery and instability that prepares the way for a supernatural story. Miéville's more earthbound intention is to anchor her characters and her audience in a world suited to the all-too-human narrative she will unfold – a world at once crisply recognizable, visually rich (the images have a harmonious precision worthy of Renaissance painting), and aesthetically complex (the characters are not wholly in sync with the neatness of their surroundings).

After this prelude, "The Book of Mary" continues with a pointed reference to something that always fascinates Godard and Miéville: vision, both physical and psychological. A remarkable dialogue takes place just as we see Mary for the first time, during another argument between her feuding parents:[4]

MOTHER: I want to see clearly. . . . I wish you understood.
FATHER: Understanding is scarce. Truth is often deadly. Your truths are fatal, so don't complain afterward.
MOTHER: I'm not complaining. I'm just trying to see clearly. Why is everyone so afraid of clarity?

We now see the father in close-up, his eyes covered by conspicuously dark glasses. Mary asks if his eyes hurt, and he says no while removing the glasses. The argument goes on at the dinner table, with the mother pleading for a new approach to their relationship, not copied from the past but reinvented for the future. The father responds that "women don't invent much. Even the soul was invented by a man."

At this point Mary interrupts (she is a budding Brechtian, it appears) by grasping a small nut with her fingers, pushing it into the center of an apple that has been cut in half, and "explaining" her actions thus:

Good morning! We continue with our operation. Now we cut the eye in half. It's black, if you can see that. Put this inside; it's the pupil. The pupil, seen from outside – magnified, of course – is brown. The eye is huge, but the pupil takes up a lot of space. The rest is water. That's right, water. The pupil floats like a baby in its mother's belly. When you look at things, it's because of the pupil, because it floats; and when we move, as you see, it shifts. Understand what I'm saying?

Her mother replies that it's "complicated" and "a bit technical," but Mary pushes on:

Yes, it's mechanical and technical, and surgical too. You operate once for this illness. If you do it twice, the patient dies. In any case, the eye withers. It's a very serious operation. Yes, I entirely agree there. You undergo it after you've almost been sick. Because this gentleman . . . you see his eye . . . has been completely . . . shaken, see? It's had a shock. This eye has been completely terrorized, so we can't do much for it. Well, that's all for this program. Goodbye!

The mother who longs for clarity, the father in sunglasses at the table, the child who witnesses their dispute – all have undergone a shock, all have terrorized eyes. "Seen from outside," this household is normal and comfortable; but when it is cross-sectioned, like the apple, we can tell it is dogged by the "fatal truths" that weigh on all humans. The pun on *pupil* (a part of the eye / a learning child) is similar in French and English, making Mary the still-forming *pupille* who floats in the belly of her home, lectures to others as if *they* were pupils, and offers a dire prognosis ("we can't do much for it") for a malaise that is actually her own. She is the apple of her parents' eyes, and the resources for emotional survival on which she will draw during the movie – her imaginary classroom, the solace she finds in music and poetry, her taste for difficult films like *Contempt,* which she watches on television – are charged with energy and creativity. However, the eye that envelops her is withering away, and if her warnings go unheeded the patient may very well die, spiritually if not materially. Although the title of Miéville's film suggests a biblical account, the book of Mary that we see in the story is a volume of Charles Baudelaire's poetry from which the child reads. "My spirit with a heavy fear forebodes!" begins the passage she recites, and a bit later it ends, "How strange and wicked was our act? Can you explain my trouble and my fright?" This is hard, heavy stuff for an eleven-year-old, suggesting that her inner world may be in poignantly close touch with the sort of "forbidden things" toward which Godard and Miéville crept as *Numéro deux* reached its conclusion.

In an elegant integration of story and style, Miéville gives Mary three key scenes that correspond to fundamental building blocks of cinema: the eye-operation scene, focusing on imagery and the eye; the Baudelaire scene, focusing on the spoken and printed word; and finally a scene in which Mary dances to a recording of a Mahler symphony, focusing on music and choreographic motion.[5] Mary also dominates the last portion of Miéville's movie. In a tender moment, her mother tries to ease her discomfort over the family's changes: "Nothing can stay the same. . . . When a thing stops moving, it's dead. You must have confidence." She then performs a Godardian language game, showing *Marie* that her name is an anagram of *aimer,* the verb "to love." This leads to a scene in which Mary

"The Book of Mary": The title character (Rebecca Hampton) of Anne-Marie Mié-ville's brief drama sings Beethoven while scrutinizing an egg about to acquire much mysterious meaning.

assumes a newly mature and sophisticated relationship with her mother as the latter leaves for a date with a new boyfriend.

Alone at the dinner table, Mary sings a bit of Beethoven's familiar "Für Elise" while "conducting" with a knife from her place setting; then she scrutinizes the soft-boiled egg on her dinner plate. Her first words have an oblique political meaning that seems unconnected with the film's main-ly domestic concerns: "It would be killing the unification of Europe in the egg. This business must be smothered in the egg. Can't make an omelet without breaking eggs." It is unlikely that Mary spends much time think-ing about European unity or pondering the old French proverb about omelets; yet the personal is political to Miéville and Godard, and Mary's words refer evocatively to her household's rifts and realignments as well as to Europe's future. (One recalls the young hero of *Citizen Kane* shout-ing "The Union forever!" just as his family splits itself apart; perhaps this is why Miéville has Mary hum a line of "When Johnny Comes Marching

Home," an American song of the Civil War era, just before her egg soliloquy.)

Continuing the woman-centered focus on domestic concerns (food,
parenting, the home itself) that makes "The Book of Mary" a sort of gentle sequel to *Numéro deux,* the screen now fills with Mary's neatly cooked
egg. "I don't know," she says in voice-over. "Get lost! It's the only way."
And with this she cracks the eggshell open, chipping the top off vigorously enough to knock it out of the frame. This is the last image of Miéville's
movie, and I see it as a (literal) opening into Godard's story, which follows
directly. It also foreshadows the many round images (the moon, the basketball, the adult Mary's open mouth) that will punctuate Godard's film.
On the most immediate level, though, we are looking at an egg – an object strongly connected to the feminine (through its origin), to procreation
(through its primary purpose), and to abjection (through its links with
the "lowness" of bodily function, whether to germinate a chick or feed
a growing girl).

Godard's portion of *Hail Mary* takes these very matters as its main interests, and I suspect that the furor over it was sparked less by its interpretation of a Christian myth than by its insistence on probing that myth's
connections with aspects of bodily life that today's Western religions are
regrettably eager to overlook, undervalue, or deny.

Godard's feature-length contribution to *Hail Mary* opens and closes with
evocations of femininity and abjection. This chapter will refer frequently
to the film's mysterious final image, a full-screen close-up of Mary's mouth
with a striking red lipstick tube hovering alongside it; and the beginning
also involves a woman's mouth. The first scene starts with the intertitle
AT THAT TIME, followed by shots of water shimmering with ripples from
splashing stones. We then see a café table occupied by Joseph and Juliette,
one of his girlfriends. He munches a pastry, and we hear a female voice
utter the film's first spoken words: "Out of my mouth is shit."

We cannot be entirely sure that Juliette is the person speaking, since
her face is not in view. Taking this as a sign of the movie's rich ambiguity,
critic Charles Warren notes three ways we might interpret the voice. We
may associate it (a) with Godard, since the speaker is outside the frame,
as is the filmmaker; (b) with God, since invisibility often suggests author-
ity, and also since Bach organ music accompanies our first look at Juliette
a moment later; or (c) with the Virgin Mary, again because of the music,
and because the film's title calls her to mind. While this makes an interesting trinity of possible readings, I would add that the circumstance of

being off-screen has complicated implications in Godard's work, since he and Miéville associate "the invisible" with controlling powers that may be unfriendly or even dangerous.

Warren observes that the lowly word "shit" does not make a very imposing start for a film about mythic sublimities; but it is the business of *Hail Mary* to intertwine low and high with a spiritual audacity that no previous Godard film had achieved. Warren sees this process at work in the last shot of the credits sequence, where the water has a reddish tinge that evokes another series of meanings: the blood Jesus shed, the blood he instructed his followers to drink, and the blood of Mary's menstruation. (Later she will tell a doctor that her period was "intense" on a Friday, which is the day of the week when Jesus was crucified.) Juliette's statement certainly sounds self-deprecating, but Warren points out that "shit is also fructifying. Excrement nourishes the earth. Menstrual blood is excrement. Any blood . . . is excrement. Speech, writing, art, are all in a sense excrement."[6]

So is motion-picture film, which carries visible traces of bodies, actions, and ideas. André Bazin, the theorist who most influenced Godard's early career, built his commitment to realism on the notion that the cinematic image is a "tracing" of the material world, and therefore shares in the actuality of that world. Françoise Dolto, a theorist who appears to have strongly influenced Godard's conceptualization of *Hail Mary,* evokes a different sort of tracing when she observes that "thought may be fecundated by an idea coming from elsewhere, without knowing who gave it to us."[7] This is what the film's Professor character will claim for all human existence when he says a bit later, "Life was willed, desired, anticipated, organized, programmed by a determined intelligence." Mary will say the same in more personal terms: "I think the spirit acts on the body, breathes through it, veils it to make it fairer than it is."

Godard echoes Dolto when he calls Mary a "virgin image. No traces. No imprints. . . . *To be virgin is to be available,* to be free."[8] But not surprisingly, Godard's conception of the uncontaminated virgin points to low imperatives of the body as well as high potentialities of the soul. "Let the soul be body," Mary says in the film. During her night of torment before Jesus' birth, her pain comes partly from seeing herself as "a body fallen from a soul" and "a soul imprisoned by a body," rather than a harmonious unity in whom body and soul are indistinguishable. Wresting wholeness from plurality is a key theme of *Hail Mary,* and Godard grapples with this challenge no less than his heroine does, shaping a singular cinematic work from a multitude of visibly (and audibly) fractured components.

All this is set in motion by the first portion of the first scene, with the suggestive splits we have noted among word, image, music, and action. Also established here is the film's ambience of modern, everyday reality, against which the story's biblically inspired events will be placed.

The scene continues with painfully commonplace bickering between Joseph and Juliette, who are sadly at odds over their obviously poor relationship. A couple of their statements are significant with regard to the movie's larger concerns. Juliette says, "all women want something unique," a sentiment Mary will echo with specific reference to herself. Turning to bodily interests, Joseph says with an ironic tone that "men think they enter a woman"; this indicates his skepticism about rapport between the sexes, and makes an unwitting joke vis-à-vis the virgin pregnancy that Mary, his soon-to-be fiancée, will undergo.

We then meet the film's title character. She is playing in a basketball game – the sort of everyday, "profane" touch that outraged the movie's detractors – but it is evident that other, deeper concerns preoccupy her. Godard signals this with sound-track music (a well-known Bach prelude, also familiar from Schubert's popular "Ave Maria") and with a striking close-up revealing her pensive, distracted attitude. Her thoughts become clear to us when she speaks in voice-over:

> I wondered if some event would happen in my life. I've had only the shadow of love . . . in fact, the shadow of a shadow, like the reflection of a water-lily in a pond, not quiet but shaken by ripples in the water, so that even the reflection is deformed and not yours.

Her thoughts are also reflected by Godard's editing, as he cuts between the moon and Mary poised with her basketball. This suggests that her mundane activity is the earthly counterpart of a more cosmic *something*, which might become hers if she is able to leave herself sufficiently open, available, virginal.

We have met two women, Mary and Juliette, so far in the story. Now we meet a third: Eva, a university student. We also meet a Professor who is closely linked with her in the narrative as he teaches her, romances her, and tries to initiate her (with other pupils) into a sort of cosmic philosophy he is developing.

Holding a Rubik's Cube in her hand, Eva gazes with an expression as distracted as Mary's – it is hard to say whether she is looking inward, outward, or (most likely) both – while the Professor states his hypotheses. He begins by repeating the widely held theory that life on earth originated from a primordial soup excited by solar heat; but then he refutes this argument, claiming that the universe has not existed long enough for this to occur through random action. He illustrates his point with a diagram showing a patch of the universe as seen from an edgewise angle. (This image resembles a closed mouth, anticipating the shot of Mary's open mouth at the very end of the film.) He explains that the diagram shows light being absorbed by a common form of bacteria, demonstrating his theory that life on earth came from outer space – and that earthly creatures may therefore be called true extraterrestrials!

This statement brings into *Hail Mary* the kind of boundary-blurring that Godard has always loved. Humans and aliens, past cause and present result, the swarming earth and intergalactic space – all are pretty much the same if you take the Professor's long view of things. He carries this another step when he says that life arrived on our planet by design rather than chance. To support this notion, he asks a student named Pascal to "solve" a Rubik's Cube while Eva covers his eyes and directs his actions by saying "yes" and "no." Random twisting would provide a solution in 1.35 trillion years, the Professor informs them, but intelligent thought reduces this to a couple of minutes.

This is interesting stuff, and Godard gives the Professor enough time to make an impression on us as well as the students – not surprisingly, since Godard is a science buff himself, and probably thinks about this sort of thing quite a lot. His films of the eighties and nineties sometimes show a healthy streak of self-mockery, however, and here he throws a couple of gentle jibes at the Professor that may also be aimed at his own pretentions. When the Professor mentions extraterrestrials, the camera shows no reverence for his lecture, but cuts to an unexpected close-up of Pascal's weird (unearthly?) haircut – which keeps filling the screen while the teacher discusses the proliferation of life, as if Pascal's wild foliage were an amusing stand-in for more primitive forms of existence. The scene retains an underlying seriousness, though, emphasized by Bach on the sound track and immaculately textured lighting in shots of Eva's face and Pascal's hands, as they solve the cube in almost no time at all.

Two other details of this scene deserve comment. One is a brief exchange of dialogue: Pascal asks the Professor if he was "exiled for these ideas," and the teacher replies, "These and others." This makes him one of the displaced intellectuals – Jerzy in *Passion* is another – with whom Godard strongly identifies, partly because of his mixed Swiss and French background, and partly because his artistic predilections have led him closer to the margin than to the mainstream of the cultural world.

The other is a pair of references (perhaps unwitting) to James Joyce's great *Ulysses*. The first: As she guides Pascal's twisting of the cube, Eva's instructions of "yes" and "no" culminate in a zesty "yes ... yes ... yes" worthy of Molly Bloom's soliloquy. The second: Pascal's final question to the Professor – "Is the law of falling bodies because life fell from the sky?" – recalls Joyce's use of falling-body velocity as a metaphor for original sin. Godard remarked in a 1965 interview that Joyce is "of no interest to the cinema," and in a 1957 article he cited *Ulysses* as the sort of book that "conclusively seals all exits round it."[9] Could be, but perhaps Godard doth protest too much. His best films contain such strong echoes of Joyce's punning ambiguity and rambunctious carnivalism that denials of influence are difficult to credit.

Hail Mary is heading toward matters more mystical than Rubik's Cubes and velocity measurements, of course; yet the supernatural side of Mary's life is introduced in a naturalistic way, with flourishes exemplifying Godard's patented mix of the comic, the portentous, and the paradoxical. An airplane swoops low over a wintry woods at night; Mary reacts to its noise while brushing her hair at a mirror; the plane sweeps over a tangle of power and communication wires; wind howls as the sun sets behind a distant horizon. Then a wide-eyed girl gazes through a light-dappled window and walks through an airport lobby, where she and an adult man – Gabriel, the angel sent to inform Mary of her extraordinary destiny – stoop to fasten the lace of his red-white-and-blue saddle shoe. They do the job together with one hand each, like a party stunt.

Now we meet Joseph again, reading philosophy (to his dog!) in the front seat of the taxi that he drives for a living. The angel and his little-girl assistant scuffle with strangers in the terminal, then slide into Joseph's cab, where the girl chides Gabriel – or the actor playing him – for getting his dialogue wrong. Setting off to find Mary, they locate her at her father's service station. All this activity makes for a lively sequence, full of change and movement, yet hard to pin down in terms of a consistent mood. Much of it is accompanied by Antonín Dvořák's cello concerto, which lends a keenly dramatic atmosphere at some moments, but stops and starts almost comically at others. Similarly, the early shots cue us to expect something momentous, yet misunderstandings abound when Gabriel and his helper finally arrive at Mary's place: She is angry at Joseph for showing up when they don't have a date, and her father is so furious that he almost clobbers the startled boyfriend with a wrench.

Wind howls again as Mary asks what's going on. "Mary, it is you," Gabriel answers – not a very informative reply, but she accepts it with intuitive reverence, calmly bowing her head. We cut to the darkened sky with a tiny crescent moon on the right, balanced by a glowing traffic light on the left. (As we watch, it changes to red, a color of passion and danger.) Joseph sits in the taxi while Gabriel and Mary enact the Annunciation, their mood serious but hardly melodramatic or even particularly emotional. The angel tells Mary she will have a child. "By whom?" she asks, adding, "I sleep with no one." Not unreasonably, Joseph is instantly suspicious of the whole arrangement, urging the visitors away and telling Mary not to "play innocent."

Mary repeats her plaintive, entirely sensible question – "By whom?" – and Gabriel's helper now speaks up: "Be pure. Be rough. Follow thy way." (Her words in French have a chantlike cadence: "Sois pure. Sois dure. Ne cherche que ta voie.") Again, it is hard to fault Mary for being perplexed by the reponses she's getting. Like many religious texts, they seem to promise profundity; but when one actually tries to figure them out, they are less like the Professor's scientific charts than like the slippery "word games" that Godard has always valued for their improvisatory freedom.

"My way? But the voice or the word?" asks Mary, new to the game but quickly getting into its spirit.[10] "Don't be silly," the child retorts."I know where you're going, and soon you will, too. Don't forget!"

Gabriel repeats the last words, adding a subtle touch of abject philosophy: "Don't forget, what goes in goes out. And what goes out goes in!" Whereupon the visitors zoom away in Joseph's taxi, leaving Mary to slump exhausted upon a gasoline pump, then rise and skip almost merrily to the building. The cab's departure reveals a crisp white arrow painted on the pavement; it points to a sign reading "bonne route" (i.e., "happy motoring!") on a wall behind Mary, who seems both mystified and exhilarated by these strange events.

Her skipping walk rhymes with the beginning of the next shot, which shows the uneven progress of the Professor and several students along a rough-hewn strip of rock thrusting from the coast into the sea. (A couple of stones are thrown into the water, also rhyming this scene with the first moments of the film.) The group pauses to rest, chatting about Hölderlin and *Scientific American* magazine; one student describes how a friend "rigged wiring to warm the ants in winter. He wanted to keep them awake . . . hoping they'd use that leisure time to invent things. . . . Music, maybe."

Music swells, in the form of Dvořák's cello concerto, as we cut to Mary ironing her basketball jersey and murmuring to herself, "There's no escape." We have seen her jersey before, at the basketball court, when she exercised in dancelike movements to the "Ave Maria" prelude. The number it prominently displays – 10 – would be a throwaway detail in a conventional movie, but in a Godard film we might expect it to carry various connotations, which indeed it does. Three of these will be enough to suggest the density of meaning that runs through *Hail Mary*, as through most of Godard's other works:

- Mathematically, the number 10 is fundamental to the decimal system, deeply ingrained in Western scientific and philosophical thought.
- Graphically, it suggests a stylized sexual metaphor – an upright 1 followed by an open 0, corresponding with many other images in the movie, such as Mary's lipstick and open mouth in the closing scene.
- Symbolically, it represents the point where the numerical system (like the human hand) runs out of single digits, and proceeds to infinity by recombining the previous ones. It is therefore a symbol of limitation, culmination, renewal, and unending possibility.

The film now begins a period of rapid scene shifting between Mary and Joseph, who are trying to gain some understanding of what is happening to them, and the Professor and his students, who are seeking a similarly cosmic knowledge through more secular means.

Joseph arrives to see Mary, honking his taxi horn and charging up to her house. "Miracles don't exist," he aggressively declares. "Kiss me," he wistfully demands. His most revealing phrase, though, is a plaintive "What is this?" as he stands against the sky in a low-angle shot, clearly more mystified than angered at his current predicament. So is Mary, who responds, "There's no escape for us," touching her pubic area in wonder over the new set of significances her body has acquired.

"Let's go on with our story!" the Professor suggests, as an intertitle (AT THAT TIME) reminds us of the movie's biblical provenance. Imagine our descendants 100 million years from now, the teacher continues, addressing Eva as birds fly above. Using their unimaginable wisdom, this future society will observe that "the supposedly fixed balance of the universe is subtly changing." And naturally, the Professor concludes, the future citizens will try to preserve life as they know it. Such is the resistance of human beings to change and evolution,

This scholarly speculation is interrupted as we cut to Mary and Joseph walking grumpily out of Mary's house. Mary fidgets with her basketball as Joseph demands some physical affection. "Kiss me . . . just once," he asks.

"I do kiss you. You should trust me," she replies, and the meaning of this moment lies in the fact that while her words and behaviors do not match – she says "I do kiss you" while not kissing him at all – she is not merely substituting empty words for authentic action. Rather, she is reassuring Joseph that on some other existential level – one that runs parallel to their present situation, exquisitely close but never quite intersecting with it – she *is* kissing him, perhaps spiritually rather than physically, yet with all the joy and fervor he might desire.

At the moment, however, Joseph is not tuned into such a high philosophical plane. Frustrated and unconvinced, he knocks away her basketball and pushes her roughly onto the hood of his taxi, thrusting his face toward hers. Dvořák swells dramatically. Pinned beneath him, she turns her face to one side, making her lips inaccessible; then she turns toward him, fixing her eyes directly on his; then she turns to the other side, hiding her face completely. He retreats from the shot as she relaxes her body but remains in the same subdued position.

Also subdued is the moon, peeking tentatively from a bank of clouds as we cut to the night sky. On the sound track, the Professor continues his hypothesis that earthly life was set in motion by a "prior intelligence," which then left it to struggle for existence in "a pitiless universe." The words "pitiless universe" bring a quick flashback to Mary pinned beneath Joseph on the taxi hood – a facile trope on Godard's part, or perhaps a touch of dark humor, contrasting cosmological angst with romantic emotionalism.

More obviously ironic is the Professor's remark that the astonishing intelligence of computers is what led him to think life was "programmed" by a very smart outsider. The images following his praise of computers – silent shots of rippling water; a gentle sun shining through branches and sinking behind the horizon; Eva's earnest, thoughtful face – have a natural grace and beauty that seem decisively distant from the clicking, whirring world of artificial intelligence. To his credit, the Professor appears to realize this. He rattles on about life being "encoded" in materials like magnesium or borium; but on his notepad he circles the word "God," and he agrees with Eva that the "secret of Creation" is simply "that Voice deep in our consciences [that] whispers, if we listen: You are born of something, somewhere else, in Heaven. Seek, and you will find more than you dream of." He then takes his group out of the woods, in a long-distance profile shot that vaguely recalls Ingmar Bergman's journey into the land of myth and memory, *The Seventh Seal*.

Continuing the film's alternation between the Professor's group and the escalating troubles of Joseph and Mary, we return to the young couple and their quarrel.[11] They have made little progress, still hashing out the same contentious points. Joseph demands "the truth" and accuses Mary of "sleeping around" with "guys with big cocks." Mary defends her innocence, insists on her sincerity – "Maybe the words come out wrong, or it's my voice, but it's the truth" – and says again, "I do kiss you," still steadfastly keeping her distance. Prominent props within this scene include Joseph's dark glasses (recalling "The Book of Mary," where sunglasses symbolized a refusal to "see clearly") and Mary's basketball, associated with the moon and with her ethereal dreams. The ball also rhymes with Mary's swelling abdomen; at one point Juliette pushes it directly at her romantic rival's belly, mingling athletic playfulness with jealous aggression.

Another important image shows the sky filled with clouds just as Joseph says, "A child must come from somewhere!" This may lead us to think of heaven; or to ponder the vastness and variety of nature; or simply to remember the general direction of outer space, where the Professor's bacteria live. In any case, we soon come back to earth, ringing with the commingled sounds of Dvořák's concerto, Bach's choral music, and the noise of Mary's basketball game.

"It's over, Mary! Ciao!" calls Joseph in a last angry voice-over, but his words make little impression on Mary, who is already ensconced in the next part of the story. Seated in a doctor's office, waiting for a gynecological examination that may cast more light on her situation, she passes the time by perusing a magazine and smiling at a little boy. Godard throws in more humor here, as Mary eavesdrops on the conversation of two men, one of whom wants to understand the dreams that have been troubling him. Their dialogue sounds like a surreal comedy routine:

FIRST MAN: There must be a reason [for your dreams]. You should take notes.
SECOND MAN: Yes, but I can't write, so I draw.
FIRST MAN: If it's a picture, you can't forget.
SECOND MAN: So I must learn to write if I want to forget!

Godard's message has changed little over the years. Images have too much power for their own good, but words have a power that is greater still – the power to be forgotten, erased, expunged. Mary listens with a smile.

The physician is a stereotypical doctor, distracted by phone calls but questioning Mary with the familiarity and concern of an old family friend. "I have a pain!" she blurts out, adding "in my belly" more quietly. She appears somewhat distraught before the examination begins, but doesn't hesitate to confront the doctor with a question on her mind: "Does the

Mary and Joseph: Emotions run high between the frequently confused and troubled protagonists (Myriem Roussel, Thierry Rode) of *Hail Mary*.

soul have a body?" He answers that it's the other way around, and she appears surprised.

The doctor good-naturedly acknowledges that men aren't very good at understanding women. "All you can know is what a man already knew: There's a mystery there," he admits. Still, he seems as skeptical as Joseph about the cause of Mary's pregnancy, laughing off her claim that her conception "wasn't with any body." She reaffirms her ideal of physical and spiritual integrity, saying that virginity "should mean being available, or free, not being hurt." The doctor is impatient, but after examining her internally he states his inescapable conclusion: "It's true that it's true."

This scene's cinematic tone is a mixture of cool precision, with its crisply clinical setting, and emotional warmth, framing Mary in affectionate close-ups and allowing the doctor moments of clear compassion and empathy. Mary's most notable gesture is to assume a near-fetal position – curling almost into a ball, embracing her knees with her arms – as if she needed to convey the reality of her unborn child to the unbelieving world.

Bach's music also comes and goes during the episode, underscoring its miraculous dimension.

Joseph, meanwhile, is hovering between the enlightenment he needs and the stubbornness he can't seem to shake. "It must be mine!" he mutters while standing near his taxi, even though the impossibility of this should be more obvious to him than anyone. His refusal to accept the reality of divine intervention is understandably human, but higher powers – perhaps Gabriel the angel, perhaps Godard the filmmaker, perhaps a combination of both – are evidently trying to raise his consciousness. Two shots show him at the doors of his taxi, and between these images – just after he gazes intently toward the camera – there is a quick shot of Mary climbing into her bathtub, closing a door to hide her nudity. A second vision follows as he climbs into the taxi: Gabriel and the little girl, standing with motionless intensity against a slowly flowing river. Joseph walks toward the river to look around, and the place where they stood is empty – but again his glance touches off an image of Mary, in the water of her bathtub. Although the skeptical Joseph and the blessed Mary are separated by physical distance and metaphysical misunderstanding, the film seems determined to align them on some sort of spiritual wavelength.

Since nudity plays a significant role in *Hail Mary,* and since Godard's use of nudity has caused considerable commotion among skeptical critics – sometimes with good reason – this is an opportune time to pause and discuss the issue.

Godard's fondness for female nudity dates back to the early 1960s and has elicited a wide range of responses. Some have praised it for raising an audacious challenge to prudish limitations on screen portrayals of the body; others have condemned it as yet another instance of male-controlled cinema objectifying and exploiting the female form. All such responses have been appropriate with regard to one Godard film or another, but it's important to note that his uses of nudity (and other expressions of female sexuality) have been much too varied for any single formula to take into account.

Even an example as brief and unerotic as the image of Mary in her bathtub allows for more than one interpretation. It might be called a typical case of Godard's incorrigible voyeurism, as clinical and uncomprehending as the doctor's touch in the examining-room scene; or one might find it a lyric celebration of the body as a sublime substance, approaching spiritual enlightenment not through *transcendence* of the physical but through scrupulous *awareness* of materiality. One could even find both

Female forms: Issues of gender exploitation and objectification have arisen peri-
odically with regard to Godard's works, including *2 or 3 Things I Know about
Her* with Marina Vlady and Anny Duperey, one of several films in which he uses
prostitution for metaphorical purposes.

readings to be valid, given Godard's penchant for ambiguity and ambivalence.

This said, it is incontestable that Godard's rebellion against the commercial film establishment has missed a beat or two when it comes to the
subject of commodified nudity. In the early *Contempt* he ruthlessly sati-
rized a character representing a Hollywood-style producer (Jeremiah Prokosch, played by Jack Palance) for ogling projection-room footage of a
naked actress playing a mermaid; but twenty-two years later, how do we
separate Godard from Prokosch as we watch his *Hail Mary* images of an
all-woman basketball team prancing gorgeously around a gym, or gaze
at the conventionally attractive actresses he uses in so many of the movie's
important roles?

Turning specifically to Joseph's vision of Mary in her bathtub, the first
things we notice are (a) that she is naked and (b) that this is a *vision* in
more than one sense of that multilayered term. To the extent that the vision exists in Joseph's imagination, it suggests that his sexual desires are

185

still alive and hungry at this stage of the story. To the extent that the vision is provided by God, it suggests that the Supreme Being is not averse to communicating with mortal man by means of imagery with a surprising degree of feminine allure. To the extent that the vision is designed and executed by Godard, it suggests that he takes a conscious and specifically masculine pleasure in the godlike powers of being a movie director. The latter observation is supported by Mary's voice-over as she bathes, photographed in a sustained high-angle shot:

> Yet I rejoiced in giving my body to the eyes of Him who has become my Master forever, and glanced at this wondrous being. For in truth, He was that, then and always, not for His looks nor for what He did, but in the silent power of what He was, the power gathered up in Him, vast as a mountain raised toward the sky [*élevée vers le ciel*] that you can't measure or name, but only feel.

When she rejoices in giving her body to the eyes of a "master" too vast, removed, and powerful for a mere human to understand, could Mary be celebrating her submission to the pleasure of visibility itself, including the visibility afforded by cinema, which in this case means Godard and his movie camera? And given the improvisatory and personal nature of Godard's filmmaking, could actress Myriem Roussel be speaking for herself to some extent? Neither possibility can be excluded, any more than Mary's divine revelations and the Professor's scientific theories can be said to cancel each other out, or to be displaced by some other "correct" viewpoint. There is a troubling undertone to the idea of Mary/Roussel reveling in exposure to film's mechanical apparatuses and anonymous audiences; after all, the history of cinema is partly a history of performers "giving their bodies" to narratives and images over which they have little control, and women have been especially deprived of such control on both sides of the camera.

Still, many signs point to *Hail Mary* as a serious and even reverent work of art, and in this context the vision scene conveys a sense of genuine devotion toward both God and cinema. Godard has always seen film as a means toward some end that is greater and more life-enhancing than spectacle for its own sake, and Mary's submission to its power is a vicarious expression of his own willingness to serve its potential for social, aesthetic, and spiritual good. Perhaps this is why an exquisitely setting sun replaces Mary's body soon after her voice-over begins, remaining until the scene concludes with bird cries and a brief reappearance of the sensuous Dvořák theme.

As a final note on Mary's nakedness, there is a long tradition of nudity in religious painting and sculpture. This resonates throughout *Hail Mary,* and not only in connection with the heroine. Adam and Eve, the Bible's most famous nudes, provide models for the Professor and Eva; indeed, the Professor repeatedly calls his companion Eve rather than Eva, and she munches on a heavily symbolic apple in a place called the Paradise Villa, as well as displaying her naked body there.

Mary does not customarily appear nude in traditional art, so Godard may be accused of breaking with the past in this regard. Still, the genre of painting known as *Maria lactans* has focused attention on her breasts ever since the fourteenth century.[12] Mary's breasts have a dual meaning in these images. On one hand, they are the physical organs that nourished Christ as a child so he could live in human form; on the other, they symbolize the divine nourishment given to Him – and all who believe in Him – by God through His holy mother. One purpose of *Maria lactans* is therefore to convey the materiality and mortality of both Mary and her divine yet human son.

It is also worth noting that Jesus appears fully or partially nude in many significant paintings, sometimes with his genitals exposed and even aroused. Art historian Leo Steinberg argues that such pictures represent "God's assumption of human weakness," affirming not the "superior prowess" ascribed to the penis in other contexts but rather "condescension to kinship" with humanity, and "the Creator's self-abasement to his creature's condition."[13] Jesus' nudity in Renaissance art is therefore a sign of humility and vulnerability. Mary embraces the same qualities in Godard's film when she speaks of bodily submission to a "wondrous being" charged with great and silent power. This gratification transforms her nudity from the stuff of exploitative prurience to that of transcendent ecstasy.[14]

Mary is clothed, casual, and back in the everyday world as we see her on the phone with Joseph, bickering with him while eating an apple. (The apple links her with young Mary's apple-eye operation in Miéville's film, and also with Eva of the present story.) She and Joseph trade wisecracks related to water, a leitmotif of the film, and to *Hamlet,* with which Joseph doesn't appear to be familiar – even though Mary, also from a working-class background, quotes it readily. Still deeply frustrated, Joseph angrily slams the phone booth with his hand, and Godard boldly cuts to a sun-filled sky populated only by a tiny bird. Its dizzy flight (accompanied by the soaring Dvořák theme) evokes the human confusion nagging Joseph, while suggesting the inklings of spiritual acceptance that may at last be starting to penetrate his thoughts.

The references to *Hamlet* foreground the movie's subtheme of worldly knowledge, and this remains in focus as we cut to Eva and the Professor in a comfortable lakeside room. "Night changes its own look and meaning," he says, as they stand before a window tinted blue by the darkness outside; together they identify the source (Heidegger) and date (winter 1959) of that sentence.

This moment is an intellectualized mirror image of the childish banter that Mary and Joseph have just exchanged. Still, the thoughtfulness of Eva and the Professor has limits. Eva complains that the Professor always "clams up" when talk turns to politics. His response is significant: "I think politics today must be the voice of horror." Eva answers with a variation of the question posed by Mary to Gabriel's assistant: "The voice? But the way or the word?" And the Professor answers with a finality that hovers between realism and nihilism: "The voice of horror of which nothing can be said."

His statements recall the scene in *Weekend* when Tom Thumb demands extermination of "the big thieves," meaning the capitalists whose power/knowledge manipulations have created a "world . . . full of horror." We may also remember that the revolutionary Kalfon, another user of this carefully chosen word, wishes to traumatize the world with "even more horror." The mention of "horror" in *Hail Mary* thus connects this mystically *religious* film to one of Godard's most aggressively *political* works. This directs our attention to a chain of political references that are often overlooked because the biblical content of *Hail Mary* tends to overshadow them.

Some of these allusions refer to Czechoslovakia, apparently the Professor's homeland. That country was also the subject of Godard's collage-documentary *Pravda,* made in 1969 and focusing on the nation after its invasion by Soviet forces. Czechoslovakia was still part of the Soviet Union's socialist bloc in the mid-1980s, which points to a complex set of intellectual and emotional associations for Godard, the erstwhile Marxist/Maoist who is now more concerned with aestheticized and spiritualized interests. We know the Professor was "exiled" from his country because of his theories, including his view that human life was preordained; and Eva has told him that their Paradise Villa is "as pretty as Czechoslovakia," using the name of his country as a ready-made "paradise lost" metaphor. He refers to his origins again while placing a John Coltrane record on the phonograph. ("You can't find that in Prague," he says.) These fleeting references are both nostalgic *for* and critical *of* a place that (a) sets a standard for beauty, yet (b) casts people out for having unapproved ideas – and, adding insult to injury, allows no access to exquisite American jazz like the music we now hear on the sound track.

In other words, the Professor is depicted as political and apolitical at the same time. If he "clams up" about politics, this is because he is aware of the power it carries ("the voice of horror") and also because he dislikes the responsibilities it entails. "A smoke, a sax solo, that's all a man wants," he apathetically muses. Such ambivalence aligns the Professor closely with Godard himself. (As noted, Godard uses an Eastern European man as an on-screen alter ego more than once.) The logic behind this is not hard to figure out. Well into middle age, Godard has come to see himself as a marginalized figure quite similar to the Professor – a dreamer of daring hypotheses now cast out of the country/industry that ought to be his rightful place, seeking a modicum of comfort while passing his courageous ideas along to the bold (and beautiful) new generation that must carry on his grand endeavor when the time comes for him to smoke his last smoke and savor his last sax solo.

Godard does not seem happy about this situation, but like the Professor he would rather explore its existential contours and ponder its aesthetic, psychological, and spiritual possibilities than wage an active struggle to escape from it. Interestingly, his attitude in 1985 can easily be traced to views he expressed much earlier, as in the 1966 narration for *2 or 3 Things I Know about Her.* "I'm only looking for reasons to be happy," he said in that film, sounding very much like the Professor in his tobacco-and-saxophone stage. "I discover that memory is our chief reason for living, if we have one," the *2 or 3 Things* monologue continued, prefiguring the nostalgia of *Hail Mary,* "and secondly . . . the capacity to live in the present and to enjoy it . . . just as one found it, in its own unique set of circumstances."

Here is a concise affirmation of Godard's improvisatory spirit, still clearly felt in *Hail Mary.* Here also is his love for the chance moment ("just as one found it") that erases the division between human planning and the endless potential of the world surrounding us. Like most Godard movies, *Hail Mary* is deliberately fractured by narrative leaps, visual incongruities, and verbal digressions. While such gestures have many different causes, as we have noted in discussions of other films, a key motivation is Godard's effort to locate his works in a sort of eternal present or continuous now that acknowledges little debt to the past or obligation to the future. If memory is really a "chief reason for living," this is not because it revivifies the past but because it enlivens the here-and-now by making the past a part of it. By being so fragmented and collaged, Godard's movies make their own past events hard to remember and future ones impossible to anticipate. This is another interest he shares with Beat writers like Kerouac and Ginsberg, and with avant-garde filmmakers like Stan Brakhage and Paul Sharits, who also strive to conquer time's tyranny in works characterized by mercurial flux and flow.

Despite the challenging structures of individual films, Godard's consistency in these matters indicates a solid sense of continuity among past, present, and future within his cinema as a whole. This is illustrated by the multiple links connecting *Hail Mary* with prior works like *Weekend* and *2 or 3 Things I Know about Her*. The narration in the latter film about memory and living in the present, for instance, occurs in a scene that features a car, a gas station, and a woman named Juliette, long before those elements showed up in *Hail Mary*.

Also prefigured in *2 or 3 Things* is the Professor's ambivalence about politics. "My aim," the off-screen whisperer in *2 or 3 Things* says, is "for the simplest things to come into being in the world of humans, for man's spirit to possess them, a new world where men and things would interrelate harmoniously. This is really more of a political issue than a poetic one." Politics are favored over poetics in this sentence, but it is revealing that Godard frames the statement in a subtly defensive way. Even in *2 or 3 Things*, produced during his highly politicized years, he sees the conjunctions between "people" and "things" as being so ephemeral that poetics are never far away from a meaningful exploration of them. "Should I have described Juliette or the leaves?" asks the narrator. "It was really impossible to describe both, so let us just say that the leaves and Juliette fluttered gently in that late October afternoon." In the end, it is the here-and-now beauty of a landscape and a person – the different faces of nature merged into an immediate, encompassing moment – that matters most to the self-described "writer and painter" who speaks to us from the sound track with Godard's own voice.[15]

While the narrator of *2 or 3 Things* seeks a harmonious unity between humanity and materiality, the heroine of *Hail Mary* seeks something even more profound: an awareness of the physical and the spiritual as inseparable aspects of a single grand continuum. This is a philosophical extension of Godard's longtime refusal to see a contradiction between images and objects, or between "fiction" and "documentary" forms.

After the romantic scene between Eva and the Professor, we hear Mary quote from a book she's reading, ignoring her father as he leaves the house muttering about business and gas-pump figures:

I think the spirit acts on the body, breathes through it, veils it to make it fairer than it is. For what is flesh alone? You may see it and feel only disgust. You may see it only in the gutter, drunken, or in the coffin, dead. The world's as full of flesh as a grocer's counter is of candles at the start of winter. But not until you've brought a candle home and lit it can it give you comfort.

On one level, this is another statement about cinema, in itself a mere photochemical process containing only the life "breathed through it" by artists. More important, it is a tribute to the elevated status acquired by the body when we see it as more than flesh alone. Mary knows the gratification that comes from realizing the oneness of body and spirit. The joy she expressed in her bathtub monologue, about giving her body to the eyes of the master, resulted partly from her alertness to the fact that body without spirit is inconsequential, whereas body veiled by spirit is sublimity itself. No wonder she still skips with happiness as she checks the gas pumps and goes back indoors; no wonder nature responds by veiling her father's business in a flurry of snow almost photogenic enough for a Jacques Demy musical.

As for the other characters, Joseph's dogged pursuit of Mary indicates a spiritual as well as material itch that will lead him to perceive the interrelatedness of body and spirit quite soon. Eva and the Professor are harder cases; the last thing we see during their romantic interlude is naked Eva smoking a cigarette while sax music plays, fulfilling the Professor's lazy pronouncement about "all a man wants."

Also trapped on the level of body-as-biology is Juliette, a character we haven't spent much time with lately. She keeps flirting with Joseph; he keeps resisting; and all she can think to ask is, "Don't you like my body?" He offers vague rejoinders like, "That's not it" and "I don't know." She responds with displays of frustation as futile (yet understandable) as his own anger toward Mary's elusiveness. "I'm a real woman," she reasonably points out, only to be met with "I'd like to love you, but I don't know how." Giving up, for now at least, she leaves for home.

So does Joseph, but a lingering shot of a quarter-moon in the cloud-filled sky suggests that another significant event may be imminent. The pint-sized moon even foreshadows the form this event will take: an encounter with the little girl who accompanies Gabriel on his mission, and then a bizarre session with her and the angel himself.

Joseph spots the girl through a shop window, steps inside, and chases her to a clothing rack where Gabriel is trying on jackets. Joesph paws the angel and his garment, as if making sure the angel is getting a good fit; the girl reprimands him for complicating things. "If God exists, nothing's allowed," Joseph mutters. A close-up of Juliette cuts in, and Gabriel asks Joseph about this sort-of-girlfriend who keeps hovering around the edges of their story. "What are you doing with that tramp?" the angel demands. This upsets the little girl ("No, Uncle Gabriel. Not like that!") and Gabriel starts whining ("When he's around I forget my lines!").

The heavenly visitors then start a lengthy critique of Joseph; at different moments it resembles a therapy session, a schoolroom exercise, a surreal catechism, and even a parody of the "criticism" sessions promoted by Maoist ideology. Picking up a notepad, the girl ticks off a hilariously diverse list of flaws in Joseph's personality: "He wants to know everything. He doesn't even know how to walk his dog. He's scared of the hole. He has no taste in ties. He lacks trust. He wears blind man's glasses." Throwing off his tough-guy demeanor and displaying a merciful side – quite a change for this unangelic angel – Gabriel whispers forgiving responses to each point. "Like everyone," he says repeatedly. "That's no fault."

One function of this scene is to continue the rambunctious relationship between Joseph and Gabriel, who engage in a sort of theological slapstick. Another is to draw Joseph a step closer to accepting an obedient role in the great events that have overtaken his life. The scene also develops what might be called the movie's spiritual algebra, whereby a scattered set of signs and symbols gradually converge into a diffuse but suggestive whole.

The notion of spiritual algebra can be taken almost literally, given Godard's fondness for scientific concepts. (This is another taste – along with jazz, smoking, and attractive women – that he and the Professor share.) When the angel says that Joseph is "a real nothing," therefore, we can read this mathematically: Joseph = zero.

Joseph is naturally displeased with this remark. "Zero equals zero," he murmurs a little later, in what's apparently meant as a snappy retort. Gabriel stays on a mathematical track, questioning Joseph with the bullying air of a nasty teacher. "What's the common denominator between zero and Mary?" he asks, pulling off Joseph's glasses, waving his hand before his face, and hitting him on the head. "Mary's body!" he cries when his "pupil" fails to respond, adding, "Answer, nitwit!" The best Joseph can come up with is, "She'll make a fool of me" and "If some guy's knocked her up. . . ." He still isn't grasping the heavenly message, so Gabriel literally slaps him around, incongruously trying to knock some sense ("We're not *some* guy!") and humility ("Trust! And love, you jerk!") into the hopelessly confused human.

For all the craziness of this scene, its play with the nothing–zero equation has connotations that are quite serious. Gabriel's assistant carries these further when she accuses Joseph of being "scared of the hole," another seemingly offhand phrase with many meanings. Most immediately, it refers to Joseph's dread of being a zero or a "real nothing," with no significant role in the mysterious drama surrounding him. It also conveys his trepidations about the body, and particularly the orifices or "holes" through which bodies (including women's bodies, which are currently troubling him) open out to the larger world: the vagina that Mary withholds from him, the anus to which Juliette alludes in the film's first scene, the mouth that Mary will display in the last. In line with this, and with Godard's psychoanalytical interests, the phrase also refers to Joseph's castration anxieties, caused by his powerlessness in relation to Mary and Gabriel.

Most profoundly, it refers to Joseph's fear of losing his grasp on the material realm, which he thinks will happen if he abandons his familiar human perspectives in favor of the spiritual perceptions being urged on him by Mary and the angels. Mary foresees the glories to be gained by submitting to Gabriel's message and the supernatural task she's been assigned; but Joseph's lack of vision ("He wears blind man's glasses, the dolt!") makes him dread the loss of physical certainty that a leap into metaphysical adventure would entail.

The scene ends inconclusively, but Joseph's last word – a muttered "love," echoing Gabriel's exhoration to love and trust – indicates a ray of hope for him. Gabriel's helper underscores this by silently mouthing the phrase "Yes, love is. . . ." Godard reaffirms the optimistic mood by cutting to a gorgeous seascape dappled with sunlight and then another huge, golden sun glowing in an exquisite sky.

Everything about this scene has been hectic and fragmented. While the next portion of the story is also charged with Godard's usual nervous energy, its narrative content could almost have been lifted from a conventional drama about lovers who have difficulty coming to terms.

It begins with a moment that directly anticipates the end of the film. Mary enters a store, shows interest in lipstick tubes on a cosmetics counter, then walks away without trying or buying the merchandise. It's important to note that the items she rejects have strong associations with materialism, consumerism, and the idea of femininity as a cluster of performances and masquerades dictated by social convention.

Cut to a room where Joseph is resting in bed, reading a book called *Tomorrow the Dogs*. He and Mary will surely make a good couple: Since the lipstick-counter scene she has been carrying a volume on Francis of Assisi, history's most animal-friendly saint. Mary hands her book to Joseph, who reads the hyperbolic ad copy on the jacket: "Into the maze of life goes the dashing young man . . . to be knight, lord, a great prince, he wants it all. But someone unseen awaits him without weapon, without title, without pride: God!"

Joseph wants none of this high-flown stuff, but Mary is entertained by the saint's habit of giving names to the elements like "Sister Rain" and "Brother Fire," an affectionate gesture that echoes this movie's own love of nature. Still obsessed with his own frustrations, Joseph impatiently asks what St. Francis calls the body. Mary looks up the answer – "Brother Donkey" – and seems to approve of it, perhaps because it reflects her view of the body as a support or infrastructure for the soul.

Back on the subject of bodies, Joesph starts pushing his case with Mary again. "Why does my body repel you?" he plaintively asks. Then he adds, "Don't say 'I kiss you, I do,'" hoping to forestall a dull repetition of the go-round they had earlier.

Mary's reply is poignantly honest. "I'm scared too," she says. "All this doesn't happen every day," she continues, in a full-screen close-up that brings out the vulnerable, almost girlish humanity in her thoughtful face. Acknowledging that she and Joseph still share a special bond, she observes that "one's better as a pair." After a pause, she then springs another version of the theological question that nags her, asking why he doesn't believe that the spirit affects the body. He answers that the reverse of this is true, and Mary admits that this makes her afraid.

Their conversation continues in the vein of a banal dramatic scene, shifting from sympathetic to querulous to tender. Joseph accuses Mary of not loving him, demands to know who got her pregnant, denies his attachment to Juliette, and reaffirms his desire to stay as close as possible to Mary if she will help him understand what's happening to them. Mary responds with more of her mystifying phrases ("It's a big secret. . . . We don't know how to say it") but her explanations grow more direct as the scene develops. "The hand of God is upon me and you can't interfere," she says, noting that it is not Joseph's body but his "lack of trust" that remains their biggest problem.

The scene culminates with a variation on the doctor's medical examination. Joseph pushes Mary onto the bed, with the nasty sound of an off-screen slap. She takes hold of his hand, guiding it to her knee. (This is oddly framed in a foot-of-the-bed shot, with Joseph in the foreground and Mary stretched obliquely away from the camera.) "Feel," she instructs him, and gradually he slides his hand toward her pubic area. The shot is poetic rather than clinical, with no indication that Joseph's fingers are actually penetrating her; but she speaks as if her virginity had again been proved: "You see, I'm sleeping with no one."

She then reaffirms her pregnancy, and just as the doctor accepted this paradox ("It's true that it's true") after his examination, Joseph abruptly changes his attitude. "I'll only be your shadow," he says, his hand resting on her back after she returns to an upright position, her face hidden by the fall of her hair. She answers in a radiant close-up, "God's shadow. Isn't that what all men are for a woman who loves her man?"

Although it mentions God, this line is less a religious epigram than a romantic platitude. Only in a coda to the scene, after Joseph has gone, does Mary's deep religious insight return – and characteristically for Godard, its metaphysical ring is juxtaposed with a highly physicalized view of Mary stripping off her underwear and slipping a filmy nightgown over her naked body. "Let the soul be body," she declares. "Then no one can say the body is soul, since the soul shall be body."

At first this sounds murky, but its meaning for Godard is quite specific. The filmmaker who once wished for "harmony between people and things" still seeks equilibrium among the diverse elements of the world; only now he has raised his sights, focusing less on "people and things" than on "souls and bodies," and seeking not mere harmony but an *intermingling* or *transubstantiation* that unites soul and body into an inseparable whole. Mary gives body a subtle privilege over soul, saying not that "the body is soul," but that "the soul shall be body" – that is, the body, not the soul, is the foundation upon which their unity must be built. Again it becomes clear why Godard persists in using film, an utterly physical medium, to enter the rarified terrain that *Hail Mary* explores. However mystical or transcendental his interests become, he still sees the realm of the body – the material – as the inescapable ground for all human activity, including the most speculative flights of fiction and philosophy.

The scene ends with Mary falling asleep in bed, her open book on the pillow, her hand clenched before her mouth as if she were a little girl about to suck her thumb. "Thy will be done," she reverently murmurs, completing the image's mixture of adult materiality and childlike submissiveness to an invisible presence. In light of the film's bad reputation among some

Christians, it is worth noting that these words are taken from the Lord's Prayer, among the most fundamental of all Christian texts – hardly what one would expect from an impious character (or filmmaker) trying to offend the righteous.

Joseph's drastic change of attitude – from the aggressive "Tell me who you did it with" to the submissive "I'll only be your shadow" – indicates that he has reached a spiritual turning point. Godard confirms this wittily, cutting to several shots of Joseph cruising in his taxi to mighty Bach organ music, his car illuminated by a rooftop TAXI sign whose glow distinctly resembles a radiant halo!

Humor continues as Joseph and Mary have another tête-à-tête, this time on a pier under a lovely blue sky. Joseph's off-screen voice says, "She's married," apparently speaking to a passerby who flirted with Mary, and who couldn't possibly grasp the irony of this little phrase. Then things grow serious again as the couple strolls along the pier, Joseph reading from a letter Mary has sent him. In it, she complains about basketball and the cycle of "exhaustion . . . winning . . . exhaustion," which never seems to get anywhere. Joseph has complaints of his own, about a rich client who coaxed him into juicing up his taxi – phone, video, the works – but never comes around to use it. "He phones to say he's coming, but by evening he hasn't shown up," Joseph gripes, sounding like someone from *Waiting for Godot.* Godard evidently wants to remind his characters that God's grace does not include prompt respite from worldly cares or the endless uncertainties of the human condition.

The intertitle IN THIS TIME hints that something significant is about to happen, and sure enough, Joseph confronts Mary with an unusual request. "We're getting married," he says. "Can I see you naked? I'll only look." Godard might have gotten this idea from his old favorite William Faulkner, whose short novel *The Bear* depicts a man whose wife refuses to show her body even in lovemaking. Mary promptly agrees, but emphasizes that Joseph will only look. Their bargain recalls Mary's words about "giving my body to the eyes" of a heavenly master, and has obvious links with the visual pleasure offered by cinema.

Mary might also feel this activity will help Joseph in his still-gradual spiritual growth. The notion of seeing has cropped up earlier in this scene: "You said you could see I loved you," Joseph said. "Yes, I see it," Mary replied, shielding her eyes from the sun. Still, his very next words – "You said that's not enough" – remind us that physical sight is not equivalent to metaphysical insight, and that both characters recognize this, however imperfectly. Joseph's impending view of Mary is therefore significant from one perspective, trivial from another – depending on how you look at it, so to speak.

Godard continues this ambiguous mood in the next scene. An airy view of the pier expresses Joseph's relief and happiness at their agreement, but Mary strides away from him with a grumpy voice-over ("It's been ages since I've had a normal conversation. . . .") and takes to her bed, lying alone with an introspective look in her eyes.

"Nature prevails," her voice-over goes on. "I want to talk, like others. Because although I hide it, I'm in pain, like others. Even a bit more." This is not mere talk, since here begins one of the most intensive and painful sequences of Godard's career. Mary suddenly dives into her bed and starts thrashing around with chaotic motions, conveying an anguish and distress that are almost palpable. All we hear is her writhing body in the rustling bedsheets, plus a few fragments from stringed instruments; these finally coalesce into a Dvořák phrase, as if the harmony represented by music were belatedly regaining its balance after being torn asunder by Mary's agony.

Music and sound effects cease when her voice-over resumes, now more cryptic than before. "They'll wrest from me that which I dare not give," she says, perhaps referring to Joseph and others who would divert her sexuality from the sacred purpose for which it has been reserved. "You'll act chastely with me. Don't take from someone who never took from you," she continues, now gazing quietly at her pubic area and, despite her momentary calmness, apparently having second thoughts about baring her body for Joseph while he "only looks." To possess true chastity is "to know every possibility," she adds, "without ever straying." With this thought she resumes her near-fetal position and anxiety-filled expression.

Is the likable but limited Joseph capable of such true chastity? He doesn't seem to think so. "That's an impossible task," he reads aloud from a book on the pier. These words come from his book rather than his reaction to Mary's speech, but Godard blurs this distinction by splicing the two utterances together.

To accomplish such a daunting task, Joseph's quotation continues, one would have to admit "that the stars we see at night are vast worlds located very far from ours," contradicting the commonsense knowledge "that stars are just lamps hanging from the sky, most of which are very close to us." We see no stars as he reads, but we do see a glorious skyscape with sun and clouds, and then an exquisite full moon brightening a pitch-dark night. Rippling water and another sky view fill the screen as Joseph's voice goes on, echoing the Professor's theory that human life originated in outer space – an idea once better understood than it is today, the book suggests, known even to dogs in ancient times. Joseph's faithful dog Arthur, his equivalent of Gabriel's companion, seems pleased with that notion, judging from a close-up of his contented face.[16]

Joseph's quotation takes on extra meaning when we connect it with the monologue Mary just finished. She has brought another equation into the film –

chastity = knowing every possibility without straying

– and while Joseph immediately calls this "impossible," he then suggests (through the book he's reading) that the equation can be solved if one looks beyond the evidence of the physical senses. By way of example, he contrasts ordinary vision – which perceives the stars as little points of light – with the ability to accept a greater truth that must be taken *on faith* by those of us who are not physicists or astronomers, namely, that the stars are distant and vast despite their appearance to the untutored eye.

Joseph's capacity for chastity may still be in doubt, but he is eager for some sort of progress at this point. When we see him adjusting his necktie in the taxi, the car's open door protrudes from its body like the wing of an angel preparing for flight. "The time has come," he says. "I'll go see the boss lady. This time I think we've won."

In her room, Mary undresses before the camera (stripping for action?) in a richly ambivalent shot that serves as both (a) an elegant striptease that shamelessly gratifies the camera's male-controlled gaze, and (b) a compassionate reminder of Mary's vulnerability as an ordinary woman who never asked to be either an instrument for God's plan or a bewildering puzzle for her loved ones. "I no longer wish to understand. Does it matter what I am or am not?" she rhetorically asks, still convinced that her best chance for happiness lies in simple submission to the heavenly ordained chain of events.

It remains unclear how Joseph's role will play itself out, and Mary is clearly displeased ("No, not already!") when he arrives at her door. She might take comfort, however, since God appears to be accompanying her visitor. This is indicated by two signs: Joseph arrives in the room almost like an apparition, i.e., a supernatural guest; and next to him we see a sporting-event poster whose largest word is "Adia," resembling "a dia," or "to God." The main feature of this poster is an advertising-type image of a basketball player, but tacked over its face is a snapshot of Mary with her basketball – a minicollage, juxtaposing her specialness and individ-

God's-eye-view: Joseph (Thierry Rode) and Mary (Myriem Roussel) grapple with physical and metaphysical urges in *Hail Mary*.

uality with the generality and anonymity of humankind as a whole. A door divides our view of Joseph in half for a moment, symbolizing his divided loyalty to Mary's needs and his own. Off-screen dogs bark (connoting wisdom? nature? animal appetites?) until Mary's voice-over replaces them. "We can't escape one another any more than we can escape Him," she says – or thinks, since her lips are still. She does not watch Joseph as he crosses the room and sits beside her on the bed.

He caresses her arm in an overhead (God's-eye-view?) shot; but when his hand reaches hers, she flings it off, pushes him away, looks toward the ceiling with an imploring expression, and slides to the floor, where she pummels the oriental carpet and clasps her hands in prayer. Joseph is bewildered and concerned. So is the sound track, which pulses with traffic noise, birdsong, the Dvořák theme, and Mary's emotional breathing. The birds and occasional dog barking continue into the next part of the scene, when the characters reach another pivotal moment.

This again takes the form of an encounter that has mystical and para-doxical overtones. Mary has been wearing just a camisole since undress-ing at the start of the scene, and now she stands to face Joseph, whose face fills the screen in close-up. "Tell me you love me," she asks, and he obeys, his hand reaching out-of-frame toward her abdomen. "No," she replies. He repeats the words "I love you" more gently, and again she says "No," her voice briefly mixed with a dog's whimpering. The shot changes to a medium-close view of Mary from ribs to knees, placing her naked pubic area dead-center in the frame – a shot that could be considered ei-ther clinical or pornographic in other contexts, but here seems simply in-nocent in its candor and forthrightness. She says "No" more forcefully, thrusting Joseph's hand away from her body. The exchange of words and gestures is repeated twice more, climaxing when Mary almost shouts "No, no, no, no!"

There is an abrupt cut to Mary's face in close-up, her mouth open (one of the film's key motifs) and a dramatic orchestral passage swelling on the sound track. Returning to the overhead view, we see that Gabriel has rushed from behind Mary and tackled Joseph onto the bed. Mary kneels by his side as Joseph asks "Why?" and Gabriel shouts "Because!" The an-gel then pushes Joseph's head toward the floor and says a bit more calm-ly, "Because it's law."

The tone of this last moment has been rough, startling, violent. These qualities persist as Gabriel slaps Joseph and calls him an "asshole." Noth-ing gentle or "saintly" is going on here – yet a spiritual breakthrough is clearly taking place, signaled by an out-of-nowhere shot of gently sway-ing wildflowers over flowing Dvořák music. If physical abuse and verbal insult seem unlikely partners for the metaphysical enlightenment that's happening here, this is because contemporary audiences have been condi-tioned by feel-good versions of Christian doctrine, which emphasize com-fort and security over the difficult task of challenging materiality and its seductive wiles. Gabriel's tough-guy approach is the narrative equivalent of Godard's cinematic style – full of naked flesh, vulgar language, frac-tured images, fragmented sounds, and other shockers meant to jar us out of the lazy patterns and perceptions in which we've allowed ourselves to be trapped. Godard and Gabriel have more in common than the letter that begins their names.

Joseph's new spiritual leap becomes plain with his next words, free of the anger and frustration that he has been expressing until now: "I'll sacrifice myself." Oddly, this is the statement that prompts Gabriel to call him an asshole; yet perhaps the angel's word is less demeaning than it first appears, given Godard's great interest in anality and abjection. "A hole isn't a hole," Gabriel immediately adds, suggesting that to be an asshole (or another orifice, such as a vagina or mouth) is not necessarily to be empty or vacuous. "Taboo wipes out sacrifice," the angel goes on, apparently meaning that Joseph needn't feel a sense of loss if he obeys the taboo placed on Mary's body for the moment. As if playing out a ritual, Joseph again asks "Why?" Gabriel answers, "Because that's the rule."

The players are now prepared for the final portion of the breakthrough scene. Gabriel has evidently left the room as silently as he arrived. Joseph sits on the bed, holding his head as if deep in thought. Mary stands directly in front of him, still naked from the waist down. Their words and gestures are choreographed as precisely as a dance or theater piece. Church bells ring in the background and –

- Mary says, "Joseph, I love you," caressing his hair and dropping her hand to her side.
- Joseph speaks her name, then raises the palm of his hand toward her abdomen.
- Mary cries "No!" and he withdraws his hand, gazing at it intently.
- Joseph moves his palm toward Mary's belly and carefully withdraws it, before quite touching her.
- Mary says "Yes" in a warm and loving tone.
- Joseph asks, "Is that it: I love you?" still gazing at his hand, then raising his eyes to Mary, who whispers, "Yes."
- Joseph repeats the gesture – hand toward Mary's stomach; hand withdrawn just before touching – and asks "Is that it? That?" as the Dvořák theme swells.
- "Yes," she answers. "I love you," he says, pulling his hand away. "Yes," she repeats.

All of this has been filmed from the side, with a chair positioned as a symbolic barrier between the two characters. Godard now cuts to an extreme close-up of Mary's abdomen, accompanied by the swelling Dvořák music. Joseph's palm touches Mary's flesh directly over her navel, then moves away as the music hits a dramatic chord. A second time Joseph's hand touches and withdraws, whereupon Mary swivels her hips to the left, swinging her pubis out of sight and her buttocks into full view of the camera. At precisely this moment, the sound track cuts from the romantic Dvořák theme to a thunderous Bach organ chord, and a quick edit zooms our eyes toward a cloudy yet peaceful sky. Lest we miss the divine significance of these events, Mary speaks on the sound track in a tone that is clearly rapturous, yet contains a hint of colloquial off-handedness that reminds us of her ongoing humanity. "Suddenly a light shone in my heart," she says, "warm and gentle as a glowing fire. What on earth, or even heaven, beats knowing you please the One you love, and Who is your Master?" The image cuts from delicate sky to four shots of earthly nature – trees, plants, flowers – as she continues, "I remembered what He said about sin, as we watched the dragonflies. If you thought of it rightly, it just wasn't there."

Then we return indoors, where Joseph waits on Mary's bed as she dresses again. "We're speaking His Word," she says. "How else can we be close to His Word than by speaking it?" Joseph speaks her name and she responds with a perfunctory "Yes? What?" while looking pensively at a flower vase on her table.

Her mind is elsewhere, and so is Godard's; the movie cuts away from the characters again, this time finding nature's splendor immediately at hand in three extreme close-ups of the flowers on the table, photographed with a radiance that is truly awesome. "We're speaking," Mary continues in voice-over as if Joseph were not present, "and we're speaking of the Word. What we're speaking of, the Word, is always ahead of us." The flower images are followed by a quick view of Mary literally dancing as she puts on her shoes and sits beside Joseph on the bed. She asks if he will stay with her, and he answers, "I'll stay. I'll never touch you. I'll stay," cradling her head on his shoulder and caressing her hair. As always in a Godard film, the specific words used by the characters are of great significance. Mary's statement that she and Joseph are "speaking His Word" indicates that unity has been established between the divine, which according to St. John literally is "the Word," and the human, which by uttering this Word becomes a vessel for spirituality. Mary's reference to "speaking His Word" thus combines a physical act (speaking) and an ineffable essence (Word) in a phrase that is itself both spoken (Mary utters it) and unspoken (we hear it as voice-over, not dialogue) by the narrative.

In this dramatic moment, bracketed by the sight of Mary's buttocks and the sound of Mary's voice, Godard's equal passion for the lower and upper body signifies a desire he shares with his heroine: to find the divine in the human and the human in the divine. Joseph's newfound obedience indicates that he now shares this aspiration as well.

The same cannot be said of the Professor, however. Going back to his homeland for a reunion with his wife and son, he now leaves the forlorn Eva for new adventures in the material world that he once scorned in favor of cosmic theories. Godard links him with Joseph in a series of three precisely composed shots: Joseph stroking Mary's hair while wearing a wristwatch, the Professor stroking Eva's hair while wearing a wristwatch, and (between these) a close-up of a watch on its own, its ornate second hand ticking past the twelve o'clock position like a planet in its orbit or a basketball in its flight.

Still, it is obvious that the Professor represents a more Faustian side of the male personality than does Joseph, and Eva dismisses him with almost the same words that Gabriel used to describe Joseph before he became enlightened: "You really are a nothing." Sadly, the Professor has no angel to raise his consciousness with inspired nonsense about zeroes, holes, and common denominators. He leaves the movie like the "nothing" he is – reciting petty "laws of nature" to Eva, making a hollow promise to repay the money he owes her, and vanishing in a train that is noticeably more earthbound than the airplane Gabriel takes when *he* travels.

It could be the Professor's train that rockets past a half-moon at the beginning of the next scene, linking Eva's romantic pain to another bout of spiritual suffering that Mary must endure. Mary felt tremendous peace ("a gentle light shone in my heart") at the end of her life-changing session with Joseph, but accomplishing a metaphysical task is hugely difficult for a physical being, even when that being is specially blessed. "What we're speaking of, the Word, is always ahead of us," Mary said near the end of the last scene, implying that catching up with it is difficult even for a privileged soul like her. Now she speaks another long monologue in voice-over, her lips moving on-screen with different words that we cannot hear. Her speech reveals the enormous pain she continues to feel, and also her fierce determination to emerge from this dark night with her spirit refreshed and renewed.

"What makes a soul is its pain," she begins, as the train rushes along a tense diagonal at the corner of the screen. This statement indicates her belief that the current agonies are a sort of purgatory in which greater strength and insight will be forged. "He'll be the first to hear my pain for them," she continues. We cut to a close-up of her face, resting in shadow with eyes closed. "And he told me: Daughter, I'm suffocating to see you suffocate."

Her eyes open wide as she starts berating God in extraordinarily blunt terms, calling Him a "creep" and a "coward who won't fight." She becomes more ferocious as we cut to a full-length shot of her body lying prone on the bed. God depends "on ass alone – that is, on a quiet heart – for existence," she continues, "an excess of ingress." Here she acknowledges her oneness with God, whose "ingress" means He has entered her; and she rebels against the "excess" this inflicts on her. At the same time, her posture on the bed literalizes the "ass alone . . . a quiet heart" of which she speaks. Naked below the waist, she is photographed at an oblique angle that gives her buttocks a heartlike shape; her nudity also suggests her continued availability to divine "penetration," which she has been simultaneously embracing and rejecting.

The next shot is very different. Mary lies on her back; her feet – the body's lowest part – loom in the foreground, while the rest of her stretches away from the camera. "I want no carnal joy," her voice continues. (In keeping with this, she now wears panties below her familiar white undershirt.) "I don't want to wear out my heart . . . or my soul in one go. Even pain won't get me in one go, and I won't disappear into it. It will disappear with me." These are spirited words, and Godard underscores their energy by filling the screen with a cloud-filled sky, and the sound track with Dvořák's fluttering trills and mellow harmonies.

These give way to traffic noise and a roll of thunder as Joseph's car rolls up beneath its glowing taxi-sign halo. The cab spends most of the shot waiting at a red light, and when we return to Mary after a view of the nighttime sky, it is as if the full moon were another traffic signal, allowing the story to proceed on its appointed course.

"It will always be horrible for me to be the Master," she says in heavily shadowed close-up, her lips still out of sync with her soliloquy. "But there will be no more sexuality in me. I'll know the true smile of the soul, not from outside but from inside, like a pain that's always deserved." The word "outside" calls up a brief landscape shot, picturing a natural world that cannot credibly compete with the particular joys that are Mary's destiny. By contrast, the reference to a "pain that's always deserved" brings a different view of Mary on the bed, still seen from a feet-first angle, but with her legs now gathered toward her body so her groin is visible in the center of the screen.

Images of idyllic nature and Mary's anguished thrashing continue to alternate, rhyming with the mixture of birdsong (cheerful) and thunder (ominous) on the sound track. In her next moments of silent anguish, Mary wrestles with her bedsheet as if it were a shroud intended for a premature burial; and she tensely rests with a clenched hand near her pubic hair, as if torn among conflicting options: the urge to protect her sex, a

The skull beneath the skin: The agonized writhing of Mary (Myriem Roussel) evokes the mortality of her human nature as she wrestles with the superhuman demands placed upon her in *Hail Mary*.

lingering wish for arousal and satisfaction, and outrage at the frictions that her divided nature forces upon her.

The scene's intensity becomes more vehement as it progresses. Seen from above with naked breasts and torso, Mary arches her back and strains toward the camera, then flops over and cries or gasps into a pillow. This is among the episode's most powerful shots, since Mary's gyrations make her ribs and spine visible beneath her writhing skin – underscoring her mortality by evoking what seventeenth-century playwright John Webster called "the skull beneath the skin," the bedrock of unalterable humanity beneath the veneer of individual personhood. "It's not a matter of experience but of total disgust, total hatred, and not of morality or dignity," she says in a hardened tone. The link between these words and her twisting body connects the loathing she feels with the inescapable physicality (beyond abstract cultural concepts like ethics and honor) that is now her blessing and curse.

As if nature itself resonated with her pain and wept with her tears, the next landscape shot is filled with rain sweeping down on reeds that wave in the wind, as they did long ago in the movie's first image. A quick zoom-in toward the swaying plants is followed by a match-cut to Mary's fingers resting in the foliage of her pubic hair. Joyce's influence may be at work again in this suggestion that *body* and *world* are the closely linked *microcosm* and *macrocosm* of a single reality.

"The Father and Mother must fuck to death over my body," Mary says, in a startling reference to the central incident of *Numéro deux,* and to Freud's primal scene, the dreaded-yet-desired vision of a passionate creative act from which the individual, originated in that act, is always already excluded. "Then Lucifer will die," she continues, "and we'll see ... who's weariest, him or me." Like much of the soliloquy, these words are obscure enough to indicate that Mary is deeply detached from ordinary ways of thinking – a condition Godard has long respected in his characters, and courted in his work. Though Mary's meditations are anguished, however, they appear to have the sort of therapeutic effect that one might seek from the free-association wordplay of psychoanalysis. Her fantasy of divine progenitors having intercourse-to-the-death over her body is at once shocking in its feral savagery, healing in its imagined outcome – the devil will die – and triumphant in its implied victory over a dark angel too weary to prevail over his indefatigable human foe.

Mary's last word, "me," accompanies a cut from her groin to her face, crossed by a diagonal shadow that symbolizes the eternally divided nature of human hearts and minds. The next portion of her speech is less ragingly emotional, more crisply philosophical; it is also appealingly hopeful in the growing spiritual knowledge it reveals. The words and images of this sequence are organized with great precision, flowing through the scene in an orderly double file, related to one another in unexpected but unerringly meaningful ways. A few examples will convey the flavor, if not the full richness, of the intuitive insights suggested here:

WORDS: "Earth and sex are in us."
IMAGE: Reeds growing from the earth, blowing in the wind yet erect like Mary's recently seen pubic hair.

WORDS: "Outside there are only stars."
IMAGE: A cloudy sky illuminated by the sun (a star) near the horizon.

WORDS: "Wanting isn't expanding by force."
IMAGE: A distant shore, framed by sky above and lake below, clear expanses sweeping gracefully across the screen.

WORDS: "It's recoiling into oneself, from level to level, for eternity."
IMAGE: A cloudy sky with a clear space in the center of the frame; the glowing sun in a fiery close-up; the open sky stretching forever beyond a ridge of clouds; water shimmering with its ghostly reflection.

And so on, in an elegant duet of verbal and visual elements that form exquisite pairs while evading any sense of being defined, determined, or delimited by each other.

Mary continues speaking. Her words do not "expand by force" or strive toward a sublimity that is more than human; instead they show her desire to embrace "earth and sex" by "recoiling" into the many levels of her bodily self, thereby connecting with the cosmos, from which humans grow as surely as reeds spring from the fertile earth. "You don't need a mouthhole to eat with," she says, and we see the sun – as round as a mouth, or a basketball, or a womb swelling with new life, all linked with spiritual "nourishment" in Mary's story. One doesn't need "an asshole to swallow infinity," she goes on, as we see a patch of grass pitted with little holes of rounded shadow.

This talk of upper and lower "holes" again inflicts healthy confusion on normal distinctions between the upper and lower body, taking us on a carnivalesque voyage from ass to head and back again; meanwhile, we watch an amiable hedgehog twist its shape into contortions not unlike those Mary describes. Although this moment seems more playful than profound, it suggests that the lowliest living things have access to bodily realities of which most humans deprive themselves by submitting to the confinements of so-called civilization.

As in other scenes and films we have discussed, Godard's celebration here of the low and abject is a means not only of rectifying a persistent imbalance in contemporary life, but also of suggesting a "cure" in the form of a radical new harmoniousness between realities of "low" and "high" in human experience. For him as for Mary, bringing these qualities into some sort of stable unity is an ideal to be devoutly sought, and wholeness of the body is both a first step *toward* and an outward signifier *of* such unity.

This is why Mary rejects the division of her body into higher and lower zones: "Your ass must go in your head," she says, scrambling conventional iconography (not to mention biology) with abandon, "and so descend to ass level, then go left or right to rise higher." She and Godard are doing some bold thinking here, abandoning a long tradition of Christian imagery that arranges different parts of the body into a carefully ordered hierarchy – the head approaching heaven, the feet planted on earth, the genitals causing trouble in between – and suggesting that every part of the human form is as precious and even sacred as every other.

In carrying out this maneuver, Godard applies to bodies the aesthetic strategy of *parataxis,* which he frequently brings to his filmmaking. This term has different meanings in different areas of art, and at least three are relevant to Godard's work. In literature, it means the accumulation of phrases ("I came, I saw, I conquered") without connective words; this is similar to Godard's use of jump cuts, narrative gaps, and abrupt transitions. In painting, it means the leveling out or democratization of the canvas, as in a collage where every portion of the composition has an equal measure of integrity and value. In cinema, it means the development of a formal pattern that has its own agenda and interest apart from the narrative that unfolds alongside it.

The latter two practices are directly relevant to Godard's treatment of Mary's body. Her call for corporeal scrambling ("your ass must go in your head . . .") could describe a modernist painting of the body intended to break down symbolic and psychological conventions for the sake of a fresh and perhaps spiritualized new vision. As for the cinematic form of parataxis, Godard is a past master of it, often subordinating plots and characters to the rigors of some formal system that shapes the film as a whole with its raison d'être and guiding artistic principles. He does exactly this in *Hail Mary,* exploring his spiritual preoccupations as much through techniques of montage (e.g., intercutting human and natural scenes) and digression (e.g., interrupting Mary's story with the Professor's subplot) as through the main narrative about Mary's pregnancy, motherhood, and relationship with Joseph.

Godard's use of this strategy is one reason why fleeting references and idiosyncratic allusions often take on unexpected weight and innovative meanings in his films. As an example, consider the issue of Mary's virginity in *Hail Mary.* As in the biblical story, much importance is attached to her vagina and its sancity. As viewed by Godard, however, this sanctity has less significance as a physical condition of the main character than as a mental reminder that bodies in general must not be taken as dominant realities in our lives. Here as in other recent films, Godard makes little fuss about the unpenetrated vagina in its usual (patriarchal) role as a marker of possession and control; he believes that sexuality can take many forms, as his references to anality have frequently suggested.[17] This helps explain how Mary's feelings about her heart, soul, and vagina can all merge into a single (angry) statetement such as one she will utter shortly: "My soul makes me sick at heart, and it's my cunt." The undifferentiated wholeness made possible by such thinking can lead beyond heartsickness, moreover, to happiness and even ecstasy. "I'm a woman," she will also say, "though I don't beget my man through my cunt. I am joy."

Preparing the ground for these declarations, Godard cuts from the sunny sky that ushers out Mary's soliloquy about earth, stars, selfhood, and eternity to a view of Mary lying on her bed, covered by a sheet that can be paradoxically read as either a potential shroud or a symbolic swaddling cloth.

Her anger at God has returned. She recognizes the ecstatic joys that counterbalance her excruciating pains; but again like a patient speaking to a psychoanalyst, she still has negative feelings to work through before she can find complete acceptance of the good that has come her way. "God is a vampire who suffered me in him," she soliloquizes, "because I suffered and he didn't, and he profited from my pain." As if exhausted by this outburst, her voice-over ceases for a long moment while she lies almost motionless on her back; neither skin nor skeleton is visible now, but the material side of her nature asserts itself in the sight of her abdomen heaving beneath the sheet in the slow, deep breaths of sleep. Traffic noises blend with Bach, carrying us to a quick shot of everyday life on a city street. When we return to Mary she is still in the same position, but now fully naked and exposed to the camera's gaze.

"Mary is a body fallen from a soul," she says, assuring us that her nudity is not a gift to Godard and his camera, but an indispensable sign of the corporeality that again preoccupies her. "I am a soul imprisoned by a body," she adds, manifesting anger by reversing her earlier comment to the doctor that "the soul has a body." For the moment, her usual view – that soul takes precedence over body – is pushed aside by a sense of her body as a stifling jail rather than a vehicle for happiness and fulfillment. "My soul makes me sick at heart. And it's my cunt," she now says. "I'm a woman, though I don't beget my man through my cunt." She is growing more angry toward the interference now being mounted by imperatives of the body (especially the private part toward which the camera peers) against the more spiritual aspects of her nature, and against the harmonious balance that is her ultimate ideal.

Mary has experienced too much enlightenment by this point, however, for her discontent and puzzlement to persist very long. She rests, her abdomen again providing the screen's only motion as it rises and falls to the rhythm of her breath. Then birdsong and frog noises creep onto the sound track as her head stirs and her words assume a very different attitude, felt not only in their literal meaning but also in the tone of her voice – still quiet, but lighter and more lilting than before. "I am joy," she says. "I am she who is joy and need no longer fight it, or be tempted, but to gain an added joy."

This embrace of happiness – she does not merely feel joy, she is joy – is both a spiritual and a material gratification. We cut to a close-up of her rising and falling belly, her hand resting upon it protectively, caressingly, maternally. (A small scar mars its surface – another fleeting reminder of the vulnerability to which all flesh is subject, and of the complex physical history that Mary shares with all mortals.) We hear her breathing deeply and fully, as if rehearsing for the birth that will soon take place. A particularly majestic passage from the Dvořák string concerto swells as we return to a shot of her face bisected by shadow. The last words of her monologue remove any lingering doubt that she has not only accepted her destiny but reached out to it with wholehearted gladness: "I am not resigned. Resignation is sad. How can one be resigned to God's will? Are we resigned to being loved? This seemed clear to me. Too clear." Tears creeping from her eyes, and a rush of wind on the sound track, give physical emphasis to the metaphysical contentment she is expressing at last.

The film moves toward its final phase with an exuberant flourish of favorite metaphors. We see a full moon glowing in the sky, intercut with a conspicuously pregnant Mary sitting with Joseph in the bleachers at a basketball game. The words AT THAT TIME reappear after a long absence. Mary and Joseph both seem interested in the game at first, but Joseph's attention wanders as he puts on his glasses and lowers his gaze to a book in his hands. (In the second gymnasium shot, a huge shadow blocks the camera's view for a fleeting moment, reminding us that mysterious forces are still at work.)

Taking no notice of miraculous Mary in their midst, the sports fans fill the gym with their cheering and noisemaking, and all but one shot of the moon is accompanied by their continuing din on the sound track. This sound–image combination can be read in different ways: We may criticize the crowd for focusing its enthusiasm on a trivial sports event that diverts attention from phenomena with profound implications (Mary's divine pregnancy, the moon's glorious beauty) that are equally close and infinitely more important; or we may take a more indulgent view, assuming that cosmic truths will generally elude the best of us, and noting that at least the crowd's cheering is paired with *symbols* of Mary and her motherhood

– the moon, the basketball – as if the fans were hailing Mary despite their own obliviousness. Either interpretation would probably please Godard, whose affection for ambiguity has not dimmed.

After the fifth and final moon shot, we cut to an outdoor plaza seen dimly on the right; the screen's left edge is filled with the curve of a lamp shaped exactly like the moon that presided over the preceding scene. Mary walks through a door in the background, moves toward us, sits directly before the camera, and breathes heavily. Joseph sits behind her, placing his hand comfortingly on her shoulder. (In another amusingly ambiguous touch, we hear barking dogs, perhaps equating Joseph with a faithful canine – or, less condescendingly, associating him with the innocence and loyalty of his own dog.) Mary looks toward the sky; Joseph looks toward Mary; the camera looks toward heaven and earth in a beautiful shot that balances the shining globe lamp with the full moon high above. Bach's bittersweet broken chords join a rush of wind on the sound track. This shot recalls the last portion of Stanley Kubrick's mystical epic *2001: A Space Odyssey*, another film in which an extraordinary fetus points the way to a new kind of future.

Now it is winter, the traditional season of Jesus' nativity. The film's last movement begins with two shots of water, a longstanding symbol for birth. Although they are identically framed, with the horizon near the top edge of the screen, the shots are different enough to form a sort of minimal narrative: The first unmoors our viewing position by placing us near rippling waves on the open sea; the second takes us back to terra firma with breakers crashing on a rocky shore.

We reenter the world of the main story with a wintry shot of Mary's gas station, and we reencounter Godard's eccentric humor – strongly felt during the concluding scenes – in the ironic details of this crisply "realistic" image. One such detail is the sardonic contrast between nature's pure, white snow and civilization's gas-burning automobiles. Another is the pair of loaded words – "self" and "change" – printed on signs in front of the establishment. Mary's long-awaited child is arriving at last, and Godard embroiders the event with touches that are often as gently amusing as they are wryly symbolic.

An automobile pulls into the gas station; then an airplane (like the one Gabriel traveled in) soars over woods and wires in the night; then we gaze through a car windshield at the rear of a heavy-duty snowplow clearing the darkened road before us, its roof light blinking like a self-important version of Joseph's taxi-sign halo. Bach's majestic violin music yields to the cries of a newborn baby. The words AT THAT TIME reinvoke a mythical mood, and new life bursts onto the screen with an affectionate parody of the Bible's manger scene –

- a cow licks its freshly born calf with a loving tongue;
- a little boy stands and stares;
- two rabbits quiver their noses at the camera;
- two horses whinny;
- and springtime blooms with a constellation of bright pink blossoms against a rich blue sky.

"Oh, Mary, what a strange road I had to take to reach you!" says Joseph, recognizing that their bewildering relationship was guided by a higher purpose all along. "Now what's wrong?" replies Mary, her peevish tone providing a down-to-earth antidote for the portentousness of Joseph's exclamation.

We have traveled a strange road, too, and now the movie gives us a well-earned respite in the everyday world – portraying Mary and her child in a bourgeois family scene that couldn't be more ordinary and unmystical. Sitting in a car with no TAXI halo to adorn it, she fiddles with a baby blanket while her father holds the infant; their conversation has a touch of domestic intrigue that would suit a TV soap opera. She asks, "Do you believe it now?" He responds with questions of his own: "Will he call Joseph 'Dad'? What will you do – tell him later that's not his father?" Her reply assures us that she has no lingering doubts about the trials she's been through. "That's life!" she philosophically observes.

Her father and Joseph drift away to discuss financial arrangements involving the gas station, and between two close-ups of a peaceful-looking donkey (perhaps alluding to *Au hasard Balthazar,* the Robert Bresson masterpiece about a donkey who is a saint) we are treated to our first close-up of the infant, lying in his mother's lap and contentedly sucking the fingers of both hands. This is another contribution to the open-mouth imagery woven through the film, from the first scene – when Juliette's words, "Out of my mouth is shit," suggest both the nourishing authenticity and the frustrated spirituality of the human condition – to the last scene, when Mary's rounded lips will consume the entire screen. Strains of Bach blend with family chitchat and the voice of a woman who says, "Thanks, Mary, for every woman," in a tone at once reverent and casual. Then the woman who apparently spoke these words (herself roundly pregnant) helps Mary carry the crying infant from her parked car to a rustic country house. One of the film's most appropriately titled musical pieces, Bach's familiar "Jesu, Joy of Man's Desiring," accompanies them as they walk.

Pink blossoms fill the screen again, followed by an abrupt cut to a smooth watery surface, which splashes asunder as Mary and the baby burst into view. The image of mother and child emerging from water is clearly another symbol of the unimaginably important birth that has taken place, but since the baby is already born, we may wonder why Godard reiterates it. The answer may be his conviction that to understand the full implications of such a profound event, we must experience it in an ongoing present (suggested here through metaphor and repetition) rather than a sealed-off past. Subsequent shots include a close-up of the rising sun and two peaceful landscapes; although they are static in appearance, they become dynamic through their evocation of reality as a cycle that never ends. The passage of the sun and the changing of the seasons are actualities in themselves, and also surrogates for the divine birth that must be continually renewed in thought if it is to retain its plenitude of meaning.

During this sequence we twice return to Mary floating the baby in a swimming pool. These images carry on the film's birth symbolism and also obviously refer to Jesus' baptism. (Theodore of Mopsuestia, an early bishop, wrote that in baptism "the water becomes a womb for him who is born.")[18] It is worth noting that although Mary has been naked in some scenes of the movie, here she is decorously covered with a bathing suit. A superficial reason is that the world (and the film) no longer need to take an intense interest in her body, now that her divine-pregnancy mission has been accomplished. There is also a deeper connotation to Mary's hidden body, which points to the hidden nature of God and the ultimate truth He represents.

"How did He look? What was He like?" she asks, bearing out the film's reminder that much has been revealed but more remains unseen. "There are no looks in love, no outward seeming. No likeness. Only our hearts will tremble in the light," she continues, as we cut to a grassy glade where her child, now a little boy, is playing with three young friends. "I can't describe Him as He stood there," Mary goes on, "but I can tell you how the women looked on seeing Him."

We never hear the rest of her account, since the movie now turns its attention to her son. As in the manger scene, the tone of this episode is one of gentle parody, supplementing its biblical material with touches of good-natured humor.

"Come with me," the boy says to his companions, interrupting their ball game. Bringing them to a different part of the field, he asks two of them their names – Fabian and Florent, they reply – and informs them that they will be called Peter and James from now on.

This moment is amusing in its off-handed mix of historical and contemporary flavors, but it is also a key incident in Godard's film, since it provides our first sign that we are definitely dealing with Jesus here. Along with its echoes of biblical events, after all, this story of a woman named Mary has been full of symbolic, allusive, and simply indeterminate elements; and every minute of it has taken place in modern Switzerland, not the Holy Land of ancient times. It is possible that our Mary has always been a contemporary woman *similar* but not *identical* to the Mary of the Bible – in which case, her child would not be Jesus but, at most, a Jesus-like little boy. Just as Mary's pregnancy-in-virginity identified her as an authentic incarnation of her biblical counterpart, however, so her child's actions show him to be an equally genuine Jesus figure. His renaming of the "disciples" confirms this. So does his dialogue, when he starts saying things like "I am He who is" and, accompanied by a roll of thunder, "I must tend to my Father's affairs."

That thunder is impressive, but ostentatious signals from the boy's heavenly Father can't prevent his earthly father (stepfather?) from aiming some discipline at the unruly kid, who has just run off after refusing to get into the family car. "He'll be back," Mary says to calm Joseph down. "At Easter or Trinity Sunday," she casually adds.

Godard positions the camera very close to Joseph's visual perspective during part of this scene; when Jesus looks at Joseph, he stares almost directly at us too. We shouldn't feel embarassed, the camera angle tells us, if we're still somewhat bewildered by all this. So is Joseph, and he's been even closer to the story than we have.

The last scene begins with a roar of Joseph's engine. Cutting abruptly from the countryside to a city street, we see a woman's shapely legs and fashionable high-heeled shoes as she strides across the pavement, followed by a man in jeans and sneakers. A second street-level shot is dominated by enormous arrows painted on the pavement – pushy signs of urban-type "civilization," to borrow a word from *Weekend,* but utterly ignored by the walkers, who proceed in their own direction without hesitating. The man strolls ahead of the woman in the next shot, which is slashed with the yellow diagonals of a crosswalk.

Not until they arrive at their cars do we see who they are: Mary and Gabriel, now opening their doors and preparing to drive away. Gabriel pauses to call a friendly "Hey, madam!" but Mary appears not to recognize him. He calls again, adding an impatient horn honk. "Yes? What?" she brusquely asks. "Nothing," he replies in close-up, adding, "Hail, Mary!" with a breezy wave of his arm.

Alone in the next shot, Mary stands in thought, perhaps listening to the church bells that ring in the distance. She tilts her face briefly toward the sky, then back to earth as she climbs into her car. Except for this momentary sign of alertness to some other dimension, everything about this scene suggests that she is again firmly rooted in the secular world. Underscoring this, the camera peers through her car window while she lights a cigarette.

Strains of Bach's choral music suggest that the moment may not be as worldly as it first appears, however. This impression grows as Mary glances briefly but significantly at the flame springing from her lighter, rhyming with the sunshine that flickers across her face. She looks pensive as she takes another puff on her cigarette, then breaks into a half-smile that covers her lips exactly as the smoke enters her lungs; the camera comes closer as she inhales and exhales a second time.

These cigarette shots may easily be written off as an atmospheric touch, or grouped with the pauses for unoccupied "dead time" that give many "serious" movies (including many New Wave movies) part of their lifelike atmosphere. Being lifelike is not a major priority for *Hail Mary,* however, and we may expect that the film's last moments will somehow connect with the *deepened* sense of being-in-the-world that Mary's spiritual adventures have bestowed upon her. Health hazards aside, cigarettes are remarkable instruments that allow an ambivalent blurring of boundaries between (inner) body and (outer) world, "transubstantiating" an ordinary substance (tobacco) into a vaporous essence that passes through the self with no more visible trace than the ephemeral airplane-trails that sweep the sky in some Godard films. For the rest of us, smoking may be a sign of indulgence or dependence; for Mary it is a sign of *inspiration* in the lowest (physical) and highest (metaphysical) sense.

Mary herself may not realize the implications of this moment, but she seems to know instinctively that her days of divinely ordained obscurities are mostly over. She rests her head against the back of the car seat, then raises her hand again to her mouth. Now it holds a lipstick instead of a cigarette, recalling the earlier scene when she paused in front of a cosmetics counter, then continued on her way without buying anything.

She touches the red tube to her lips with tentative gestures, as if testing some new and unfamiliar pleasure. Keeping her in profile as she abruptly withdraws the lipstick, Godard cuts to a tighter shot; indeed, every shot in this sequence is slightly closer than the last, indicating that Godard has resumed his role of visual invesigator, using the camera as a research instrument as well as an aesthetic tool. Bach's music, which ceased just before the lipstick appeared, returns and grows louder as she raises the tube again, drawing it toward her lips as if it were a miniature rocketship on its way to test the Professor's theories about the distant reaches of our galaxy. (One may recall his diagram resembling a mouth much earlier in the film.) Its redness dances near the center of the screen as she pokes it tantalizingly at her slightly open lips. The music fades as she speaks the film's last words in voice-over: "I am of the Virgin, and I didn't want this being. I only left my imprint on the soul that helped me."

With this sentence, the camera jumps to a very close position at the side of her head, filling much of the screen with her luxuriant brown hair as the music crescendoes, her mouth opens wider, and she begins to apply the lipstick. The film's final cut brings one of the richest, most mysterious shots of Godard's rich, mysterious career: a full-screen close-up of Mary's open mouth, ringed by the redness of her lips but dominated by the dark, gaping emptiness at its center.

The eccentricity of this image is overwhelming, and has received much notice. A key element in that eccentricity is the framing of the shot, not wholly symmetrical, but favoring the upper lip and leaving the lower lip out of view. By avoiding the mechanically "balanced" image that a Hollywood cinematographer might have offered, this "imperfect" picture serves to emphasize the distinctiveness and individuality (that is, the humanity) of the character before the camera and the filmmaker behind it.

The most obvious interpretation of the shot is an old-fashioned Freudian one: The lipstick is a phallic symbol, representing the sensual realm to which Mary is returning after her spiritual odyssey; and her mouth represents her body, now freshly available for material interaction with the world. This reading is reasonable as far as it goes, but to leave things at that would be regrettably simplistic, reducing a resonant enigma to a picture puzzle with an easily decodable meaning. It might also be downright misleading, since the lipstick (which never enters the mouth) is nowhere visible when the mouth takes over the screen. Indeed, little of anything is visible, and this emptiness breathes a darkness into the visual field that would do a horror movie proud. (One thinks of the zoom into a mute, morbid mouth at the end of Roman Polanski's nightmarish 1976 film, *The Tenant*.)

The most productive course of interpretation is ultimately not to read this shot too closely with the intellect but to absorb it with the imagina-

Multifaceted metaphor: Mary (Myriem Roussel) applies lipstick in the enigmatic last sequence of *Hail Mary*.

tion, and to appreciate how perfectly its visual impact meshes with the Bach choral piece that recurs again here. Adding to the shot's conscious and unconscious resonance is its harmony with many earlier images in both of the *Hail Mary* films. In the short "The Book of Mary" these include the father's dark glasses (another void in the optical field) and young Mary's broken egg (another opening into an unseen space). In the Godard story they include the opening dialogue ("Out of my mouth is shit") and various moments when some substantial, seen object materializes with such arbitrary insistence (e.g., the taxi-lamp halo, the shining moon) that its uncanny presence calls paradoxical attention to ephemeral, unseen dimensions hovering just beyond our ken. Also relevant, of course, are the film's multiple references to bodily openings.

This web of images is difficult to parse; but one could hardly expect it to be otherwise since, after all, the aim of the *Hail Mary* films is to explore the unshowable and unsayable through an artistic medium that takes showing (picture, montage) and saying (sound, narrative) as basic principles. We must remember that much of Godard's cinema (especially his later work) rests on the paradoxical hypothesis that our existential environment has a dual nature. One one level, it is a material realm that can be known by the five senses and recorded by cinematic technologies. On another level, it is the shadow or veil of a spiritual dimension that is imperceptible to our senses and impenetrable to our conscious thoughts. Attempting to manifest the immaterial through material (filmic) devices can lead only to eminently ambiguous results. In the particular effort called *Hail Mary*, this ultimately takes the form of a movie screen occupied by the unmoving darkness of a mouth that does nothing we can hear or see.

Why a mouth, though, rather than some other body part, or a different sort of image entirely? One answer is that mouths have been important throughout *Hail Mary*. Another is that mouths have fascinated Godard ever since *Breathless*, when Michel celebrated life by thumbing his lips[19] and greeted death by twisting them at Patricia (who repeated the grimace in a foreshadowing of Mary's lipstick gesture). The list threads through film after film: Nana's horror at a client's kiss; Corinne's feast on Roland's remains; Sandrine's efforts to fellate Pierre; and so on. At other times the mouth becomes conspicuous through its invisibility or its radical disconnection from speech (e.g., the "Oval Portrait" scene in *My Life to Live* and the voice-overs in various films).

What most of the mouths just mentioned have in common – with many others in additional movies – is that they are silent. Godard characters often talk a lot, to be sure, and Mary herself has spoken prolifically during her story. If we have approached that story with our usual moviegoing habits, we have used her words, her inflections, and the grain of her voice as clues for understanding her inner psychological self – the "inside" that we find when we strip away the "outside" of physical appearance.

We recall from *My Life to Live*, however, that another step is possible: removing the "inside" to discover the soul itself. In the period leading up to *Hail Mary*, Godard tried numerous methods (freeze-frame photography, tableaux vivants, etc.) that he hoped would bypass or transcend both the "outside" of photographic reality and the "inside" of psychological experience. The enigmas of *Hail Mary* result from his willingness to act on a new insight. He now believes that the way to the soul cannot be found by *transcending* or *eluding* or *evading* the body. Rather, one must go *into* and *through* the "outside," whose fascinating complexity is an eloquent sign of the spiritual self residing there.

Words are of little help in this journey, and the close-up of Mary's mouth pays tribute to the idea of silence as an active choice rather than a passive absence. Mary's last sentence is uttered by her body *as a body,* saying, "I only left my imprint on the soul that helped me." In accord with this, the film's concluding image simultaneously underscores her physicality (by showing an expressive and compelling part of her body) and reaffirms the mystery that all physicality must have (signified by the dark void between her lips) when we approach it with merely human means of perception.

Seeking to pin down and "understand" the conclusion of *Hail Mary* would therefore be beside the point. Like the threads of meaning woven through the film – the richness of selfhood as exemplified by Mary, the history of humanity as traced by the Professor, the potentialities of cinema as conceived by Godard – it is literally and figuratively *open-ended.*

In sum, the image of Mary's mouth is an opening into mysteries greater than our everyday ways of thinking, knowing, and perceiving can coherently contain. Hence, as we have noted, it resembles the metaphorically ambiguous egg – at once utterly mundane and utterly enigmatic – cracked open by young Mary at the end of Miéville's film, and the Professor's diagram of the galaxy, a reddish horizontal line with a sort of pucker in the middle, very much like a closed mouth. Mary uncloses this, cracking open the universe to reveal an exquisitely sensual space fraught with possibilities that are as exhilarating for us to sense as they are impossible for film to circumscribe.

The camera does not enter this space any more than it enters young Mary's egg; nor does the Mary of either film try to verbalize her feelings at her story's end. ("I can't describe Him as He stood there," says adult Mary, perhaps echoing the end of *The Divine Comedy,* when Dante faces the impossibility of describing his ultimate encounter with God's image.) It is also significant that neither Mary places anything in her mouth during her last moments on the screen: Young Mary shows no interest in eating the egg she has just decapitated, and adult Mary trades her cigarette for a lipstick.

This distinguishes both Marys at the ends of their stories from Eva/Eve, who bit her apple in a full-screen close-up, reminding us that ever since Genesis, the mouth has been associated not only with nourishment and expression but also with learning and all its privileges, uncertainties, and dangers. The two Marys of *Hail Mary* have learned a great deal, and at the conclusions of their respective stories they know the time has come simply to live, love, and digest the experiences they have undergone. In keeping with Godard's increasing desire to respect physical *and* metaphysical realities in all their fullness, thickness, and volatility, we will do best to follow their example, treasuring the *Hail Mary* films not for neatly taught lessons but for a stream of ontological, epistemological, and philosophical adventures, the likes of which few other films can offer.

7

Nouvelle Vague

Me, my memory, I can't help it. I would if I could, but I can't forget anything. . . .
Of course, there are things I would like to remember, but. . . .

– *A Married Woman*

The controversies over *Hail Mary* brought Godard's name into public view more prominently than at any time since *Breathless*. Indeed, his debut feature never achieved such widespread fame – or infamy, some would say – despite its importance to film history.

Nonetheless, the *Hail Mary* brouhaha did little to shore up his highly uncertain status as a commercially viable filmmaker. Audiences who had lost interest in him during the period between *Le Gai Savoir* and *Here and Elsewhere* found subsequent pictures like *Numéro deux* and what some critics[1] call the "trilogy of the sublime" films – *Passion, First Name: Carmen, Hail Mary* – almost as rarified and demanding as their highly politicized predecessors. *Détective,* the fractured thriller-comedy made to raise money for the completion of *Hail Mary,* gained an international release but satisfied few moviegoers except the diminishing band of Godard enthusiasts. This is ironic, since *Détective* might have been a crowd pleaser with its snappy title, genre-film plot, and big-name cast including Nathalie Baye, Claude Brasseur, Jean-Pierre Léaud, Laurent Terzieff, and Johnny Halliday; but as a viewing experience it proved little more accessible than *Sauve qui peut (la vie),* one of the comeback pictures that (like *Numéro deux* before it) seemed designed to challenge rather than seduce everyday moviegoers. Unsurprisingly, they did not rise to the challenge.

Nobody had commercial illusions about *Grandeur et décadence d'un petit commerce de cinéma,* a 16mm short made in 1986, focusing on the rigors of the movie-producing game. Ditto for the 1986 video productions

Soft and Hard (A Soft Conversation between Two Friends on a Hard Subject), centering on a discussion between Godard and Miéville, and the interview tape *J. L. G. Meets W. A.*, also known as *Meetin' W. A.*, a spinoff from the *King Lear* project in which Woody Allen was involved.

King Lear itself originated as a spur-of-the-moment deal between Godard and Cannon Films, a money-driven production company. Cannon hoped Godard would deliver an updated Shakespearean melodrama with all sorts of celebrities – ranging from Woody Allen and Molly Ringwald to Norman Mailer and Peter Sellars – playing hip new versions of the tragedy's characters. Instead, the company received a postmodern pastiche as freewheeling and collagelike as any of Godard's other recent films. True to his ornery habits, moreover, he brought the company's bewilderment directly into the movie, which is extraordinarily self-reflexive even by Godard's high standard. It begins with a telephone conversation between the filmmaker and a couple of Cannon executives, who say things like, "People do not believe already that the movie will ever be done. We are losing confidence." Godard breathes into the receiver while the Cannon folks complain and cajole; the screen displays printed words (A PICTURE SHOT IN THE BACK) and alternate subtitles (FEAR AND LOATHING; A STUDY; A CLEARING) as well as painterly images of a falling angel and a laughing woman. Cannon may have been as eager to market this "product" as its representatives claimed in the phone call, since the company proceeded to release it in theaters despite its wildly unconventional content. There it became Godard's lowest-visibility release since the disbanding of the Dziga-Vertov Group.

A little more attention was accrued by "Armide," a twelve-minute short set to music from Jean-Baptiste Lully's baroque opera of that title. It was included in *Aria*, producer Don Boyd's anthology of sketches inspired by operatic music. The collection as a whole was a speciality item aimed at limited audiences, so there was not a great deal of theatrical exposure for Godard's sketch, about a gleaming gymnasium where two gorgeous cleaning women try to seduce a pair of male body builders who can't see beyond their own barbells. *Soigne ta droite,* a comedy also completed in 1987 and unveiled at the prestigious Cannes International Film Festival, was seen by even fewer people despite radiant images and a cast including Jane Birkin and Godard himself.

Taking a break from this string of apathetically received films, he spent 1988 in his video laboratory, making the brief *On s'est tous défilé*, a nonnarrative pastiche of music, random sounds, and slow-motion imagery; the slightly longer and visually stunning *Power of the Word*, which amused critics by privileging images and music over the verbal potency announced by the title; and "The Last Word/The French Heard By," a meditation on war and language (produced for *The French Seen By,* a TV series) that anticipates aspects of the later feature *For Ever Mozart.*

The following year was more auspicious, bringing the video *Le Rapport Darty* – a seminarrative about business, culture, and the urban scene, focusing on a store owner having trouble with the local police – and also the start of a major work that would occupy much of Godard's time and attention for the next decade: *Histoire(s) du cinéma,* a video exploration of film's first century, mulled over in terms that are at once enormously learned and profoundly personal.

Godard's interest in video, which is discussed at length in Chapter 8, has clearly been motivated by aesthetic and expressive considerations as well as the economics of production, distribution, and exhibition. He has always remained a cinéaste at heart, however, and few observers doubted that he would make his way back to 35mm production when circumstances permitted. This happened in 1990 when he wrote and directed *Nouvelle Vague,* his first feature film since 1987. It is a work of such astonishing beauty as to constitute a powerful argument for the indispensability of full-scale cinema in the seductive age of small-screen electronic substitutes.

This notwithstanding, *Nouvelle Vague* was received less than rapturously in some of its first appearances. After transfixing some spectators and bewildering others at the Cannes filmfest, where it was highly enough regarded by the programmers to be selected for the Official Competition, it made its way to the New York Film Festival at Lincoln Center, home of many American milestones for Godard, including the *Hail Mary* screenings that had stirred so much attention five years earlier. As a member of the festival's five-member selection committee, I was eager to revive Godard's reputation among critics and audiences at this closely watched event, which had not featured his work for the previous few seasons. Godard arrived in Manhattan, the film had its first U.S. screening before a packed auditorium – and then Vincent Canby, the powerful and generally insightful critic of the *New York Times,* published a review so savage (and so unexpected, given his longtime support for New Wave cinema) that Godard left town early, hopes for timely distribution of the movie were dashed, and those of us who deeply admired it were left wondering how its point could so profoundly have been missed, not only by Canby but also by numerous other observers who might have risen to its defense.[2]

Canby's review so concisely captures the dismissive tone of moviegoers who fail to understand Godard's motives and methods that it is worth quoting at length. After calling the film "featherweight" in his first paragraph, he speculates that perhaps "a better movie is still waiting to be found in the editing room, where Mr. Godard composes his movies, it seems, from whatever pieces of exposed film are at hand." Calling it "as pretty as a feature-length lipstick commercial," he states that there is little beyond its foliage shots "to occupy either the mind or the eye." Noting a plot element about a corporate takeover, he suggests that "someone is bound to describe [the film] as a sendup of the Age of the Conglomerate," but that this "would be to be credit the movie with more than it can deliver." He concludes:

> Mr. Godard's passion for Cinema now seems perfunctory, as do his tracking shots, his use of pretty actresses (often seen reading books), and the chapter headings (in French, Italian, English and German) that divide the movie. Only people who despise the great Godard films . . . from "Breathless" . . . through "Every Man for Himself" . . . could be anything but saddened by this one. The party's over.

It has never been clear what party Canby had in mind, but such details hardly mattered as his *Times* pan sank the film's prospects for reaching American art theaters any time soon. A few thoughtful critics tried to undo the damage – an article by Robert Stam in *Film Comment* was perhaps the most perceptive – but the rest was silence. *Nouvelle Vague* eventually saw a very limited release, courtesy of an unusually venturesome distribution company, and even made its way to the home-video market. Still, half a decade passed before its credibility had recuperated enough for a critic like Armond White not to sound like a contrarian when he accurately praised it as "a movie by an artist trying to make full sense of our sensual and intellectual experience, a celebration of the felicities held in common between cinema and nature."[3]

Nouvelle Vague begins with a declaration, spoken by an off-screen voice at the start of the opening titles: "But I wanted this to be a narrative. I still do."

Godard's ambivalence has never been more obvious, or more poignant; nor has it ever been more directly applied to the question of storytelling. Since the statement refers to the film we have just started watching, it probably stands for the filmmaker's point of view – but what is the filmmaker saying? If he wanted to make a narrative movie, why didn't he? If he changed his mind, why is he bothering to fill us in on his original intention? Why, moreover, is he using the present tense – "I still do" – since the filmmaking process was over and done with before the movie ever reached the screen?

Only two sentences have been spoken, and already the coordinates of conventional film are discombobulated. If anything is clear, it's that Godard remains haunted by narrative as both a goal devoutly to be wished and a trap assiduously to be avoided.

Since the very first moments of *Nouvelle Vague* invoke that slippery word "narrative," it is tempting to take the idea of narrative intent "literally" and analyze the movie in terms of plot and character development. Many critics have steered in the opposite direction, however, claiming that the film is too totally disjointed – either brilliantly or preposterously so – for a narrative to be clearly detected, much less studied and evaluated. I agree that the dialogue, settings, and characters of *Nouvelle Vague* are (to state the obvious) stitched together in unorthodox ways that defy traditional readings. However. the movie does have a story, coherent enough to be followed and enjoyed despite Godard's insistence on breaking it into kaleidoscopic fragments interspersed with digressions, distractions, and diversions too copious for a single adjective like "Brechtian" to explain them all away.

Briefly, the story goes like this: The main setting is a luxurious estate, owned by a prosperous family that makes its money in multinational finance and manufacturing. Walking down a nearby road, a handsome male wanderer named Roger Lennox is almost hit by a car; a beautiful Italian countess, Elena Torlato-Favrini, is at the wheel. Although we do not witness this incident ourselves, we do see Roger lying on the ground as Elena bends over him, soothing injuries he has apparently suffered. She takes him home, where he encounters a variety of wheeler-dealers with fancy clothes and cars. There are also numerous servants who maintain their own strict hierarchy, with upper-level domestics mistreating lower-rank colleagues almost as brutally as the upper-class gentlefolks abuse them all. The family owns various factories, one of which Roger visits, observing the interactions among self-assured executives, workers of assorted ranks, and impressive high-tech machines.

After hanging around at the estate a while longer, Roger and Elena go for a speedboat ride on the adjoining lake. She hops into the water, splashes around happily, and teases Roger to join her, refusing to listen when he says he can't swim. As with the automobile accident a little earlier, a sudden cut abruptly changes the situation: Roger is now in the water and Elena is sitting in the boat, coolly watching as he flails, sinks, and evidently drowns.

Life and business proceed as usual back at the estate, until a conversation between a servant and a visitor reveals a new puzzle facing the household. According to the servant, a man exactly like Roger Lennox recently showed up at the door, announcing himself as Roger's brother. Elena claims to believe the man's story, although the servant thinks Roger himself has somehow returned to life. Listening to another conversation, we learn that the newcomer – Richard Lennox – is wrestling for control of a company owned by the Torlato-Favrini family, blackmailing them by threatening to make dangerous revelations.

We cannot know for certain whether Richard is really Richard, or whether he is Roger resurrected, or whether Roger never drowned in the first place. Nor can we know whether Richard's blackmail plan centers on the ambiguous "murder" of Roger, if that's what it was, or on his inside knowledge of the family's shady schemes. A bit of dialogue that promises to shed light on these mysteries is, not surprisingly, rather mystifying itself.

> LAWYER FOR FAMILY: We say someone leads a double life, Mr. Lennox.
> LENNOX NO. 2: Richard Lennox.
> LAWYER: Doesn't he often lead one life, full and complete – his own life – by seeming to lead two?
> LENNOX: True. But how many lead only half a life, lacking guts for a whole one, which seems double to *others*.

Whew. In any case, Richard's personality seems to be quite different from Roger's in the earlier part of the movie. Whereas the first Lennox mostly lounged around the estate and took little interest in its many intrigues, the second Lennox is as much of a hard-shelled capitalist as anyone in sight, striding around in an expensive-looking suit and keeping an assistant on hand to carry his umbrella. His materialism is most emphatic in an airport scene, when he debarks from a plane with Francesco Goya's legendary painting *The Naked Maja* in his hand – somehow extricated from a Beirut cellar – and promptly gives it to some money men, who comment crassly on the "splayed breasts" and other physical qualities of the nude figure.

Lennox and Elena still have a close relationship. Perhaps this is because she believes he is Roger's brother, although it's unclear why this would bind them together, considering how she treated the late (?) Roger; or perhaps it's because he is an effective enough blackmailer to hold her in his clutches indefinitely. Repeating the movie's most dramatic sequence, they again climb into a boat – not a powerboat but a small rowboat this time – as music swells and clouds obscure the sun. "I'm a trap for you," says Richard as they prepare to shove off. "[Despite] whatever I told you, the more faithful I am, the more I'll deceive you. My candor will ruin you."

Stopping the boat after some energetic rowing, he jumps playfully into the water and – now reversing rather than repeating the earlier boat scene – teases Elena to join him as he splashes merrily about. She demurs. He reaches up to put a hand on the back of her neck, and playfully asks for a kiss. Suddenly their places are switched; she thrashes and sinks while he watches, with the wide-eyed gaze of a villain in some old melodrama. It is the flip side of the sequence that "killed" the first Mr. Lennox, and this time the outcome is different in tone as well as victimhood: As her hand emerges from the water one last time, his hand darts into the frame to grasp her wrist. Before we can be certain that he has rescued her, a light-ning-quick cut returns us to dry land, with an elegant tracking shot that eventually catches both Richard and Elena scurrying toward her mansion. "Don't look back!" he cautions her, recalling the biblical admonition to Lot's wife, who was turned into a pillar of salt for disobeying.

Our story has a happier ending than Lot's, heralded by an intertitle say-ing LOVE CONQUERS ALL in Latin, one of several languages used during the movie. The last sequence begins with the unexpected sight of Elena bidding a friendly farewell to her servants – one of them gets to keep a Mercedes as a gift – and bending down to tie Richard's shoelace. He lik-ens this to a tennis player receiving tribute from a defeated opponent; then he reaches down to take her upraised hand, reprising one of the film's most significant gestures.

Elena then solves the Lennox mystery by discovering around Richard's neck a slender chain bearing the same symbolic ornament – an Egyptian ankh – that she found on Roger at the time of his mishap on the roadway. "So it was you?" she asks. "It's you, it's me," he responds, passing his hand vertically between their faces, as if making a magic sign. CONSUM-MATUM EST reads a final intertitle, brimming with sarcasm and sincerity as the couple drive off to further adventures that we shall never see.

This plot outline is brief and incomplete, but it demonstrates that *Nou-velle Vague* indeed has a story, complete with dialogue and character de-velopment. I emphasize the point because, as already noted, even some critics who respect Godard have suggested that the film's nods to linear structure function less as a narrative than as a sort of glue "to hold the lively sounds and ravishing images together," in White's phrase.[4] (The plot synopsis in Wheeler Winston Dixon's book on Godard seems completely unaware that Lennox has more than one identity; here is one critic who appears to have found the movie's manifest content too much to absorb, not to mention the meanings and implications of that content.)[5] While the plot does serve the purpose indicated by White – providing a skeleton upon which Godard hangs more important and compelling elements – the characters and their activities are still of considerable interest to the filmmaker, who could easily have dispensed with them altogether (as he did in some Dziga-Vertov Group experiments) had he actually wanted to create the sort of "purely cinematic" abstraction that some observers apparently see here. As much in *Nouvelle Vague* as in *Breathless,* he means not to evade "normal" cinema – which inspires much of the movie's content, from its financial intrigues and household tensions to its love-story interludes and whodunit finale – but rather to dissect and reconfigure Hollywood-type conventions, savoring their aesthetic beauty while attempting to drain away their power as agents of commonsense ideologies. Stam is right to observe that the film "applies the usual Godardian electroshock to the story it tells," but saying that the movie is ultimately *about* its "images . . . camera movement . . . cinematic rhythm and temporality . . . the passage of shot to shot, and sound to sound"[6] is overstating the case. Films that *are* made according to that recipe, such as Stan Brakhage's abstract *Roman Numeral Series* and some of Harry Smith's animations, look and sound much less like "movie-movies" than *Nouvelle Vague* does. Godard's film is no action painting, tranced-out hallucination, or exercise in "closed-eye vision," as worthy as such avant-garde ventures often are. It certainly embodies a radical reconstruction of narrative-film procedures, but those procedures remain distinctly visible in the completed work, much as the chord changes of an old song can be heard beneath the exfoliating flights of a bebop jazz improvisation.

This said, I must add that the intertwined components of *Nouvelle Vague* – its interstitial story, flow of luxurious images, and mixture of complicated sounds – are less engaging as not-quite-narrative cinema than as emblems of Godard's filmic philosophy as he heads into the 1990s. His films of this decade are marked by an unrelenting radicalism of expression as well as a deeply felt commitment to recouping cinema's past. The subjects he deals with are eclectic, ranging from the ethos of a continent assaulted by war, ideology, and technology (*Germany Year 90 Nine Zero, For Ever Mozart*) to relationships between the human and the divine (*Hélas pour moi*) and the genealogy of film itself, which *Histoire(s) du cinéma*

Unrelenting radicalism: Berengère Allaux in *For Ever Mozart* (1997).

explores with peripatetic, anything-goes intuitiveness. What unites these very different works is their way of combining now-familiar interests – most notably a search for hidden sociocultural and/or philosophical-mystical dimensions in whatever phenomena come under his gaze – with fresh, often drastically eccentric storytelling techniques.

Nouvelle Vague delves into sociopolitics through its parodic approach to life-styles of the rich and famous, and into mysticism through the surreal clarity with which it conveys the sights and sounds of a tale that frequently promises to make sense but consistently backs away from actually doing so, causing even such emphatic events as love and death to come and go with the elusive almost-reality of a dream or hallucination.

One way to enter the film's apparently ungraspable world is to recognize its roots in Godard's own recollection of childhood idylls on the comfortable estate of his maternal grandparents. "Godard's memories of his childhood are of a paradise full of affection and wealth," writes Colin Myles

MacCabe in his account of the filmmaker's life. "Everything centered on Julien Monod and his large estate on the French side of Lake Geneva, the site of endless family gatherings, as the pious Protestant banker commemorated the feasts of the year with his numerous children and grandchildren."[7] Godard's recollections might not be wholly accurate – whose are? – but there is no question about the power they have retained for him in later life. For a small but telling sign of this, note how the name Monod crops up in his work, as early as *Band of Outsiders* in 1964 and as late as *Hélas pour moi* in 1992. (A character in *Band of Outsiders* even turns it into a pun: monod-on-nous.) Note also the increasing appearance of nature imagery in his films, gathering momentum after *Sauve qui peut (la vie)* and taking on great importance in nature-saturated productions like *Hail Mary* and *King Lear.*

Thinking of *Nouvelle Vague* as a memory movie helps explain such characteristics as the vividness of its images – the mind's eye sometimes "sees" long-past recollections in amazing detail – and the emotional charge that these images frequently carry, quite apart from the incidents and encounters that they contain and convey. Considering the film as an exercise in memory also sheds light on the arbitrariness with which the images relate to one another. Like dreams, memories often follow a non-logic of their own; given Godard's lifelong interest in escaping the limitations of logic and rationality, it is not surprising that he would eventually use the prerogatives of memory to anchor an entire work.

The film's most important intersection with the meanings and mechanisms of memory is found in Godard's continuing pursuit of a decades-old objective still not attained to his satisfaction: the creation of a new form of cinema that bypasses the ego of the individual artist, and the cultural habits of society at large, to tap into a greater reality not accessible through customary creative methods.

As we have seen, this goal animates most periods of Godard's career. The improvisatory quality of his early works is both a means of implementing the auteur theory, through spontaneous shooting and a sort of directorial ventriloquism, and an attempt to use high-speed filmmaking in ways that blur the "reality" of the filmed event with the "artifice" of the completed movie. The radical separation of sound and image by the Dziga-Vertov Group aims at destroying cinema's ability to manipulate audiences by reproducing decadent ideologies. The movies made immediately before, during, and after the "trilogy of the sublime" take on the most ambitious agenda of all, seeking to capture – or glimpse, or sense, or *something* – the spiritual dimension that Godard now suspects is an integral part of the everyday world. All this activity can be seen as a multi-faceted effort to destabilize cinema so it will reflect a reality larger than that of the individual artist, however "inspired" or "committed" that artist may be.

At first glance, *Nouvelle Vague* might look like a headlong retreat from this endeavor. By this skeptical view, Godard withdraws here into a cocoon of memories from an idealized past – highly personal memories, at that – to the point where much of his movie is impenetrable to anyone not sharing his private store of recollections, or at least his album of ancestral photos from the Monod family archive.

However, it is more productive to see *Nouvelle Vague* as an effort by Godard to renew his creative energies through a risky technique: fusing the *private* and *individualistic* aspects of memory with the *public* and *collective* aspects of cinema. Using personal recollections as a starting point offers two advantages. For one, it is a way of short-circuiting the superficially communal aspects of moviegoing – fostered by the shared, often nostalgic emotions of popular film – in order to probe deep recesses of the filmmaker's own personality, excavating oddities and idiosyncrasies that others may recognize as (paradoxically) similar to qualities they believed were unique to themselves. For another, it provides a powerful means of relativizing the "real world" captured by cinema technology, thereby cracking it open for fresh scrutiny and analysis. Memories are the residues of contingency, accumulated in the course of life experiences (including the very earliest) that we may or may not have chosen to undergo; while we may treasure some of the images and sounds that we have stored away, others may be unpleasant or even hateful to us. All of which means that memory is not always subject to the "control" that we usually want to exercise over our lives, actions, and thoughts. A part of consciousness that eludes control is a natural habitat for someone who seeks to push film beyond the controls foisted upon it by a long history of conventional practice. The very arbitrariness of memory makes it an antidote to the calculated strategies of "normal" storytelling, and an exciting source of material for a filmmaker who values cinema as a vehicle for intuition, speculation, and discovery.

This is why memory inspires the content and style of *Nouvelle Vague*. As noted, the content recalls Godard's sun-drenched seasons on a family estate during his childhood, when the moods and machinations of grown-ups must have seemed as mysterious to *him* as the behavioral intrigues and verbal gobbledygook of the movie's characters often seem to *us*. The style is of course inseparable from this content, dividing the plot into memorylike fragments while maintaining just enough storylike continuity to link the movie with recognizable ways of processing information and experience.

The focus on memory in *Nouvelle Vague* is made explicit by a character with a minor role in the narrative but a central role in conveying the film's meaning: Jules the gardener, whose intermittent speeches are a combination of soliloquy, narration, and running commentary on the action. "Nothing from outside to distract memory," he says at one point, savoring his intimate relationship with the estate and its gorgeous grounds. "I barely hear, from time to time, the earth's soft moan, one ripple breaking the surface," he continues. "I am content with the shade of a single poplar, tall behind me in its mourning." In these sentences, the interior landscape of memory and the exterior landscape of nature form a single continuum, like the Möbius strip that Godard has likened to cinema's intermingling of fiction and reality.

Near the end, Jules's ruminations come even closer to identifying the film as a memory experience; and although he is speaking of the characters within the story, he could easily be referring to Godard himself. "It was as if they had already lived all this," the gardener says. "Their words seemed frozen in the traces of other words from other times. They paid no heed to what they did, but to the difference that set today's acts in the present and parallel acts in the past. They felt tall, motionless, with past and present above them: identical waves in the same ocean." These words have a Proustian ring, evoking *Le Temps retrouvé* so vividly that Godard must have intended the connection.

In describing *Nouvelle Vague* as a memory film, I am obviously calling attention to specific aspects that spring directly from Godard's history and sensibility. I do not mean to suggest that it is a self-involved or solipsistic work, however. The opposite is true, since Godard manages to use the memory mechanisms that interest him in ways that go far beyond the inward-turning indulgences of nostalgic remininiscence. As already noted, his turn toward personal recollection is a means of evading the narrative clichés and manufactured feelings that fill conventional film stories; it also enables him to bypass the ingrained habits of conscious thought so as to draw on wellsprings of mental energy (and experience) that lie in deeper levels of the mind.

Beyond this, Godard uses the film's fascination with memory to grapple with political concerns raised by his "story" of shady capitalists flaunting their assumed superiority. In a typical Hollywood movie about characters living a posh and privileged life, the appropriateness of their pampered status would hardly be questioned, much less criticized. *Nouvelle Vague* takes a different tack, by viewing the situation as yet-unborn generations might someday remember it. Again it is Jules the gardener who makes this point:

> Soon certain social conventions, customs, principles, inbred sentiments will vanish. We can take as defunct the society we've lived in. Future ages will recall it only as a charming moment in history. They'll say . . . , "It was a time when there were rich and poor, fortresses to take, heights to scale, treasures well-enough guarded to preserve their appeal. Luck was in the running."

So much for the notion that *Nouvelle Vague* is a long day's journey into pointlessness and incongruity, as its hostile critics have charged. So much also for the idea that Godard abandons sociopolitical concerns in the wake of his aesthetically and spiritually attuned "sublime" films. Almost every facet of this complicated work, from the class interactions of its characters to its rejection of narrative clichés, can be read as a critique of commonsensical ideologies that Godard has long despised. Even the movie's astonishing physical beauty takes on a subversive edge, since the primary settings are presented as a mosaic of discontinuous surfaces rather than a series of smoothly flowing images linked by narrative logic and conventional montage. Summoning up the comfortable surroundings in which his youthful consciousness was formed, Godard proceeds to interrogate their social meaning (suggesting that rich, poor, and fortresses will not always be taken as inevitable parts of the natural order) and to deconstruct the roles they played in shaping his own values and identities (bourgeois, Protestant, educated, etc.) in later life. The disjointedness of this process, hindering the effortless visual pleasure that might otherwise come from the imagery, reflects his desire less to *re*-member than to *dis*-member the scattered pieces of his past.[8]

Nouvelle Vague also serves a second agenda for Godard, related to his sociopolitical goals yet taking off in very different directions. Once more the trusty Jules provides an important clue to this.

"A garden is never finished. Like prose," he says in one of his voice-overs, sounding again like Godard, a *poète maudit* who sows his films with words as religiously as Jules nourishes the estate's foliage. "It always needs touching up: its pattern, its colors," the groundskeeper adds. "It's as if it suggests its own corrections. But if you neglect it. . . ." And his head sinks as he ponders this awful possibility.

Jules appears to be Godard's surrogate in *Nouvelle Vague,* commenting on the action with a wit and detachment worthy of the filmmaker himself. When he talks about the estate's garden, we can take his words literally, as a part of the movie's fictional story; and we can also take them figuratively, as a metaphorical statement regarding the film we are watching – never definitive, always incomplete, forever germinating new ideas that could lead to its own improvement.

Jules has deeper things on his mind than the responsibilities of the creative spirit, however. Soon he utters what are probably the most resonant and suggestive words in the film: "Let the world be without name for a time. Let things listen to what they are. In silence, in their own time and their own way."

On its face, this is a surprising statement to hear in a Godard film. One of his most constant qualities has been a steady fascination – obsession, even – with words and language. In film after film, his characters have chattered away whether or not they had anything significant to say; and they have turned to writing (journals, etc.) when speaking was inconvenient. His camera has photographed words, dissected words, and integrated words with nonverbal scenes and images. His editing has incorporated written words, syllables, and letters into visual montage. Using documentary-style (direct-sound) recording techniques, his microphones have captured speech along with the ambient sounds around it, preserving not only the sense of the words but the expressive "grain of the voice" that says them. His cinema has always been "driven by a logocentric vocation," as Angela Dalle Vacche puts it, displaying a deeply rooted "love for language in all its manifestations: alphabetical and literary, graphic and acoustic."[9]

So why does Jules, after comparing his own artistic project (the garden) with prose, call for "silence" and a "world without name," in which "things listen to what they are" instead of the words we use to label, tame, and possess them?

One answer lies in another of Godard's longtime goals: his desire to make films in which fictional elements are inseparably linked with the physical realities that surround them. In his later films, this is joined by a greater-than-ever fascination with the material presence of words (words as sound) and a greater-than-ever suspicion toward the signifying power of words (words as meaning).

Though the effort to mingle fiction and reality can be traced back to *Breathless,* with its real-world locations and improvisational acting, it emerges as a major preoccupation in *My Life to Live* and makes another leap in *Pierrot le fou,* which can be seen as an extended study of how a particular pair of human bodies (Belmondo and Karina) look, sound, and comport themselves under a wide range of circumstances presented by the film's peripatetic camera setups. When we watch Ferdinand teeter precariously along a tree trunk within the fiction, we are also watching Belmondo teeter precariously along a tree trunk within reality. If he were to slip and fall on his head, we would have the dual experience of seeing Ferdinand undergo a mishap in his (make-believe) adventures and Belmondo undergo a disaster in his (actual) life; and we would have to choose our own balance between shrugging off the misfortune of the character, on one hand, and recoiling from the tragedy of the actor, on the other. This truism would go without saying if conventional movies did not labor so successfully to cover physical actuality with the veneer of fantasy, encouraging us to see all aspects of a film as parts of a story-based illusion.[10] That is exactly the sort of cinematic attitude Godard wants to expose and eradicate, of course, and capturing human figures in their irreducible reality – proving anew that "existence preceeds essence," in movies as in life – is one of his favored strategies.

He did some of his basic thinking about this around 1965, when *Pierrot le fou* was made and when *Cahiers du cinéma* published his essay "*Pierrot* My Friend," which puts great emphasis on the "physical" part of film; it ends by stating that "the cinema, by making reality disgorge, reminds us that one must attempt to live."[11] Also helpful is a statement he made in an interview that year. "What you do . . . is simply try to create a kind of object out of the person, like in painting or sculpture," he says. As a movie director, he naturally tries to coax performers into following his instructions; but as an artist, he seems most pleased with the results when his instructions are ignored:

> I'm always surprised by the fact that I never succeed in obtaining what I want. . . . I say to an actor: "You walk like this," and he doesn't walk that way. "You laugh at that spot," and he doesn't laugh. But each time I am struck by the fact that that person *exists* nevertheless. Exists independently of me regardless of his performance being good or bad. So I try to make use of that existence and to shape things around it so he can continue to exist. Nothing should be sacrificed to the film. The idea of the film is nothing, just a few lines.

And later in the same interview, "That's what I like to do above all, place people in situations like that where they . . . you don't know if it's good or bad . . . but you know they exist."[12]

Godard's restless sensibility grappled with many stories, styles, and ideas between *Pierrot le fou* and *Nouvelle Vague*, but his interest in this aspect of cinema remained keen. This is why he was able to say, regarding *Nouvelle Vague,* that the presence of a movie star like Alain Delon had the same attraction for him as a tree in a landscape – and that he photographed Delon accordingly, showing "the same reverence for nature [as with] a dark closeup of a tree's sinewy trunk," as White describes it.[13] In practice, this meant filming Delon from behind more often than would normally happen, denying him the glamorous star-gazing shots that big-name performers usually command. Godard is not particularly concerned with Delon as a star, or even as an actor. He *is* interested in Delon and others (including the nonprofessionals who appear in many of his films) as existential beings-in-the-world, whose sheer presence constitutes a mystery as profound and seductive as anything the screenplay cooks up for them to do or say.

Nouvelle Vague plugs directly into Godard's conception of cinema as simultaneously a builder of spectacle and a recorder of reality. This makes it a direct descendant of all his works, going back to *Breathless,* which aim at flummoxing the boundaries between fiction and documentary. It has especially strong links to *Hail Mary* and the other "sublime" movies, since it also strives to penetrate the hard shell of material reality (like young Mary cracking her enigmatic egg) and glean some sense of the higher energies that may have left their traces there.

This brings us back to the question of Jules the gardener, and why he wishes the world could be "without name for a time," full of things listening "to what they are" in the peaceful silence of their own fundamental natures. In this moment, emphasized by its position near the end of the film, Godard is suggesting that we transcend the limitations of conventional thought by erasing the words – imposed on us by society – that both express and circumscribe our perceptions.

We may understand this better if we recall that Godard has singled out the prison house of language for sharp analysis in previous films. One is *2 or 3 Things I Know about Her,* where his first-person narration complains about a society in which "there are so many signs . . . that I end up wondering what language is about." By contrast, "images can get away with everything, for better or worse. . . . Objects are there, and if I study them more carefully than people, it's because they are more real than people."

Nouvelle Vague acts on this insight by making all the world into objects. A movie star is photographed in the same manner as a tree – not for the purpose of degrading or diminishing the human figure, but with the opposite aim of appreciating people as parts of a grand cosmic continuum, and allowing them to appreciate themselves with similar intensity.

Images, signs, people: Marina Vlady as Juliette Janson, and her self-reflective mirror image, captured by the camera in *2 or 3 Things I Know about Her* (1966).

(Juliette does this in *2 or 3 Things* when, as she puts it, "I suddenly had the feeling that I was the world and that the world was me.") Promoting this romantic oneness among people, places, and things is a goal of all the major devices in *Nouvelle Vague,* from the evasion of stable identity (are we watching Richard or Roger or both?) to the fracturing of the story into a kaleidoscopic array of exquisitely filmed fragments.

The effort to explore reality without passing through conventional sign systems also explains the proliferation of random speech in *Nouvelle Vague;* this makes language not a privileged carrier of dramatic meaning, but just another part of the landscape we are visiting. Once more we can look back to Godard's early work – indeed, the first shot of *Breathless,* with Michel hidden behind an ad-packed newspaper – for the roots of this practice. And again, two films of the mid-1960s show this strategy reaching its mature form. The first is *Pierrot le fou,* with its images of Ferdinand's blotchily scrawled journal and Rimbaud's portrait crazily covered with printed letters.[14] The second is *2 or 3 Things,* which features the characters Bouvard and Pécuchet (from Gustave Flaubert's eponymous novel) sitting in a café with a huge stack of books in various languages, identified by the published screenplay as "fiction, history, guidebooks, telephone directories, etc."[15] In what seems a never-ending process, Bouvard reaches for volume after volume and recites a few lines from each, which Pécuchet dutifully writes down in what appears to be a mushrooming "commonplace book" made up entirely of quotations chosen at random from previously published works. These two are astute precursors of the postmodern notion that originality is dead, everything has already been said, and today's only authentic route to expression is a candid commitment to quotation, pastiche, collage, and montage – methods Godard has embraced from his earliest days, as we have seen in virtually all the works we have examined.

The screenplay for *Nouvelle Vague* could have been copied from this copybook. Stam reports that the movie's "aleatory collage of sententious phrases" was "apparently compiled at the last minute by Godard and his collaborators," and that "the director himself claims scarcely to remember its diverse sources," which include Rimbaud, Dante, Lucretius, Friedrich Nietzsche, Raymond Chandler, and of course William Faulkner, that perennial Godard favorite.[16] Since the script does convey a plot and allow human relationships to develop, as odd and minimal as these may be, it is certainly more coherent than Stam indicates when he says that "dialogue here becomes a kind of decoy, signifying little beyond its own quotability." Stam is exactly right, however, when he notes that "what is said is less important than how it is said." Conducting his investigation-cum-spectacle, Godard finds more significance in tones of voice and nuances of gesture than in specific words and actions. Along with his penchant for pastiche and assemblage, this allies him with other dramatists having a postmodern bent – the American stage director Robert Wilson, for instance, who habitually cares more about how a speaker *sounds* than what is actually being *said*. Wilson has referred to the spoken words of his early theater pieces (such as the majestic *Einstein on the Beach*, which blends a nonsensical script with Philip Glass's pulsating music) as a kind of "weather," indicating that their contribution to the overall atmosphere of the work – as material presence, not poetic expression – is all that really matters to him. Although some of the dialoguing and monologuing in *Nouvelle Vague* serves a dramatic purpose, a good deal of it is precisely like "weather," providing mood and ambience in much the same way as the quality of light, the rustle of outdoor and indoor noises, and indeed the literal weather – sun, clouds, breezes – that envelops the exterior scenes. Godard explores these word-sounds with the same sensuous fascination he displays toward other natural phenomena.

By treating words as material objects rather than privileged meaning-machines, then, Godard accomplishes two things: First, he creates a seamless cinematic fabric in which every component – words and voices as well as shapes, colors, textures, movements – has an equal measure of importance, and an equal chance to be valued for its contribution to the aesthetic whole. Second, he records the individual elements of this fabric so meticulously and lovingly that new, possibly profound insights can emerge from our contact with them.

In order for this to happen, the social and cultural import of words must not be allowed to take undue control of our attention, as happens all the time in "normal" movies that give dialogue and/or narration an expressive power that is virtually authoritarian in its effects. As we have seen, Godard has long believed we must bypass our personal egos if we are to participate in a greater, more cosmic reality; in earlier films he was motivated by the lust for Beat-style freedom and the utopian yearning of collective politics, and now he is inspired by spiritual and metaphysical hopes. The fragmented visuals and precarious memory-narrative of *Nouvelle Vague* are ways of pushing his own ego out of the picture, as is his rejection of speech as a meaning-full activity.

Jules the gardener again conveys what appear to be Godard's thoughts on these matters. "Whatever I say," he declares near the trees and water so dear to his heart, "within me are only words that will resurrect me." This resurrection of self, of individuality, of ego are exactly what Godard wants to avoid; yet like the seminal romantic Jean-Jacques Rousseau, he and Jules find that the internal self can never submit entirely to an exterior nature realm, since that outside world can only be known by the individual who perceives it. "All this grass, is it within me?" asks Jules, grappling with this question. "Is it grass when it's without me?"

He then asks a short, pithy question that carries his inquiry to a level even more challenging: "If no one labels it, gives it a name, what then is grass?" Godard returns here to the existentialist notion that "existence precedes essence," freshly integrating it with his own desire to shape a sort of spiritual algebra. If we take "existence" to mean being-in-the-world, and "essence" to mean the defining of a thing by human understanding and language, then Godard's form of cinema – so often separating image and language into parallel but disconnected tracks – can be seen as an attempt to know *things* in a way uncontaminated by *conceptions* formed in our imperfect, ego-centered minds.

Godard's concern with relationships between things and names became not just an interest but a central, even urgent preoccupation in the so-called sublime films, as he indicated in comments on *First Name: Carmen,* the centerpiece of that trilogy. A question asked in that movie – "What is there before the name?" – directly prefigures the exploration of this issue in *Nouvelle Vague* seven years later. "People always want to know what things are called," Godard told Gideon Bachmann in a 1983 interview. "I think that the cinema should show things before they receive a name, so that they can be given a name, or that we can give in to the business of naming them." Although it is true that Godard was shifting his emphases in the 1980s from predominantly political matters to subjects with greater spiritual and aesthetic dimensions, his focus on language here retains a clear political thrust. "Today we live in an epoch of total power being given to all forms of rhetoric," he says, "a time of terrorism of language which is further accentuated by television." Speaking as a filmmaker, he continues, "I . . . have an interest to speak of things before words and names take over, to speak of the child before daddy and mummy give it a name. To speak of myself before I hear myself being called Jean-Luc. To speak of the sea, of liberty, before they are being called sea, waves or freedom."[17]

Nouvelle Vague is a radical effort to capture a world free of names and labels, which inevitably promote power/knowledge agendas more than they serve transcendent truth and sublimity. Stam recognizes this when he says the film "has some of the visual exhilaration of discovering the world before names – as if we were back with the Lumières' primitive delight in everyday sights."[18] Moviegoers still puzzled by the fractured, disjointed nature of *Nouvelle Vague* may indeed find another rationale for it by remembering that many of the earliest films ever made – including those of Louis and Auguste Lumière, movie pioneers in the late nineteenth century – were brief, varied "actualities" shown to audiences in freewheeling programs that jumped from one subject to another every minute or so. While individual films often evoked a strong (if illusory) sense of unmediated reality, what many spectators valued was less the authenticity of particular images than the thrill of a constantly surprising "cinema of attractions," as critics have subsequently called it.

A passionate admirer of Lumière-style film, Godard feels that the promise it originally held out – of an art both spectacular and investigatory – has been betrayed by the temptations of commercialism.[19] *Nouvelle Vague* shows the possibility of a different outcome, not by mobilizing new technologies and innovative effects, but by revisiting and rethinking the past – the *personal* past of Godard's own memory, and the *artistic* past of a cinema based on the sincerity of primitive filmmaking rather than the fabrication, manipulation, and superficiality of Hollywood's later days. Returning to Jules's example, Lumière movies do not label grass, name grass, or exploit grass for seductive narrative purposes. They simply *show* grass for our enjoyment and contemplation, thereby exploring and celebrating the world in ways that more "sophisticated" cinema has sadly forgotten. Godard underscores the dual nature of this moment in *Nouvelle Vague,* at once personal and professional, with two intertitles. The first, just before Jules speaks of things without labels, reads SINCE THE BEGINNING, indicating that we are probing a timeless question here. The second, just after Jules's words, reads YOUR HUMBLE SERVANT, inscribing both Jules and Godard as mere laborers in the vineyards of aesthetics and philosophy.

Godard's wish to conjure up a world-before-names through a cinema-without-language recalls not only the best aspects of the pioneering Lumière brothers but also the work of a contemporary American filmmaker who is as much a radical, a romantic, and a modernist as Godard has ever been. There is no clear evidence that American avant-gardist Stan Brakhage has exerted a direct influence on Godard, and I must strongly emphasize that there is a very long list of very great differences between the two filmmakers, in both theory and practice. Most particularly, Godard has never gone as far as Brakhage in disavowing virtually all traces of narrative and characterization, and he certainly doesn't share Brakhage's preference for a silent cinema that draws entirely on "optical thinking" and addresses its audience exclusively through the eye. Still, despite their many differences they have many priorities, predilections, and strategies in common; and since Brakhage has pushed some of these to even greater extremes than Godard, study of his work can illuminate Godard's project.

One desire they share is to escape the visual domination of Renaissance perspective, which is anchored in ideologies of "realism" and "self-evidence" that both filmmakers find simplistic and redundant. They prefer a forthrightly *presentational* aesthetic that celebrates the flatness and artifice of cinema over illusions of presence and depth. This leads them to highly stylized filmmaking, articulated by conspicuous editing and self-consciously poetic mise-en-scène. Both also feel strong connections to the world of nature; the lakes, fields, and woods in Godard's work have a more kinetically filmed equivalent in Brakhage's countless shots of the Rocky Mountains region.

On the deepest level, what links these filmmakers most closely is their belief in the necessity of bypassing the individual ego so that greater cosmic forces can permeate their artistic work and enlarge its philosophical or spiritual meanings. Brakhage found motivation for this in poet Charles

Olson's notion that Western traditions cause us to be "alienated from the real" by false ways of knowing and feeling, and that "the sensuous presence of our contact with the world is constantly deferred by generalized logical classification," in critic David E. James's words. In order for people to be reintegrated "as continuous with reality rather than discrete from it," they must circumvent "historically and socially conditioned consciousness and the grammar of its language." This means rejecting "the intending role of the humanist ego" and "ideas that *refer* to reality rather than *embody* it," thus allowing the artist "to go beyond the imagination to unmediated perception, to that place where consciousness and nature are in direct contact."[20]

These words address key aspects of Godard's work as accurately as they describe some of Brakhage's ideals. For all the differences between their actual films, this profound distrust of what James calls "large mental structures that satisfy the desolate modern ego" unites Godard and Brakhage in what might almost be called a shared aesthetic-philosophical project. Brakhage was there first, shaping his radically poeticized approach as early as 1952, and refusing such cinematic mainstays as linear narrative and conventional space–time coordinates from the beginning of his career. Godard traveled a different path, as we have seen, taking years to throw off narrative structures and rarely doing so (except in wild mid-career experiments like, say, *One Plus One*) as drastically as his American contemporary; nor has he ever been attracted to the hand-held cameras and manipulations of film stock (scratching, painting, growing mold on the emulsion) that Brakhage has steadily used. Still, we would do well to see this pair as fellow travelers rather than unconnected individualists. Listen to Jules asking his unexpectedly profound question – "If no one labels it, gives it a name, what then is grass?" – and then ponder Brakhage's meditation on the same issue in a 1963 statement that has become his most widely cited contribution to film theory. It begins:

> Imagine an eye unruled by man-made laws of perspective, an eye unprejudiced by compositional logic, an eye which does not respond to the name of everything but which must know each object encountered in life through an adventure in perception. How many colors are there in a field of grass to the crawling baby unaware of "Green?" How many rainbows can light create for the untutored eye? How aware of variations in heat waves can that eye be? Imagine a world alive with incomprehensible objects and shimmering with an endless variety of movement and innumerable gradations of color. Imagine a world before the "beginning was the word."[21]

As different as Godard's works are from Brakhage's, this world before "beginning was the word" is what he hopes to unveil in *Nouvelle Vague*, as in his "sublime" movies and his most daring video productions.

Like his American counterpart, Godard is on an intuitive journey toward what he hopes will be Eden, a mythical destination that has fascinated him at least since Mary and Eva/Eve munched their apples in *Hail Mary*, linking that movie's New Testament story with Old Testament resonances. Eva bit her apple in the Paradise Villa, a setting not unlike the Swiss estate of *Nouvelle Vague*, which also comes equipped with comfy furniture, well-appointed fixtures, and working-class domestic help for supercilious residents to command. Such decadent surroundings made only a momentary appearance in *Hail Mary*, just long enough to tempt the Professor into dreams of an easy life full of sax solos and good smokes. By contrast, natural and humanly made luxuries consistently surround most of the *Nouvelle Vague* characters – even the servants, who willingly accept gifts from the countess while bidding her a fond farewell at the end.

It might be argued that Godard filmed this movie in a splendiferous setting merely to exploit the visual pleasure it provides. Perhaps, but the logic of his career suggests that his visit to a site of wealth and indulgence has more complex motivations. I have already noted two sides of his artistic personality that the opulent estate allows him to explore: personal memories of childhood contentment and adult political views that hold overprivileged capitalists in great suspicion. A third object of Godard's concern is a nagging sense of emotional ambivalence over his own position as a world-renowned media artist operating on the fringes of European cinema in terms of both geography (Switzerland) and aesthetics (avant-garde narrative). The estate in *Nouvelle Vague* vividly embodies the contradictions among these three areas of interest, allowing the bad and the beautiful to coexist in fascinating tension as Roger/Richard pursues his slippery course(s) among materialistic manipulators spinning their money-driven wheels in incongruously idyllic splendor.

The slipperiness of the story itself echoes the ambiguity of Godard's feelings toward all this. Still, critics who accuse his later films of too much gloominess should note that the ultimate outcome of *Nouvelle Vague* is clearly transcendent if not actually triumphant, with the camera rising to frame an immaculately composed image that brings landscape and humanity into a picture-perfect synthesis. Dialogue in the film's last portion also steers us in a sunny direction. "From the moment I saw you," says the countess to Lennox, "you robbed me of my existence." This line might lead us to expect a fit of film-noir anguish as the scene continues, but robbery becomes inseparable from liberation when she continues, "By delivering me from my existence, you stole it." Finally she adds, "You came from outside, and through love installed yourself in me, and I welcomed you through love." These words have a religious ring that echoes *Hail Mary*, with its view of inside and outside as permeable and interchangeable categories; they also anticipate *Hélas pour moi*, where God inhabits a mortal man's body in order to cohabit with a woman. In addition to their spiritual overtones, the words convey a romantic happiness that becomes explicit when Lennox and the countess join hands and he quotes his mother's phrase, "Giving a hand is all I asked of joy."

Hands have been an important motif in *Nouvelle Vague*, going through all sorts of motions – from grasping one another with affection to flailing for life in a threatening sea – connoting more meanings than a simple symbolic scheme can explain. Ultimately the film associates hands with joy, but like most of this movie's utterances, Lennox's aphorism makes more poetic than literal sense. Fortunately, the commonsense attribute of intellectual consistency is not what Godard seeks, as we are well aware. In the spiritually motivated odysseys of *Nouvelle Vague* and other late films, he pursues a sense of harmony between the physical and the metaphysical that parallels but does not equal the harmony between people and things that was his goal in *2 or 3 Things* and other previous works. Now he seeks a oneness with the world that is also a oneness with some sort of supreme being or ultimate reality, which he cannot define but can apparently sense, intuit, and dream.

Finding this oneness would provide not only artistic success of the most profound sort, but also an answer to the endless sets of questions he has confronted since his days as a youthful moviegoer and critic. Like a few other filmmakers who see cinema more as an exploratory tool than a narrative device – including Brakhage, who likewise considers "birth, sex, death, and the search for God" to be the true artist's inevitable subjects[22] – he uses film to probe his own obsessions, on the assumption that they are not unique to him and will strike chords of recognition in many who accompany him on his adventures in perception. In this way he hopes to assuage his existential anxieties even as he opens new vistas for communication, or *communion,* to use a term that Brakhage prefers for the sharing of meaningful truths rather than mere information.

In the end, Godard seeks an atonement for his middle-class sins (and origins) that will also be an at-one-ment with the God of nature, humanity, and art. By carrying this quest into one of its most provocative phases,

Nouvelle Vague demonstrates that postmodern pastiche, avant-garde assemblage, and the unmoored significations of a philosophically ambivalent age can be as spiritually productive as they are aesthetically tantalizing and personally provocative.

In addition to rejuvenating the spiritual interests probed by the "sublime" films a few years earlier, *Nouvelle Vague* anticipates later works that explore tensions between the natural and supernatural through adventures of disoriented characters caught in beguiling yet mysterious landscapes. *Germany Year 90 Nine Zero,* released in 1991, resurrects the *Alphaville* hero Lemmy Caution – still played by Eddie Constantine, a quarter-century older but as bold and bulky as ever – and sends him on another quest through space and time. This time his mission takes him from the crumbling communist enclave of Eastern Europe to the triumphantly capitalistic West, retracing Godard's own ideological journey from days of unsustainable Marxist ideals to a recognition that *where* one lives is less important than *how* one lives, and that how one lives is a matter calling for unending thought, negotiation, and self-scrutiny. Since this attitude is fueled by roughly equal measures of hope and resignation, both dispositions pervade the film's atmosphere. Lemmy finds little to choose between East and West, which together have produced the muddle of modern Europe, home of great possibilities and mind-boggling disappointments. Godard films the muddle lovingly, dispelling any sense of cynicism while also suggesting that aesthetics are the surest means of escaping despair over what has become of the twentieth century's great sociopolitical experiments.

Historical rumination also plays a part in *Hélas pour moi,* but this 1992 production is more intimate than Lemmy Caution's last adventure. It recalls *Hail Mary* in its overtly religious concerns, and *Nouvelle Vague* in its fascination with a diverse group of individuals whose luxurious yet limited lives are challenged by a mysterious, possibly dangerous stranger. His arrival prompts a wide range of responses, from personal consternation to musings on the search for meaning in a spiritually exhausted time.

The stranger in *Hélas pour moi* is not a highway-walking enigma like Lennox in *Nouvelle Vague* but a figure with a far more impressive résumé: He is God himself, played by Gérard Depardieu in a larger-than-life performance that suggests good-natured complicity with Godard's apparent intention of giving Europe's grandest (and busiest) screen star one of the few roles that might match his noisily hyped reputation. (Unfortunately, this complicity proved short-lived, since Depardieu walked out of the picture when shooting reached the halfway mark.)[23] Taking its cue from ancient legends about intercourse between gods and humans, the film chronicles what happens when the Supreme Being takes over a man's body in order to experience earthly pleasures.

"Our age is in search of a lost question," says one character, summing up a key theme of the tragicomedy, "weary of all the right answers." This precisely echoes Godard's aim in *Nouvelle Vague,* as well as in most of the investigations-cum-spectacles that precede and follow it. We have seen ample evidence that he has no interest in producing the facile "right answers" used by conventional art to coddle its customers. Instead he seeks deep and thrilling *questions* that can renew our zest for living, thinking, and creating despite the overwhelming disillusionments that our materialistic era has piled up around us.

8

Video and Television

And if cinema today still works on television, it's because television itself has no love. ... On television you can find power in its pure state, and the only things that people like seeing on TV at all are sports and cinema films, and that is because they seek love. ...

– Jean-Luc Godard, 1983[1]

Godard's interest in video, including mass-market television and offbeat "video art" formats, did not grow into a strong preoccupation until the middle of the 1970s. This makes him something of a latecomer to the field, since alternative or "guerrilla" television had already picked up a good deal of steam among American artists and activists.

It goes without saying that his tardiness was not caused by timidity or conservatism. The main thing at issue was his longstanding loyalty to the apparatus of motion pictures: the professional 35mm equipment he had worked with during most of his career, and the flexible 16mm format (carrying many of the benefits associated with portable TV equipment) used for many of the Dziga-Vertov Group films.

His first production using video as a major tool was *Numéro deux* in 1975. This was a full five years after the American video underground had started its efforts to satirize, subvert, and ultimately replace the establishment-bound institutions of commercial TV, inspired by the countercultural mood of the 1960s in general, and the writings of fashionable theorists like Marshall McLuhan and Buckminster Fuller in particular.[2] Some of these TV guerrillas wanted to produce in-depth documentaries and "specials" that would promulgate their radicalized views on specific social and political issues. Others wanted to produce regular series or miniseries that would challenge conventional notions of TV programming as a whole. Once he embraced video, Godard wanted to do both; and within the next five years he did, also finding time to pioneer a whole new genre – the video *scénario,* a short work made as a commentary or supplement to a 35mm feature. He may have arrived at the video party late, but once in the group, he made his presence forcefully felt.

Godard's video productions, many of them codirected or otherwise aided by Miéville, have been as controversial as his films. Some critics damn them with faint praise, saying his turn to video has mainly been a savvy economic move, allowing him to make individualistic works without too much financial risk. Others praise them with faint damns, regretting the reduced image quality of his video pieces compared with his "real" movies, yet acknowledging that video's flexibility and malleability make it useful for personal, spontaneous creation. Still others see them as the last refuge of a marginalized artist whose eccentricities have sadly limited his access to mainstream production, distribution, and exhibition.

There is some truth in each of these views. The image quality of video is indeed inferior to that of movie film, although the medium compensates for this by allowing a range of manipulations and "special effects" that are relatively simple to accomplish. It is also true that video encourages low-budget production, but this should enhance rather than diminish its prestige, since it allows for an individualism and experimentalism that adventurous filmmakers have found increasingly hard to practice, especially since cultural politics turned more conservative in the 1980s and 1990s, reducing financial support (and ticket-buying audiences) for innovative work.

Godard himself has lent credence to the notion that video offers a haven from the slings and arrows of commercial cinema, characterizing himself as an incorrigible experimenter who will never be the kind of media celebrity he could have become if he'd pursued a more conventional path. As an artist who has made the sociocultural margin his home, he appears to have realized at some point, he can't profess too much surprise at finding himself a marginalized artist. He amplified on this at a 1995 press conference, giving it a distinctly positive spin: "I am something of a loner. . . . I've always considered myself marginal. In a book, the primordial space is the margin, because it joins with that of the preceding page. And you can write in the margin, and take notes, which is as important as the 'main text.'"[3]

Godard's admirers have long maintained that, under the influence of his strong creative personality, the margin *becomes* the center when he is occupying it. It is certainly true that his excursions into video have helped legitimize that medium as a valid option for serious artistic expression.

Conversely, video has served him well – not only as a flexible, low-budget medium for some of his more audacious ventures, but also as a new arena in which to pursue his longtime fascination with spontaneous creation and (always at the top of his agenda) challenging commonsense notions of socially productive art, entertainment, and communication.

Asked by an interviewer about his growing interest in video during the mid-to-late 1970s, he responded with a revealing statement, noting that when a technology is new,

> it is less rigid, and there are less instructions from the police, the law or circulation. There is not less law, but it hasn't been made, it isn't written down. It is before the written. . . . You have no rules so you have something to live with, you have to invent some rules and to communicate with other people. . . . I was interested because there were no rules. . . . You have to find rules in yourself and when to work more or to love.[4]

When he observes that the "law" governing new technologies is "before the written," Godard recalls his desire to capture a state of innocence and innovation that stands above or beyond the everyday realities of our socially conditioned world. His affection for light-gathering and sound-recording equipment with not-yet-written rules is clearly connected to his quest for perceptions that predate "beginning was the word" consciousness, to cite Stan Brakhage once again. Approaching a new audio or video technique, Godard can be imagined asking the question posed by Jules the gardener: If nobody labels it or gives it a name, what then *is* this phenomenon? One possible answer: whatever we choose to make of it. As Godard said of video in another portion of the interview just quoted, "I don't know why I got interested. Maybe because it wasn't run by movie people so there was no law. So I was authorised."[5]

The idea of video as an escape route from "law" crops up more than once in his statements over the years. Speaking in 1993 of his "videoscript" for *Passion,* Godard says, "I have always been against writing. It represents the laying down of the law," which becomes "fixed and constraining" like a straitjacket. "I want to work like a painter with images and details," he adds. "Delacroix painted five hundred hands before drawing a full human figure." And later, "The scenario should be an inquest, an investigation, not a certainty, a written law."[6] Video thus represents a way to evade the coercive tendencies of the written word, allowing the artist to circumvent verbal preconditions and draw upon visionary resources that are comparatively free of well-worn sociocultural habits.

Godard's engagement with video was not sudden or arbitrary. It emerged from tendencies that were already visible in his filmmaking, and picked up strength from two further developments that touched his life, one personal and one political.

The personal development has been pithily described by French critic Philippe Dubois, who notes that "the appearance of video in Godard's work corresponds fairly precisely to the appearance of Anne-Marie Miéville in his life and work."[7] Miéville has been less public than Godard about her background, although it is known that she is also Swiss; that she had a brief singing career in Paris during the 1960s; and that she acquired some filmmaking experience before joining her new companion – who shared her urgent interest in the Palestinian crisis – as still photographer for *Tout va bien,* and then helping him establish the Sonimage production company.[8] Serving as cowriter and (usually) codirector of his next several projects, she helped him appropriate video as a weapon against what they perceive as the cultural degradation and dehumanization caused by contemporary society's mass-media blitz, a major contributor to which has been (ironically) video itself.

The political event was the 1974 election of Valérie Giscard-d'Estaing as president of France, bringing a series of liberal reforms that included the decentralization of the Organisation de Radio et Télévision Français – which regulated broadcasting activities – into a number of smaller units with some degree of independence from one another. This allowed Godard and Miéville to make a coproduction deal with the Institut National Audiovisuel, calling for two miniseries that would certainly not have seen the light of day under France's previous media regime.

Even before video became a primary concern for Godard and Miéville, the first three films they worked on together dealt as much with questions of media and communication as with the sociopolitical problems that appear to be their main subjects. This is conspicuously true of *Here and Elsewhere* in 1974 and *Comment ça va* in 1976, which discuss how mass media transform our perceptions of globally important events and concepts; it is more subtly true of *Numéro deux* in 1975, which shows (indeed, reproduces) the impact of media technologies on emotional dynamics within a household. The filmmakers' goal in these works, as Dubois summarizes it, is to respond *"in images and sounds* to the set of questions that address why we no longer know how to communicate, speak, see, and think, and how we can still try to speak and create with images and sounds." Among their key devices are various forms of direct or spontaneous address, manipulation of the image by electronic means, and experiments in slowing and "de-composing" the image, thus reducing its power to mesmerize and confuse.[9]

In retrospect, the three films that launched Godard's collaboration with Miéville seem like relatively straight continuations of the Dziga-Vertov Group's overall project. Their political overtones are overt, and their styles make absolutely no concessions to popular movie conventions. Godard and Miéville readmitted a certain degree of mass-market appeal in 1979 when they gave *Sauve qui peut (la vie)* a reasonably linear story, along with movie stars and a great deal of truly sensuous cinematography; such later works as *First Name: Carmen* and *Détective* continued this trend, mixing a few crowd-pleasing ingredients (dramatic acting, narrative suspense, etc.) with the unusual and demanding elements that were obviously their primary interest. This phase of their partnership also produced a pair of large-scale experiments that stand with their most audacious achievements. These are the video series coproduced by Sonimage for broadcast by French television: *Six fois deux/Sur et sous la communication,* six episodes made in 1976, and *France/tour/détour/deux/enfants,* a dozen episodes made in 1977 and 1978.

Although these programs have baffled media critics unfamiliar with Godard's avant-garde sensibility, thoughtful observers have noted the essential point about them: They do not represent an effort to *employ* or *exploit* television, but rather to *intervene* in the cultural scene that TV has dominated throughout its reign as the world's most pervasive and influential communications medium. Godard is not "moving into television" with the hope of revitalizing his career – if that had been his goal, he could surely have found more realistic ways of approaching it! – or of "reforming" an institution sunk so deeply into triviality that even commercial movies appear sophisticated by comparison. His aim is to radicalize popular attitudes toward TV by pushing to the limit the elements and capabilities that he finds most potentially valuable within it. These include

- the closeness and potential intimacy between the medium and its viewers, who consider the TV screen a comfortable part of their everyday surroundings;
- the extended time frame of the TV series, which allows a set of subjects to be explored for hours and hours without necessarily seeming odd or long-winded;
- the ease with which images and sounds can be handcrafted via advanced video technology;

- and, related to all of these, the unforeseen possibilities that might arise from defamiliarizing the taken-for-granted ordinariness of the medium itself, and of the questionable social structures it currently mirrors.

Instead of spinning stories, inventing characters, and diverting viewers from the cares of the day, therefore, Godard and Miéville use television as a sort of scientific probe. Their method is to fill the living-room TV set with faces, bodies, and voices taken from ordinary life, and allow the personalities, histories, mannerisms, and other traits of these persons a dignity and *attention* that conventional programming would never have the patience or imagination to allow. It's unlikely that the artists expect a large number of viewers to sit and consume this slowly evolving material with the same avidity granted to traditionally "entertaining" shows; but they do hope spectators will realize that as a *component* of contemporary life, TV should not merely echo but actually *absorb* and *embody* contemporary experience. We should be able to switch on the tube, that is to say, and find our world encapsulated there in all its unadorned actuality. If the planet's most powerful medium is to discover the truth that existence precedes essence, then the sheer presence of material reality must precede the artificial constructions and definitions that conventional television (like conventional cinema) works so hard to bestow on it.

To understand the aims and accomplishments of *Six fois deux* and *France/tour/détour/deux/enfants,* it is helpful to recall a slightly later work that comes closer to those programs in spirit than any of the other films made immediately before and after them. This is (ironically) the only film of the period that does not carry Miéville's name in its credits: *Passion,* the 1982 drama that investigates painting and mise-en-scène as intently as *First Name: Carmen* explores music and as intuitively as *Hail Mary* burrows into religious material.

As noted earlier, *Passion* chronicles the experiences of a filmmaker named Jerzy as he directs a movie involving soundstage re-creations of great paintings. Near the beginning, a worker on the film-within-the-film mentions the "rules" of cinema – presumably the very rules that drove Godard to experiment with video, which he considered free of regulations and constraints. "There's a story, and you have to follow it," says the worker, in tones resembling those of Betty Berr, a host of the *France/tour/détour* series. Jerzy then appeals to cinematographer Raoul Coutard, who momentarily becomes a character in the film, reassuring Jerzy that cinema has no rules – yet mumbling a bit later that there *are* two rules: "minimum effort canceled by maximum nuisance."

All this is clearly meant to seem more sardonic than serious, especially since Jerzy is having great trouble holding his production together, much less creating motion-picture art. The mood turns more earnest, however, when he starts working with a video recorder. Two scenes involving Jerzy and his video setup help us understand Godard's own attitudes toward TV technology.

The first comes shortly after a factory worker, played by Isabelle Huppert, observes that work and pleasure are similar since they share the same gestures. This casts light on Godard's theory of acting, which refuses sharp distinctions between different categories of behavior. It also shows his continuing (Marxian) distaste for divisions of labor, which inevitably divide the human spirit, too.

Back at Jerzy's place, Jerzy and an actress played by Hanna Schygulla watch a videotaped scene from the movie they're making; the scene involves Hanna, an unnamed male actor, and an operatic voice halfheartedly synced with Hanna's lips. "It's our work," Jerzy reminds Hanna, who appears reluctant to view her image on the screen. "Love working, work at loving – show me the difference," he then says to a telephone caller.

Meanwhile, the video scene runs on and on, as if it were not an episode in a drama but some kind of interminable home movie. Hanna, never becoming comfortable with it, keeps grimacing and giggling. What emerges from this moment is Godard's idea that the *duration* and *intimacy* of video allow representations of living, loving, and creating to overlap with our off-screen lives more obviously and definitively than happens with any other medium. Indeed, televised material can seem to the viewer as persistent (and embarassing) as "real life" itself. The main difference between TV and existential reality, it seems, is that TV focuses our attention on details of experience that ordinarily get lost in the multilayered shuffle of everyday activity.

The other relevant scene comes during a part of the movie when Jerzy is arguing with film executives who can't understand why he doesn't tell stories like a normal director. Transfixed again by Hanna's video image – framed in a tight close-up, she speaks about "talking to myself" and "traveling into myself" – he spools the cassette forward and backward, muttering a few words over and over: "Don't forget me. . . . I'm forgetting you." On one level this seems contradictory, since film and video work against forgetting, capturing images with a permanence that memory can't equal; but the moment has a deeper meaning, since Jerzy's manipulations of the video image give it an ephemerality that underscores its artificial nature. It is not Hanna who shimmers and flickers before him;

it is only Hanna's image, and the harder he tries to grasp this, the more he risks letting the real Hanna slip away from consciousness.

As television producers, Godard and Miéville take their cue from two notions suggested by these scenes: (a) TV is the most lifelike of media and therefore the most *unlike* traditional means of expression, with imperatives and potentialities all its own; and (b) TV's vivid yet transient nature makes it a particularly seductive *competitor* and a potentially insidious *substitute* for the complex authenticities of actual experience.

What's needed, Godard and Miéville conclude, is a Brechtian television that presents itself not as a *replacement of* but rather a *complement to* the existential world. TV shows of this sort would not take the viewer out of reality – the goal of "escapist" entertainment – but would exist alongside that reality, opening our perceptual lives to new possibilities rather than sucking our attention into a commercially driven "vast wasteland."[10]

The term "antitelevision," meaning "a complete turning of television conventions against themselves," aptly describes the Sonimage approach in *Six fois deux* and *France/tour/détour*.[11] These programs challenge TV norms in many ways – replacing the tube's usual noise and chatter with intermittent stretches of silence, for instance, and developing material in fits and starts ("stammering") that deliciously subvert commercial television's "natural" flow of consumer-friendly sights and sounds.

In many respects, however, the shows don't so much invert the medium's normal functions as place them between ironic quotation marks. One sign of this is the fact that *Six fois deux* and *France/tour/détour* both fall into TV's most commonplace format: Each is a series, meant to appear in living rooms week after week with reassuring regularity.[12] Each also makes extensive use of on-camera interviewing, putting its own spin on this common device but reproducing it all the same. These and other similarities with mainstream TV indicate the producers' desire not to ignore the habits cultivated by broadcast video but rather to employ such patterns for their own purposes.

Although their goal is to recast television in a radically new form, moreover, they do not claim definitive answers as to exactly what this new form should be. Accordingly, they try to make viewers (along with other figures in the media industry) question basic assumptions about the very notion of television as it has hitherto existed. In each series, what they create is an *attempt* at a TV show, to borrow one of Godard's favorite formulations from bygone days. More precisely, it is an attempt at a new conceptualization of the medium, intended more to open minds than to gratify eyes and ears. The results of this intervention are as drastically different from mainstream norms as any of Godard's theatrical films, including the movies of the Dziga-Vertov Group, whose essayistic structures remain a source of energy and ideas for the TV ventures. It should also be stressed that *Six fois deux* and *France/tour/détour* are not intended as models for other producers to imitate; even Godard and Miéville stayed with series TV for only a short time, soon swinging back to feature-film production and nonseries video.

Of the two series, *France/tour/détour/deux/enfants* is more germane to Godard's overall trajectory, because (as Colin MacCabe has accurately noted) it gets beyond the lingering political preoccupations of *Six fois deux*, pointing less to Godard's polemical past and more to an aestheticized future in which the everyday world will be mined for instances of beauty, mystery, and transcendence. If this enterprise goes well, video will become "philosophy as chamber music" and series TV will be reborn as simultaneously "a novel and a painting," as Godard said in 1980.[13]

This is at once an exhilarating new goal and a characteristic result of Godard's longtime quest to reinvent reality in his own romantic terms. His hope for the mid-1970s television work is nowhere better expressed than in the mid-1960s film *2 or 3 Things I Know about Her*, which I have cited earlier: "My aim: for the simplest things to come into being in the world of humans, for man's spirit to possess them, a new world where men and things would interrelate harmoniously." Weekly television is a promising venue for bringing together the world of things and the world of human agency, since it combines the serial form of the nineteenth-century novel (always one of Godard's great loves) with the perceptual precision afforded by the most modern audiovisual tools. It is an excellent forum for the "passion for self-expression" that Godard admits to in the *2 or 3 Things* commentary, where he gives himself one of his most accurate signatures: "writer and painter."

Describing his approach to *Six fois deux* and *France/tour/détour*, Godard said he "functioned as a network programmer, that is, by making a programming grid."[14] This is technically correct, but Godard is being at least partially ironic when he uses the lingo of institutional TV in such a deadpan manner, as if he had merely aimed to hammer together a professionally acceptable series. The significant thing, of course, is how he and Miéville used their "programming grid" once it was sketched out. Conventional programmers fill their allotted time slots with "content" of various kinds – fictional or nonfictional, live or prerecorded, and so on – that combines the reassuring consistency of a standardized product (pretty much the same from one broadcast to the next) with the refreshing novelty of whatever small variations the programmers allow into each individual segment. Perhaps the most important single innovation that Godard and Miéville brought to this process was to minimize the notion of content – or rather to *undramatize* it, allowing the simple existence of human activity on the tube to constitute the "compelling interest" that viewers presumably demand.

The format of *Six fois deux* is as regularized as its title, presenting six "movements" of two sections each – the first exploring a social or cultural issue from a generalized or theoretical standpoint, the second focusing on some individual whose life somehow illustrates or intersects with the concerns that have been raised. The format of *France/tour/détour* is more elaborate, but just as predictable in its overall shape. The main "characters" are a boy and girl who take turns "starring" in each half-hour segment. The basic ingredients are (a) electronically altered views of the child's daily life, (b) an interview with the child, conducted by Godard off camera, (c) an oblique commentary on all this by two "hosts" in a studio, (d) a short video-essay relating to some aspect of the episode's theme, and (e) more commentary by the hosts, leading to an inconclusive ending that points toward future developments with the words, "That's another story. . . ."

Viewing these episodes for the first time, one might think Godard has lost his longtime interest in spontaneous expression. Each program seems locked into the same rigid mold as the others: same format, same hosts, even the same words at certain key moments. To some degree, this impression is correct. Determined to wring new possibilities out of TV's most familiar properties, Godard and Miéville confront the challenge of standardized programming head-on, making regularity and repetition a part of their own plan. They recognize that television is a *ritual* experience. In ordinary TV the purpose of the ritual is to mesmerize us with "entertaining" trivia. By contrast, Godard and Miéville see the ritual of the half-hour segment as a liberating concept: Giving each episode the same basic structure is like recognizing that a typical day, a typical year, or a typical lifetime has a basic structure that can either be resented as a confining straitjacket or – taking a more positive attitude – be valued as a known, dependable framework within which we're free to explore, experiment, and daydream as we wish.

The overall shape of *France/tour/détour* can certainly be compared with a day or a lifetime. The series moves through a wide range of activities and interests that engage most ordinary children, from school and family life to sports, music, fashion, even history and politics. However, this more-or-less linear development is balanced by the repetitious structure of the individual programs, as when each one begins with everyday images "de-composed" by slow-motion photography, and finishes with a promise of more to come ("That's another story. . . .") as if the hosts were parents reluctantly closing their storybooks but assuring us that the cycle will continue on its steady, reliable course.

Like the individual movements, the series as a whole also subsumes its linear elements into what ultimately becomes an orderly cycle, reinforced by having the first and last episodes begin with one of the children preparing for bed. Indeed, the series may be viewed as a recurring dream that sloughs off the purposeful agendas of conscious life – including the conventional TV shows that influence our minds – and lets us wander through various nooks and crannies of everyday existence at a leisurely pace geared to contemplation rather than accomplishment. The first segment of the first episode guides us clearly in this direction. "Preparing your body for the night," the voice-over says. "Uncovering a secret, then covering it up again. The beginning of a story, or the story of a beginning. To slow down is to decompose."

What must be decomposed is not only the imagery of ordinary television but also the mental habits that superficial entertainments plant and cultivate within us. Faced with the predictable, antidramatic events of *France/tour/détour*, we may pay full attention if we choose, scrutinizing the words and gestures and expressions of the people-just-like-us who appear on screen. Alternatively, and just as legitimately, we may treat the TV set as the piece of furniture it is, glancing at its contents when they interest us and ignoring them otherwise. Or we may alternate between these possibilities. The only option not available is the one conventional TV pitches relentlessly at us: being drawn into the hypnotic grip of false "realities" chosen not for their "truth" or "beauty" but for their compatibility with commercial needs.

All this having been said, it must now be added that the regularity and predictability of the episodes are actually far from hostile to Godard's perennial love of spontaneity and improvisation. Indeed, the very sameness of the week-to-week structure enables him to experiment in fresh ways with "last-minute focusing," as he dubbed his ever-flexible style back in 1962.[15] Taking a hint from Godard's jazz references in *Hail Mary* and elsewhere, we might say (as with narrative-film procedures cited in the previous chapter) that the standardized shape of each episode serves the same function as the underlying chord structure of a bebop composition:

It provides a basic framework that's familiar to artists and audience alike, and thus enables the performers/producers to take off in any direction they desire with no fear that communication or understanding will break down.

To use another analogy, the rigid "rules" of the series serve the same purpose as the genre conventions that Godard employed in his early films – the gangster genre in *Breathless* and *The Little Soldier,* the musical genre in *A Woman Is a Woman,* the science-fiction genre in *Alphaville,* and so forth. These provide a reliable, ritualized base upon which the producers can extemporize as they wish. At times Godard and Miéville work within the conventions they have chosen, respecting the time-tested links between these protocols and enduring human interests and values. At other times the artists eagerly subvert those same conventions, foregrounding their weaknesses and turning them back upon themselves in the sort of aggressive parody called *détournement* by members of France's radical Situationist movement, which shared Godard's hostility toward the modern "society of the spectacle," as theorist Guy Debord called it.[16]

It is a wish to capitalize on both of these implicit models – improvisation and *détournement* – that leads Godard and Miéville to some of their fundamental choices in *France/tour/détour,* such as the decision to focus most of its attention on the children of a middle-class family. True, the depiction of domestic life in *France/tour/détour* veers far from the narratives found in ordinary shows: There is no story to shape the school and household events that dawdle along from week to week; parents are rarely glimpsed; the children spend large amounts of time on mundane activities like eating, doing homework, and responding to meandering questions from an interviewer we never see. Still and all, everyday family life provides the backdrop for a great deal of commercial TV, and Godard knows that a certain portion of the French viewing audience can be depended upon to watch for at least a little while when family-related images flicker across the living-room screen. During this time, as during a bop composition or a genre movie, any reasonably attentive viewer will always have a basic grasp of where we are (a TV show about kids), what's going on (commonplace situations at home and school), and what the time frame is (a half-hour per show). Within these parameters, Godard and his collaborators can improvise, ruminate, and free-associate with a fair degree of freedom before commercially conditioned viewers start switching their dials to something more conventionally entertaining.

Spectators who share the producers' interest in freeing TV from its traditional formulas have greeted this experiment with applause on the infrequent occasions when it has been publicly screened. Those with no such interests have found themselves bored or befuddled, but their unexamined notions of TV programming have received a bit of salutary shaking up for however long they did stay tuned. By the mid-1970s stage of their careers, it's unlikely that Godard or Miéville expected viewers in the latter category to emerge much changed from a momentary encounter with improvisatory, norm-challenging television. Surely a few seeds have been planted in a few receptive minds, however, and certainly the *gesture* of contesting consumer-driven TV has had sociocultural significance beyond the number of spectators measured by ratings-survey statistics.

Video work by Godard and/or Miéville has taken sundry forms in the years since *Six fois deux* and *France/tour/détour,* still their most audacious forays onto the turf of commercial television. In 1978, shortly after those ventures, the pair returned to the arena of international politics by arranging with the government of Mozambique to work on a multifaceted project that involved TV production – five hours of programming called *North against South* was envisioned – as well as surveying the country's own capacity to develop TV communications, and empowering residents to operate video equipment for their own purposes. More recent years have seen everything from videotaped interview sessions – such as the rambling *Soft and Hard (A Soft Conversation between Two Friends on a Hard Subject)* and the concise *J. L. G. Meets W. A. (Meetin' W. A.)*, both produced in 1986 – to two treatments of film history that couldn't be more dissimilar: the lean *2 x 50 Years of French Cinema* and the extravagant *Histoire(s) du cinéma.*

Linking a good deal of the video work, emphatically excluding the *Histoire(s) du cinéma* series, has been a desire to take advantage of the spareness and economy (aesthetic as well as economic) that video readily provides. This ties in with Godard's abiding wish, encountered so many times in these pages, to evade the seductive superficialities that make conventional cinema a diversion rather than an education, an enlightenment, an epiphany.

It is true that his films of the 1990s, from *Nouvelle Vague* through *For Ever Mozart,* have a sensuous quality arising from their saturated cinematography, rich if cut-and-spliced musical tracks, and appealing performers (even when, like Alain Delon in *Nouvelle Vague,* they are shot more like objects than personalities). Still, this sumptuousness arises from Godard's effort, first crystallized in the "sublime" trilogy, less to exploit the physicality of cinema than to undermine it by segmenting, fragmenting, and collaging it in ways that suggest – and even produce – the metaphysical dimensions that increasingly preoccupy him.

Video works like the mid-1970s television programs, *J. L G. Meets W.A. (Meetin' W A.)*, and *2 x 50 Years of French Cinema* represent the other side of this coin, as he strips away superficially enticing moments in hopes of finding a "zero degree" of cinematic language – an objective dating back (with different sets of inflections) to the Dziga-Vertov Group films and even to *The Little Soldier* and portions of *Breathless*. The goal of this effort is made clear by an exchange I cited in the introduction to this book, between Émile Rousseau and Patricia Lumumba, the punningly named protagonists of *Le Gai Savoir*, near the beginning of that movie. "I want to learn," says Patricia, "to teach. . . that we must turn against our enemy the weapon with which he fundamentally attacks us: language." Émile agrees, adding, "Let's start from zero." Patricia then refines their task by asserting that "first we have to go back there, return to zero," a process that will mean dissolving "images and sounds" in order to grasp how these are constituted and capitalized on in the modern world.

As noted in Chapter 5, this invocation of "zero" has much in common with that of cultural critic Roland Barthes, who coined the expression "writing degree zero" in his 1953 book of that title. In describing a "colourless writing, freed from all bondage to a pre-ordained state of language,"[17] Barthes is testing a possible resolution of certain tensions that have emerged in modern literature – tensions between writing as *communication,* using language to engage the attention and action of one's reader, and writing as *silence,* probing the limits of language (Robbe-Grillet, Camus, Burroughs, et al.) as a pathway to interiority, desublimation, and ultimately the transcendence (or eradication) of verbality itself.

As he explores this "style of absence," Barthes is not so much advocating its usefulness as teasing out whatever theoretical possibilities it might contain. Like him, Godard finds it seductive as a concept but problematic as a model for actual practice, which helps explain why he has oscillated so frequently between the minimalist tendencies of, say, *France /tour/ détour* and the more effusive qualities found in, say, the "trilogy of the sublime" films. Even in works that approach a zero-degree style through deliberate flatness and repetition – much of *France /tour /détour,* for instance – he often balances his cinematic spareness with prolix linguistic highjinks. What he seeks here might be called a colorless visual technique – not literally colorless, of course, but one that denies ordinary pleasures to achieve a Brechtian emphasis on intellectual content – coupled with a verbal radicalism that strives not so much for absence as for a mercurial,

Man with a movie camera: A reflexive moment in the sensuously filmed *For Ever Mozart* (1997).

ungraspable fluidity that offers precisely the liberation from "pre-ordained language" of which Barthes wrote.

The results of this endeavor are works that fuse the image-wary *iconoclasm* found in his career by some critics (such as Angela Dalle Vacche) and the language-wary *semioclasm* found by others (such as James Monaco) into an unprecedented whole. Godard embraces this fusion for many reasons; as we have seen, there are complex motivations behind nearly all of his artistic decisions. Before closing this study, however, I would like to suggest that his evident hostility toward preordained languages (visual and verbal) might be productively explored in the terms of French psychoanalytic theorist Jacques Lacan, who argues that male children resolve their prepubescent Oedipal crises (giving up desire for the mother, accepting the prohibitive Law of the father) by submitting to a Symbolic order represented by the preexisting domain of language. This is the very domain that Godard's twin "clasms" so vigorously contest in a valiant effort to regain the utopian "zero" of presocialized plenitude, boundlessness, and freedom. Evidence of such unconscious struggles is as easy to find in his work as are the obliquely Oedipal cinematics that often embody them – from the partial erasure of grown-ups in *France/tour/détour* to the videographed abjections in *Numéro deux* and the key moment in *Sauve qui peut (la vie)* when the character named Paul Godard stands before a blackboard emblazoned with the words "Caïn et Abel/Cinéma et Vidéo."

Cain and Abel were brothers as well as rivals for the affection of a paternal deity, and Godard seems to regard cinema and video as the same – complements and opposites, partners and competitors, potential lovers and possible annihilators of one another, depending on whose "laws" are governing their technologies, their economic structures, their relationships with producers and consumers. At some moments Godard has turned to video as a path to renewed flexibility and productivity, and at other times he has returned with unabashed eagerness to luxuriant 35mm cinema. In the magnificently abundant *Histoire(s) du cinéma* he succeeds in having it both ways, assembling a history of film in a video format that coaxes extraordinary crispness, precision, and sheer beauty from that medium, and demonstrates that breaking the laws of standard either/or production can open new horizons hardly dreamed of in the past.

Here and elsewhere in his work, Godard's ever-shifting efforts to slip around the "laws" of creating, writing, naming, social conditioning, and other common practices of our complicated era produce some of the most profoundly personal yet richly communicative moments ever to grace the film or video screen. In the end, what has drawn so many devotees to his videos and movies is not the proliferation of intricate psychological clues, or the allure of a Beat-like spontaneity, or the prospect of a verbal-visual purity that might cleanse moving-image expression of its many sins. Rather, it is the boundless creativity of a dedicated artist (with gifted collaborators) who has refused to budge from the socioaesthetic margin despite the allure of a mainstream career that might once have been his for the asking. In the 1990s, as cinema has moved toward its second century, his most ambitious efforts have again moved in a sensuous direction, and it is possible that *Histoire(s) du cinéma* will prove the most enduring of his many monuments. All that appears certain as he approaches a half-century of cinephilia is that his cameras will stay busy, his imagination will stay alert, and his sensibility will stay as ornery as ever.

"I live on the border," Godard told critic Jonathan Rosenbaum in a 1980 interview[18] that illuminates his lifelong refusal to settle for film *or* video, images *or* words, France *or* Switzerland, stories *or* essays *or* experiments too singular to be named. "Our only enemies are the customs people," he continued, "whether these are bankers or critics. . . . People think of their bodies as territories. They think of their skin as the border, and that it's no longer them once it's outside the border. But a language is obviously made to cross borders. I'm someone whose real country is language, and whose territory is movies."

Notes

Chapter 1. Introduction

1. Jean-Luc Godard in *Le Nouvel Observateur*, Oct. 12, 1966. Quoted in Marie-Claire Ropars-Wuilleumier, "Form and Substance, or the Avatars of the Narrative." Reprinted in Royal S. Brown, ed., *Focus on Godard* (Englewood Cliffs, N.J.: Prentice–Hall, 1972), pp. 90–108, cited at 95.
2. The first two comments appeared in the British film journal *Sight and Sound* when *Contempt* was reissued in 1996. The third appeared in the American magazine *Film Comment* in 1997.
3. Quotes taken from Jean Clay, "Jean-Luc Godard: The French Cinema's Most Negative Asset." Originally published as "Le Paradoxe de Jean-Luc Godard, nihiliste et créateur" in *Réalités* 212 (Sept. 1963).
4. Ibid.
5. Keith Reader, review of Maryel Locke and Charles Warren, eds., *Jean-Luc Godard's Hail Mary: Women and the Sacred in Film*, in *Modern & Contemporary France* (1994), p. 464.
6. Biographical information on Godard comes from several journalistic and scholarly sources. Among the most helpful is Colin Myles MacCabe, "Jean-Luc Godard: A Life in Seven Episodes (to Date)," in Raymond Bellour with Mary Lea Bandy, eds., *Jean-Luc Godard: Son + Image, 1974–1991* (New York: Museum of Modern Art, 1992), pp. 13–21.
7. Interview with Jean-Luc Godard, *Cahiers du cinéma* 138 (Dec. 1962). Reprinted in Jean Narboni and Tom Milne, eds., *Godard on Godard* (New York: Da Capo Press, 1986), pp. 171–96, cited at 177.
8. Ibid., pp. 178–9.
9. Ibid., p. 182.
10. Quoted from Colin MacCabe with Mick Eaton and Laura Mulvey, *Godard: Images, Sounds, Politics* (Bloomington: Indiana University Press, 1980), p. 116.
11. Jean-Luc Godard, "One Should Put Everything into a Film." *L'Avant-scène du cinéma* 70 (May 1967). Reprinted in Narboni and Milne, eds., *Godard on Godard*, pp. 238–9, cited at 239.

12. Jean-Luc Godard, "*Pierrot* My Friend." *Cahiers du cinéma* 171 (Oct. 1965). Reprinted in Narboni and Milne, eds., *Godard on Godard*, pp. 213–15, cited at 215. Godard gave the same description ("not a film, but an attempt at film") in a *Cahiers* interview published in the same issue: Jean-Louis Comolli, Michel Delahaye, Jean-André Fieschi, and Gérard Guégan, "Let's Talk about *Pierrot.*" Reprinted in Narboni and Milne, eds., *Godard on Godard*, pp. 215–34, cited at 223.

13. Interview with Godard, reprinted in Narboni and Milne, eds., *Godard on Godard*, cited at 179.

14. Quoted in David Sterritt, "Ideas, Not Plots, Inspire Jean-Luc Godard." *Christian Science Monitor,* Aug. 3, 1994, p. 12. Reprinted in David Sterritt, ed., *Jean-Luc Godard: Interviews* (Jackson: University Press of Mississippi, 1998), pp. 175–8, cited at 177.

15. Jean-Luc Godard, "*The True Story of Jesse James.*" *Cahiers du cinéma* 74 (Aug.–Sept. 1957). Reprinted in Narboni and Milne, eds., *Godard on Godard*, pp. 59–61, cited at 60–1.

16. Jean-Luc Godard, "*Bitter Victory.*" *Cahiers du cinéma* 79 (Jan. 1958). Reprinted in Narboni and Milne, eds., *Godard on Godard*, pp. 64–6, cited at 64–5.

17. James Monaco, *The New Wave: Truffaut, Godard, Chabrol, Rohmer, Rivette* (New York: Oxford University Press, 1976), p. 109.

18. MacCabe with Eaton and Mulvey, *Godard: Images, Sounds, Politics,* pp. 115–16.

19. Interview with Godard, reprinted in Narboni and Milne, eds., *Godard on Godard*, cited at 173.

20. Comolli et al., "Let's Talk about *Pierrot,*" reprinted in Narboni and Milne, eds., *Godard on Godard*, cited at 216.

21. Jean-Luc Godard, "Defence and Illustration of Classical Construction." *Cahiers du cinéma* 15 (Sept. 1952). Reprinted in Narboni and Milne, eds., *Godard on Godard*, pp. 26–30, cited at 28, 30.

22. Jean-Louis Leutrat, "The Declension," in Bellour with Bandy, eds., *Jean-Luc Godard*, pp. 23–33, cited at 26. Leutrat is paraphrasing Barthélemy Amengual's 1967 essay "Jean-Luc Godard et la remise en cause de notre civilisation de l'image."

23. Gilles Deleuze, *Cinema 2: The Time-Image,* trans. Hugh Tomlinson and Robert Galeta (Minneapolis: University of Minnesota Press, 1989), p. 185.

24. Godard, "Defence and Illustration," reprinted in Narboni and Milne, *Godard on Godard*, cited at 27.

25. Sterritt, "Ideas, Not Plots," p. 12.

26. Jonathan Rosenbaum, "Theory and Practice: The Criticism of Jean-Luc Godard," in *Placing Movies: The Practice of Film Criticism* (Berkeley: University of California Press, 1995), pp. 18–24, cited at 20. Rosenbaum is referring to Godard's criticism, noting the similarities between its breathless style and the parallel quality found in Godard's films.

27. Jonathan Rosenbaum, "The Importance of Being Perverse: Godard's *King Lear,*" in *Placing Movies,* pp. 184–9, cited at 189.

28. MacCabe with Eaton and Mulvey, *Godard: Images, Sounds, Politics,* p. 57.

Chapter 2. *Breathless*

1. Jean-Luc Godard, "*Strangers on a Train.*" *Cahiers du cinéma* 10 (March 1952). Reprinted in Jean Narboni and Tom Milne, eds., *Godard on Godard* (New York: Da Capo Press, 1986), pp. 22–6, cited at 24.

2. Interview with Jean-Luc Godard, *Cahiers du cinéma* 138 (Dec. 1962). Reprinted in Narboni and Milne, eds., *Godard on Godard*, pp. 171–96, cited at 175.

3. The original treatment, published in the journal *L'Avant-scène cinéma* 79 (March 1968), runs to about seven pages in the English translation by Dory O'Brien published in Dudley Andrew, ed., *Breathless* (New Brunswick: Rutgers University Press, 1987), pp. 153–60. My sources for quotations from *Breathless* in this chapter are the English-subtitled version of the film and Andrew's edition of the film's continuity script, modified when my understanding of the spoken French dialogue differs from these translations.

4. This is discussed in Mark Rappaport's documentary film *From the Journals of Jean Seberg* (1995).

5. Colin MacCabe with Mick Eaton and Laura Mulvey, *Godard: Images, Sounds, Politics* (Bloomington: Indiana University Press, 1980), p. 84.

6. Jim Hillier, ed., *Cahiers du cinéma: The 1950s: Neo-Realism, Hollywood, New Wave* (Cambridge, Mass.: Harvard University Press, 1985), pp. 7–8. Hillier quotes from Thomas Elsaesser, "Two Decades in Another Country: Hollywood and the Cinéphiles," in C. W. E. Bigsby, *Superculture* (London: Elek, 1975), p. 210.

7. See especially David Sterritt, *Mad to Be Saved: The Beats, the '50s, and Film* (Carbondale: Southern Illinois University Press, 1998).

8. Interview with Godard, reprinted in Narboni and Milne, eds., *Godard on Godard*, cited at 193–4.

9. Ibid., p. 172.

10. Among the commentators who have discussed this is James T. Jones in *A Map of Mexico City Blues: Jack Kerouac as Poet* (Carbondale: Southern Illinois University Press, 1992), p. 151.

11. Interview with Godard, reprinted in Narboni and Milne, eds., *Godard on Godard*, cited at 172–3.

12. Ibid., p. 173.

13. Notes on continuity script, in Andrew, ed., *Breathless*, p. 148.

14. Interview with Godard, reprinted in Narboni and Milne, eds., *Godard on Godard*, cited at 174.

15. Norman Mailer, "The White Negro." *Dissent* 4 (1957). Reprinted in Ann Charters, ed., *The Portable Beat Reader* (New York: Viking, 1992), pp. 586–609, cited at 586, 588. The description of a hipster is from Mailer's quotation of Caroline Bird, "Born 1930: The Unlost Generation," *Harper's Bazaar* (Feb. 1957).

16. Interview with Godard, reprinted in Narboni and Milne, eds., *Godard on Godard*, cited at 173.

17. Colin Myles MacCabe, "Jean-Luc Godard: A Life in Seven Episodes (to Date)," in Raymond Bellour with Mary Lea Bandy, eds., *Jean-Luc Godard:*

Son + Image, 1974–1991 (New York: Museum of Modern Art, 1992), pp. 13–21, cited at 14, 16.

18. John Clellon Holmes, "The Game of the Name" (1965), in his collection *Passionate Opinions: The Cultural Essays,* published shortly after his death (Fayetteville: University of Arkansas Press, 1988). Excerpted in Charters, ed., *Portable Beat Reader,* pp. 619–26, cited at 621–2.

19. MacCabe with Eaton and Mulvey, *Godard: Images, Sounds, Politics,* p. 132.

20. In keeping with the hyperactive spirit of the film as a whole, *Breathless* has no opening credits beyond its title and this dedication, and the dedication is not included in English-subtitled prints. See Andrew, ed., *Breathless,* p. 29.

21. Interview with Godard, reprinted in Narboni and Milne, eds., *Godard on Godard,* p. 180.

22. Jean-Luc Godard, "Montparnasse-Levallois." *Cahiers du cinéma* 171 (Oct. 1965). Reprinted in Narboni and Milne, eds., *Godard on Godard,* pp. 211–13, cited at 211–12.

23. Jean-Luc Godard, "*Pierrot* My Friend." *Cahiers du cinéma* 171 (Oct. 1965). Reprinted in Narboni and Milne, eds., *Godard on Godard,* pp. 213–15, cited at 214–15.

24. Jean-Luc Godard, "Africa Speaks of the End and the Means." *Cahiers du cinéma* 94 (April 1959). Reprinted in Narboni and Milne, eds., *Godard on Godard,* pp. 131–4, cited at 132–3.

25. Godard, "*Pierrot* My Friend," reprinted in Narboni and Milne, eds., *Godard on Godard,* p. 215.

26. The character ascribes this quotation to Soviet revolutionary Vladimir Ilyich Lenin, but it actually comes from Russian author Maxim Gorky, as Godard noted in a 1960 interview: "That's a quote from Gorky; but in the film I have him say it's Lenin, because I like Lenin better." Michele Manceaux, "Learning Not to Be Bitter: Interview with Jean-Luc Godard on *Le Petit Soldat,*" *L'Express* (June 16, 1960), p. 38. Reprinted in Royal S. Brown, ed., *Focus on Godard* (Englewood Cliffs, N.J.: Prentice–Hall, 1972), pp. 25–7, cited at 17.

Chapter 3. *My Life to Live*

1. Jean-Luc Godard, "What Is Cinema?" *Les Amis de cinéma* 1 (Oct. 1952). Reprinted in Jean Narboni and Tom Milne, eds., *Godard on Godard* (New York: Da Capo Press, 1986), pp. 30–1, cited at 30.

2. Interview with Jean-Luc Godard, *Cahiers du cinéma* 138 (Dec. 1962). Reprinted in Narboni and Milne, eds., *Godard on Godard,* pp. 171–96, cited at 179.

3. Ibid., p. 182.

4. Ibid., p. 172. This section of my chapter and some material to follow draw substantially from Godard's reflections in this important *Cahiers du cinéma* interview.

5. Dudley Andrew, "Jean-Luc Godard: A Biographical Sketch," in Dudley Andrew, ed., *Breathless* (New Brunswick: Rutgers University Press, 1987), pp. 21–4, cited at 21.

6. Interview with Godard, reprinted in Narboni and Milne, eds., *Godard on Godard,* pp. 180, 182.

7. Ibid., p. 180.

8. Godard acknowledged later that "one or two scenes were re-shot." Tom Milne, "Jean-Luc Godard and *Vivre sa vie*." *Sight and Sound* 36:1 (Winter 1966): 9–12, cited at 11. Reprinted in David Sterritt, ed., *Jean-Luc Godard: Interviews* (Jackson: University Press of Mississippi, 1998), pp. 1–8, cited at 6.

9. Interview with Godard, reprinted in Narboni and Milne, eds., *Godard on Godard*, p. 186.

10. Ibid., p. 187.

11. Ibid.

12. Richard Schickel, *D. W. Griffith: An American Life* (New York: Simon & Schuster, 1983), p. 489.

13. Interview with Godard, reprinted in Narboni and Milne, eds., *Godard on Godard*, p. 187. My source for quotations from *My Life to Live* is the English-subtitled version of the film, modified where my understanding of the spoken French dialogue differs from this translation.

14. Quoted in Ib Monty, "*La Passion de Jeanne d'Arc*," in Christopher Lyon, ed., *The International Dictionary of Films and Filmmakers* (New York: Perigee Books, 1985), pp. 356–8, cited at 357–8.

15. Raymond Carney, *Speaking the Language of Desire: The Films of Carl Dreyer* (Cambridge and New York: Cambridge University Press, 1989), p. 153.

16. Antonin Artaud, *The Spurt of Blood*, in *Selected Writings* (Berkeley: University of California Press, 1988), pp. 72–6, cited at 75–6.

17. Speaking in 1962 of *The Little Soldier* and its protagonist, Godard said that "since it is a film about confusion, I had to show it. . . . Moreover, my character, often theoretical, increases the confusion by seeking in a sense to simplify things. The important thing was that one should believe in the character. One must be able to see that what he says is wrong, that he is wrong, and that suddenly something he says is right. One must be able to say then: what he said before was maybe not so wrong after all. Or, what he says now may not be so right after all. In any case, his way of saying these things is touching. Bruce Parain, in *Vivre sa vie*, says that error is necessary for the discovery of truth." Interview with Godard, reprinted in Narboni and Milne, eds., *Godard on Godard*, p. 178.

18. Dalle Vacche sees in Godard's cinema a quest for "voids where the mind, through language, can project all its abstractions" as well as an "intense antipictorial vocation, even though the appeal of painting constantly resurfaces in his images." Angela Dalle Vacche, *Cinema and Painting: How Art Is Used in Film* (Austin: University of Texas Press, 1996), p. 11. See also chap. 4 of that book, "Jean-Luc Godard's *Pierrot le Fou*: Cinema as Collage against Painting," pp. 107–34.

Chapter 4. *Weekend*

1. These words from Brecht's *Saint Joan of the Stockyards* (1929–30) appear as the subtitle of the 1964–5 film *Not Reconciled* by Jean-Marie Straub and Danièle Huillet.

2. Jean-Luc Godard, *Weekend* (London: Lorrimer Publishing, 1984). The source for quotations in this chapter (including full-screen intertitles) is the published version of Godard's screenplay in English – actually a descriptive transcript assembled from the finished film – modified where my understanding of the original French, or translations provided by film (or video) subtitles, appear more true to the spirit of the work.

3. Warhol also had a wry interest in the deeper meanings of red-white-and-blue as colors of chauvinism and arrogance, as critic Anne M. Wagner notes in her discussion of his *Little Race Riot,* a 1963 silkscreen depicting racial conflict in images tinted with "those eminently nationalist hues." Anne M. Wagner, "*Little Race Riot,*" *Representations* 55 (Summer 1996): 98–119, esp. p. 110.

4. Angela Dalle Vacche, *Cinema and Painting: How Art Is Used in Film* (Austin: University of Texas Press, 1996), p. 114.

5. Jean-Luc Godard, "Towards a Political Cinema." *Gazette du cinéma* 3 (Sept. 1950). Reprinted in Narboni and Milne, eds., *Godard on Godard*, pp. 16–17, cited at 16.

6. The motivations behind these attacks may have been professional jealousy and Situationist hostility toward Godard's habit of interpreting and interrogating revolutionary texts (Marx, etc.) held in something like awe by Debord and his cronies. For an insightful account see Brian Price, "Plagiarizing the Plagiarist: Godard Meets the Situationists," *Film Comment* 33:6 (Nov.–Dec. 1997): 66–9.

7. Pauline Kael, "Weekend in Hell," in *Going Steady: Film Writings 1968–1969* (New York: Marion Boyars, 1994), pp. 138–44, cited at 139. Originally published in the *New Yorker* 44 (Oct. 5, 1968).

8. Quoted in Jean Collet, "No Questions Asked: Conversation with Jean-Luc Godard on *Bande à part.*" *Télérama* 761 (Aug. 16, 1964): 49–50. Reprinted in Royal S. Brown, ed., *Focus on Godard* (Englewood Cliffs, N.J.: Prentice-Hall, 1972), pp. 40–5, cited at 45.

9. Joel Haycock, "The Sign of the Sociologist: Show and Anti-Show in Godard's *Masculin/Féminin,*" *Cinema Journal* 29:4 (Summer 1990). Quoted in Yosefa Loshitzky, *The Radical Faces of Godard and Bertolucci* (Detroit: Wayne State University Press, 1995), p. 143. Haycock and Loshitzky describe this ersatz porno movie as a parody of Ingmar Bergman's film *The Silence* (1963), although Godard himself was noncommital on this point when asked about it in a 1968 discussion. (See Gene Youngblood, "Jean-Luc Godard: 'No Difference between Life and Cinema,'" *Los Angeles Free Press,* March 8, 1968, pp. 15, 20. Reprinted in David Sterritt, ed., *Jean-Luc Godard: Interviews* [Jackson: University Press of Mississippi, 1998], pp. 9–49, cited at 15.) More interesting is that Loshitzky compares the "bestial sexuality" in *Masculine/Feminine* with that in Bernardo Bertolucci's film *Last Tango in Paris* (1973), suggesting that while the "grunts and whimpers of the porno movie are ridiculed in the context of Godard's film," such sounds are "elevated" in Bertolucci's picture, in which the "meaning of true liberation . . . resides not in language, but instead in an escape from language." *Radical Faces,* p. 144.

10. Haycock, "Sign of the Sociologist," quoted in Loshitzky, *Radical Faces,* p. 144.

11. Loshitzky, *Radical Faces*, p. 144.

12. Robert Stam, *Subversive Pleasures: Bakhtin, Cultural Criticism, and Film* (Baltimore: Johns Hopkins University Press, 1989), p. 124. Stam is writing here about Brazilian modernism of the 1920s, a hotbed of cultural combat against imperialism. Later he cites Brazilian filmmaker Joaquim Pedro de Andrade's words about the 1969 film *Macunaíma*: "Cannibalism is an exemplary mode of consumerism adopted by underdeveloped peoples. . . . The traditionally dominant, conservative social classes continue their control of the power structure – and we rediscover cannibalism. . . . The present work relationships, as well as the relationships between people – social, political, and economic – are still, basically, cannibalistic. Those who can, 'eat' others through their consumption of products, or even more directly in sexual relationships. Cannibalism has merely institutionalized and cleverly disguised itself." P. 146.

13. Ibid., p. 155.

14. Ibid., p. 148. Stam quotes the description of Menippean satire in Mikhail Bakhtin's essay "Forms of Time and of the Chronotope in the Novel," in *The Dialogic Imagination: Four Essays,* ed. Michael Holquist, trans. Caryl Emerson (Austin: University of Texas Press, 1981), pp. 84–258, quotation at 219.

15. Julia Kristeva, *Powers of Horror: An Essay on Abjection,* trans. Leon S. Roudiez (New York: Columbia University Press, 1982), p. 141.

Chapter 5. *Numéro deux*

1. Julia Kristeva, *Powers of Horror: An Essay on Abjection,* trans. Leon S. Roudiez (New York: Columbia University Press, 1982), p. 45.

2. Harun Farocki and Kaja Silverman, "In Her Place." *Camera Obscura: Feminism, Culture, and Media Studies* 37 (Jan. 1996), pp. 92–122, cited at 93. This useful article, constructed as a series of alternating comments by its two authors, is taken from a book-in-progress that had not yet appeared when my manuscript was completed. It has since been published as *Speaking about Godard* (New York University Press, 1998).

3. My source for translations from *Numéro deux* is the English-subtitled version of the film, modified where my understanding of the dialogue or printed text seems truer to the intentions of the filmmakers.

4. Georges Bataille, "The Use Value of D. A. F. de Sade (An Open Letter to My Current Comrades)," in *Visions of Excess: Selected Writings, 1927–1939,* trans. Allan Stoekl with Carl R. Lovitt and Donald M. Leslie Jr. (Minneapolis: University of Minnesota Press, 1985), pp. 91–102, cited at 97.

5. I cite the grandmother's quotations of *The Female Eunuch* from the film's subtitles, since this is the rendition of Greer's text that Anglophone viewers will be reading, but note that it differs from the original. The first quotation, for example, appears as follows in the book: "Women have very little idea of how much men hate them. . . . Punished, punished, punished for being the object of hatred and fear and disgust, through her magic orifices, her cunt and her mouth. . . ." Germaine Greer, *The Female Eunuch* (New York: McGraw–Hill, 1971), pp. 245, 154 (from the chapter called "Loathing and Disgust";

the portion beginning "Punished . . ." refers to a gang-rape in Hubert Selby Jr.'s boisterous 1964 novel *Last Exit to Brooklyn,* and to the real-life horrors paralleled by this scene). Here is some of Greer's writing on male fetishizing of women, quoted by the grandmother a bit later: "The sun shines only to burnish her skin and gild her hair; the wind blows only to whip up the color in her cheeks; the sea strives to bathe her; flowers die gladly so that her skin may luxuriate in their essence. She is the crown of creation, the masterpiece. The depths of the sea are ransacked for pearl and coral to deck her. . . . Baby seals are battered with staves, unborn lambs ripped fom their mothers' wombs, millions of moles . . . and other small and lovely creatures die untimely deaths that she might have furs. . . ." P. 47 (from the chapter called "The Stereotype").

6. The word "behind" will gain further resonances in *Comment ça va,* the next Godard–Miéville film, which says an "invisible" presence – e.g., an editor who runs a publication *behind* the scenes – is often the controlling factor in human affairs.

7. Jean-Luc Godard, photo caption in Raymond Bellour with Mary Lea Bandy, eds., *Jean-Luc Godard: Son + Image, 1974–1991* (New York: Museum of Modern Art, 1992), p. 158.

8. Ibid.

9. Herbert Marcuse, *Eros and Civilization: A Philosophical Inquiry into Freud* (Boston: Beacon Press, 1955), p. 221.

10. Ibid., p. 201.

11. Jean-Luc Godard, "What Is Cinema?" *Les Amis de cinéma* 1 (Oct. 1952). Reprinted in Jean Narboni and Tom Milne, eds., *Godard on Godard* (New York: Da Capo Press, 1986), pp. 30–1, at 31.

Chapter 6. *Hail Mary*

1. Jacques Derrida, *The Gift of Death,* trans. David Wills (Chicago: University of Chicago Press, 1995), p. 84. Thanks to Nancy Ten-Jung Tewksbury for calling these words to my attention.

2. Interviewed by David Sterritt, 1980, New York City.

3. Among the best sources for information on the *Hail Mary* controversy are Maryel Locke, "A History of the Public Controversy," in Maryel Locke and Charles Warren, eds., *Jean-Luc Godard's Hail Mary: Women and the Sacred in Film* (Carbondale: Southern Illinois University Press, 1993), pp. 1–9; and Charles Lyons, *Don't Watch That Movie! Censorship and Protests of Films in America, 1980–1992* (Ph.D. dissertation, Columbia University, 1994), pp. 251–5.

4. My source for the verbal content of *Hail Mary,* including "The Book of Mary," is the English-subtitled version of the film and its printed version in the "Shot Breakdown" portion of Locke and Warren, eds., *Jean-Luc Godard's Hail Mary,* pp. 135–83, modified when my sense of the spoken dialogue differs from this translation. Locke and Warren note that "Godard cares greatly about his English subtitles" and cite a translator's endorsement of the subtitles in this film as "an excellent translation of the French dialogue in both content and style or register" (p. 132).

5. For more on this see David Sterritt, "Miéville and Godard: From Psychology to Spirit," in Locke and Warren, eds., *Jean-Luc Godard's Hail Mary,* pp. 54–60.

6. Charles Warren, "Whim, God, and the Screen," in Locke and Warren, eds., *Jean-Luc Godard's Hail Mary,* pp. 10–26, cited at 16.

7. Quoted in Sandra Laugier, "The Holy Family," in Locke and Warren, eds., *Jean-Luc Godard's Hail Mary,* pp. 27–38, cited at 36. Laugier makes the important point that chapters of Dolto's book *The Gospel at Risk of Psychoanalysis* correspond precisely with portions of Godard's screenplay, and quotes Godard on the as-yet-unproduced movie in 1983, when he joked about an ideal computer program that could take his chosen ingredients – "a book by Françoise Dolto on religion and psychoanalysis . . . two characters, Joseph and Mary . . . three cantatas by Bach, a book by Heidegger" – and "[put] it all together." P. 29 (originally in *Le Nouvel Observateur,* Dec. 30, 1983).

8. Laugier, "Holy Family," p. 37.

9. For the "no interest" comment see "Let's Talk about *Pierrot,*" interview with Jean-Luc Godard conducted by Jean-Louis Comolli, Michel Delahaye, Jean-André Fieschi, and Gérard Guégan, *Cahiers du cinéma* 171 (Oct. 1965). Reprinted in Narboni and Milne, eds., *Godard on Godard,* pp. 215–34, cited at 234. For the "seals all exits" comment see Jean-Luc Godard, "*Hollywood or Bust,*" *Cahiers du cinéma* 73 (July 1957). Reprinted in Narboni and Milne, eds., *Godard on Godard,* pp. 57–9, cited at 58.

10. In my text I have followed the film's English subtitles: "My way! but the voice or the word?" The original French (from the dialogue text supplied to Locke and Warren by Godard and Miéville) is somewhat different: "Ma voie, mon chemin ou le son de ma voix?" which I translate literally as "My way, my road or the sound of my voice?" See "Repérage Cinétitres – The French Dialogue" in Locke and Warren, eds., *Jean-Luc Godard's Hail Mary,* pp. 185–228, cited at 203.

11. A brief squabble between Joseph and Juliette, appearing just before this scene in the shot list assembled by Locke and Warren, is mostly missing from the English-language edition of *Hail Mary* released on videocassette. See Locke and Warren, "Shot Breakdown," p. 158.

12. I draw here on Leo Steinberg, *The Sexuality of Christ in Renaissance Art and in Modern Oblivion* (New York: Pantheon/October, 1983), esp. pp. 14–15.

13. Ibid., pp. 47–8.

14. Commenting on Mary's nudity, Godard has said his purpose "was to try and shoot a woman naked and not make it aggressive, not in an X-rated-picture way. There are several shots which have more the purpose of an anatomical drawing. . . . I was trying to make the audience see not a naked woman, but flesh, if that's at all possible." Godard has also indicated his knowledge of how Mary is portrayed in traditional art: "Very often in painting, the Virgin is depicted half-naked, or at least with the breast naked or revealed, because of the Christ child. This has always caused problems: in the time of Martin Luther, there was a great deal of opposition to Raphael, for instance. The German soldiers came to Rome and scratched up many Raphael paintings. They thought it was offensive, too much of a *Playboy* style of paint-

ing." Quoted by Katherine Dieckmann, "Godard in His 'Fifth Period,'" *Film Quarterly* 39:2 (Winter 1985–6), pp. 2–6, cited at 3. Reprinted in David Sterritt, ed., *Jean-Luc Godard: Interviews* (Jackson: University Press of Mississippi, 1998), pp. 167–74, cited at 169.

15. My source for the quotations from *2 or 3 Things I Know about Her* is the English translation by Marianne Alexandre in *Three Films by Jean-Luc Godard* (London: Lorrimer Publishing, 1984).

16. Arthur is not among the most common names that people bestow on dogs, so it's interesting to speculate on this detail. If dogs once possessed great wisdom, as Joseph's book suggests, does the name echo King Arthur's legendary goodness and sagacity? (Clive Donner's fantasy film *Arthur the King*, about a woman who enters Camelot by falling down a rabbit hole in Stonehenge, also dates from 1985.) Alternatively, since the close-up of the dog's friendly but uncomprehending face has a gently humorous effect, is "Art" a playful symbol for "art" and cinema? Does it matter that George Harrisons's haircut was named "Arthur" in *A Hard Day's Night*? The possibilities seem endless. Lest such speculation seem irrelevant, consider that in a 1964 interview Godard made extensive remarks about the names of characters in *Band of Outsiders*, concluding with the explanation that the protagonist named Arthur in that movie "has the same first name as Rimbaud, and so I used a text by Rimbaud in one of my commentaries...." See Jean Collet, "No Questions Asked: Conversation with Jean-Luc Godard on *Bande à part*." *Télérama* 761 (Aug. 16, 1964): 49–50. Reprinted in Royal S. Brown, ed., *Focus on Godard* (Englewood Cliffs, N.J.: Prentice–Hall, 1972), pp. 40–5, cited at 41.

17. One recalls not only *Numéro deux* but such other films as *Sauve qui peut (la vie)*, with Paul Godard's incest fantasy, and *Passion*, where Jerzy and Isabelle have tender intercourse "now from behind ... mustn't leave a trace."

18. Steinberg, *Sexuality of Christ*, p. 134. In the biblical account, of course, Jesus' baptism was performed not by Mary but by John the Baptist.

19. Gerald O'Grady pointed out the link between *Breathless* and *Hail Mary* lips, and between Mary's open mouth and the Professor's cosmic diagram, in comments at a 1987 conference on *Hail Mary* held at the Carpenter Center for the Visual Arts at Harvard University.

Chapter 7. *Nouvelle Vague*

1. One such critic is Philippe Dubois, "Video Thinks What Cinema Creates: Notes on Jean-Luc Godard's Work in Video and Television," in Raymond Bellour with Mary Lea Bandy, eds., *Jean-Luc Godard: Son + Image, 1974–1991* (New York: Museum of Modern Art, 1992), pp. 169–85, cited at 177. Dubois borrows the "happy expression" from Marc Cerisuelo's 1989 book *Jean-Luc Godard*.

2. Vincent Canby, "Nature's Splendor and Aphorisms in Godard's Latest," *New York Times*, Sept. 29, 1990, Sec. I, p. 16.

3. Armond White, "Double Helix: Jean-Luc Godard," *Film Comment* 32:2 (March–April 1996): 26–30, cited at 29. White's enthusiasm runs away with

him when he continues, "I feel [*Nouvelle Vague*] is the most beautiful movie made since *The Magnificent Ambersons.*" Still, it is refreshing to see the film embraced so wholeheartedly after its earlier dismissal by reviewers who perceived it with far less care and imagination. *Film Comment* is published by the Film Society of Lincoln Center, incidentally, which also sponsors the New York Film Festival and other cinematic activities; but neither White's article nor Stam's in the wake of the movie's Lincoln Center premiere would have been influenced by the festival's support of the film.

4. Ibid.
5. Wheeler Winston Dixon, *The Films of Jean-Luc Godard* (Albany: State University of New York Press, 1997), pp. 185–9.
6. Robert Stam, "The Lake, the Trees," *Film Comment* 27:1 (Jan.–Feb. 1991): 63–6, cited at 64.
7. Colin Myles MacCabe, "Jean-Luc Godard: A Life in Seven Episodes (to Date)," in Bellour with Bandy, eds., *Jean-Luc Godard*, pp. 13–21, cited at 14.
8. The notion of past events as pieces to be "re-membered" or "dis-membered" is evocatively used by Margaret Olin in an essay on Claude Lanzmann's documentary *Shoah*, a very different film in which topography also plays a key structural and dramatic role. See her "Lanzmann's *Shoah* and the Topography of the Holocaust Film," *Representations* 57 (Winter 1997), pp. 1–23.
9. Angela Dalle Vacche, *Cinema and Painting: How Art Is Used in Film* (Austin: University of Texas Press, 1996), p. 112
10. An exception to this may be nudity on the screen, since we are aware of seeing the real performer's naked body; yet the power of film-as-pretending may explain why many performers display their bodies for the camera while remaining conventionally modest in other public situations. Godard makes a wry comment on this when Michel Piccoli's character in *Contempt* says, "Show women a camera and they show their backsides." (Needless to say, this character's alertness to media seductiveness far exceeds his sensitivity to feminist concerns – a charge many would level at Godard himself.)
11. Jean-Luc Godard, "*Pierrot* My Friend." *Cahiers du cinéma* 171 (Oct. 1965). Reprinted in Narboni and Milne, eds., *Godard on Godard*, pp. 213–15, cited at 215.
12. James Blue, "Excerpt from an Interview with Richard Grenier and Jean-Luc Godard," in Toby Mussman, ed., *Jean-Luc Godard* (New York: E. P. Dutton & Co., 1968), pp. 245–53, cited at 249, 253. Ellipses of second quotation in original.
13. White, "Double Helix," p. 29.
14. Dalle Vacche suggests that the "colored vowels marking Rimbaud's face" conjure up the possibility of "aphasia, a speaking block based on the inability to organize the linguistic chain." *Cinema and Painting*, p. 114.
15. *Three Films by Jean-Luc Godard* (London: Lorrimer Publishing, 1984), p. 164.
16. Stam, "The Lake, the Trees," p. 64.
17. Quoted in Gideon Bachmann, "The Carrots Are Cooked: A Conversation with Jean-Luc Godard," *Film Quarterly* 27:3 (1984): 13–19, cited at 14. Reprinted in David Sterritt, ed., *Jean-Luc Godard: Interviews* (Jackson: Univer-

sity Press of Mississippi, 1998), pp. 128–39, cited at 129. "I like dealing with things that may soon no longer exist or dealing with things that do not exist yet," Godard adds a little later. "Thus the real title of the film [*First Name: Carmen*] could be *Before the Name*. Before language, in other words, *Before Language (Children Playing Carmen)*."

18. Stam, "The Lake, the Trees," p. 64.

19. In the portion of *Contempt* set in the projection room of a crass American producer, we see a Lumière quotation – "Cinema is an invention without a future" – blazoned below the screen, perhaps implying that the Lumières began the sellout themselves by treating their works as money-making commodities. In his 1995 video *2 x 50 Years of French Cinema*, commissioned as part of a celebration of cinema's first century, Godard notes that 1995 marks not the centenary of film's invention – a complicated process that can't be pinned down to one occasion – but the hundredth anniversary of the Lumières' first public exhibition, i.e., the centenary of money changing hands at the box office!

20. David E. James, *Allegories of Cinema: American Film in the Sixties* (Princeton: Princeton University Press, 1988), p. 40. James is one of very few critics to notice connections between Godard and Brakhage, pointing out that Brakhage started making his epic *Dog Star Man* in the same year (1959) that Godard made *Breathless,* and citing an interesting coincidence of sensibilities centered on the concept of home movies as a paradigm for nonindustrial film production. Brakhage, who has often called his works home movies, said in 1967, "I believe any art of the cinema must inevitably arise from the amateur, 'home-movie' making medium." James, *Allegories of Cinema,* p. 55. Godard said in a later comment, cited by Colin MacCabe in 1980 (*Godard: Images, Sounds, Politics*): "As for me, I've become aware, after fifteen years of cinema, that the real 'political' film that I'd like to end up with would be a film about me which would show to my wife and daughter what I am, in other words a home-movie – home-movies represent the popular base of the cinema." James, *Allegories of Cinema,* p. 55.

21. Stan Brakhage, *Metaphors on Vision* (New York: Film Culture, 1963), n.p.

22. Ibid.

23. Andrew Sarris, "Jean-Luc Godard Now," *Interview* 24 (July 1994): 5–6, cited at 6. Godard says in this interview that production of *Hélas pour moi* was made possible because he is "still associated with a heroic period in French cinema," and therefore it can happen that "a big star decides that he wants to take some time off to make a 'Godard' film." Sarris asks how he got along with Depardieu in shooting the picture, and Godard replies, "Not at all. He was supposed to work six weeks. He walked out after three. The extras did more acting than he did. But without him there would have been no money."

Chapter 8. Video and Television

1. Gideon Bachmann, "The Carrots Are Cooked: A Conversation with Jean-Luc Godard," *Film Quarterly* 27:3 (1984): 13–19, cited at 15. Reprinted in

David Sterritt, ed., *Jean-Luc Godard: Interviews* (Jackson: University Press of Mississippi, 1998), pp. 128–39, cited at 132.

2. Deirdre Boyle's study *Subject to Change: Guerrilla Television Revisited* (New York: Oxford University Press, 1996) provides an informative and readable overview of these developments. Boyle also cites the French priest, paleontologist, and philosopher Pierre Teilhard de Chardin as a highly influential figure in American countercultural-media circles of the 1960s, especially after a revised English translation of his book *The Phenomenon of Man* appeared in 1965, coinciding with the advent of portable video equipment. "The history of the living world," wrote Teilhard in this volume, "can be summarized as the elaboration of ever more perfect eyes within a cosmos in which there is always something more to be seen. To see or to perish is the very condition laid down upon everything that makes up the universe." The resonance of these words with Godard's ideas is not difficult to detect. Pierre Teilhard de Chardin, *The Phenomenon of Man* (New York: Harper, 1959), p. 31; quoted in Boyle, p. 10.

3. Excerpts from a 1995 press conference at the Cannes International Film Festival, transcribed by Henri Behar for the Film Scouts website. Godard's thinking might be influenced here by some of Jacques Derrida's ideas, such as his notion of the "supplement."

4. Colin MacCabe with Mick Eaton and Laura Mulvey, *Godard: Images, Sounds, Politics* (Bloomington: Indiana University Press, 1980), p. 132.

5. Ibid., p. 133.

6. Don Ranvaud and Alberto Farassino, "An Interview with Jean-Luc Godard," *Framework* 83 (1993): 8–9, cited at 8.

7. Philippe Dubois, "Video Thinks What Cinema Creates: Notes on Jean-Luc Godard's Work in Video and Television," in Raymond Bellour with Mary Lea Bandy, eds., *Jean-Luc Godard: Son + Image, 1974–1991* (New York: Museum of Modern Art, 1992), pp. 169–85, cited at 169.

8. See the biographical sketch by John Gianvito in Maryel Locke and Charles Warren, eds., *Jean-Luc Godard's Hail Mary: Women and the Sacred in Film* (Carbondale: Southern Illinois University Press, 1993), p. 125. Gianvito reports that Miéville has "revealed few details about her life and given few interviews."

9. Dubois, "Video Thinks What Cinema Creates," p. 170.

10. The term "vast wasteland" became a catchphrase among alarmed Americans after Newton Minow, chair of the Federal Communications Commission in the 1950s, used it to describe the overall quality of America's favorite medium.

11. Dubois, "Video Thinks What Cinema Creates," p. 174.

12. This is how Godard and Miéville intended them to be seen, and MacCabe reports that *Six fois deux* was shown "on the third channel in France on six successive Sundays in the late summer of 1976," although he adds that the third channel is a "minority" venue and that most of the broadcast took place during the August holiday season. MacCabe with Mulvey and Eaton, *Godard: Images, Sounds, Politics*, pp. 141, 147. Presentations of *France/tour/détour* have generally taken the form of special events spotlighting the se-

ries as "art video" rather than a radical intervention in daily programming practices.

13. Interview with Claude-Jean Philippe, *Les Nouvelles Littéraires* (May 30, 1980), quoted in Dubois, "Video Thinks What Cinema Creates," p. 177.
14. Interview with Philippe, quoted in ibid., p. 174.
15. Interview with Jean-Luc Godard, *Cahiers du cinéma* 138 (Dec. 1962). Reprinted in Jean Narboni and Tom Milne, eds., *Godard on Godard* (New York: Da Capo Press, 1986), pp. 171–96, cited at 173.
16. This phrase provides the title for Guy Debord's most widely known work, *Society of the Spectacle* (Detroit: Black & Red, 1983). Godard was roundly criticized by Situationist writers, however; see n. 6 to Chapter 4 above.
17. Roland Barthes, *Writing Degree Zero* (New York: Noonday Press, 1968), p. 76.
18. Quoted in Jonathan Rosenbaum, "Bringing Godard Back Home," *Soho News* (Sept. 24–30, 1980), pp. 41–2, cited at 41. Reprinted in Sterritt, ed., *Jean-Luc Godard: Interviews,* pp. 100–6, cited at 102.

Select Bibliography

Andrew, Dudley, ed., *Breathless* (New Brunswick: Rutgers University Press, 1987).

Bachmann, Gideon, "The Carrots Are Cooked: A Conversation with Jean-Luc Godard," *Film Quarterly* 27:3 (1984): 13–19.

Barthes, Roland, *Writing Degree Zero* (New York: Noonday Press, 1968).

Bellour, Raymond, with Mary Lea Bandy, eds., *Jean-Luc Godard: Son + Image, 1974–1991* (New York: Museum of Modern Art, 1992).

Brakhage, Stan, *Metaphors on Vision* (New York: Film Culture, 1963).

Brown, Royal S., ed., *Focus on Godard* (Englewood Cliffs, N.J.: Prentice–Hall, 1972).

Canby, Vincent, "Nature's Splendor and Aphorisms in Godard's Latest," *New York Times*, Sept. 29, 1990, Sec. I, p. 16.

Dalle Vacche, Angela, *Cinema and Painting: How Art Is Used in Film* (Austin: University of Texas Press, 1996).

Dieckmann, Katherine, "Godard in His 'Fifth Period,'" *Film Quarterly* 39:2 (Winter 1985–6): 2–6.

Dixon, Wheeler Winston, *The Films of Jean-Luc Godard* (Albany: State University of New York Press, 1997).

Farocki, Harun, and Kaja Silverman, "In Her Place," *Camera Obscura: Feminism, Culture, and Media Studies* 37 (Jan. 1996): 92–122.

Godard, Jean-Luc, *Alphaville* (London: Lorrimer Publishing, 1972).

Three Films by Jean-Luc Godard: A Woman Is a Woman, A Married Woman, Two or Three Things I Know about Her, trans. Jan Dawson, Susan Bennett, and Marianne Alexandre (London: Lorrimer Publishing, 1984).

Weekend (London: Lorrimer Publishing, 1984).

Hillier, Jim, ed., *Cahiers du cinéma: The 1950s: Neo-Realism, Hollywood, New Wave* (Cambridge, Mass.: Harvard University Press, 1985).

James, David E., *Allegories of Cinema: American Film in the Sixties* (Princeton: Princeton University Press, 1988).

Kristeva, Julia, *Powers of Horror: An Essay on Abjection,* trans. Leon S. Roudiez (New York: Columbia University Press, 1982).

Locke, Maryel, and Charles Warren, eds., *Jean-Luc Godard's Hail Mary: Women and the Sacred in Film* (Carbondale: Southern Illinois University Press, 1993).

Loshitzky, Yosefa, *The Radical Faces of Godard and Bertolucci* (Detroit: Wayne State University Press, 1995).

Lyons, Charles, *Don't Watch That Movie! Censorship and Protests of Films in America, 1980–1992* (Ph.D. dissertation, Columbia University, 1994).

MacCabe, Colin, with Mick Eaton and Laura Mulvey, *Godard: Images, Sounds, Politics* (Bloomington: Indiana University Press, 1980).

Marcuse, Herbert, *Eros and Civilization: A Philosophical Inquiry into Freud* (Boston: Beacon Press, 1955).

Milne, Tom, "Jean-Luc Godard and *Vivre sa vie.*" *Sight and Sound* 36:1 (Winter 1966): 9–12.

Monaco, James, *The New Wave: Truffaut, Godard, Chabrol, Rohmer, Rivette* (New York: Oxford University Press, 1976).

Mussman, Toby, ed., *Jean-Luc Godard* (New York: E. P. Dutton & Co., 1968).

Narboni, Jean, and Tom Milne, eds., *Godard on Godard* (New York: Da Capo Press, 1986).

Price, Brian, "Plagiarizing the Plagiarist: Godard Meets the Situationists," *Film Comment* 33:6 (Nov.–Dec. 1997): 66–9.

Ranvaud, Don, and Alberto Farassino, "An Interview with Jean-Luc Godard," *Framework* 83 (1993): 8–9.

Rosenbaum, Jonathan, "Bringing Godard Back Home," *Soho News* (Sept. 24–30, 1980), pp. 41–2.

   Placing Movies: The Practice of Film Criticism (Berkeley: University of California Press, 1995).

Sarris, Andrew, "Jean-Luc Godard Now," *Interview* 24 (July 1994): 5–6.

Stam, Robert, "The Lake, the Trees," *Film Comment* 27:1 (Jan.–Feb. 1991): 63–6.

   Subversive Pleasures: Bakhtin, Cultural Criticism, and Film (Baltimore: Johns Hopkins University Press, 1989).

Steinberg, Leo, *The Sexuality of Christ in Renaissance Art and in Modern Oblivion* (New York: Pantheon/October, 1983).

Sterritt, David, "Ideas, Not Plots, Inspire Jean-Luc Godard." *Christian Science Monitor,* Aug. 3, 1994, p. 12.

   ed., *Jean-Luc Godard: Interviews* (Jackson: University Press of Mississippi, 1998).

White, Armond, "Double Helix: Jean-Luc Godard," *Film Comment* 32:2 (March–April 1996): 26–30.

Youngblood, Gene, "Jean-Luc Godard: 'No Difference between Life and Cinema,'" *Los Angeles Free Press,* March 8, 1968, pp. 15, 20.

Filmography

Abbreviations: D, director; P, producer; S, screenplay; E, editor; Ph, cinematography; So, Sound; M, music; AD, assistant director (if any); AP, associate producer (if any); C, principal cast.

Opération Béton. 1954. D, P, S, E – Jean-Luc Godard; Ph – Adrien Porchet; M – G. F. Handel, J. S. Bach. Actua-Films. 35mm. 17 min.

Une Femme coquette. 1955. D, P, E, Ph – Jean-Luc Godard. S – Hans Lucas (Jean-Luc Godard) from "Le Signe" by Guy de Maupassant; M – J. S. Bach; C – Marie Lysandre, Roland Tolma, Jean-Luc Godard. Jean-Luc Godard. 16mm. 10 min.

All Boys Are Called Patrick (Tous les garçons s'appellent Patrick; a.k.a. *Charlotte et Véronique).* 1957. D – Jean-Luc Godard; P – Pierre Braunberger; S – Eric Rohmer; Ph – Michel Latouche; E – Cécile Decugis; So – Jacques Maumont; M – L. van Beethoven, Pierre Monsigny; C – Jean-Claude Brialy, Anne Colette, Nicole Berger. Les Films de la Pléiade. 35mm. 21 min.

A Story of Water (Une Histoire d'eau). 1958. D, E – Jean-Luc Godard, François Truffaut; P – Pierre Braunberger; S – François Truffaut; Ph – Michel Latouche; So – Jacques Maumont; C – Jean-Claude Brialy, Caroline Dim, Jean-Luc Godard. Les Films de la Pléiade. 35mm. 18 min.

Charlotte et son Jules. 1959. D, S – Jean-Luc Godard; P – Pierre Braunberger; Ph – Michel Latouche; E – Cécile Decugis; So – Jacques Maumont; M – Pierre Monsigny; C – Jean-Paul Belmondo, Anne Colette, Gérard Blain, Jean-Luc Godard. Les Films de la Pléiade. 35mm. 20 min.

Breathless (À bout de souffle). 1960. D – Jean-Luc Godard; P – Georges de Beauregard; S – Jean-Luc Godard, from a treatment by François Truffaut; Ph – Raoul Coutard; E – Cécile Decugis, Lila Herman; So – Jacques Maumont; M – W. A. Mozart, Martial Solal; C – Jean Seberg, Jean-Paul Belmondo, Henry-Jacques Huet, Daniel Boulanger, Jean-Pierre Melville, Jean Domarchi, André-S. Labarthe, Jean Douchet, Philippe de Broca, Jean-Luc Godard. Société Nouvelle de Cinéma. 35mm. 90 min.

The Little Soldier (Le Petit soldat). 1960. D, S – Jean-Luc Godard; P – Georges de Beauregard; Ph – Raoul Coutard; E – Agnès Guillemot, Nadine Marquand, Lila

Herman; So – Jacques Maumont; M – Maurice Leroux; C – Michel Subor, Anna Karina, Henri-Jacques Huet, Paul Beauvais, Georges de Beauregard, Jean-Luc Godard. Sciéty Nouvelle de Cinéma. 35mm. 88 min.

A Woman Is a Woman (Une Femme est une femme). 1961. D – Jean-Luc Godard; P – Georges de Beauregard, Carlo Ponti; S – Jean-Luc Godard, from an idea by Geneviève Cluny; Ph – Raoul Coutard; E – Agnès Guillemot, Lila Herman; So – Guy Villette; M – Michel Legrand; C – Anna Karina, Jean-Paul Belmondo, Jean-Claude Brialy, Marie Dubois, Jeanne Moreau. Rome-Paris Films/Unidex, Euro International. 35mm. 84 min.

"Sloth" ("La Paresse"), in anthology film *The Seven Capital Sins (Les Sept péchés capitaux)*. 1961. D, S – Jean-Luc Godard; Ph – Henri Decae; E – Jacques Gaillard; So – Jean-Claude Marchetti, Jean Labussière; M – Michel Legrand; AD – Marin Karmitz; C – Eddie Constantine, Nicole Mirel. Les Films Gibe/Franco–London Films/Titanus. 35mm. 15 min.

My Life to Live (Vivre sa vie). 1962. D, S – Jean-Luc Godard; P – Pierre Braunberger; Ph – Raoul Coutard; E – Agnès Guillemot, Lila Lakshmanan; So – Guy Villette, Jacques Maumont; M – Michel Legrand; C – Anna Karina, Sady Rebbot, André-S. Labarthe, Peter Kassovitz, Laszlo Szabo. Les Films de la Pléïade. 35mm. 85 min.

"The New World" ("Le Nouveau Monde"), in anthology film *RoGoPaG*. 1962. D, S – Jean-Luc Godard; Ph – Jean Rabier; E – Agnès Guillemot, Lila Lakshmanan; So – Hervé; M – L. van Beethoven; C – Alexandra Stewart, Jean-Marc Bory, Jean-André Fieschi, Michel Delahaye. Société Lyre/Arco Film. 35mm. 20 min.

Les Carabiniers (The Riflemen; a.k.a. The Soldiers). 1963. D – Jean-Luc Godard; P – Georges de Beauregard, Carlo Ponti; S – Jean-Luc Godard, Roberto Rossellini, Jean Gruault, from *I Carabinieri* by Benjamino Joppolo; Ph – Raoul Coutard; E – Agnès Guillemot, Lila Lakshmanan; So – Jacques Maumont; M – Philippe Arthuys; C – Marino Masé, Albert Juross, Geneviève Galéa, Catherine Ribeiro, Jean Gruault, Jean-Louis Comolli, Barbet Schroeder. Rome–Paris Films/Les Films Marceau/Laetitia Films. 35mm. 80 min.

"Le Grand escroc," in anthology film *Les Plus belles escroqueries du monde*. 1963. D, S – Jean-Luc Godard; P – Pierre Roustang; Ph – Raoul Coutard; E – Agnès Guillemot, Lila Lakshmanan; S – Hervé; M – Michel Legrand; C – Jean Seberg, Charles Denner, Laszlo Szabo. Ulysse Productions/Primex Films/Lux/CCF/Vides Cinematografica/Toho/Caesar Film Productie. 35mm. 25 min.

Contempt (Le Mépris). 1963. D – Jean-Luc Godard; P – Georges de Beauregard, Carlo Ponti, Joseph E. Levine; S – Jean-Luc Godard, from *Il Disprezzo* by Alberto Moravia; Ph – Raoul Coutard; E – Agnès Guillemot, Lila Lakshmanan; So – William Sivel; M – Georges Delerue; C – Brigitte Bardot, Michel Piccoli, Jack Palance, Fritz Lang, Giorgia Moll, Jean-Luc Godard. Rome–Paris Films/Les Films Concordia/Compagnia Cinematografica Champion. 35mm. 105 min.

Band of Outsiders (Bande à part). 1964. D – Jean-Luc Godard; S – Jean-Luc Godard, from *Fool's Gold* by Dolores and Bert Hitchens; Ph – Raoul Coutard; E – Agnès Guillemot, Françoise Collin; S – René Levert, Antoine Bonfanti; M – Michel Legrand; C – Anna Karina, Sami Frey, Claude Brasseur, Louisa Colpeyn. Anouchka Films/Orsay Films. 35mm. 95 min.

A Married Woman; a.k.a. *The Married Woman* (*Une Femme mariée*). 1964. D, S – Jean-Luc Godard; Ph – Raoul Coutard; E – Agnès Guillemot, Françoise Collin; So – Antoine Bonfanti, René Levert; M – L. van Beethoven, Claude Nougaro; C – Macha Méril, Bernard Noël, Philippe Leroy, Roger Leenhardt. Anouchka Films / Orsay Films. 35mm. 98 min.

Alphaville: Une Étrange Aventure de Lemmy Caution. 1965. D, S – Jean-Luc Godard; P – André Michelin; Ph – Raoul Coutard; E – Agnès Guillemot; So – René Levert; M – Paul Mizraki; C – Eddie Constantine, Anna Karina, Akim Tamiroff, Howard Vernon. Chaumiane Production / Filmstudio. 35mm. 98 min.

"Montparnasse-Levallois," in anthology film *Paris vu par . . . (Paris Seen by . . . ; a.k.a. Six in Paris*). D, S – Jean-Luc Godard; P – Barbet Schroeder; Ph – Albert Maysles; E – Jacqueline Raynal; S – René Levert; C – Joanna Shimkus, Philippe Hiquily, Serge Davri. Les Films du Losange. 16mm / 35mm. 18 min.

Pierrot le fou. 1965. D – Jean-Luc Godard; P – Georges de Beauregard; S – Jean-Luc Godard, from *Obsession* by Lionel White; Ph – Raoul Coutard; E – Françoise Collin; So – René Levert; M – Antoine Duhamel; C – Jean-Paul Belmondo, Anna Karina, Dirk Sanders, Raymond Devos, Samuel Fuller. Rome–Paris Films / Dino de Laurentiis Cinematografica. 35mm. 110 min.

Masculine/Feminine (*Masculin/Féminin*). 1966. D – Jean-Luc Godard; S – Jean-Luc Godard, from "La Femme de Paul" and "Le Signe" by Guy de Maupassant; Ph – Willy Kurant; E – Agnès Guillemot; So – René Levert; M – Francis Lai, W. A. Mozart; C – Jean-Pierre Léaud, Chantal Goya, Marlène Jobert, Michel Debord. Anouchka Films / Argos Films / Svensk Filmindustri / Sandrews. 35mm. 110 min.

Made in U.S.A. 1966. D – Jean-Luc Godard; P – Georges de Beauregard; S – Jean-Luc Godard, from a novel by Richard Stark; Ph – Raoul Coutard; E – Agnès Guillemot; So – René Levert, Jacques Maumont; M – L. van Beethoven, R. Schumann, Mick Jagger, Keith Richard; C – Anna Karina, Laszlo Szabo, Jean-Pierre Léaud, Yves Afonso. Rome–Paris Films / Anouchka Films / SEPIC. 35mm. 90 min.

2 or 3 Things I Know about Her (*2 ou 3 Choses que je sais d'elle*). 1966. D, S – Jean-Luc Godard; Ph – Raoul Coutard; E – Françoise Collin, Chantal Delattre; So – René Levert, Antoine Bonfanti; M – L. van Beethoven; C – Marina Vlady, Anny Duperey, Roger Montsoret, Raoul Lévy. Anouchka Films / Argos Films / Les Films du Carosse / Parc Films. 35mm. 90 min.

"Anticipation; ou, L'Amour en l'an 2000," in anthology film *The Oldest Profession* (*Le Plus vieux métier du monde*). 1967. D, S – Jean-Luc Godard; Ph – Pierre Lhomme; E – Agnès Guillemot; M – Michel Legrand; C – Jacques Charrier, Anna Karina, Marilu Tolo, Jean-Pierre Léaud. Francoriz / Les Films Gibé / Rialto Films / Rizzoli Films. 35mm. 20 min.

"Camera-Eye" ("Caméra-oeil"), in anthology film *Far from Vietnam* (*Loin du Viêtnam*). 1967. D, S – Jean-Luc Godard; Ph – Alain Levent; C – Jean-Luc Godard. SLON. 16mm. 15 min.

La Chinoise; ou, Plutôt à la chinoise. 1967. D, S – Jean-Luc Godard; Ph – Raoul Coutard; E – Agnès Guillemot, Delphine Desfons; So – René Levert; M – Karlheinz Stockhausen, F. Schubert, A. Vivaldi; C – Anne Wiazemsky, Jean-Pierre Léaud, Michel Semeniako, Lex de Bruijn, Juliet Berto. Anouchka Films / Les Productions de la Guéville / Athos Films / Parc Films / Simar Films. 35mm. 96 min.

"L'Aller et retour andate e ritorno des enfants prodigues dei figli prodighi," in anthology film *Amore e rabbia/vangelo 70.* 1967. D, S – Jean-Luc Godard; Ph – Alain Levent; E – Agnès Guillemot; So – Guy Villette; M – Giovanni Fusco; C – Nino Castelnuovo, Catherine Jourdan, Christine Guého, Paolo Pozzesi. Anouchka Films/Castoro Film. 35mm. 26 min.

Weekend. 1967. D, S – Jean-Luc Godard; Ph-Alain Levent; E – Agnès Guillemot; So – René Levent; M – Antoine Duhamel, Guy Béart, W. A. Mozart; C – Mireille Darc, Jean Yanne, Jean-Pierre Kalfon, Jean-Pierre Léaud, Paul Gégauff, Ernest Menzer, Jean Eustache. Films Copernic/Ascot Cineraid/Comacico/Lira Films. 35mm. 95 min.

Le Gai Savoir. 1968. D, S – Jean-Luc Godard; Ph – Georges Leclerc; E – Germaine Cohen; M – Cuban songs and fragments from classical repertoire; C – Jean-Pierre Léaud, Juliet Berto. Anouchka Films/Bavaria Atelier/ORTF/Suddeutschen Rundfunk. 35mm. 95 min.

Ciné-Tracts. 1968. D, P, S, E – Jean-Luc Godard et al. 16mm. 2–4 min. each.

A Film Like the Others (Un Film comme les autres). 1968. D, S, Ph, E – Dziga-Vertov Group (Jean-Luc Godard, Jean-Pierre Gorin). Anouchka Films. 16mm. 100 min.

One Plus One (Sympathy for the Devil). 1968. D, S – Jean-Luc Godard; P – Michael Pearson, Iain Quarrier; Ph – Anthony Richmond; E – Ken Rowles, Agnès Guillemot; So – Arthur Bradburn; M – The Rolling Stones; C – The Rolling Stones (Mick Jagger, Keith Richards, Brian Jones, Charlie Watts, Bill Wyman), Anne Wiazemsky, Iain Quarrier, Danny Daniels. Cupid Productions, Inc. 35mm. 99 min.

British Sounds (See You at Mao). 1969. D – Dziga-Vertov Group (Jean-Luc Godard, Jean-Henri Roger); P – Irving Teitelbaum, Kenith Trodd; Ph – Charles Stewart; E – Elizabeth Koziman; So – Fred Sharp. Kestrel Productions for London Weekend Television. 16mm. 52 min.

Pravda. 1969. D, S, Ph, E, So – Dziga-Vertov Group (Jean-Luc Godard, Jean-Henri Roger, Paul Burron); P – Claude Nedjar; C – Vera Chytilova. Centre Européen Cinéma Radio Télévision. 16mm. 58 min.

Wind from the East (Vent d'est). 1969. D – Dziga-Vertov Group (Jean-Luc Godard, Jean-Pierre Gorin, Gérard Martin); S – Jean-Luc Godard, Daniel Cohn-Bendit, Sergio Bazzini; Ph – Mario Vulpiani; E – Jean-Luc Godard, Jean-Pierre Gorin; So – Antonio Ventura, Carlo Diotalleri; C – Gian Maria Volonté, Anne Wiazemsky, Paolo Pozzesi, Christiana Tullio Altan. CCC/Poli Film/Anouchka Films/Kuntz Film. 16mm. 100 min.

Struggle in Italy (Luttes en Italie; a.k.a. *Lotte in Italia).* 1969. D, S – Dziga-Vertov Group (Jean-Luc Godard, Jean-Pierre Gorin); C – Christiana Tullio Altan, Anne Wiazemsky, Jérôme Hinstin, Paolo Pozzesi. Cosmoseion for RAI. 16mm. 76 min.

1 P.M. (One Parallel Movie). 1971. Includes footage from *One American Movie* (*1 A.M.*), left uncompleted in 1968, and footage from an uncompleted film about that production. D, S – Jean-Luc Godard, D. A. Pennebaker; Ph – Richard Leacock, D. A. Pennebaker; E – D. A. Pennebaker; C – Jean-Luc Godard, Richard Leacock, Anne Wiazemsky, Eldridge Cleaver, Rip Torn, Tom Hayden, Tom Luddy. Leacock-Pennebaker. 16mm. 90 min.

Vladimir and Rosa (*Vladimir et Rosa*). 1971. D, S, Ph – Dziga-Vertov Group (Jean-Luc Godard, Jean-Pierre Gorin); C – Anne Wiazemsky, Jean-Luc Godard, Jean-Pierre Gorin, Juliet Berto, Ernest Menzer, Claude Nedjar. Grove Press Evergreen Films/Telepool. 16mm. 106 min.

Tout va bien. 1972. D, S – Jean-Luc Godard, Jean-Pierre Gorin; P – Alain Coiffier, J. P. Rassam, Jean-Luc Godard; Ph – Armand Marco; E – Kenout Peltier; So – Bernard Ortion, Armand Bonfanti; M – Eric Charden, Thomas Rivat, Paul Beuscher; C – Jane Fonda, Yves Montand, Vittorio Caprioli, Jean Pignol, Anne Wiazemsky, Pierre Oudry, Elisabeth Chauvin. Anouchka Films/Vicco Films/Empire Film. 35mm. 95 min.

Letter to Jane: Investigation of a Still. 1972. D, S – Jean-Luc Godard, Jean-Pierre Gorin; P – Sonimage; C – Jane Fonda, Jean-Luc Godard, Jean-Pierre Gorin. Jean-Luc Godard, Jean-Pierre Gorin. 16mm. 52 min.

Here and Elsewhere (*Ici et ailleurs*). 1974. Includes footage from *Jusqu'à la victoire*, left uncompleted by the Dziga-Vertov Group in 1970. D, S – Jean-Luc Godard, Anne-Marie Miéville; P – Coralie International/JR Films; Ph – William Lubtchansky; E – Anne-Marie Miéville. Sonimage/INA. 16mm. 60 min.

Numéro deux (*Number Two*). 1975. D – Jean-Luc Godard; S – Jean-Luc Godard, Anne-Marie Miéville; Ph – William Lubtchansky; So – Jean-Pierre Ruh; M – Leo Ferré; C – Sandrine Battistella, Pierre Oudry, Alexandre Rignault, Rachel Stefanopoli. Sonimage/Bela Productions/SNC. 35mm, video. 88 min.

Comment ça va. 1976. D, S – Jean-Luc Godard, Anne Marie Miéville; Ph – William Lubtchansky; M – Jean Schwartz; C – Anne-Marie Miéville, M. Marot. Sonimage/INA/Bela Productions/SNC. 16mm. 78 min.

Six fois deux/Sur et sous la communication (*Six Times Two/Over and Under Communication*). 1976. Pt. 1: "Ya personne/Louison"; Pt. 2: "Leçons de choses/Jean-Luc"; Pt. 3: "Photo et cie/Marcel"; Pt. 4: "Pas d'histoires/Nanas"; Pt. 5: "Nous trois/René(e)s"; Pt. 6: "Avant et après/Jacqueline et Ludovic." D, S, E – Jean-Luc Godard. Anne-Marie Miéville; Ph – William Lubtchansky, Gérard Teissedre. Sonimage/INA. Video. 100 min. each part.

France/tour/détour/deux/enfants (*France/Tour/Detour/Two/Children*). 1977–8. Pt. 1: "Obscur/Chimie." Pt. 2: "Lumière/Physique." Pt. 3: "Connu/Géométrie/Géographie." Pt. 4: "Inconnu/Technique." Pt. 5: "Impression/Dictée." Pt. 6: "Expression/Français." Pt. 7: "Violence/Grammaire." Pt. 8: "Désordre/Calcul." Pt. 9: "Pouvoir/Musique." Pt. 10: "Roman/Economie." Pt. 11: "Realité/Logique." Pt. 12: "Rêve/Morale." D, S – Jean-Luc Godard, Anne Marie Miéville; Ph – Pierre Binggeli, William Lubtchansky, Dominique Chapuis, Philippe Rony; C – Camille Virolleaud, Arnaud Martin, Betty Berr, Albert Dray, Jean-Luc Godard. INA for Antenne 2/Sonimage. Video. 26 min. each part.

Sauve qui peut (la vie) (*Every Man for Himself*; a.k.a. *Slow Motion*). 1979. D – Jean-Luc Godard; P – Alain Sarde, Jean-Luc Godard; S – Anne-Marie Miéville, Jean-Claude Carrière; Ph – William Lubtchansky, Renato Berta, Jean-Bernard Menoud; E – Jean-Luc Godard, Anne-Marie Miéville; So – Jacques Maumont, Luc Yersin, Oscar Stellavox; M – Gabriel Yared; C – Isabelle Huppert, Jacques Dutronc, Nathalie Baye, Cécile Tanner, Roland Amstutz, Marguerite Duras. Sara Films/MK2/Saga Productions/Sonimage/CNC/ZDF/SSR/ORF. 35mm. 87 min.

Scénario de Sauve qui peut (la vie). 1979. D – Jean-Luc Godard. JLG Films. Video. 20 min.

Lettre à Freddy Bouache (Letter to Freddy Bouache). 1981. D – Jean-Luc Godard, with Pierre Binggeli, Gérard Rucy; S, E – Jean-Luc Godard; Ph – Jean-Bernard Menoud; So – François Musy; M – M. Ravel. Film et Vidéo Productions. Video. 35mm. 11 min.

"Changer d'image," for broadcast *Le Changement a plus d'un titre*. 1982. D – Jean-Luc Godard; C – Jean-Luc Godard. Video. 9 min.

Passion. 1982. D, S, E – Jean-Luc Godard; Ph – Raoul Coutard; So – François Musy; M – W. A. Mozart, A. Dvořák, M. Ravel, L. van Beethoven, G. Fauré; C – Isabelle Huppert, Hanna Schygulla, Michel Piccoli, Jerzy Radziwilowicz, Laszlo Szabo. Sara Films/Sonimage/Films A2/Film et Vidéo Production SA/SSR. 35mm. 87 min.

Scénario du film Passion. 1982. D – Jean-Luc Godard, with Jean-Bernard Menoud, Anne-Marie Miéville, Pierre Binggeli; C – Jean-Luc Godard, Hanna Schygulla. JLG Films/Studio Trans-Vidéo/Télévision Suisse Romande. Video. 54 min.

First Name: Carmen (Prénom: Carmen). 1983. D – Jean-Luc Godard; P – Alain Sarde; S – Anne-Marie Miéville; Ph – Raoul Coutard, Jean Garcenot; E – Suzanne Lang-Villar, Jean-Luc Godard; So – François Musy; M – L. van Beethoven, Tom Waits; C – Maruschka Detmers, Jacques Bonnaffé, Myriem Roussel, Christophe Odent, Jean-Luc Godard. Sara Films/Jean-Luc Godard Films. 35mm. 85 min.

Petites notes à propos du film Je vous salue Marie. 1983. D – Jean-Luc Godard; P – JLG Films; C – Jean-Luc Godard, Myriem Roussel, Thierry Rode, Anne-Marie Miéville. JLG Films. Video. 25 min.

Hail Mary (Je vous salue Marie). 1985. D, S – Jean-Luc Godard; Ph – Jean-Bernard Menoud, Jacques Firmann; E – Anne-Marie Miéville; So – François Musy; M – J. S. Bach, A. Dvořák, John Coltrane; C – Myriem Roussel, Thierry Rode, Philippe Lacoste, Anne Gauthier, Johan Leysen, Juliette Binoche, Manon Andersen, Malachi Jara Kohan. Pégase Films/SSR/JLG Films/Sara Films/Channel 4. 35mm. 72 min. Preceded by "The Book of Mary" ("Le Livre de Marie"), D – Anne-Marie Miéville.

Détective. 1985. D – Jean-Luc Godard; S – Jean-Luc Godard, Anne-Marie Miéville, Alain Sarde, Philippe Setbon; Ph – Bruno Nuytten; E – Marilyne Dubreuil; So – Pierre Gamet, François Musy; M – F. Schubert, R. Wagner, F. Chopin, F. Liszt, A. Honegger, C. Chabrier, Ornette Coleman, Jean Schwartz; C – Nathalie Baye, Claude Brasseur, Stéphane Ferrara, Johnny Hallyday, Jean-Pierre Léaud, Julie Delpy, Laurent Terzieff. Sara Films/JLG Films. 35mm. 95 min.

Grandeur et décadence d'un petit commerce de cinéma (Grandeur and Decadence of a Small-Time Filmmaker). 1986. D – Jean-Luc Godard; P – Pierre Grimblat; S – Jean-Luc Godard, from a James Hadley Chase novel; Ph – Caroline Champetier, Serge Le François; So – François Musy, Pierre-Alain Besse; M – B. Bartók, Leonard Cohen, Bob Dylan, Janis Joplin, Joni Mitchell; C – Jean-Pierre Léaud, Jean-Pierre Mocky, Marie Valera, Jean-Luc Godard. Hamster Productions/JLG Films. 16mm. 52 min.

Soft and Hard (A Soft Conversation Between Two Friends on a Hard Subject). 1986. D – Jean-Luc Godard, Anne-Marie Miéville; C – Jean-Luc Godard, Anne-Marie Miéville. JLG Films/Channel 4. Video. 48 min.

J. L. G. Meets W. A. (Meetin' W. A.). 1986. D – Jean-Luc Godard; C – Jean-Luc Godard, Woody Allen, Annette Insdorf. Jean-Luc Godard. Video. 26 min.

"Armide," in anthology film *Aria.* 1987. D, E – Jean-Luc Godard; P – Don Boyd; Ph – Caroline Champetier; M – J.-B. Lully; AD – Rénald Calcagni, Jacques Lobeleux; AP – François Hamel; C – Marion Peterson, Valérie Allain, Jacques Neuville, Luke Corre. Lightyear Entertainment/Virgin Vision. 35mm. 12 min.

King Lear. 1987. D, E – Jean-Luc Godard; P – Menahem Golan, Yoram Globus; S – Jean-Luc Godard, after *King Lear* by William Shakespeare; Ph – Sophie Maintigneux; So – François Musy; C – Peter Sellars, Burgess Meredith, Molly Ringwald, Norman Mailer, Kate Mailer, Woody Allen, Léos Carax, Julie Delpy, Jean-Luc Godard. Cannon Films (Golan–Globus). 35mm. 90 min.

Soigne ta droite (Keep Up Your Right). 1987. D, S, E – Jean-Luc Godard; P – Philippe DeChaise Martin; Ph – Caroline Champetier de Ribes; So – François Musy; M – Rita Mitsouko; C – Jean-Luc Godard, Jacques Villeret, Philippe Rouleau, Jane Birkin, François Périer. Gaumont/JLG Films/Xanadu Films. 35mm. 82 min.

On s'est tous défilé. 1988. D – Jean-Luc Godard. JLG Films. Video. 13 min.

Puissance de la parole (Power of the Word). 1988. D – Jean-Luc Godard; Ph – Caroline Champetier, Pierre-Alain Besse; So – François Musy, Pierre-Alain Besse, Marc-Antoine Beldent; M – J. S. Bach, L. van Beethoven, R. Strauss, C. Franck, M. Ravel, John Cage, Bob Dylan, Leonard Cohen; C – Jean Bouise, Laurence Cote, Lydia Andrei, Michel Iribarren. Gaumont/JLG Films/France Télécom. Video. 25 min.

"Le Dernier mot"/"Les Français entendus par" ("The Last Word"/"The French Heard by"), for the broadcast *Les Français vus par.* 1988. D – Jean-Luc Godard; P – Anne-Marie Miéville, Hervé Duhamel, Marie-Christine Barrière et al.; Ph – Pierre Binggeli; So – Pierre Camus, Raoul Fruhauf, François Musy; M – J. S. Bach; C – André Marcon, Hans Zichter, Catherine Aymerie, Pierre Amoyal. Erato Films/Socpresse/Le Figaro/JLG Films. Video. 13 min.

Le Rapport Darty. 1989. D – Jean-Luc Godard, Anne-Marie Miéville; C – Jean-Luc Godard, Anne-Marie Miéville. Video. 50 min.

Nouvelle Vague. 1990. D, S, E – Jean-Luc Godard; P – Alain Sarde, Ruth Waldburger; Ph – William Lubtchansky; So – François Musy; C – Alain Delon, Domiziana Giordano, Roland Amstutz, Laurence Cote. Sara Films/Périphéria/Canal+/Véga Film/Télévision Suisse Romande/Films A2/CNC/Sofia Investimage/Sofia Créations. 35mm. 89 min.

"L'Enfance de l'art," in anthology film *Comment vont les enfants (How Are the Kids).* 1990. D, S – Jean-Luc Godard, Anne-Marie Miéville. JLG Films/UNICEF. 35mm. 8 min.

Germany Year 90 Nine Zero (Allemagne année 90 neuf zéro). 1991. D – Jean-Luc Godard; S – Jean-Luc Godard, from *Nos solitudes* by Michel Hanoun; P – Nicole Ruelle; Ph – Christophe Pollock, Andréas Erben, Stépan Benda; So – Pierre-Alain

Besse, François Musy; M – Gavin Bryars, Gianni Scelsi, F. Liszt, W. A. Mozart, J. S. Bach, I. Stravinsky, P. Hindemith, L. van Beethoven, D. Shostakovitch; C – Eddie Constantine, Hanns Zischler, Claudia Michelsen, André Labarthe, Nathalie Kadem, Kim Kashkashian. Antenne 2/Brainstorm Production. 35mm. 62 min.

Lest We Forget (*Contre l'oubli*), segment in anthology film. 1992. D – Jean-Luc Godard with Anne-Marie Miéville, Chantal Akerman, René Allio, Constantin Costa-Gavras, Claire Denis, Alain Resnais, et al.; M – Mino Cinelli; C – Jean-Luc Godard, Catherine Deneuve, Jane Birkin, Henri Cartier-Bresson, Sami Frey, Isabelle Huppert, Philippe Noiret. Les Films du Paradoxe/PRV/Amnesty International. 35mm. 110 min.

Hélas pour moi (*Oh Woe Is Me*). 1993. D – Jean-Luc Godard; P – Ruth Waldburger; S – Jean-Luc Godard, from *Amphitryon 38* by Jean Giraudoux; Ph – Caroline Champetier; So – François Musy; M – J. S. Bach, L. van Beethoven, P. Tchaikovsky, A. Honegger; C – Gérard Depardieu, Laurence Masliah, Bernard Verley, Jean-Louis Loca, François Germond, Anny Romande. Les Films Alain Sarde/Véga Film. 35mm. 85 min.

JLG/JLG – Autoportrait de décembre (*JLG/JLG – December Self-Portrait*). 1994. D, P, S – Jean-Luc Godard; Ph – Yves Pouliquen, Christian Jaquenod; E – Catherine Cormon; C – Jean-Luc Godard, Denis Jadót. Gaumont/Périphéria. 35mm. 63 min.

Les Enfants jouent à la Russie (*The Kids Play Russian*). 1994. D, S, E – Jean-Luc Godard; P – Ruth Waldburger; Ph – Christophe Pollock; C – Laszlo Szabo, Bernard Eisenschitz, André-S. Labarthe, Jean-Luc Godard. JLG Films. Video. 63 min.

2 x 50 Years of French Cinema (*2 x 50 ans de cinéma français*). 1995. D, S, Ph – Anne-Marie Miéville, Jean-Luc Godard; E – Jean-Luc Godard, Anne-Marie Miéville; C – Jean-Luc Godard, Michel Piccoli. Périphéria/BFI TV/La Sept/ARTE. Video. 51 min.

For Ever Mozart. 1997. D, S – Jean-Luc Godard; P – Alain Sarde, Ruth Waldburger; Ph – Christophe Pollock, Katell Djian, Jean-Pierre Fedrizzi; So – François Musy, Olivier Burgaud; M – David Darling, Ketil Bjornstad, Jon Christensen, Ben Harper, Gyorgi Kurtag; C – Madeleine Assas, Ghalia Lacroix, Bérangère Allaux, Vicky Messica, Frédéric Pierrot. Avventura Films/Périphéria/CEC Rhône Alpes/France 2 Cinéma/Canal Plus/CNC/Véga Film/TSR/Eurimages/DFI. 35mm. 81 min.

Histoire(s) du cinéma. 1989–97. (More episodes may follow.) Pt. 1A: "Toutes les histoires" ("All the Stories"); Pt. 1B: "Une Histoire seule" ("A Single Story"); Pt. 2A: "Seul le cinéma" ("Only the Cinema"); Pt. 2B: "Fatale beauté" ("Fatal Beauty"); Pt. 3A: "La Monnaie de l'absolu"/La Réponse des ténèbres" ("The Currency of the Absolute"/The Reply of the Shadows"); Pt. 3B: "Montage, mon beau souci/Une Vague nouvelle" ("Montage, My Beautiful Care/A Vague Piece of News"); Pt. 4A: "Le Contrôle de l'univers" (Control of the Universe"); Pt. 4B: "Les Signes parmi nous" (The Signs among Us"). D, S, E, C – Jean-Luc Godard. Gaumont/JLG Films/La Sept/Fr 3/Centre National de la Cinématographie/Radio Télévision Suisse Romande/Véga Film. Video. Pts. 1A–2A, 50 min. each; Pts. 2B–4B, 25 min. each.

Le Cinéma mis à nu par ses célibataires, même. 1999. D,S – Jean-Luc Godard, Anne-Marie Miéville. C – Jean-Luc Godard. Périphéria Suisse/The Museum of Modern Art. Video. 60 min.

Additional Films Cited

All That Heaven Allows, dir. Douglas Sirk (Universal International, USA, 1955)

Amadeus, dir. Milos Forman (Saul Zaentz, USA, 1984)

Anatomy of a Murder, dir. Otto Preminger (Columbia/Carlyle/Otto Preminger, USA, 1959)

Arthur the King, dir. Clive Donner (USA, TV film, 1985)

Au hasard Balthazar (Balthazar), dir. Robert Bresson (Argos Films/Parc Film/ Athos Films/Swedish Film Institute/Svensk Filmindustri, France, 1966)

Battleship Potemkin (Bronenosets Potemkin), dir. Sergei Eisenstein (Mosfil'm, USSR, 1925)

Bicycle Thief, The (Ladri di biciclette), dir. Vittorio De Sica (PDS–ENIC, Italy, 1948)

Bitter Victory, dir. Nicholas Ray (Columbia/Transcontinental/Robert Laffont, USA, 1957)

"Book of Mary, The" ("Le Livre de Marie"), dir. Anne-Marie Miéville (Pégase Films/SSR/JLG Films/Sara Films/Channel 4, France, 1985; paired with Godard's *Hail Mary [Je vous salue Marie]* in the release *Hail Mary [Je vous salue Marie]*)

Citizen Kane, dir. Orson Welles (RKO, USA, 1941)

Dog Star Man, dir. Stan Brakhage (Stan Brakhage, USA, 1962–4)

Exterminating Angel, The (El Angel Exterminador), dir. Luis Buñuel (Ininci/Films 59, Mexico, 1962)

400 Blows, The (Les Quatre Cents coups), dir. François Truffaut (Les Films du Carrosse/SEDIF, France, 1959)

From the Journals of Jean Seberg, dir. Mark Rappaport (USA, 1995)

Hard Day's Night, A, dir. Richard Lester (Proscenium Films, Great Britain, 1964)

Harder They Fall, The, dir. Mark Robson (Columbia, USA, 1956)

Hiroshima mon amour, dir. Alain Resnais (Argos/Comei/Pathé/Daiei, France, 1959)

Horse Soldiers, The, dir. John Ford (UA/Mirisch, USA, 1959)

Imitation of Life, dir. Douglas Sirk (Universal International, USA, 1959)

Jules et Jim, dir. François Truffaut (Les Films du Carrosse/SEDIF, France, 1961)

La Terra Trema, dir. Luchino Visconti (Universalia, Italy, 1948)

Last Tango in Paris (Ultimo tango a Parigi; Le Dernier Tango à Paris), dir. Bernardo Bertolucci (Les Artistes Associés/PEA/UA, France/Italy/USA, 1972)

Last Temptation of Christ, The, dir. Martin Scorsese (Universal/Cineplex Odeon, USA/Canada, 1988)

Macunaíma, dir. Joaquim Pedro de Andrade (Brazil, 1969)

Magnificent Ambersons, The, dir. Orson Welles (RKO/Mercury, USA, 1942)

Miracle, The (Il miracolo), dir. Roberto Rossellini (Tania Film, Italy, 1948; U.S. release in anthology film *The Ways of Love,* 1950)

North by Northwest, dir. Alfred Hitchcock (MGM, USA, 1959)

Not Reconciled; or, Only Violence Helps Where Violence Rules (Nicht Versöhnt; oder, Es Hilft nur Gewalt, wo Gewalt Herrascht), dir. Jean-Marie Straub and Danièle Huillet (Straub–Huillet, West Germany, 1964–5)

October (Oktiabr) (a.k.a. *Ten Days That Shook the World*), dir. Sergei Eisenstein (Sovkino, USSR, 1927)

Out One: Spectre, dir. Jacques Rivette (Sunchild Productions, France, 1972)

Paisan (Paisà), dir. Roberto Rossellini (Foreign Films Productions/OFI, Italy, 1946)

Paris Belongs to Us (Paris nous appartient), dir. Jacques Rivette (AJYM/Les Films du Carrosse, France, 1961)

Passion of Joan of Arc, The (La Passion de Jeanne d'Arc), dir. Carl Dreyer (Société Générale des Films, France, 1928)

Psycho, dir. Alfred Hitchcock (Shamley/Alfred Hitchcock, USA, 1960)

Ride Lonesome, dir. Budd Boetticher (Columbia, USA, 1959)

Rio Bravo, dir. Howard Hawks (Warner/Armada, USA, 1959)

Roman Numeral Series, dir. Stan Brakhage (Stan Brakhage, USA, 1979–81)

Scarface, dir. Howard Hawks (Caddo, USA, 1932)

Seventh Seal, The (Det sjunde inseglet), dir. Ingmar Bergman (Svensk Filmindustri, Sweden, 1957)

Shoah: An Oral History of the Holocaust, dir. Claude Lanzmann (Les Films Aleph/Historia Films, France, 1985)

Silence, The (Tystnaden), dir. Ingmar Bergman (Svensk Filmindustri/Janus, Sweden, 1963)

Suddenly Last Summer, dir. Joseph L. Mankiewicz (Columbia, USA, 1959)

Tenant, The (Le Locataire), dir. Roman Polanski (Paramount/Marianne, France, 1976)

True Story of Jesse James, The, dir. Nicholas Ray (Twentieth Century–Fox, USA, 1957)

2001: A Space Odyssey, Stanley Kubrick (MGM/Stanley Kubrick, Great Britain, 1968)

Umberto D, dir. Vittorio de Sica (Dear Films, Italy, 1952)

Vertigo, dir. Alfred Hitchcock (Paramount, USA, 1958)

Vincent, François, Paul . . . and the Others (Vincent, François, Paul . . . et le autres), dir. Claude Sautet (Lira Films/President Produzione, France, 1974)

Westbound, dir. Budd Boetticher (Warner, USA, 1959)

Index

N.B.: Titles in languages other than English are alphabetized under the initial article, if any.

Abel, 262
À bout de souffle, see Breathless
Absalom, Absalom! (Faulkner), 123
Afonso, Yves, 107
Albee, Edward, 44
Algerian National Cinematography, 136
Alice in Wonderland (Carroll), 39
Allaux, Berengère, 229
All Boys Are Called Patrick (Godard), 6, 7
Allemagne année 90 neuf zéro, see Germany Year 90 Nine Zero
Allen, Woody, 222
Alliance against Racism and for the Respect of French and Christian Identity, 163–4
All That Heaven Allows (Sirk), 82
Alphaville (Godard), 9–12, 13, 14–15, 80, 166, 245, 258
Althusser, Louis, 62
Amadeus (Forman), 2
Anatomy of a Murder (Preminger), 44
Andrade, Joaquim Pedro de, 271n12
Anouilh, Jean, 43
Antonioni, Michelangelo, 65
Ardent Marial Youth and World Fatima Movement, 164
Arendt, Hannah, 37
Aria (anthology film), 222
"Armide" (Godard), 13, 222
Arnheim, Rudolf, 4
Arriflex (camera), 47
Artaud, Antonin, 73, 75
Arthur, King of the Britons, 274n16

Arthur the King (Donner), 274n16
Arts, 4, 45
Astruc, Alexandre, 5
Atkinson, Michael, 1
Au hasard Balthazar (Bresson), 212
"Ave Maria" (Schubert), 176, 179

Bach, Johann Sebastian, 7, 174, 176, 177, 182, 184, 196, 201, 209, 211, 212–13, 215, 216, 217, 273n7
Bachmann, Gideon, 240
Bakhtin, Mikhail, 122, 127, 143, 153
Balzac, Honoré de, 96, 118
Bande à part, see Band of Outsiders
Band of Outsiders (Godard), 9, 13, 100, 230, 274n16
Barthes, Roland, 29, 129, 260–1
Bataille, Georges, 143, 144
Battistella, Sandrine, 157
Battleship Potemkin, The (Eisenstein), 54, 122
Baudelaire, Charles, 172
Baye, Nathalie, 162, 221
Bazin, André, 4–5, 6, 32, 175
Bear, The (Faulkner), 196
Beat/Beat Generation, 44, 45–6, 47, 48, 50, 56, 62, 64, 97, 136, 190, 239, 262
Beauregard, Georges de, 137
Becket; or, The Honor of God (Anouilh), 43
Beethoven, Ludwig van, 29, 111, 162, 173

"Belief & Technique for Modern Prose" (Kerouac), 44
Belmondo, Jean-Paul, 7, 39, 41, 43, 49, 52, 234–5
Benjamin, Walter, 90
Bergman, Ingmar, 181, 270n9
Berlin Film Festival, 166
Berr, Betty, 252
Berto, Juliet, 9
Bertolucci, Bernardo, 270n9
Bible, 168, 212, 214, 243
Bicycle Thief, The (De Sica), 4
Birkin, Jane, 222
Bitter Victory (Ray), 18
Bizet, Georges, 162
Blake, William, 107
Boetticher, Budd, 44
Bogart, Humphrey, 57, 58
"Book of Mary, The" (Miéville), 33, 169, 170–4, 182, 217
Boyd, Don, 222
Brakhage, Stan, 190, 228, 241–3, 244, 249
Braque, Georges, 32
Brasseur, Pierre, 221
Breathless (Godard), 1, 6, 7, 8, 13, 19, 30, 37, 39–60, 62, 63, 64, 69, 79, 85, 97, 102, 111, 118, 120, 133, 134, 148, 170, 218, 221, 224, 228, 234, 236, 237, 258, 260, 276n20
Brecht, Bertolt/Brechtian, 2, 36, 37, 64–5, 67, 68, 69, 70, 71, 74, 75, 76, 79, 82, 89, 92, 96, 99, 102, 107, 109, 110, 113, 118, 120, 124, 125, 134, 162, 171, 225, 254, 260
Bresson, Robert, 212
British Sounds (Dziga-Vertov Group), 130
Brontë, Charlotte, 39
Brontë, Emily, 107–9, 117
Buñuel, Luis, 102, 105
Burroughs, William S., 44, 260

Cage, John, 111
Cahiers du cinéma, 4, 6, 7, 29, 45, 49, 235
Cain, 262
Camus, Albert, 260
Canby, Vincent, 223–4
Cannes International Film Festival, 1, 44, 164, 222, 223
Cannon Films, 222
Carmen (Bizet), 162
Carney, Raymond, 74
Carrière, Jean-Claude, 162

Carroll, Lewis, 106–7
Chabrol, Claude, 4
Chandler, Raymond, 238
Chaplin, Charles, 62
Charlotte et son Jules (Godard), 7
Charlotte et Véronique, see All Boys Are Called Patrick
Ciné-Tracts (Godard et al.), 130
Citizen Kane (Welles), 173
Coltrane, John, 188
Columbia Pictures, 167
Comment ça va (Godard–Miéville), 25, 132, 161, 170, 250, 272n6
Constantine, Eddie, 69, 72, 245
Contempt (Godard), 1, 4, 9, 98, 118, 123, 172, 185, 275n10, 276n19
Coutard, Raoul, 47, 67, 68, 70, 76, 79, 86, 97, 110, 252
Cukor, George, 89

Dalle Vacche, Angela, 86, 91, 234, 261
Dante, 219, 238
Darc, Mireille, 95, 101, 111, 117
Debord, Guy, 92, 258
"Defence and Illustration of Classical Construction" (Godard), 33
Delacroix, Eugène, 249
Deleuze, Gilles, 34
Delon, Alain, 236, 259
DeMille, Cecil B., 104
Demy, Jacques, 191
Depardieu, Gérard, 245–6
Derrida, Jacques, 161, 277n3
Détective (Godard), 13, 161–2, 168, 221, 251
Dharma Bums, The (Kerouac), 46
Divine Comedy, The (Dante), 219
Dixon, Wheeler Winston, 228
Doctor Sax; or, Faust Part Three (Kerouac), 44
Dog Star Man (Brakhage), 276n20
Dolto, Françoise, 175
Doniol-Valcroze, Jacques, 4
Donen, Stanley, 45
Donner, Clive, 274n16
Dostoyevsky, Feodor, 30, 122
Doude, Van, 55
Dreyer, Carl, 71, 72, 73–4, 76, 88
Dubois, Philippe, 250
Dumas, Alexandre, 83, 102
Duperey, Anny, 185
Duras, Marguerite, 44
Dutronc, Jacques, 163

Dvořák, Antonin, 178, 179, 181, 182, 186, 187, 197, 199, 200, 201, 204, 210

Dziga-Vertov Group, 9–10, 28, 38, 116, 130, 131, 132, 133, 134, 222, 228, 230, 247, 255, 260

Edwards, Blake, 45
Einstein on the Beach (Wilson–Glass), 238
Eisenstein, Sergei, 4, 18, 122, 125
El Cid, 116
Elsaesser, Thomas, 45
Engels, Friedrich, 116
Eternal World Television Network, 167
Evergreen Review, 44
Every Man for Himself, see Sauve qui peut (la vie)
Exterminating Angel, The (Buñuel), 102, 105

Falconetti, Maria, 73
Farocki, Harun, 133
Faulkner, William, 30, 53, 111, 123, 196, 238
Federal Communications Commission, 277n10
Female Eunuch, The (Greer), 152
Ferré, Leo, 154, 158
Film Comment, 224, 275n3
Film Like the Others, A, see Un Film comme les autres
Film Society of Lincoln Center, 167, 275n3
First Name: Carmen (Godard), 10, 111, 162, 168, 169, 170, 221, 239–40, 251, 252, 276n17
Fitzgerald, F. Scott, 53
Flaubert, Gustave, 237
Fonda, Jane, 131, 132
Ford, John, 44, 122
For Ever Mozart (Godard), 10, 111, 223, 228, 229, 259, 261
Foucault, Michel, 21, 23, 26, 29, 62, 159
400 Blows, The (Truffaut), 6, 44
France/tour/détour/deux/enfants (Godard–Miéville), 161, 251–2, 254–9, 260, 262
France/Tour/Detour/Two/Children, see France/tour/détour/deux/enfants
Francis of Assisi, Saint, 194
French Seen By, The (TV series), 223
Freud, Sigmund/Freudian, 122, 123, 139, 142, 143, 206, 216
Fuller, Buckminster, 247

Fuller, Samuel, 44
"Für Elise" (Beethoven), 173

"Garden of Love, The" (Blake), 107
Gaulle, Charles de, 43, 106
Gaumont, 167
Gazette du cinéma, 4, 44
Gégauff, Paul, 110–12
Genesis, 168, 219
Germany Year 90 Nine Zero (Godard), 13, 228, 245
Gift of Death, The (Derrida), 161
Ginsberg, Allen, 46, 190
Giscard-d'Estaing, Valérie, 250
Glass, Philip, 238
Gorin, Jean-Pierre, 9, 130–1, 132
Gorky, Maxim, 268n26
Goya, Francesco, 226
Grandeur and Decadence of a Small-Time Filmmaker, see Grandeur et décadence d'un petit commerce de cinéma
Grandeur et décadence d'un petit commerce de cinéma (Godard), 221
Greer, Germaine, 152, 153
Griffith, D. W., 8, 66

Hail Mary (Godard–Miéville), 10, 17, 18, 26, 38, 104, 161–220, 221, 223, 230, 236, 243, 244, 245, 252, 257
Halliday, Johnny, 221
Hamlet (Shakespeare), 187, 188
Handel, George Frederick, 7
Hard Day's Night, A (Lester), 274n16
Hawks, Howard, 44
Heidegger, Martin, 188, 273n7
Hélas pour moi (Godard), 10, 18, 170, 228, 230, 244, 245
Hampton, Rebecca, 173
Harder They Fall, The (Robson), 57
Harrison, George, 274n16
Here and Elsewhere (Godard–Miéville), 132, 133, 135, 161, 221, 250
Hillier, Jim, 45
Hiroshima mon amour (Resnais), 44
Histoire(s) du cinéma (Godard), 3, 10, 30, 38, 161, 223, 228, 259, 262
Hitchcock, Alfred, 44, 45, 48, 82
Hölderlin, Friedrich, 179
Hollywood, 44, 45, 48, 53, 57, 68, 82, 89, 93, 104, 105, 111, 119, 120, 127, 162, 167, 168, 185, 216, 232, 240
Holmes, John Clellon, 50
Horse Soldiers, The (Ford), 44

How's It Going?, see Comment ça va
Huillet, Danièle, 111, 269n1
Huppert, Isabelle, 162, 163, 253
Hustler, The (Rossen), 82

Ici et ailleurs, see Here and Elsewhere
Imitation of Life (Sirk), 44
Institut National Audiovisuel, 250
International Catholic Cinema Office,
   166
Internationale Situationniste, 92
Ionesco, Eugène, 108

James, David E., 242
Jeanson, Blandine, 107
"Jesu, Joy of Man's Desiring" (Bach), 213
Jesus (Christ), 100, 175, 187, 211, 213,
   214
Je vous salue Marie, see Hail Mary
JLG/JLG – Autoportrait de décembre
   (Godard), 31
JLG/JLG – December Self-Portrait, see
   JLG/JLG – Autoportrait de décembre
J. L. G. Meets W. A. (Meetin' W. A.)
   (Godard), 222, 259, 260
Joan of Arc, 72, 73, 74, 76, 88
Johnny Guitar (Ray), 125
John Paul II, Pope, 164–5
John, Saint, 169, 202
John the Baptist, 274n18
Johnson, Lyndon, 112
Joyce, James, 177–8, 206
Jules and Jim (Truffaut), 86
Jusqu'à la victoire, see Until Victory

Kael, Pauline, 97
Kalfon, Jean-Pierre, 95
Karina, Anna, 63, 64, 67, 71, 72, 73, 75,
   77, 79, 81, 84, 85, 87, 88, 132, 234
Kazantzakis, Nikos, 167
Keep Up Your Right, see Soigne ta droite
Kerouac, Jack, 44, 45, 46, 47, 48, 50, 63,
   190
King Lear (Godard), 13, 16, 19, 36, 168,
   222, 230
Koch, Joanne, 167
Kristeva, Julia, 128, 129, 143, 144–6
Kubrick, Stanley, 211

Lacan, Jacques, 261
La Chinoise; ou, Plutôt à la chinoise
   (Godard), 9, 16, 90, 92, 129, 170
Lady Chatterley's Lover (Lawrence), 44

"La Marseillaise," 140
Lang, Fritz, 45
Lanzmann, Claude, 275n8
L'Arnaqueur, see Hustler, The
Last Exit to Brooklyn (Selby), 272n5
Last Tango in Paris (Bertolucci), 270n9
Last Temptation of Christ, The (Scorsese),
   167
"Last Word, The" (Godard), 223
La Terra Trema (Visconti), 4
Lawrence, D. H., 44
Léaud, Jean-Pierre, 9, 106, 221
Le Gai Savoir (Godard), 9, 19, 26, 91,
   112, 129, 221, 260
Legrand, Michel, 67, 76, 82, 85
Leibnitz, Gottfried Wilhelm von, 84
"Le Livre de Marie," *see* "Book of Mary,
   The"
Le Mépris, see Contempt
Lenin, Vladimir Ilyich, 268n26
Le Petit soldat, see Little Soldier, The
Le Rapport Darty (Godard–Miéville),
   223
Les Amis du cinéma, 4
Les Carabiniers (Godard), 8, 13, 80
"Le Signe" (Maupassant), 7
Le Temps retrouvé (Proust), 232
Letter to Jane (Godard–Gorin), 130, 132
Lettrist International, 92
Leutrat, Jean-Louis, 33
L'Humanité, 1
Light in August (Faulkner), 123, 124
Lincoln Center, 166, 168, 223, 275n3
Little Race Riot (Warhol), 270n3
Little Soldier, The (Godard), 8, 13, 16, 56,
   61, 62, 63, 64, 68, 83, 115, 258, 260,
   269n17
Locke, Maryel, 167, 168
Lord's Prayer, 196
Loshitzky, Yosefa, 103
L'Osservatore Romano, 165
Lot, 227
Louvre, 86
Lucas, Hans (Jean-Luc Godard), 4, 7
Lucifer, 206
Lucretius, 238
Lully, Jean-Baptiste, 222
Lumière, Auguste, 123, 240–1, 276n19
Lumière, Louis, 240–1, 276n19
Luther, Martin, 273n14
Lycée Buffon, 3
Lyons, Charles, 167

MacCabe, Colin (Myles), 1, 22, 36, 229–30, 255
McLuhan, Marshall, 247
Macunaíma (Andrade), 271n12
Made in U.S.A. (Godard), 9
Maggie Cassidy (Kerouac), 44
Magnificent Ambersons, The (Welles), 275n3
Mahler, Gustave, 172
Mailer, Norman, 47, 50, 222
Malcolm X, 115
Mankiewicz, Joseph L., 44
Mann, Anthony, 45
Mao Zedong/Maoist, 10, 36, 112, 132, 188, 192
Marcuse, Herbert, 159
Married Woman, A (Godard), 1, 9, 16, 118, 129, 221
Marx Brothers, 6
Marx, Karl/Marxian/Marxist, 1, 92, 99, 100, 116, 130, 188, 245, 253, 270n6
Mary, *see* Virgin Mary/Mary
Masculine/Feminine (Godard), 1, 7, 16, 91, 103, 109, 119, 129
Masculin/Féminin, see Masculine/Feminine
Massieu, Jean, 73
Maupassant, Guy de, 7
Maysles, Albert, 34
Meetin' W. A., see J. L. G. Meets W. A.
Melville, Jean-Pierre, 1
Metro–Goldwyn–Mayer (MGM), 136
Mexico City Blues (Kerouac), 44
Miéville, Anne-Marie, 10, 25, 33, 38, 132–3, 135, 142–3, 148, 151, 154, 156, 158, 160, 161, 162, 168, 169, 170–1, 172, 173, 174, 175, 187, 219, 222, 248, 250–2, 254–9
Minnelli, Vincente, 44
Minow, Newton, 277n10
Miracle, The (Rossellini), 166
Monaco, James, 261
Monod, Julien, 230, 231
Monogram (Rauschenberg), 44
Monogram Pictures, 53
Montand, Yves, 131
"Montparnasse-Levallois" (Godard), 34, 54
Mosfil'm, 136
Mozart, Wolfgang Amadeus, 110–12
My Life to Live (Godard), 8, 17, 30, 37, 61–88, 94, 97, 103, 118, 126, 129, 139, 218, 234

Naked Lunch (Burroughs), 44
Naked Maja, The (Goya), 226
National Confederation of Catholic Family Relations, 163
Newman, Paul, 82
New Testament, 243; *see also* Bible
New Wave, 1, 4, 5, 6, 7, 17, 32, 35, 37, 44, 61, 62, 63, 69, 71, 110, 215, 223
New Yorker Films, 167, 168
New York Film Festival, 2, 166, 223, 275n3
New York Herald Tribune, 40
New York Times, 223–4
Nietzsche, Friedrich, 26, 238
North against South (Godard–Miéville), 259
North by Northwest (Hitchcock), 44
Not Reconciled; or, Only Violence Helps Where Violence Rules (Straub–Huillet), 269n1
Nouvelle Vague (Godard), 17, 18, 26, 30–1, 38, 104, 170, 221–46, 259
Number Two, see Numéro deux
Numéro deux (Godard–Miéville), 38, 94, 129–60, 161, 163, 172, 174, 206, 221, 247, 250, 262

O'Connor, Flannery, 165
O'Connor, John Cardinal, 166
October (Eisenstein), 125
Odyssey, The (Homer), 9
Oh Woe Is Me, see Hélas pour moi
Old Testament, 243; *see also* Bible
Olson, Charles, 241–2
1 A.M./One American Movie (Godard), 132
One Plus One (Godard), 91, 112, 130, 242
1 P.M./One Parallel Movie (Godard–Pennebaker), 132
On s'est tous défilé (Godard), 222
On the Road (Kerouac), 46
Opération Béton (Godard), 7
Organisation de Radio et Télévision Français (ORTF), 250
Orson Welles Cinema, 167
Out One: Spectre (Rivette), 73
"Oval Portrait, The" (Poe), 84–6, 218

Paisan (Rossellini), 4
Palance, Jack, 185
Parain, Brice, 83–4, 269n17

Paris Belongs to Us (Rivette), 6
Paris Cinémathèque, 4
Paris-Flirt, 57
Paris vu par . . . (anthology film), 34
Passion (Godard), 3, 10, 55, 159, 161,
    162, 169, 177, 221, 249, 252, 274n17
Passion of Joan of Arc, The (Dreyer), 71–4,
    81
Paul, Saint, 165
Pennebaker, D. A., 1, 132
Phenomenon of Man, The (Teilhard de
    Chardin), 277n2
Picasso, Pablo, 32, 111
Piccoli, Michel, 162, 275n10
Pierrot le fou (Godard), 9, 16, 31, 80, 91,
    119, 129, 234–5, 237
"*Pierrot* My Friend" (Godard), 235
Playboy, 273n14
"Plenitude of Eros in the Spontaneity of
    Human Love, The" (John Paul II),
    165
Poe, Edgar Allan, 30, 84, 85, 86, 119
Polanski, Roman, 216
Positif, 1
Power of the Word (Godard), 222
Pravda (Dziga-Vertov Group), 9, 130, 188
Preminger, Otto, 44
Prénom: Carmen, see First Name: Carmen
Production Code, 44
Proust, Marcel/Proustian, 232
Psycho (Hitchcock), 48, 54, 82, 119
Puissance de la parole, see Power of the
    Word
Purcell, Henry, 97

Rabelais, François, 122
Raphael, 273n14
Rauschenberg, Robert, 44
Ray, Nicholas, 18, 45
Rembrandt, 56
Renoir, Auguste, 58, 59
Renoir, Jean, 5, 34
Resnais, Alain, 43
Rhinoceros (Ionesco), 108
Ride Lonesome (Boetticher), 44
Riflemen, The, see Les Carabiniers
Rimbaud, Arthur, 75, 76, 237, 238,
    274n16, 275n14
Ringwald, Molly, 222
Rio Bravo (Hawks), 44
Rivette, Jacques, 4, 6, 73, 111
Robbe-Grillet, Alain, 260
Robson, Mark, 57

Rode, Thierry, 183, 199
Roger, Jean-Henri, 130–1
Rohmer, Eric, 4, 7
Rolling Stones, 91, 130
Roman Catholic Church, 164
Roman Numeral Series (Brakhage), 228
Rosenbaum, Jonathan, 35–6, 262
Rossellini, Roberto, 5, 8, 54, 166
Rouch, Jean, 63
Rousseau, Jean-Jacques, 100, 239
Roussel, Myriem, 183, 186, 199, 205, 217

Sack Theaters, 167
Saint-Just, Louis Antoine Léon de, 105,
    106, 115
Sanctuary (Faulkner), 123
Sartre, Jean-Paul, 42
Sautet, Claude, 138
Sauve qui peut (la vie) (Godard), 159, 161,
    162, 163, 168, 169, 170, 221, 224,
    230, 251, 262, 274n17
Scarface (Hawks), 39
Scénario du film Passion (Godard et al.),
    161
Schatz, Thomas, 29
Schnabel, Artur, 110
Schönberg, Arnold, 111
Schubert, Franz, 176
Scientific American, 179
Scorsese, Martin, 167
Schygulla, Hanna, 162, 253
Searchers, The (Ford), 122
Seberg, Jean, 40, 41, 43, 55, 59
See You at Mao, see British Sounds
Selby, Hubert, Jr., 272n5
Sellars, Peter, 222
Seven Capital Sins, The (anthology film),
    62
Seventh Seal, The (Bergman), 181
Shakespeare, William/Shakespearean,
    222
Sharits, Paul, 190
Shoah (Lanzmann), 275n8
Silence, The (Bergman), 270n9
Sirk, Douglas, 44, 45, 82
Situationist International, 92, 258
Six fois deux/Sur et sous la communication
    (Godard–Miéville), 161, 251–2, 254–
    6, 259
Six Times Two/Over and Under Commu-
    nication, see Six fois deux/Sur et sous
    la communication
"Sloth" (Godard), 62

Slow Motion, see Sauve qui peut (la vie)
Smith, Harry, 228
Soft and Hard (A Soft Conversation Between Two Friends on a Hard Subject) (Godard–Miéville), 222, 259
Soigne ta droite (Godard), 222
Soldiers, The, see Les Carabiniers
Solomon R. Guggenheim Museum, 44
Sonimage, 135, 250, 251, 254
Sorbonne, 3, 40, 50
Spurt of Blood, The (Artaud), 75
Stam, Robert, 116, 127, 224, 228, 238, 240
Stanislavski, Konstantin, 65
Steiger, Rod, 57
Steinberg, Leo, 187
Sterling, Jan, 57
Story of Water, A, see Une Histoire d'eau
Straub, Jean-Marie, 111, 269n1
Subterraneans, The (Kerouac), 46
Suddenly Last Summer (Manciewicz), 44
Sympathy for the Devil, see One Plus One

Tashlin, Frank, 44
Teilhard de Chardin, Pierre, 277n2
Tenant, The (Polanski), 216
Terzieff, Laurent, 221
Theater and Its Double, The (Artaud), 73
Theodore of Mopsuestia, 213
Theology of the Body (John Paul II), 165
Three Stooges, 94, 101
Totem and Taboo (Freud), 122, 123
Tous les garçons s'appellent Patrick, see All Boys Are Called Patrick
Tout va bien (Godard–Gorin), 130, 131, 132, 250
Triumph Films, 167
True Story of Jesse James, The (Ray), 18
Truffaut, François, 4, 6, 7, 17, 19, 39, 44, 46, 61, 86
Twentieth Century–Fox, 7, 136
Twenty Years After (Dumas), 83
2 ou 3 Choses qui je sais d'elle, see 2 or 3 Things I Know about Her
2 or 3 Things I Know about Her (Godard), 9, 16, 22, 23, 27–8, 60, 91, 92, 103, 129, 170, 185, 189, 190, 236, 237, 244, 255
2001: A Space Odyssey (Kubrick), 211
2 x 50 ans de cinéma français, see 2 x 50 Years of French Cinema
2 x 50 Years of French Cinema (Miéville–Godard), 259, 260, 276n19

Ulysses (Joyce), 177–8
Umberto D. (De Sica), 4
Une Femme coquette (Godard), 7
Une Femme est une femme, see Woman Is a Woman, A
Une Femme mariée, see Married Woman, A
Une Histoire d'eau (Godard–Truffaut), 7
Un Film comme les autres (Dziga-Vertov Group), 130
United States Supreme Court, 166
University of Alabama, 167
University of Nebraska, 167
Until Victory (Dziga-Vertov Group), 132

Vent d'est, see Wind from the East
Vertigo (Hitchcock), 82
Vertov, Dziga, 36
Vincent, François, Paul . . . and the Others (Sautet), 138
Virgin Mary/Mary, 10, 164, 166, 170, 174, 187, 214, 216, 274n18
Vivre sa vie, see My Life to Live
Vlady, Marina, 185, 237

Waiting for Godot (Beckett), 196
Waits, Tom, 162
Warhol, Andy, 90
Warren, Charles, 174, 175
Webster, John, 205
Weekend (Godard), 9, 16, 38, 89–128, 129, 134, 144, 188, 190, 214
Welles, Orson, 4, 5
Westbound (Boetticher), 44
"When Johnny Comes Marching Home," 173
White, Armond, 224, 228, 236
Wiazemsky, Anne, 110, 132
Wild Palms, The (Faulkner), 53
Wilson, Robert, 238
Wind from the East (Dziga-Vertov Group), 130
Wittgenstein, Ludwig, 28
Woman Is a Woman, A (Godard), 8, 13, 62, 63, 64, 258
Wright, Frank Lloyd, 44
Writing Degree Zero (Barthes), 260
Wyler, William, 4–5

Yanne, Jean, 95, 101, 107, 111

Zoo Story, The (Albee), 44